1973
THE MYSTERY & DETECTION ANNUAL

THE MYSTERY & DETECTION ANNUAL

Donald K. Adams, *Editor*

Lawrence D. Stewart, *Associate Editor*

Consulting Editors

Daniel R. Barnes

Leon Howard

Martin Roth

Julian Symons

W. B. Vasels

THE
MYSTERY & DETECTION
ANNUAL

DONALD ADAMS

BEVERLY HILLS, CALIFORNIA

1973

DONALD K. ADAMS, *Editor*
The Mystery & Detection Annual
152 South Clark Drive
Beverly Hills, California 90211

First printing
US ISSN: 0000-0302
ISBN: 0-913288-01-2

Library of Congress Catalog Card Number: 72-87432

Designed and printed by Grant Dahlstrom at The Castle Press, Pasadena, California.

Table of Contents

ILLUSTRATIONS

The sketches on pages i, v, xi, 141 and 306 are by Editha Spencer.

The drawings and sketches to illustrate "The Mystery Poem," pages 83 to 96, and the drawings on the title page and dust jacket, are the work of Eric Spencer.

On page xii the dust jacket of *The Great Gatsby* is reproduced through the courtesy of Charles Scribner's Sons; the illustration is that used in Matthew Bruccoli's *F. Scott Fitzgerald, a Descriptive Bibliography* (1972). The dust jacket of *The Long Goodbye* is reproduced through the courtesy of Houghton, Mifflin Company and photographed from a copy owned by Lawrence D. Stewart.

The photographs on page 52 were taken by Lawrence D. Stewart.

All illustrations to " 'Who Can Be Trusted?': *The Detective*, an Early Journal of Detection" (pages 167-92) and "Mystery Fiction in the Nineteenth Century" (pages 193-205) are provided through the kindness of the authors and of the Department of Special Collections, University Research Library, University of California, Los Angeles.

Other illustrations are acknowledged in the text.

Editor's Preface

THE TWENTIES and early thirties saw a renaissance in American poetry, drama and fiction: Eliot, Pound and Jeffers; Fitzgerald, Hemingway and Dos Passos; O'Neill and Wilder. That burst of creative energy naturally spread to the detective story. Dashiell Hammett, Raymond Chandler, Erle Stanley Gardner, Horace McCoy, and other writers emerged from the *Black Mask* school to provide American crime fiction with a vitality and frankness which continues in 1973 to shape the genre of mystery and detection not only here in the United States but also abroad in Britain and France.

As fans of the books of Chandler, Gardner and Ross Macdonald — and of countless films — know, Southern California in particular has been the favorite haunt of the hard-boiled detective and the sharp-eyed criminal lawyer. The easy money, social mobility, glamor, cynicism, and amorality associated in the public mind with California, especially the southern half of the state, have made the detective novel virtually an indigenous form. In books and on film it has been long established as the most appropriate artistic approach to the frantic and seductive life of the West Coast.

The 1973 issue of *The Mystery & Detection Annual* focuses on this golden age of realistic American detective fiction. A perceptive analysis of Chandler's *The Long Goodbye*; a chronological discussion of Ross Macdonald's novels and their pervasive search for justice; an interview with Ross Macdonald; and the first appearance in print of Horace McCoy's important novella, "Death in Hollywood," originally written in 1933 — these contributions shed light on "The Southern California Scene" in detective fiction.

This issue of *The Mystery & Detection Annual* has another theme, one that is alluded to openly or through implication in the essays on Chandler's and Ross Macdonald's novels and on Paul Bowles's *Up Above the World*, and in the interviews with Georges Simenon and Macdonald. It is the point made by Ngaio Marsh in her personal comments. Crime and detective fiction that counts wholly on plot, especially on the increasingly predictable surprises of even the most sophisticated plot, is doomed to bankruptcy. No matter how colorful the settings and eccentric the sleuths, such novels are enslaved to their denouements. After over a century of experience the genre clearly recognizes that character analysis and thematic development must bear a heavier burden for the justification of such novels. The plot should retire somewhat to take its place as one element (admittedly a very important element) among several ingredients in the dynamic novel.

Indeed, as Julian Symons has implied in the final pages of his *Mortal Consequences*, crime fiction that depends ultimately on its core of sensationalism can approach, but not achieve, artistic greatness. The future of the form, if it is to escape from mechanical repetition of threadbare formulae, must lie in the merging of crime and detective novels into the more general concept of "mystery fiction." The best and most imaginative "mystery" fiction will tend to become indistinguishable in design and execution, emotional and artistic effect, form and technique, from any other kind of fiction. Ideally, the mystery novel, even the detective novel, will ultimately become, simply, the novel.

The 1972 issue of *The Mystery & Detection Annual* was dedicated to Edgar Allan Poe, widely and justly regarded as the father of the detective story. Few admirers of the genre will deny Poe that accolade. Similarly, few will quarrel with the preeminence among fictional detectives of Conan Doyle's brilliant and intuitively perceptive creation, Sherlock Holmes. In the "Editor's Preface" a year ago I commented on the strange behavior of Sherlock Holmes, his almost total absence from the contents of that volume. "It is hoped," I wrote, "that in the 1973 issue of the *Annual* will appear essays on Conan Doyle and his great detective." Alas, editors propose but contributors dispose. Few such articles appeared, with the result that the celebrated Mr. Holmes will remain elusive for another year. The serious student of the genre may see in this circumstance some hint — in the proliferation of Holmesian encyclopedias, topographical surveys and annotated editions — of a literary surfeit. But the editors of *The Mystery & Detection Annual* continue, for another year, to look forward to serious discussions of the Conan Doyle mystery stories.

THE
SOUTHERN CALIFORNIA
SCENE

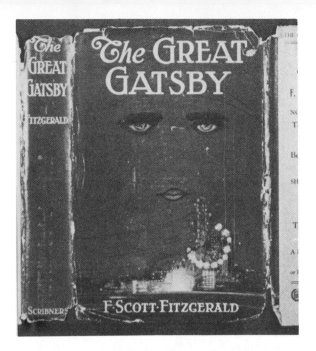

The dust jackets of the first American editions of *The Great Gatsby* and *The Long Goodbye*. For a discussion of these jackets, see pp. 331-34.

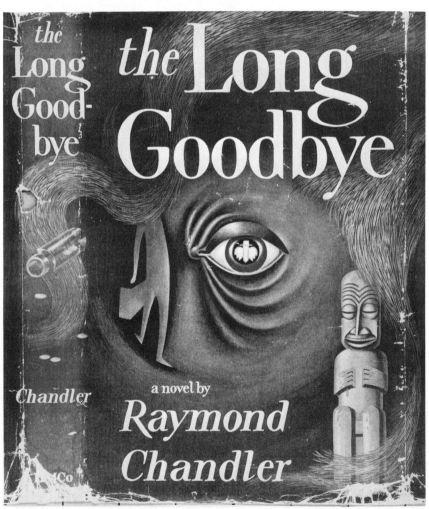

RAYMOND CHANDLER'S

NOT-SO-GREAT GATSBY

By Leon Howard

I

FEW DETECTIVE NOVELS invite comparison with specific works of "serious" fiction, and when one does it not only becomes an object of curiosity in itself but raises certain questions. On what basis may such a comparison be made? Are the differences between the two—which may be more evident than the resemblances—attributable to the peculiar demands of a particular literary genre? Does the comparison lead to any observations, otherwise unlikely, about the book which invites it? Raymond Chandler's *The Long Goodbye* is such a book, and, since Chandler was a purveyor of mysteries with an acknowledged claim to serious consideration, it may be interesting to see what happened when he became serious about something other than a mystery-writer's craftsmanship.

The novel with which *The Long Goodbye* invites comparison is F. Scott Fitzgerald's *The Great Gatsby*, and the first basis for it may be found in the background situation common to both books: An attractive young soldier, given the social freedom of his uniform, meets a "golden girl" and falls romantically and lastingly in love with her before going into military action which separates them for the duration of the war and for some time thereafter. When he returns to civilian life he realizes that he has neither the social background nor the financial means to meet her on the old terms. He forms criminal associations and eventually acquires, through dubious means, money enough to move in her circles. She preserves her romantic attachment throughout the war, but by the time they meet again she is unromantically married to another man.

Neither author, we know, worked in a Jamesian fashion from this sort of story idea. Fitzgerald has said that his book grew out of the im-

1

pression made upon him by his meeting with the notorious gambler Arnold Rothstein. Chandler could have abstracted it from Fitzgerald's much earlier novel, but if he did so it was not because the situation was of any great importance to him. His imagination was primarily stimulated by the conception of a series of vivid scenes loosely strung together by a mystery plot, and his background situations were not genetic but were merely incidental to them. Nevertheless the common situation produced a certain similarity between several important characters in Chandler's book and those who formed the substance of Fitzgerald's.

Fitzgerald's soldier, Jay Gatsby, is the central figure in his novel and is a vigorous individual whose romantic disposition is concealed by a casual and sometimes tough exterior. Born Jimmy Gatz, he had been introduced to the ways of the rich by an eccentric yachtsman and had made good use of his Army commission as officer and gentleman and his single term as an Oxford student to improve his language and manners. His criminal connections are through Meyer Wolfsheim, an important figure in organized crime, and he has risen high in the syndicate. When the book opens he is the owner of a large house across the bay from the current home of his former sweetheart and entertains extravagantly in an effort to achieve a place in her social circle. No one quite believes he is the wealthy gentleman he pretends to be, because he is too careful, too jovial, and too gauche, but he has a rare smile that reveals an inner charm which captivates his more sensitive associates. The reader is assured at the beginning that he "turned out all right" at the end, and faith in that assurance is maintained throughout the book.

Chandler's equivalent to Gatsby is Terry Lennox, formerly Paul Marston, who is introduced as a "nice young guy" with prematurely white hair, a face half immobilized by scar tissue, and impeccable manners even when drunk. Superficially, at least, he is an improvement on Fitzgerald's hero: he has none of the vulgarity suggested by Gatsby's familiar "old sport," his display of wealth is unostentatious and in good taste, and he has acquired his English affectations by service in the British army rather than by a term at Oxford. His criminal connections are with Randy Starr, who operates a casino in Nevada, and Mendy Menendez, who bosses gambling in Los Angeles County; but they are not of a business nature: Terry had saved the lives of the two gamblers during the war when the three had been commandos together, and, although he had met his wealthy wife while working in Starr's casino, there is no indication of any past or present involvement in criminal activities. Such money as he has was acquired by marriage, and he is inclined to consider it a symbol of shame rather than success. On the other hand, he is weaker than Gatsby, and instead of pursuing his former sweetheart when he meets her again he walks out of his marriage and out of the circles in which she moves. Later he remarries his former wife, but he and the golden girl never acknowledge each other, and he disappears, in person, from the novel before it is one-tenth finished. His continued existence in the memory of his former associates and the ambiguity of his supposed suicide, however, keep him a dominant figure in the story around whom much of the action revolves.

Fitzgerald's Daisy Buchanan is like a "king's daughter, the golden girl." She is not clearly visualized, but she has dark shining hair and there is a singing compulsion in her voice which suggests "an arrangement of notes that will never be played again"; and she is vivacious and capable of genuine warmth. She had preserved her love for Gatsby until the end of the war and had become restless and insecure only when Gatsby had failed to come home immediately. She had married the enormously wealthy Tom Buchanan while Gatsby was still at Oxford and had settled into his athletic, hard-drinking style of life with apparent ease. She is disillusioned enough with Tom and his current "woman in New York" to have an affair with Gatsby after they meet again but not to love him or live up to his expectations, although she remains perfect in his eyes. In comparison with her, Chandler's Eileen Wade is the visible perfection of feminine charm. When she first appears in *The Long Goodbye* she is seen as slim and tall with violet eyes and hair shining with "the pale gold of a fairy princess." She too is called "the golden girl" and has "a voice like the stuff they line summer clouds with." More poised and articulate than Daisy, she was able to describe her feeling for the young soldier as "the wild, mysterious, improbable kind of love that never comes but once" and still insist upon a genuine mature love for her husband. She had married Roger Wade in the conviction that Paul Marston was dead, but after he reappeared in her life as Terry Lennox, she still insisted on her devotion to Roger: Roger "drank, he didn't know what he was doing. He worried about his work and he hated himself because he was just a mercenary hack. He was a weak man, unreconciled, frustrated, but understandable. He was just a husband." But Terry had become "less than nothing."

It is not impossible that both Terry and Eileen were designed to be superficial improvements on Fitzgerald's originals. Both had appeared in an earlier short story, "The Curtain," where some of Terry's scenes in the later novel were acted out by Larry Batsel, "a big, handsome brute with eyes like a cow" who had formerly been "a liquor runner" and had returned to "the rackets" as a gambler. When he was revived for *The Long Goodbye* he was given the charm and the gift for intimacy attributed to Dud O'Mara in the earlier story and was consistently revised, deliberately or not, in a way that enabled his surface and his background to stand favorable comparison with Gatsby's. Eileen's peculiar charm had been attributed to Mona Mersarvey, who was known as "Silver Wig" in "The Curtain" before she was given golden hair and made to appear, at first, as perfect and as "nice" as Daisy appeared to Gatsby.

Roger Wade, Chandler's equivalent of Tom Buchanan, is also an improvement over his prototype. A philanderer, a hard drinker, and reputedly violent, he is nevertheless represented as a sensitive, talented man whose excessive drinking does not normally interfere with a successful literary career and whose eventual crack-up is explained by an emotional disturbance deeper than any doubts he might have about his ability to finish his current novel. There may be some pointed significance in the fact that he is a writer of books instead of being the sort of man, as Tom was, who shocked a friend by the improbable fact that he had been depressed by reading one. Roger is altogether a more likeable character than Tom, and his occasional mistress, Sylvia Lennox, has none of the obvious coarseness of Tom's Myrtle Wilson.

There are other characters who play comparable roles in the two books, but the most obvious of these, the narrators Nick Carraway and Philip Marlowe, play them in such different ways that they may be seen as representative of the demands of two different genres rather than as characters related to each other. The only remaining Fitzgerald character in *The Long Goodbye* is Terry's local gangster friend, Mendy Menendez, who, with Randy Starr, is the equivalent of Meyer Wolfsheim. He too might be considered an improvement over the original insomuch as his relationship to Terry was warm rather than cold-blooded, although Chandler had to make his fictional gambler display a ruthlessness and brutality which Fitzgerald could simply imply by identifying Wolfsheim with the real and well-known "fixer" of the 1919 World Series.

The final basis of resemblance between *The Great Gatsby* and *The Long Goodbye* is to be found in the major incident which is crucial in both books: in each story the girl kills her husband's mistress, and, although in each instance her former soldier-lover voluntarily takes the blame, the killing reveals her as more selfish and less "perfect" than she had appeared even in the eyes of the narrator. This incident is handled, however, in such completely different ways in the two novels that its use in Chandler's plot is almost completely disguised. Some of the difference may be attributed to the sort of disguised resemblance found in the characters. But the most important contrast in handling is the result of a difference inherent in the plot of a traditional novel and that of a murder mystery.

Of the various categories which have been invented to describe the plot of a novel that which best fits Fitzgerald's is the "dramatic." The action is centered in a New York suburb and takes place during a single summer which begins with the narrator renewing his acquaintance with the Buchanans and meeting Gatsby for the first time. It rises with the introduction of the Wilsons and the revelation of Tom's affair with Myrtle and with the renewal of Daisy's affair with Gatsby, and it falls rapidly after Daisy kills Myrtle in a hit-and-run accident, although the story itself is prolonged by the narrator's reminiscences before Gatsby is shot by Wilson and by his account of his disillusioning efforts to get somebody to attend Gatsby's funeral. The death of Myrtle is thus the catastrophe. It meets the obligations of the novel to conform to the probabilities of everyday life by being a genuine accident, with a plausible reason for Myrtle's being the victim; and Gatsby's willingness to let it be assumed that he was driving the car is entirely in character. It leads immediately, however, to a solidification of Tom and Daisy's relationship, to Nick's realization of their instinctive attachment to wealth and position rather than to other human beings, and to Gatsby's death before he fully realizes that he has been cast aside. It is a unified event in its proper dramatic place.

The death of Sylvia Lennox in *The Long Goodbye* bears an equally crucial but entirely different relationship to the plot. In the sense that it is a calamitous event which overturns the order of various lives, it too may be called a catastrophe. But it is not a unified incident which has a single dramatic place in the plot. It is divided into two parts: the killing which provides the mystery, and the revelation of the killer which provides the denouement. Between them, as in the plot of most detective novels, is a series of events by which the author maintains a bridge of excitement or suspense between the two parts of a split catastrophe. Since Chandler was always more concerned with excitement than suspense, the plot of *The Long Goodbye* consists primarily of successive scenes of violence in which the detective Marlowe is thrown in jail for helping Terry escape the country, rescues Roger Wade from a weird sanitarium, becomes involved in Roger's death and afterwards with his household, and resists the efforts of Mendy Menendez and others to stop his investigation of Terry's supposed death. Most of it, in short, is characteristic of the detective-story genre and the hardboiled school to which Chandler belonged, and it is therefore completely irrelevant to the sort of novel represented by *The Great Gatsby*.

For the first forty-three chapters of his fifty-three-chapter novel Chandler conformed closely to the demands of his genre. He makes it clear that Marlowe did not believe Terry Lennox killed his wife and that there was a murderer still to be found. He keeps alive the question whether the supposed death of Terry and the shooting of Roger was murder or suicide and does so in a way that motivates Marlowe without committing him to a conclusion. Eileen Wade is gradually revealed as something less than the dream girl she is supposed to be. She is first made to appear prim, then cold, and finally neurotic, and her professed devotion to the memory of her war-time lover is revealed as a protective device which might well drive her husband to a crack-up. But it is not clear until just before the final show-down that Marlowe considers her a murder suspect, and it takes the show-down itself to produce evidence that she has killed both Sylvia Lennox and Roger Wade. The denouement of the concluding line of Chapter 42, "Of course not. She killed both of them," is classic; and the following chapter, in which she leaves a confession and commits suicide, is within the well-established conventions of a genre which is more concerned with poetic justice than with that found in the courtroom.

But the last ten chapters, in comparison with such a perfectly wrought story as Dashiell Hammett's *The Maltese Falcon* for example, are anti-climactic. In them Marlowe makes his peace with the working detectives in the sheriff's office and seriously offends the district attorney and Sylvia's multi-millionaire father by having Eileen's confession published. He spends a night with Sylvia's sister (the first sexual affair in his recorded career) and sends her off to Paris alone with her millions. He manages to get Mendy Menendez permanently removed from the Los Angeles scene, gets impeccable evidence of Terry Lennox's suicide, and finally receives a visit from Terry himself—who, as it turns out, was not dead at all but had established a new identity in Mexico. Some of the substance of these chapters might be justified as the conventional tying up of loose ends, some perhaps might be attributed to an excessive distribution of poetic justice, and some may have been the result of other motives about which we will speculate later. But the revival of Terry Lennox makes mockery of a well-designed plot by revealing that the detective had been engaged in solving a problem of which the reader was entirely unaware:[1] Marlowe had not been trying to clear a friend's name by bringing a real criminal to justice but had been engaged in smoking the supposed friend out of hiding—for no other purpose, it would seem, than to show him that (as Sam Spade told Brigid O'Shaughnessy in *The Maltese Falcon*) "I won't play the sap for you."

The implications of what might be called the secret plot of *The Long Goodbye*, and of the seemingly anti-climactic chapters generally, are that Chandler was attempting something more than a simple detective story. That he was making his attempt within the genre, however, is clearly indicated by his style, which conformed more consistently and successfully to the requirements of the mystery story than did his plot.

Since both Fitzgerald and Chandler used first person narrators, the easiest way to consider the stylistic differences between their two novels is in terms of the personalities, purposes, positions attributed to the fictitious storytellers. Fitzgerald's Nick Carraway was specially created for *The Great Gatsby* and reflected some of the qualities of the author himself and some that the author might expect from a sympathetic reader. He is telling in retrospect the story of a summer's events which have acquired a profound meaning for him, and his purpose is not only to recount the events but reveal their meaning as he becomes aware of it while telling the story. His abstract conclusions appear at the very beginning: "When I came back from the East last autumn I felt that I wanted the world to be in uniform and at a sort of moral attention. . . . Only Gatsby . . . who represented everything for which I have an unaffected scorn . . . turned out all right at the end; it is what preyed on Gatsby, what foul dust floated in the wake of his dreams that temporarily closed out my interest in the abortive sorrows and short-winded elations of men." His narrative is carefully designed to present the concrete facts which will enable the reader to understand and share his conclusions. His position within the story, like that of Conrad's narrators, is one of intimacy with the reader, trying to get him to see what he has seen and respond to it as he responds.

Fitzgerald is therefore not committed to a simple chronicle. He can let Nick re-live some of the events with dramatic immediacy, summarize some of them, and reconstruct others from hearsay in a narrative which sometimes withholds information at the time it is acquired and sometimes anticipates it, which sometimes involves commentary and interpretation and sometimes lets the facts speak for themselves, but which is always controlled by a skilled storyteller's evident desire to reveal to others what had been revealed to him. The narration is free from all mannerisms that might stand between narrator and reader and violate their intimacy, and the general stylistic effect is that of striving toward some larger vision in which objects, actions, and people become increasingly suggestive and symbolic.

Such a style would be inappropriate if not impossible in a detective novel, which, by its very nature, is committed to concealment rather than to revelation, obfuscation rather than illumination. Usually this is achieved without any stylistic problems. The traditional first person narrator in the detective story is a relatively slow-witted individual, such as Dupin's anonymous companion, Holmes's Watson, or even

Nero Wolfe's Archie Goodwin, who shares the reader's own mystification by the detective's eccentricity and brilliance. When the story is told by an omniscient author a greater stylistic discipline is required, but it is normally no more than that demanded by Poe of the author of *Barnaby Rudge* when he pointed out the stylistic slips which put Dickens in the inexcusable position of misleading his readers directly instead of using the indirect method of letting his characters do so. The members of the school to which Chandler belonged, however, made extraordinary demands upon themselves by making their detectives tell the story and solve the mystery without deliberately confusing the reader or withholding information in the process. This required a severe stylistic discipline which had its effect upon the character of the narrator.

Unlike Nick Carraway, Philip Marlowe was a fully realized character before he appeared in this new story. He had evolved from various detectives in Chandler's *Black Mask* stories and acquired a permanent identity in *The Big Sleep*. For fourteen years he had been firmly registered in the public's mind as Chandler's trademark. His style was laconic, tough, and idiomatic, and he had a gift for striking and picturesque imagery which had become characteristic of the Chandler stamp. He, too, told his story in retrospect, but without any evidence of having reflected upon it and without any anticipation of the conclusions he had reached.

This disciplined reserve is the stylistic quality necessary to preserve secrecy in the sort of detective novel Chandler wrote. The most appropriate way of describing it might be to say that it was based upon the normal style of an experienced witness testifying in court. Sworn to tell the truth, the whole truth, and nothing but the truth, he defines truth as what he knows of his own acts and words and what he observes by his five senses. He is permitted incidental reflections ("I'm supposed to be tough but there was something about the guy that got to me") and the opinions implicit in his picturesque speech, but is allowed no interpretations of the evidence. He gets no closer to the reader than the man in the witness chair gets to the jury or spectators in the courtroom. Telling his story in this way, he can never achieve the intimacy that Nick Carraway does. He can engage in no confidences. He must always remain a sort of stage figure.

The stylistic technique of detached perceptiveness has brought a new illusion of realism into the detective story, but it does not lend itself readily to the sort of suggestive realism of Fitzgerald's novel in which particulars tend to become symbolic. Just as the plot of a mystery novel prevents an anticipation that so-and-so will turn out all right—or all wrong—in the end, the style of Chandler's novel prevents an enlarging vision of what might be considered morally "right." The murder mystery in particular had been developed around the concept of guilt and innocence, and the new realism did not lessen the difficulty it had in dealing with the subtler concepts of right and wrong.

II

Although the murder mystery, in the hey-day of Hercule Poirot, Dr. Fell, and Lord Peter Wimsey, has been hailed as the last stronghold of morality in literature, the more modern hard-boiled type is not usually associated with moral values. Raymond Chandler, in fact, was unusual in his insistence upon them. In the most frequently quoted passage from what he himself called his too-often quoted essay, "The Simple Art of Murder," he described his own type of fictional detective in the real world of crime: "Down these mean streets a man must go who is not himself mean, who is neither tarnished nor afraid. . . . He is the hero; he is everything . . . a complete man and a common man and yet an unusual man . . . a man of honor . . . the best man in his world and a good enough man for any world." It was the story of "this man's adventure in the search of hidden truth" that he wanted to tell. It was this kind of story that he admired in Dashiell Hammett's *The Glass Key*, "the record of a man's devotion to a friend," which Hammett himself "thought the most of"; and it was this kind of story that Hammett told in *The Maltese Falcon*, which Chandler considered the finest work of its kind.

In the latter novel Sam Spade turns Brigid O'Shaughnessy over to the police for reasons which are relevant to the moral values implicit in Chandler's *The Long Goodbye*. Two of them reflect a feeling of loyalty—an irrational loyalty to his murdered partner, regardless of the low opinion he had of him, and a reasoned loyalty to his profession. One was the sort of instinctive aversion to criminals which had made him a detective. Others represent practical considerations: his recognition of an involvement in criminal activities which he can escape only by standing with the law, and his knowledge that Brigid either might use her knowledge of him for blackmail or might murder him to protect herself against his knowledge of her. His last reason was that he didn't "even like the idea of thinking that there might be one chance in a hundred that you'd played me for a sucker." This, in the light of Spade's character, seems to be a trivial afterthought; but it is this that he stresses, over and over again, when he says "I won't play the sap for you." And it is this reiteration of the most trivial of reasons which humanizes Spade by revealing him in the position of trying to be and to appear as tough as Brigid really is.

The relevance of this to *The Long Goodbye* is that Marlowe might have invoked most or all of these reasons if he had confronted Eileen Wade with an intention to turn her over to the police. That there was no confrontation was Chandler's fault: he simply had not prepared a sound case against her. The firm logic of Hammett was not one of his gifts, and, lacking it, he could only do what many other mystery writers have done under similar circumstances — substantiate his detective's charges with a confession and a suicide. But Spade's reasons were implicit in everything that had been revealed in the story up to that point. Marlowe's strongest visible motive was loyalty to a dead friend, however poorly he thought of him, and he had preserved the integrity of his profession by refusing to take a fee from anybody else involved in the case. He had certainly demonstrated his inbred aversion to crooks of all sorts on every possible occasion, and he had every practical reason to cooperate with the police with whom he was in bad standing. He could have adduced some danger from Eileen, and it would have been quite natural for him, had he been forced to it, to play tough by showing her that she could not play him for a sucker.

These reasons carried over into most of the ten concluding chapters of the book. Marlowe told Lonnie Morgan, the newspaperman who arranged for the publication of Eileen's confession, that he had been "a long, long time" saying good-bye to a friend and that the publication was it. Afterwards Morgan called him and said: "You did it for him . . . I don't figure what made it worth your time. Lennox wasn't that much man." "What's that got to do with it?" Marlowe replied. Morgan "was silent for a moment. Then he said: 'Sorry, Marlowe. Shut my big mouth. Good luck.'" In these chapters Marlowe also made his rough peace with the sheriff's men — at least with those who shared his aversion to crooks and the smooth boys in the D.A.'s office — and cooperated with them in making Mendy Menendez aware that there was no future in abusing either the official police or a private detective. He played Sam Spade's role, in fact, up until the last two chapters.

Chandler's revival of Terry Lennox, however, produced some curious reversals of motivation. Menendez rather than Marlowe, as it turned out, had been acting out of loyalty to a friend. Since it developed that Marlowe had known all along that Terry had neither committed suicide nor been murdered, his conflict with Menendez became, in retrospect, a battle of egos in which the gangster had the more admirable motives. The *noblesse oblige* to which Marlowe tacitly laid claim in his telephone conversation with Lonnie Morgan lost its nobility. His brutal comment to Terry that his former friend would not have come back at all "if I hadn't smoked you out" doesn't suggest the tough front of a man who is hiding a heartache in conflict with justice but a real desire to tell Terry that "I won't play the sap for you." For the first and only time in Chandler's fiction Marlowe appears, in these last two chapters, as a man who is himself mean.

This is a harsh charge and certainly one that Chandler did not consciously intend to invite. Yet it is, I think, a legitimate one; and the reason why Chandler made Marlowe behave in this unusual way toward Terry — and in an equally unusual way toward Linda Loring — may be suggested by a return to the Fitzgerald comparison.

The explicit moral values in *The Great Gatsby* to which Nick Carraway wanted the world to stand at attention were incorporated in Gatsby himself. He "turned out all right," we are told at the beginning, because of his "heightened sensitivity to the promises of life" and "his extraordinary gift for hope." Or, as Nick put it at the very end, "Gatsby believed in the green light" which had physically identified Daisy's place but which had come to symbolize the sign to go ahead into a future which existed in hope rather than in reality. He also exemplified a generosity and a capacity for love and compassion which set him distinctly apart from the other characters Nick observed. "They're a rotten crowd . . . you're worth the whole damn bunch put together" were nearly the last words Nick said to Gatsby, and he remembered later that he had "always been glad" he said them. That Gatsby was also a crook, holding a high position in a criminal syndicate, seems to have been a matter of indifference to Fitzgerald and only one of the many things about Gatsby of which Nick disapproved.

There are other values implicit in the book, and the most important of these is Fitzgerald's respect for wealth—particularly the inherited wealth he attributes to Tom Buchanan. His often-quoted conviction that the very rich were "different" from the rest of mankind underlies his portrayal of Tom and Daisy, and it enables him to let Nick dismiss them, plausibly enough, from the story by saying: "They were careless people, Tom and Daisy — they smashed up things and creatures and then retreated back into their money or their vast carelessness, or whatever it was that kept them together, and let other people clean up the mess they had made." However squeamish Nick was about Tom, he parted from him with a handshake because he suddenly felt as though he were "talking to a child" — but he doesn't seem to realize that he is representing him as a child from another world where men like Gatsby are but flies for boys to kill for sport.

The Long Goodbye provides a strong contrast to this tacit respect for wealth because Chandler was aggressively convinced that the rich were just like everybody else and usually more so. Wherever his ideal detective might be supposed to go, Philip Marlowe was most often seen driving along Hollywood Boulevard, the winding roads of Bel Air, and the broad avenues of Pasadena, where he found people considerably worse than the more timid souls who inhabited the mean streets of South Santa Monica and Venice. In *The Long Goodbye* Harlan Potter, the father of Sylvia Lennox and Linda Loring, is the richest of the rich, but Marlowe defies him to his face and gives him and all his creatures their comeuppance when he keeps the scandal of Sylvia's death alive and uses Eileen's confession to reveal the attempted cover-up. Chandler made it somewhat excessively evident that Marlowe isn't a man to be either brushed off or bought.

It may be that this explains why he allowed Marlowe to abandon his usual celibate role long enough to spend a night with Linda Loring. His refusal, under such circumstances, of her proposal of marriage is the ultimate demonstration of Marlowe's financial integrity, for a share of her millions, even though the marriage might last for only a few months, would be a greater reward than all of the fees he had refused during the case or could expect to earn in the future. But Marlowe is given another reason: "This way you will remember me," he says after his refusal. He admits that he may be overstating his case, but it was the best he could do to keep her from retreating into the vast carelessness of the very rich in the way her father had retreated until he was shaken up again by the publication of Eileen's confession.

If a substantial portion of the anti-climactic section of *The Long Goodbye* is devoted to provoking the rich, a larger portion is devoted to destroying the crooks — even though they are not, as fictional crooks go, very vicious ones and are completely innocent of any crimes represented in the novel. Mendy Menendez is the tough and rather stupid boss of Los Angeles County gambling, but his acts of brutality are from motives which seem admirable in the Sam Spade of *The Maltese Falcon*: professional responsibility and loyalty to a friend whose security, he thinks, is being jeopardized by Marlowe's investigation. This sort of loyalty had been notably absent among Gatsby's friends, and Nick Carraway had shown a sentimental concern for it in his efforts to get Meyer Wolfsheim to attend his associate's funeral. Marlowe seems completely unimpressed by the loyalty of a crook for an associate. He is willing to save Mendy's life but not to prevent his punishment and exile. When Terry, at their last meeting, says "He has a heart," Marlowe's cynical reply is "So has a snake."

Terry Lennox, though guilty of running away from the scene of a crime and of faking suicide, is not a crook at all in any ordinary sense. He had accepted a legitimate job from Randy Starr, twice when he needed it, in a Las Vegas casino, and had accepted a settlement of a quarter of a million dollars the second time he married Sylvia. Marlowe's worst charge against him was that he was "just as happy with mugs or hoodlums as with honest men" provided they spoke good English and had good manners. This made him, in Marlowe's words, "a moral defeatist" and worthy of the sort of contempt which hurt Terry enough to bring "a glint of tears in his eyes." Marlowe refused to drink with him in memory of their former friendship, but shakes hands, in parting, as Nick did with Tom Buchanan. But before doing so he tells him off: "You're a very sweet guy in a lot of ways. I'm not judging you. I never did. It's just that you're not here any more. You're long gone. You've got nice clothes and perfume and you're as elegant as a fifty-dollar whore." This may not have been intended as a judgment, but if Terry had been following the green light of hope Marlowe was certainly trying to put it out.

The last two chapters of *The Long Goodbye* place Marlowe in a role so different from that of the knight-errant he is in the rest of the book (and in the other novels) that one is inclined to speculate on what was going on in Chandler's mind. The transformation of his hero was surely inadvertent. It is possible that he felt he had made Terry Lennox too charming, too generous, and too self-sacrificing and was so determined to destroy any favorable image of him that he was blind to the devastating effect his effort would also have on Marlowe. In any event he made sure that Terry did not turn out all right in the end.

The contrast between Chandler's attitude toward Terry Lennox and Fitzgerald's toward Jay Gatsby is so striking that it seems calculated. Yet there is no external evidence that Chandler planned it that way. There is some indication within the novel, however, that Chandler was thinking about Fitzgerald when he was writing *The Long Goodbye*. The book contains an unusual number of literary allusions, but the relationship between Roger Wade and Fitzgerald is more than an allusion. Roger himself calls attention to it in a note he leaves after his mysterious disappearance: "I do not care to be in love with myself and there is no longer anyone else for me to be in love with. Signed: Roger (F. Scott Fitzgerald) Wade. P.S. This is why I never finished *The Last Tycoon*." When Marlowe asked about the meaning of the note, Eileen explained: "He has always been a great admirer of Scott Fitzgerald. He says Fitzgerald is the best drunken writer since Coleridge, who took dope." The relationship was not only in Wade's mind but in the mind of his creator: Wade was represented as a Princeton graduate, a genuinely fine writer who knew that he was wasting his talents on popular stuff, and an excessive drinker who was struggling with an unfinished novel at the time of his Hollywood crack-up. He also, as we learn later, was deeply affected by his wife's mental condition. There were numerous differences between Wade and Fitzgerald, too, but these parallels are enough to suggest that the author of *The Great Gatsby* was on the mind — if not on the conscience — of the author of *The Long Goodbye*.

Chandler sent his book off to his agents and, as Philip Durham says, "made the mistake of asking for criticism." The criticism he got was an opinion, strange in the light of the published novel, that "something unfortunate had happened to Philip Marlowe — he had gone sentimental and become Christ-like." Durham reports that Chandler "spent many months in rewriting but was unable to reconcile himself to the criticism of his agents" and so severed connections with them and brought out the "new" version of his book in England.[2] Whether he wrote the last two chapters in an effort to reconcile Marlowe with the criticism I do not know, but, with reference to the pervading values in his book, he could have used a Fitzgerald comparison in order to defend himself against the charge of sentimentality. He could have said that he was a lot tougher than Fitzgerald had been — tougher on crooks, tougher on the rich, tougher in his insistence that people be responsible for their actions, and tougher in his determination to make his world stand "at a sort of moral attention" instead of joining Nick Carraway in merely wishing it would.

It is difficult, though, to imagine Chandler comparing his finished book with Fitzgerald's, just as it is difficult to imagine that, while writing it, he could have been aware of the many parallels that can be abstracted from the two such different novels. Chandler was too proud of his own individuality and independence to have consciously bound himself to the work of another writer as closely as he seems to have done in *The Long Goodbye*. But it is also difficult to imagine that he could have added so much anti-climactic material to a coherent story without having a serious reason for doing so. He certainly evinced in this material a powerful antipathy for the respect for wealth Fitzgerald had shown in *The Great Gatsby* and such a strong determination to draw a line between crooks and honest men that he was willing to convict Terry Lennox of guilt by association and to jeopardize the nobility of Marlowe by doing it. The last two chapters seem especially designed to insist that Terry belonged with the "rotten bunch" and to give Marlowe the chance to tell him so.

However obscure the motives of a writer may and must be, a comparison of these two books suggests that Chandler was serious about something other than his craftsmanship. He was genuinely serious about moral values and apparently so offended by those he found implicit in Fitzgerald's novel that he sacrificed his own craftsmanship to an attack on respect for wealth and tolerance for crooks. How constantly Fitzgerald was in his mind during the composition of *The Long Goodbye* is uncertain. But it is easy to imagine that at some time during the inception of his book Chandler had the notion of creating his own Gatsby and of making sure that his could not be called a "great" one.

NOTES

[1] The reader of course is given the same information that enables Marlowe to infer that Terry's farewell letter is a fake — i.e., the reference to a mailbox which would not be found in a Mexican village. The validity of this clue for the reader, however, depends upon his faith in Chandler's conformity to a reality that exists outside the novel itself; and this faith cannot be claimed by an author who asks the reader to believe that Terry could be presumed dead and still maintain control over a substantial fortune which he could not have taken with him in his sudden flight. Chandler also seems to ask the reader to believe that some "person or persons unknown" moved Sylvia's body and mutilated it after she had been shot outside the guest house.

[2] For Durham's comments see *Down These Mean Streets a Man Must Go* (Chapel Hill: The University of North Carolina Press, 1963), pp. 100-01. I have not examined the Chandler correspondence or any of the Chandler manuscripts in the UCLA library which might cast light on the Fitzgerald connection.

A FOREWORD TO

"DEATH IN HOLLYWOOD"

By Thomas Sturak

IN THE COURSE of an essay, "Horace McCoy, Captain Shaw, and the *Black Mask*," in the 1972 *Mystery & Detection Annual*, I mentioned the existence of a half-dozen unpublished manuscripts dating from the early thirties.[1] The title of one of these—"Death in Hollywood"—and my noting that it contained an allusion to Dashiell Hammett aroused the curiosity of the editors of the *Annual* who prevailed upon me to unearth the yellowing 57-page typescript. Here it appears in print for the first time, some forty years after its creation in McCoy's modest Hollywood apartment on North Beachwood Drive.

This story, whose hero-narrator is a kind of Continental Op in Movieland, at first glance seems in the Hammett mold. But in substance it is the real McCoy. Though superficially "hardboiled" in sound and texture, its uncomplicated linear plot rides on no compelling scenes of physical violence. And the real "mystery," it seems to me, resides not in the unravelling of the murder but rather in the vagaries of the story's composition. For example, the half-stated yet perfectly clear underlying theme of homosexuality and deviant sex: surely, as a veteran pulp writer, McCoy knew *that* wouldn't sell (especially not to the notoriously prudish Captain Shaw). He may have been trying to be as honest about a part of the Hollywood world as he could. That his presentation of that nether world is totally readable today and his hints early in the story about the nature of his characters are entirely effective, says much for his mastery of a difficult subject matter. He handled the theme in a manner far ahead of its time in detective fiction.[2] But for practical purposes of making a sale to *Black Mask* (or any other pulp) in 1933, such literary license was fatally perverse.

Other intriguing disparities between style and substance are also reflected in the allusion to Hammett. At the time—1932-1933— Hammett was making big money as a studio writer and McCoy was eager to follow in his ex-*Black Mask* colleague's footsteps.[3] McCoy's fortunes, however, were at their nadir. He had come to California from Dallas early in 1931, leaving behind a ten-year career as a newspaperman and bearing a national reputation as a little theatre actor (note the hero's acid remark about Mrs. Talley in the story). Full of self-confidence and the highest ambitions, he seems immediately to have sought out Hammett, who may well have helped him gain entree to the studios.⁴ But for the next two years, while waiting for the "big break," both as an actor and a scenarist, McCoy lived the down-and-out existence common to the 20,000 extras during these cruelest years of the Great Depression.⁵ Desultorily, he also wrote pulp stories, but sold few. The implied compliment to Hammett as a writer is tinged with the pathos of his own growing fears of failure. In a passage cut from the story, the narrator asks an (utterly) extraneous character, a girl who composes songs, why she doesn't publish: "She said she was going down hill and that it was a nice hill and that she didn't want to be a success because success was a worse bore than failure."

McCoy's experiences in Hollywood during the early thirties were crucial and determinative in his career as a novelist. Besides providing him with the raw materials for two books, the initial shock of failure and the compromising struggle for success set the emotional bent of his creative imagination. Even in his earliest pulp stories we catch glimpses of an inward-turning artistic sensibility and of a personality capable of being at one and the same time acute observer and naive participant. By 1933, McCoy's sense as a reporter had seen through the slick patina of Hollywood glamor and smelled out the underlying corruption of talent; and his romantic temperament was always repulsed by the perversion of genius peculiar to the movie business. As emotional autobiography, "Death in Hollywood" is aptly titled. (It is interesting that the manuscript carries the title "Murder in Hollywood" on every page after the first—perhaps a feeble attempt to make it sound more "pulpy.")

Technically, "Death in Hollywood," like McCoy's other pulp stories from this period, is less interesting for its skilled but mannered "hardboiled" style than for the flashes of lyricism and "symbolism" that are the dominant aesthetic characteristics of his best fiction. Consider his half-hearted—always with the faintest pencil marks—major excisions: for example, the early sailor/girl image, which seems meant to serve as a "normal" (heterosexual) contrast to the later allusion of "perverted" (homosexual) assignations on Waterloo Bridge (an allusion also meant for excision). Of course, some words and cuts—especially the profanity and overwritten descriptions—are kinds McCoy knew Captain Shaw (and other pulp editors) would frown upon. But others are either graceful, even poetical, or psychologically revealing. (All the cuts have been restored here, enclosed within square brackets.)

Whatever its failings as gripping, action-packed pulp literature, "Death in Hollywood" from beginning to end shows the hand of an accomplished writer. For example, the opening dialogue concerning the missing former "movie star" is matched with references to the "California sky"—and both images are suggestively reflected in the story's concluding paragraph. Certain details are chosen to lend verisimilitude—as Hammett had done in the Continental Op stories set in San Francisco—the use of concrete place names (the Brown Derby, and the Oxford telephone exchange, which at that time served West Hollywood and Beverly Hills) or of current events (recent political murders in Hollywood, and book titles). McCoy's impressionistic description is aimed to evoke an ambience:

> The street on which Randolf Morris lived looked like any other street where it crossed Hollywood Boulevard near the Chinese theater, and for three blocks northward it maintained that orthodox appearance, lined with palms and neat little bungalows. Then, as if it were far enough from the eyes of the crowds to do as it pleased, it suddenly and crazily went haywire. It became a narrow, dimly-lighted alley, twisting tortuously up hill and finally spending itself against the belly of a mountain.

Set off by judicious cutting of the next three paragraphs, this passage strikingly foreshadows descriptive techniques to be used by Raymond Chandler in his own "hardboiled" tales set in Hollywood. (Compare Randolf Morris's narrow white house in the Hollywood hills with the one in *The Big Sleep*; and the air of danger is the same.)

But at the time "Death in Hollywood" was written (and Chandler was still only thinking about submitting his first pulp effort to *Black Mask*), McCoy was moving in new directions. At the very moment, he was once again worrying at the manuscript of an earlier short story, originally called "Marathon Dance," that he'd retitled, sent to his New York agent, and received back. In a personal letter dated 3 September 1932, he complained that editors objected to "the length and the rawer profanity, but . . . I'm getting right to work on it to shove it back East as God knows I need the money."[6] This cut and expurgated manuscript also bounced, as did another, even shorter version late in 1933; and now Horace McCoy was at work doing something else with "They Shoot Horses, Don't They?" . . . but that's another story.

NOTES

[1] (Beverly Hills, Calif.: Donald Adams, 1972), p. 151.

[2] See Vern L. Bullough, "Deviant Sex and the Detective Story," in this volume, pp. 326-30.

[3] In the February 1932 *Black Mask*, Shaw answered the "many letters" asking when

another story by Hammett would appear in the magazine: "When a fellow is pulling $100,000.00 a year out in Hollywood, we don't just have the heart—or is it nerve?—to suggest that he knock off coupon cutting for a bit and turn us out one of those great old Continental Op stories" ("Behind the Mask," p. 120).

4 "Horace McCoy, Captain Shaw, and the *Black Mask*," p. 151. As early as 1929, McCoy had submitted one of his *Black Mask* stories ("Renegades of the Rio," pub. December 1929) to a Hollywood agent, Al Bridges, who encouraged him to send more (letter, 17 Dec. 1929). And in a long letter to the editor of *Detective-Dragnet Magazine* (December 1930, pp. 121-22), McCoy wrote that "one talkie has been made from one of my pulp-paper stories." But I have never found evidence of any screen credits prior to his arrival in Hollywood.

5 The figure represents the round number of extras registered by the Central Casting Corporation during the thirties and is given in many sources (e.g., Carey McWilliams, *Southern California Country*; and McCoy's novel, *I Should Have Stayed Home*).

6 To Helen Vinmont, who became McCoy's second wife in November 1933. The late Mrs. McCoy kindly allowed me to make notes from her personal correspondence with McCoy.

DEATH IN HOLLYWOOD[1]

By Horace McCoy

I

WHEN THE clerk handed me the telegram, I said, "I've got a hunch this means trouble. I oughtn't to open it. I ought to let you send it back, marked, 'Not at This Address.' I ought to change hotels."

The clerk did not say anything.

I took the telegram to my room. All the way up I had a feeling of indomitable despair, like that of a man carrying through choice a bomb, which, at a certain hour each day, may or may not explode. I knew the telegram was from the agency because nobody else had my address. They had sent me to Hollywood for a thirty day vacation and now, after five days, they were calling me in. Well, the hell with them, I thought. I won't report back.

I opened the telegram. It was from the Old Man. *"Imperative you see Menefee at once stop regards,"* it read and the signature was J.K.

Menefee was branch manager of the International on the west coast. A couple of hours later I scuttled into his office and asked him what it was all about.

"Sorry to interfere with your party," he said, "but we've got to have some help."

I asked him what kind of help. He asked me if I had been reading the papers. I told him I'd been having too much fun. He rolled a fat black cigar around in his mouth and took in a lot of the California sky with his big brown eyes.

"Helen Brockton's disappeared," he said.

I asked him who was Helen Brockton.

"Well, then, Helen Ridley," he said.

"I remember her," I said. When I was pounding pavements ten years ago she was the most popular movie star of them all.

"Sure, you remember her. She dropped out of circulation when she married Hobart Brockton, a guy with practically all the money in the world. She's been gone ten days."

"Gone where?" I asked.

"Nobody knows. I'm surprised you haven't read about it," he said, looking fretful. He looked at the California sky again. He had a curving scar across his left cheek. "There's certainly been little else in the papers." He buzzed a dictaphone. "Sara, tell Mr. Brockton our New York office has located Mr. Palmer," he said, and then looked at me. "I'll let him tell you."

"All right," I said [and looked out the window. A girl down on the the corner was crying into the blue chest of a sailor, who was shaking his head emphatically]. The sun was spinning into the window. Menefee sat in a cone of heat, playing with the black cigar. [The sun was dripping down in a golden paste over his face and hands. He talked about the International, gave me the inside dirt on a couple of political murders in Hollywood and then switched to a job I had cleaned up in Chicago.] He introduced me to a young op named Carter and I got a couple of looks at Sara. Sara was better looking than any of the picture people I'd seen.

"Cute," I remarked, when she had gone out.

Menefee stopped playing with his cigar. "Lay off," he said.

The hell I will, I thought. ["All right," I said.]

Brockton finally showed up. He was tall, lean and classy. He wore fawn-colored spats and a black derby, otherwise he looked like a banker. Menefee steered him into a chair and gave me a flowery introduction, ending with, "Now, by God, we'll get somewhere."

"I hope so," Brockton said in a tone that implied he didn't expect much. He sat down. "I don't care how much money you spend or who's involved, I want results."

"Oh, you'll get results," I said.

A parallelogram of sunshine crawled over his shoes, showing up the dust on the floor. Where there was no parallelogram of sunshine the floor was clean. The city smelled through the window.

"I think I'm going to like you," Brockton said gravely.

"Then you'll be the first," I said, and asked him what about his wife.

He asked me if I knew who she was before her marriage. I told him I did.

"She gave up pictures when we married five years ago," he said. He spoke slowly as if he had difficulty in remembering. "Since then we have been rather happy."

I asked him if he had any idea what could have happened to her.

"She just disappeared," he said, shaking his head.

"What do you mean disappeared? You mean she just walked out the door and disappeared?"

"Practically," Brockton said.

Menefee licked the loose wrapper on his cigar. A string of silver spittle looped from his mouth to the cigar. He looked at me but didn't say anything.

"Go on, tell me about it," I said to Brockton.

"On the day she disappeared," he related, "she telephoned me at the office that she was going shopping. She said she'd be home around six o'clock."

"Did she telephone you every time she went shopping?"

"No —"

"Then why do you suppose she telephoned you this particular day?" I asked.

"I don't know," he said.

"Go on," I said.

He uncrossed his legs and his hat spilled to the floor. It was nothing, just a hat spilling to the floor. But it seemed to rattle him. He made a ceremony out of picking it up.

"Sorry," he said, self-consciously, putting it on the desk.

"That's all right," I said. "We'd got to the point where your wife had disappeared."

He suddenly reddened all over his face. He slid forward a little in his chair. "I resent the tone of your questions," he said, suddenly furious. "I'm not going to stand for cheap sarcasms and veiled insinuations."

I looked at him as if I were utterly bewildered.

Menefee dropped his cigar into a brass cuspidor and stood up, saying in his best placatory voice: "You're nervous, Mr. Brockton. He's trying to help you, that's all."

Nobody said anything for a minute. Brockton slid back in his chair and crossed his legs petulantly. Menefee hooked one leg over the edge of his desk. I lighted a cigarette and looked out the window. [The girl and the sailor were gone.]

"If you don't mind I wish you'd finish this up so I can get along," Brockton said crossly. "I've got business —"

"I don't mind. Go on with the story," I said.

"Yes, please," Menefee said.

Brockton went on: "The last person known to have seen her was Malone, the chauffeur. He let her out at a department store on the boulevard."

"We've checked that," Menefee said to me. "We've checked everything. Nobody in the store remembers seeing her."

"Did she go in?" I asked Brockton.

"We don't know. The chauffeur didn't see her. He drove away."

"She wasn't an unknown," I said. "People recognized her. That was your experience, wasn't it, Mr. Brockton? People recognized her?"

"Yes, they did. Often."

I nodded. "So with the newspapers carrying so much on the case it's reasonable to assume that if she'd been seen that person would have notified the police?"

"Yes," Brockton said.

"That's what we thought," Menefee said.

"Did you have reason to suspect your wife of infidelity, Mr. Brockton?" I asked.

"I'm quite sure of that," he said, faintly amused.

The parallelogram of sunshine had crawled over to my own feet. The laces in my left shoe needed replacing.

"It may be ransom," I said.

"I hope so," Brockton said warmly.

"If it's ransom they're waiting a long time," Menefee said, getting off the desk.

I looked up at nothing. I was always looking up at nothing. "I'd like to have a look at your house. Where do you live, Mr. Brockton?" I said.

He gave me an address in Los Feliz hills. He picked up his hat. "If you're going to Hollywood I'll drop you off," he said.

"Yes," I said.

"If you'll excuse us a moment —" Menefee said to Brockton. He nodded and went into the outer office. Menefee rolled a fresh cigar around in his hands, looking at me critically. "You'll have to go easy," he said. "You've been used to hoodlums. This guy's no hoodlum. Don't make him sore."

"All right, I won't make him sore," I said.

Menefee grinned. Muscles caught up heavy corners of his mouth. "What do you think about this?"

"I don't know anything about it yet," I replied.

"Well, you've got some feeling about it," he said, waving the cigar baton-wise.

"Sure, I've got that, all right, but I may be wrong."

The scar on his cheek was quivering. He smelled sweaty.

"What's your feeling?" he said.

"I think she's dead," I said.

"That's funny, I feel the same way about it," he said, showing three teeth over his lower lip.

"That *is* funny," I said, going out.

Sara stopped her typing and smiled at me as I passed by. My neck heated. I smiled back.

"Not bad-looking," Brockton said confidentially.

"Not bad," I said.

We went out together. As we stepped into the corridor there was a scuffling of feet and three or four flashlight bulbs exploded. I threw up my hands to hide my face. Reporters crowded around us.

"What about the kidnaping?" one of them asked me.

I shivered. "What kidnaping?" I said.

"Somebody kidnaped Helen Brockton," he said.

"That so?" I asked, using an utterly surprised tone. "Who did it?"

He grinned foolishly but his eyes were hard. "You won't get to first base that way," he said, joining the other reporters. They had surrounded Brockton, all talking at once. Brockton was shaking his head, saying, "There's nothing new, there's nothing new," in a weary voice. The reporters finally gave up. They moved away, muttering. Two of them turned around, glaring at me.

"They don't like you," Brockton said. "That's bad. You oughtn't have offended them."

I shivered again. "I don't care who likes me and who doesn't," I said in my slowest voice.

He led me to his car, not saying anything else.

II

The papers used the pictures the next morning. The picture of me was blurred and indistinguishable; I had got my hand up in time. The reporters sarcastically reported that now I was on the scene the mystery was practically solved. The stories had the same flavor. It looked as if I had offended them. They praised me too much. They dismissed the work of the police department in a couple of derogatory paragraphs. It was old stuff; they were trying to keep me from getting to first base by making the police department jealous of me. Before I'd got out of bed Menefee called up to ask if I'd seen the papers.

I cursed a little and told him I had.

"So has Ed Fritz, detective-lieutenant in charge of the case," Menefee said. "I wanted to tip you off what kind of a guy he is."

It was cold in the room. I was naked. "All right, hurry up and tell me," I said.

"Stay just as far away from him as you can," he said.

I said I would, thanked him and hung up. When I had finished dressing I went downstairs to the coffee shop. A nice-looking blonde sitting against the wall kept lifting her eyes coyly at me over her grapefruit, but I don't like blondes for breakfast, so I gave all my attention to my toast and marmalade. When I paid my check I noticed she had got interested in a baldheaded man.

I went to Brockton's.

I didn't like the looks of the place.

The taxi-driver let me out in front of a high-grilled gate that was padlocked on the inside. From either side of it tall hedging ran off for the rest of the block. The upper part of a red-tiled house was visible over the hedge-top on the left.

I pulled a knob and somewhere behind the hedge a bell rang. The noise brought a flat-faced young man to the gate. He walked with a decided limp. He had on a chauffeur's uniform, unbuttoned. He looked at me, frowning.

"This Brockton's?" I asked.

He said that it was, but made no move to let me in.

"I'd like to come in," [I said.] "I'm the detective he spoke about. Or did he speak about it?"

"Oh, yes, sir, we're expecting you," he said, opening the gate.

We walked up the roadway side by side. The chauffeur's left leg was shorter than his right and his foot was twisted a little. You could tell he was crippled by the way his feet crunched the gravel. The roadway curved off to the right and all I could see of the house was the red-tiled roof. There was another high-grilled gate ahead of us that let the road into another street. Through the iron bars I could see the vivid pattern of Hollywood below. The farther we moved forward the more I could see of it. We were up pretty high. There were raw cotton clouds over the Pacific.

I caught the chauffeur looking at me out of the corner of his eye. "What do you know about this?" I asked.

"Nothing, sir. Not a thing," he said.

I thought he was a little anxious to get the words out, as if he had been expecting that identical question. "You were the last person known to have seen her," I reminded him.

He admitted that but reiterated he didn't know anything about it. He smiled sadly. He had nice teeth. He needed a shave.

The road at last brought us to the house. It was a two-story stucco that rambled all over the place. It looked like a fortress. No, not a fortress, exactly. It was more like pictures of the Alhambra.

The chauffeur, limping crab-like, took me in the back way.

A short, red-faced woman of fifty or so, with her sleeves rolled up, was in the kitchen. She said, "Ah, Malone —" as if the chauffeur had just returned from a long visit.

"This is the gentleman —" the chauffeur said.

"You're another detective," she said to me, smiling with her wide mouth.

"[All right,] I'm another detective," I said.

"I certainly do hope you find Mrs. Brockton," she said, still smiling.

"I do too," I said.

Somewhere forward a voice called: "Martha, who's there?"

Martha went to a swinging door and shoved it open. It led to a small pantry, a sort of china-closet, between the kitchen and the dining room.

"That detective Mr. Brockton hired," she said.

"Bring him in," the voice called.

I was trying to figure out whether it was a man's voice or a woman's voice. Martha answered that one for me.

"That's Mill Talley, Mrs. Brockton's secretary," she whispered. "This way."

She led me through the pantry into a luxurious, deep-toned dining room that creaked under the weight of massive old furniture, through the dining room into a carpeted hall and down a short flight of steps to the drawing room. The whole thing was ornate as a motion-picture set. The drawing room was so full of flowers I had to look twice before I saw Miss Talley. She was sitting in a plush chair by the radio, a newspaper in her lap.

When I approached her she got up, saying, "Thank you, Martha," in that same confusing voice. Martha went out. Miss Talley said, "How do you do, sit down," and shook hands with me vigorously. She had strong hands. The way she moved them they seemed to be alive. Faint powder showed on her face but her lips were not painted.

She was handsome in a robust, athletic way. She wore a blue coat suit and combed her hair straight back. She took a cigarette from a brass humidor and lighted it. When she thought the suspense had been properly built, she said, "I hope I can help you," keeping her cigarette in her mouth as she talked. It jerked with her words.

"Well, thank God, everybody's giving me moral support," I said.

"I beg your pardon?"

"Nothing," I said, thinking she ought to join some Little Theater movement where she could have a legitimate outlet for her suppressed dramatic desires in order not to inflict them on strangers.

We sat down. She laid the newspaper in a small, square-backed chair. It was antique and looked it. The upholstery was badly frayed.

"I've got a chair like that at home," I remarked.

"That's very early eighteenth century," she said, looking skeptical. "That cost Mr. Brockton a small fortune."

"I traded a gallon of blood for mine. I shot a man and then gave him a gallon of blood to keep him alive," I said.

"Why?"

"So they could electrocute him," I said.

"Well, I hope somebody is electrocuted for this business," she said, speaking around her cigarette. Her eyelids were orange. "Nobody has done anything yet."

"It takes time," I said. "May I have a cigarette?"

She passed me the humidor with one hand and flicked a lighter with the other. Her nails were smooth and clean but not polished. There was a long thin scratch across the back of her right hand.

I thanked her and inhaled. The sunlight dripped through a tall cypress in the patio outside. The water in the swimming pool beyond was blue velvet. I knew Miss Talley was watching me closely. When I looked back into the room she pretended to be interested in a bowl of roses on the piano.

"Do you think you can help any?" I finally said.

"I know very little about it," she said, simulating sadness but overdoing it.

"I mean about her habits and her friends. Everybody knows she's disappeared," I said.

She threw her cigarette over a screen into an open fireplace. "Her habits were regular. She had few close friends."

"Well, what's your theory?" I asked.

"Ransom," she said promptly. "I think she was kidnaped. Mr. Brockton is very wealthy."

The fountain in the patio gushed out a wave of sounds. It was a small tumult. I often wonder why people do not hear what other people's minds are saying as they talk to them. I watched the flakes accumulate on the end of my cigarette while my mind said: This ought to be a swell show, it has got a superb set, nice props and a hell of a good plot. But the acting is awful. The cast needs more rehearsal.

"May I see her room?" I asked.

Miss Talley took me upstairs, closed the door and left me alone.

III

The room was a tent of silks which the sun made golden. Wind got through the open windows, lifting the silks briskly and making everything tremble. There were two full-length mirrors at either end of the room. The bath was black and yellow tile. The tub was sunken so that when the door closed the person bathing had a full view in the mirror. There were many bottles of bath salts, looking like striped candy in cellophane, a pair of fancy white scales built into the wall, an army of bottles such as they advertise in Vanity Fair and many, many rough towels.

Glassed in beside the tub was a shower with ten needles. I turned a couple of knobs and the water sprayed out with stinging force. Adjoining the bath was an alcove of mirrors which formed a dressing room. I pulled open the compartment doors. There were fifty or more bathing suits, at least a hundred pairs of shoes, as many dresses and a special closet for hats. This place was a crazy asylum of fashion. The hats were all standing at attention on small french-model wooden heads. I copied down some of the milliner's names from the labels and went back into the bedroom.

There were a score of framed pictures on the wall and for ten minutes I read the inscriptions. These celebrities had all inscribed pretty much the same message. Then I tackled the chests, plowing through piles of colored lingerie.

I was on the last pile when Miss Talley came in. I had a swift feeling she had been close to the room since she had left it.

"You detectives certainly do make a mess of things, don't you?" she said, looking about.

"Yes," I said.

"If you tell me what you're looking for maybe I can help you."

"I don't know what I'm looking for. I'm just looking," I said.

"If you don't know what you're looking for how will you know when you find it?" she asked.

"Oh, I'll know, all right," I told her.

She shrugged her shoulders.

"Do all those swimming suits belong to Mrs. Brockton?" I asked.

"Yes, Mrs. Brockton liked to swim."

"Most erotics do," I said, "it's a luxurious sensation."

"What makes you think Mrs. Brockton was erotic?"

"The mirrors," I said. "Too many mirrors."

"What does that indicate?" she asked.

"Don't you know?" I said in mock surprise.

She said she didn't.

"Narcissism," I said.

She nodded, looking at me, gravely thoughtful. She seemed to be trying to remember something. [A bird, its breast flashing red in the sunlight, fluttered down on the iron grill of the window, slanted its head curiously and then flew away. As the bird flew away Miss Talley's face cleared.]

"Who did that?" I asked, pointing to a mahogany plaque fastened to the wall opposite her bed.

"Mrs. Brockton," she replied.

I climbed up on a chair and took it down.

It was a woman's head done in wax—a death mask. The black hair was curly but disheveled, like the Medusa's; there was a deep two-inch gash in the forehead colored with dull red paint, there were purple bruises on the cheeks, and the lower lip was badly split and colored that same dull red. The black hair was a wig that fell back when I touched it. The wax was soft. It was supposed to be the head of a woman who had been beaten to death with a piece of steel. It was very realistic. It looked like something out of Tussaud's.

"I didn't know Mrs. Brockton was an artist," I said, looking at the death mask.

Miss Talley bulged a little. Something crept into her face, it might have been alarm. "It was a hobby," she said. "She grew roses too."

"May I see her workshop?" I asked.

"She didn't have a workshop. She always worked in here," Miss Talley said.

"Well, then, are there other samples of her work around?" I went on.

"I don't think so," Miss Talley said thoughtfully. "She was very impeccable. Not much of her work pleased her. She always destroyed it."

"That's too bad," I said. "Where did she learn this?"

"She just picked it up. Some people are like that," Miss Talley explained.

I sat down on the edge of the bed, frankly staring at her. She flushed almost imperceptibly and then, just as imperceptibly, she stiffened.

"You don't seem very anxious to help me," I said sadly.

"I am. Very much," she said, coloring.

"Then why do you keep on lying to me?"

"I'm not lying. I've nothing to hide," she said in a hurt voice.

"You're lying right now. You shouldn't do that, Miss Talley," I complained. "If I wanted to be nasty I could make it unpleasant [as hell] for you."²

"I've told you all I know," she said, looking away.

"No, you haven't," I said.

["Yes," she insisted.]

["No," I insisted.]

She looked at the wall. I knew she was getting angry inside the blue coat because her hands moved without meaning to move. "I won't listen to any more of your [—damn] nonsense," she said, and impulsively spun out of the room.

[The bird with the red breast fluttered back on the iron grill of the window. I looked at him. I didn't know much about birds, whether or not they too had crime in their own private colonies, but I got up and started for the window to tell this beautiful fellow never to become a detective because it was a lousy business and that if he wanted to keep that red breast never to become a policeman under any circumstances. Before I could deliver my advice he flew away.]

I wrapped the death mask in a yellow silk coverlet and went downstairs.

Not finding Miss Talley, I went back to the kitchen. The lame chauffeur was talking to Martha, who was peeling potatoes. The way Martha peeled potatoes would have given an army mess sergeant apoplexy. The peelings were fully a quarter of an inch thick.

They stopped talking when I entered. I asked if they'd seen Miss Talley.

"She just went out in her car," Martha said.

"I don't think she likes you," the chauffeur said.

"What makes you think that?"

"She was sore when she went through here," he said. "I'm sure she doesn't like you."

"Nobody does," I said tragically.

I asked them a few vague questions about Mrs. Brockton's hobbies and their answers were just what I had expected. I asked the chauffeur if he would take me to town. He said he would.

A buzzer sounded behind me. Martha glanced at the annunciator on the wall above the enormous electric ice-box. One of the arrows pointed to 5.

"It's the back door," she said, laying down her knife.

"I'll go," the chauffeur said.

[Martha looked at me, a mischievous smile on her face. We were both thinking the same thing, that it was Miss Talley. We were both mistaken.] He came back leading a man. He was a compactly built man with a round head under short grizzled hair and a round face behind a short-cut grizzled mustache. He wore a gray suit badly. His face was placid but not incapable of excitement. He kept his gray felt hat on.

"Hello," he said to Martha.

"Good morning, Mr. Fritz," she said politely.

Mr. Fritz then directed his attention to me, looking me up and down with an expressionless face.

"Who are you and what's that you got?" he asked in a professional monotone.

His voice kicked my nerves around a little. "Who are you and what right have you to question me?" I demanded.

He hesitated a moment, then produced a small gold badge. "I'm Fritz, Detective-Lieutenant. What's your name and what've you got in that yellow bundle?"

I was disappointed that he had flourished his badge. I had secretly hoped there would be one actor in this mystery who wouldn't overdo it. "Oh, that's different," I said, pretending to smile. "I didn't know you were an officer. My name's Adams and I work for the Modern Art Company. Mr. Brockton wanted a portrait reframed." I wanted an anticlimax to this thing, wanted Fritz to grab the bundle and look at it and get loud and tear up the kitchen. I was desperate for comic relief. For a few seconds it looked as if I might get my wish. Fritz planted his feet wide, looked undecided and chewed his tongue.

"Where's Miss Talley?" he suddenly demanded of the cook.

Martha started to reply but before she could release the words, I said: "She's in the living room upstairs, Lieutenant."

He frowned and stamped into the pantry.

"Come on," I said to the chauffeur.

He shrugged and reached for his cap.

"Hurry," I said.

We walked around to the garage. He backed out a sedan and I got in. As we rolled down the mountainside towards Hollywood, he said: "You'll get in dutch for that. Fritz is hard-boiled."

"Is he?" I said.

We threaded a few more curves. I slipped my .38 automatic out of my coat pocket and laid it on my thigh.

"It always makes me nervous to ride with a chauffeur who packs a gun," I said. He looked startled. "Don't bother," I told him. "Just keep your hands on the wheel. I'll get it."

He kept his hands on the wheel, looking straight ahead down Western, his face chagrined. I took a .32 out of his hip pocket and dropped it into my own.

"It ruins the looks of your form-fitting uniform," I said.

At the corner of Hollywood Boulevard and Western I told him to stop. I called a taxi-driver off the corner and asked him to take the package in the yellow silk coverlet to Mr. Menefee at the International Agency on South Hill Street [and how much would it be].

["Two and a half," he said.]

[I gave him three dollars of International's money and told him to be careful of the bundle. He said he would.]

"Go on," I said to Malone. "And take it easy. I'm going to South Hill Street too. I'll show you."

On the way to the agency I tried to draw him out but the process was half-hearted because we both were thinking of other things. His replies though, if noncommittal, were polite and gracious. He didn't seem in the least upset by the gun episode. I asked him why he carried one.

He assured me it was perfectly legal, that Mr. Brockton had got him a special permit.

"But that's not answering the question," I said. "I asked you why."

"Oh, I do a lot of night driving," he replied.

I didn't say anything else.

IV

I took Malone into the agency office with me. Menefee was staring at the death-mask when we entered.

"What the hell is this?" he asked fretfully.

"Exactly what it's supposed to be, a death mask," I said. I told Malone to sit down and make himself comfortable. Menefee glared at him. I said: "I sent that on ahead because I was afraid a detective might overtake us. He could have taken it from the car, but he can't get it out of the office."

"What are you talking about?" Menefee said.

"Fritz—I bumped into Fritz," I replied patiently. "He was at the Brockton house when I left. He'll be here any minute now."

"What about this?" Menefee asked, gesturing at the plaque.

"It's a death mask of and by the lady who disappeared. I wanted it down here."

"All right, who is this?" he said, jerking a thumb at Malone.

Defiance mingled with puzzlement in Malone's flat face. "The police have given me a clean bill. You can't hang anything on me," he said.

"Why, whatever gave you that idea?" I said. "I just want to ask you some questions. I hope, however, you'll cooperate with us," I went on, the shadow of a threat in my voice.

Malone seemed relieved. He stretched his lame leg.

"I'll cooperate," he said.

"I want you to tell me everywhere you've taken Mrs. Brockton for the past couple of months," I said, taking out my notebook.

His face showed further relief. He began a recital of names and addresses while Menefee paced the floor, sucking at a black cigar and giving Malone and me an equal number of surly glares.

After a while Malone ran out of names and addresses and I had a regular directory of stores, shops, theatres and people. I told Malone he could go. At the door he stopped and turned.

"May I have my gun?" he asked.

"Certainly," I said, giving him his little .32. His exit was very dignified.

Menefee waited until the door had closed and then sat down.

"And now will you please tell me what the hell this is all about?" he exclaimed. "And will you please get that —damn death mask [to hell and gone] off my desk?"

"Put it in the safe," I suggested.

He grunted and pushed a button. Outside the *clippety-clip* of a typewriter stopped and Sara came in.

"Put this in the vault," he said, pulling the coverlet over the plaque so that it now resembled a tray of dirty dishes covered with a center-piece.

"And don't look at it," I said.

Sara looked at it then, of course. Her nostrils quivered.

"Ghastly!" she exclaimed.

"You would be a woman," I said.

"So she was *that* kind of a dame, eh?" Sara said.

"It looks like it. It certainly looks like it," I said.

She pulled the yellow silk coverlet over the mask and took it out.

"Tell me," Menefee said.

"It's a funny layout," I said, and told him all that had happened. When I had finished he smiled patronizingly and shook his head.

"You've been reading too many books," he said.

I felt my face flush. I wondered wearily why my destiny had been to spend most of my adult life working with stupid asses who used 1890 methods to catch 1933 criminals. I didn't feel like arguing with him. [Oh, the hell with you, you ass, I thought.]

The sun was making a nice light in the window. Hundreds of people were in the streets. It was noon and they were pouring out of the office buildings like locusts. [I felt a faint tug of resentment that nobody could do anything about this: little people with little dreams, doing the same things by day, climbing the same steps by night, looking forward to petty infidelities; people caught in the Inquisition of life—and I was one of them. Here I was a detective when all the time I wanted to be a great novelist.] Newsboys were shouting above the din of the traffic about the Brockton case.

"I bet the circulation managers in this town could kiss you," Menefee said.

"I bet they could too," I said.

"Well, now what do you think about her?" he asked.

"She was an intellectual suicide," I said.

Menefee got up. "That's exactly what I think," he said, grinning. "Let's put on the feed bag."

I followed him out, not wanting to.

V

When we returned from lunch Detective-Lieutenant Fritz was waiting. Menefee invited him into the inner office, sensing a storm or a hurricane, but Fritz put his hands on his hips, wagged his head from side to side, and said, no, by God, he could talk right there, and by God, he was going to say plenty and that by God, we could listen or by God, we could go to jail.

"You're not so —damn fancy as you think you are!" he bellowed at me. "Who the hell do you think you are to put the bee on me like that? What'd you do with that head you swiped at Brockton's?"

"Stop yelling at me. I don't like people who yell at me," I said.

Menefee edged over, saying, "Now, wait a minute, Ed—"

"Hell with you," Fritz threw at him, and then addressed me in a voice not as loud as the one he had been using: "Where's that head?"

"That head was on the wall for a week and nobody paid any attention to it. If you think you're going to get it now, you're crazy," I told him.

"I'll get it or I'll turn the place upside down," he bellowed.

"Go right ahead and turn it upside down, that'll be all right with us," I said. "If you've got a search warrant."

He looked from me to Menefee and then to Sara. His face was excited and an unhealthy red. He could have murdered us all.

"Okay, okay," he clipped. "You guys'll get fat bucking me. Just don't get in my way from now on."

He stormed out, driving his heels into the floor.

"That's bad," Menefee said to me, "very bad. I'd rather have those guys with me than against me."

I resented the hidden note of criticism. [I'm not a —damn bit concerned,"] I said, "and any time you don't like the books I read or the way I handle this case, you know where you can stick it."

He stared at me, saying nothing. We went inside the inner office and shut the door. He drummed a letter opener against the desk, thinking it over, and finally deciding to be amenable.

"What next?" he asked.

I told him I wanted to talk with Carter. He buzzed Sara and told her to get Carter. In a few minutes Carter arrived. He was young and ambitious and thought being a private operative was romantic. Carter had a bright future with International.

"I want you to go to the Brockton house and spot the Talley woman," I directed. "You can't miss her—she's about five-six, wears coat-suits, short black hair combed straight back, smokes cigarettes incessantly and has a hand like a boilermaker."

"I know the kind. The town's full of 'em," Carter said, smiling.

"Yes? Well, not like this one. Don't you go getting cocky," I said. "This is one of those temperamental dames who's liable to ram a fingernail file into your jugular vein. That's about her speed."

"Right," he said seriously.

"Do you know the code?" I asked him. He said he did. "All right," I said, "report to me in code. I'll either be here or at the hotel."

"Right," he said.

"And stay with that dame too."

"Right," he said, going out.

"Now, get Brockton over here," I said to Menefee. "It's time he told the truth about this business."

Menefee buzzed Sara and told her to locate Mr. Brockton and to say it was urgent that he come to the office at once.

I said I wanted to write a letter to the Old Man and went outside.

I asked Sara for some plain paper and a pen. She handed me three or four plain white second sheets. I held them up to the light. They were not watermarked.

I sat down at a desk and printed a letter to Hobart Brockton, striving to make it look and sound illiterate. The letter demanded $50,000 for his wife's freedom, told him that directions would follow in another letter and to stay away from the police. I fanned it dry, and asked Sara if she had a plain envelope.

She handed me a light blue envelope from her personal stationery. It was a cheap grade and I knew it couldn't be traced. I addressed it to Hobart Brockton, Los Feliz Hills [, stamped it and put it in my pocket for future mailing].

Sara and I flirted politely for five minutes. Then Brockton arrived. He was frowning unpleasantly.

"I hear you've been up to my house," he said sharply.

I told him I thought he had an interesting house and that it was occupied by interesting people.

"Really, after the police have gone over it so thoroughly, I can't see—" he said irritably.

"The police are not infallible," I remarked.

Menefee looked as if he wanted to apologize for me. I glared the look off his face.

"There's no use being subtle about this business, Mr. Brockton," I said. "If you want results you've got to cooperate with me. You haven't done that. You didn't tell me your wife was an artist."

"She dabbled in it—yes," he admitted.

"You didn't mention that this morning."

"It seemed just as unimportant then as it does now," he said.

"It's not unimportant. Nothing's unimportant," I said, beginning to lose patience.

I called to Sara to get the death mask and took it from her at the door. I laid it on Menefee's desk and uncovered it.

"What about this?" I asked him.

"Helen made it," he said, smiling smugly. It was quite plain he attached no significance to it. "She made it a year or so ago."

"Did you see her working on it?"

"Yes," he said thoughtfully.

"What was she doing to it?"

"She was putting the wig on it," he finally answered.

I slipped the wig off and then drew it over the wax again.

"You saw me do it too. Would you say I was an artist?" I asked.

"What do you mean?" he asked furiously.

"You never saw her working on anything else, did you? You never saw anything else she had made, did you? Well, did you?"

"You're not insinuating—" he stammered, beside himself with rage.

"Oh, for —'s sake, stop being dramatic," I said, disgusted. "I don't give a —damn whether she was or whether she wasn't. I'm merely trying to get the facts straight."

"Then you don't think my wife was an artist?" he asked.

"I certainly don't. I don't think she was any more of an artist than I am. Perhaps not as much," I said. I produced the book containing the names and addresses the chauffeur had recited for me. "I've got a list of the places and people your wife visited recently," I said. "I'd like to call them off and have you identify them."

"Oh, hell," Menefee said wearily.

After a moment in which he seemed rather confused, Brockton said, "All this seems rather absurd—"

"It is rather absurd," I agreed. "It's a rather absurd case."

I read the names, checking them as Brockton called out: "That's her dressmaker, that's her beauty parlor, that's a bookshop, that's a tea-room . . . ." Towards the bottom of the list I read the name of Randolf Morris.

"I don't believe that," Brockton said, frowning heavily. "Helen hasn't seen him for a couple of years."

Menefee leaned forward on his elbows.

"Who is Randolf Morris?" I asked Brockton.

"An artist—why, my God," he exclaimed, "do you suppose he made—"

"Don't get ahead of me, Mr. Brockton," I said.

"But she hasn't seen the man in two years," he protested. "I asked her to stop seeing him and she did. I know she did."

"Why did you ask her to stop seeing him?"

Brockton moved his shoulders uneasily, but said nothing.

"Look here," I said, angry in the fashion of one who is angry at a child for not properly doing its arithmetic, "this is positively no time to become overburdened with a sense of honor or duty. By —, Mr. Brockton, I'll walk right out on this case if you don't help me." I meant it. I was ready to walk out that minute.

"Well, to tell you the truth," he said, deciding to finally rattle his family skeletons, "Morris had gone around with her when she was in pictures. There'd been some gossip in the papers about them . . . you know how those things are. I didn't want it to be started again."

"Is this the first time Morris' name has been mentioned in connection with this case?" I asked.

"Yes, but surely, you don't think—"

"I don't know what the hell to think," I said with conviction. "But I must ask you to keep in strictest confidence all that has been said here this afternoon."

Brockton stood up, his shoulders sagging a trifle. He was a helpless

individual with a terrific storm beating around his head. I no longer
was annoyed with him. I said: "Believe me, Mr. Brockton, I'm not
working on this for the fee. It's the most unusual, the most interesting
case I've ever known. I want to solve it just as much as you do."

"I believe you," he said. "Will you tell me what you honestly
think?"

"Certainly, I will. But, understand me, it's what I *think*."

"Yes," he nodded.

"Your wife was a strange woman, a fetishist. This undoubtedly led
her into association with some kind of an abnormal world we yet
haven't discovered. I dare say she herself employed Miss Talley and
the lame chauffeur—"

"Yes," Brockton nodded.

"Well, by no stretch of the imagination could you call them normal
people. Whether they are involved in this yet remains to be seen. But
in the employment of those persons something of the mental processes
of your wife are revealed. Her home, even her own room, fairly shriek
her strange and erotic tendencies. If she wandered into an abnormal
world what happened to her is entirely speculative. Your guess is as
good as mine."

"And you don't think she made that death mask?" he said.

"No. You need only one look at that to know it is the work of a fine
craftsman. And there is another angle that keeps recurring to my
mind. Before Mrs. Brockton married she had been accustomed to a
great deal of publicity—national publicity. That too is a disease.
When she went into private life that publicity had a violent stoppage.
It may be entirely possible that she is at this moment somewhere in
hiding, reading the headlines, vicariously pleased to see her name in
print once more."

"Did it ever occur to you," Brockton asked pleasantly, "that you
might be crazy?"

"Often," I said.

VI

I reached my hotel as the blood-red sun slid off the rim of the world
and the star-accoutered night came arrogantly on. Blue dusk lay on
the window-sill like a faint sifting of ash, a faint mist hung between
the iron-dark buildings and made the street, ten stories below, seem
remote. [The swiftly-gliding automobiles, the clanging trolleys, the
hurrying figures all had an aspect of frenzy. Trapped creatures in a
narrow gorge vainly trying to escape . . . a hearse passed by. I wondered whether or not it was empty. An empty hearse meant good luck,

if you spat before it passed you. Not taking any chances, I spat out the window.]

I had had a hard day. I had visited a lot of the addresses the chauffeur gave me trying to find some trace of Mrs. Brockton. I felt pretty sure before I started I would have no luck, but that was part of the routine. I needed the discipline anyway.

The telephone bell rang, loud as the crack of doom.

It was Carter, the young op. He gave me a report in code. Transposed, it meant that Fritz had revisited the house at 3 o'clock, had stayed thirty minutes, that the Talley woman was still inside and that nothing else had happened.

"Hang on," I said.

Then I called Brockton. I told him I was sorry to trouble him but a moment before I had caught an idea and would he come right over to my place. He wanted to know if I couldn't come to his house. I said that wouldn't be wise. Then he asked me to tell him over the telephone. I said I was afraid to take chances with the extensions. He said all right, he'd come.

Thirty minutes later he arrived. I told him I wanted him to get somebody who knew Randolf Morris to introduce me under a phoney name. He stared down at the red neon sign on The Brown Derby for a few seconds and then pulled out his address book.

He got a number in the Oxford exchange and talked to somebody named Timothy. Timothy didn't know Morris but gave him another number. Brockton called that. This man's name was Tomlinson.

It developed that Tomlinson knew Brockton very well. He also knew Morris very well. Brockton put his hand over the mouthpiece and looked at me.

"Ask him to call Morris and say a friend of his—George Burton— a novelist, is in town," I directed. "Ask him if Burton can drop around tonight, that they have a lot in common."

Brockton followed directions.

"I hope [to hell] you know what you're doing," he said.

"I think I do," I responded mildly.

Tomlinson called back a few minutes later to say it was all arranged. Brockton repeated the address, which I copied, exchanged trite comment, and hung up. He invited me to dine with him, not meaning it. I thanked him but refused.

When he had gone, I bathed, dressed, put on my guns and came down to eat. While I was waiting for my food I read one of the late editions. The Brockton case was red-hot again, all over page one. The agency came in for enough free advertising to please even the Old Man. There was a well-written interview with me, the only thing wrong with it was that I hadn't been interviewed. There also were statements from Fritz and his superiors. They were convinced, they were quoted, that Mrs. Brockton's disappearance could be attributed to the presence in Southern California of a huge extortion ring. An arrest was expected shortly. Nothing was said about the death mask.

When I had finished eating I went to Randolf Morris'.

VII

The street on which Randolf Morris lived looked like any other street where it crossed Hollywood Boulevard near the Chinese theater, and for three blocks northward it maintained that orthodox appearance, lined with palms and neat little bungalows. Then, as if it were far enough from the eyes of the crowds to do as it pleased, it suddenly and crazily went haywire. It became a narrow, dimly-lighted alley, twisting tortuously up hill and finally spending itself against the belly of a mountain.

[The palms and the neat little bungalows and the neat little people in the bungalows were left behind for rococo houses that somehow hang on the side of the mountain, inhabited by unconventional men and women who comprise that colony ambiguously referred to as the art group.

You are not aware of the boundary line unless you are told. It is ridiculous. It is absurd. People who differ as widely as these in tastes and temperaments and philosophies should be separated by nothing less than a Grand Canyon.

The cool air lifts a hollow reverberation to your ears, dim as the tumble of far-off rapids. You faintly hear the city just as you faintly see the aurora that comes up from its crest.]

Randolf Morris lived in the last house on the street. It was a narrow house that was a narrow white welt on the side of the black mountain. Lights were burning on all three floors. There were four or five cars in the street, one of them resting against a sign which said No Parking At Any Time.

I went slowly up the steps and rapped on the door.

It was opened by a thinnish man, slightly bald, who wore a short-sleeved white silk shirt open at the throat, and white flannel pants that bore splotches of paint at the knees.

"I'm Morris," he said. "Are you Burton?"

I said I was. He shook hands with me, pulling me inside. His hand was very small. There were seven or eight men and women in the drawing room. Morris introduced me to his guests all at once. The guests stopped talking long enough to nod and regard me appraisingly. Then they went back to former interests.

"Sit down and tell me about yourself," Morris said, piloting me into a chair. "Tomlinson said you were a writer. Novels?"

"Yes," I said.

"What do you write about?"

"Things that don't appeal to most writers," I said.

"I understand," he said, smiling and patting me on the knee.

A handsome boy of twenty trotted in from the kitchen.

"Randy, I do believe debauchery has dulled your manners. Why don't you introduce me?" he said.

Randy introduced us. The handsome boy's name was Eddie Barr. He pulled up a chair without being invited and joined us.

"So you're a writer? Do you know Hammett? He's a writer."

I said I liked his work but that I'd never met him. "I'm just back from England," I said.

["Oh, then you know about Waterloo Bridge," he exclaimed. "Is Waterloo Bridge as bad as they say it is? Tell me about Waterloo Bridge."

I didn't know what the hell he was talking about, but I said, yes, Waterloo Bridge was pretty bad.]

"Do you drink anything?" Morris asked.

"Anything," I said.

Morris scowled at Eddie Barr and went into the kitchen.

"Your face is familiar. Haven't I seen you in pictures?" I asked Barr.

"It's quite possible," he replied.

"I think I saw you in one of O'Brien's pictures. Weren't you in a western picture with George O'Brien?"

"Do I look like a cowboy?" he asked, standing up and arching his shoulder.

When I admitted he didn't he flounced haughtily away, nearly colliding with Morris, who had a drink in each hand.

"What's the matter with him?" Morris said.

"I don't know. He asked me if he looked like a cowboy and when I said he didn't, he got sore," I said.

"Don't let it upset you. Get this under your belt and you'll feel better," he said, handing me the drink.

The drink wasn't bad.

These people had an easy camaraderie and by midnight I was well acquainted with them. They talked and talked and talked. They used too many words. Most of them spoke too fast and they just flickered from one thing to another. But three or four of them were very interesting.

[A girl named Corinne Martin composed music, she played some of her own songs, singing them in a deep, resonant voice. Everybody was quiet when she sang. She seemed to have the power to make them sad and thoughtful. A couple of her songs were excellent. I asked her why she didn't try to get them published and she said she was going down hill and that it was a nice hill and that she didn't want to be a success because success was a worse bore than failure.]

There was a slender, Garboesque girl named Lavel Leblanc who said she could have been a star in pictures if she'd changed her name. [The producers and publicity men told her the name sounded too stagey and suggested Jane Gray but she told them to go to hell and they didn't take up their option after the first three months.] She was tight and said she needed a blood transfusion but that unless she could have a blood transfusion from a black panther she wouldn't have one at all.

She was pretty hard to handle. She was loud and obnoxious and Morris finally hit her a terrific blow in the jaw and knocked her out. After that it was quieter.

Morris had one room for his books. On the tops of the stalls he had various statues and wood carvings. There were half a dozen masks on plaques similar to the one I had taken from the Brockton house. None, however, was as gruesome. There was one of a wolf's head, tongue extended, fangs bared, that was so realistic it looked more like taxidermy than art. I had to touch it to be sure.

There was no doubt in my mind now that Morris had made the death mask of Helen Brockton. There was a definite similarity in all his work, that touch of sameness which betrays all artists. It was perceptible in all his work, that same rhythm by which you know Beethoven from Grieg and Giotto from Donatello.

Morris had a great many fine volumes in his book stalls. He had superb editions of Cabell and Dreiser and Karl Marx and most of the Black and Gold library. There were four volumes of Havelock Ellis, two of Freud's impressive works, Krafft-Ebing's *Psychopathia Sexualis*, minus the familiar Latin phrases, Tolstoy, Turgenev, and many, many books of erotica.

Shortly after midnight Morris joined me in a corner of the library. I was looking through the *Psychopathia Sexualis*.

"How do you like 'These Charming People?' " he asked, sitting down. His face was bloated and liquor had puffed his lips. But his eyes were brilliant.

"I like Krafft-Ebing," I said, lowering the book to my lap. "You've got some fine stuff here."

"Yes," he replied. He rubbed the palms of his hands savagely against the arm-knobs of his chair. When he had stopped rubbing his hands he looked at them. The palms were very red. In a minute, he said: "I don't

want you to think I have parties like this every night. But I'm cele-
brating. I've been below for three weeks. In my workshop, I mean. Do
you like art or does it bore you?"

"I like any art I can understand," I told him.

"Sensible answer. Whom, for instance, do you like?"

In the drawing room the Martin girl started playing and singing
again. It was one of the songs I liked.

"Rembrandt and Velasquez and Holbein and some of Whistler's
etchings and all of Leonardo," I said.

His eyes shone more brilliantly at the mention of Leonardo.

"The mightiest genius of them all," he said prayerfully. "The finest
intellect ever placed in a human skull. Only one man ever approached
him in anything."

I asked him who that was.

"Rodin," he said. He went on to say that he had known Rodin, that
the great Frenchman once praised a head he had done. So we talked
about Rodin and Isadora Duncan and Gordon Craig and Borglum and
Taft and how much superior Eisenstein and Pabst were to the American school of motion picture directors. Three or four times during
the conversation Morris rubbed his hands so fiercely against the arm-
knobs I thought surely the skin must peel off.

"You're a novelist, Burton, and although I don't ever remember
reading you, I'm satisfied you're a capable fellow. You could do a novel
about me," he said. "My life would make a good story."

"It probably would," I said.

"Yes. I used to be very effeminate. Do you know I turned myself
into an athlete by sheer will power? That's a good story."

"It certainly is," I said.

"Would you like to see some of my work?" he asked, standing
abruptly. "Would you like to go below and see some of my work."

I also stood up, saying I'd be honored and delighted.

"I don't permit everybody to see my shop," he said.

I felt certain of that. As I followed him down the steps I made sure
my guns were ready. I liked Randolf Morris. I hoped he wouldn't do
anything to make me kill him. I hate very much to have to kill people
I like.

VIII

Half-way down the steps he pressed a switch and a powerful light
popped on. The cool, dank air of the cellar was a relief after hours of
incense, perfume, liquor fumes and stale cigarettes.

We were in a spacious room filled with statues of every size and description. There were Grecian figures, grotesque nudes, dancing fauns and men in gladiatorial combat. But horror, indescribable horror, had been cut into their faces. There were a dozen animals' heads, muscles taut, fangs bared. Horror was rampant.

I followed Morris along the narrow aisleways, lost in amazement for the man's work. He indubitably was a genius of the first rank.

He was not altogether impervious to my admiration. I had the strange feeling that no praise of mine was necessary, that Morris read every thought and quiver of my face. He walked unsteadily without being conscious of it, but his tongue and brain were still brilliant and incisive.

He pointed to this and to that with quick, staccato gestures, making lightning technical comment that I could not understand. I finally interrupted to ask why he had put such terrific fear into all their faces.

"That is a genuine emotion," he said, and his tones told me that this was the subject closest his heart. "Any other expression is false. Deep within every animal that breathes is that unutterable fear. Beauty is artificial. The world is artificial. I sometimes wonder, Burton, why no writer has ever discovered that. Everything is evil."

I asked him why he did not exhibit his work.

"I'm going East very soon," he said.

We had come to the end of one of the aisleways and were standing before the life-size statue of a woman reclining on a rock. It was a nude woman of perfect body and perfect face. The light scintillated against the polished marble. There was a trace of a smile on her face.

"This is one of the few things I have ever done in repose," Morris explained, peering studiously at me. "Is it not lovely?"

I nodded. It was perfect. It was a masterpiece.

"I have just finished polishing it," Morris continued, his eyes again boring into mine.

Morris moved around the statue talking to me, to himself . . . mumbling words. It was evident that he had but recently completed the work. At the base of the statue were marble chips—and something else. As he moved momentarily out of sight I stooped and picked up four or five dead flies. I palmed them, following him around the statue and saying, "Yes, yes," although I was not certain they were the correct answers.

The statue was so close to the wall there barely was enough room to pass. The light behind it was poor and shadowy. My nostrils picked up a pungent odor. I looked at Morris. He had not smelled it or, if he had, he paid no attention.

We walked and talked but I maneuvered to keep Morris in front of me until we returned upstairs. I had another drink and complained of giddiness.

"My vanity is to blame for that," Morris said consolingly. "I took you below because I needed to see in somebody's face the thing I saw in yours. You have buoyed my confidence. You're not accustomed to horror, are you?" he asked suddenly.

Evasively, I told him I'd had a hard day. He apologized again. I told him that was all right, but that I'd better shove off before I passed out.

The guests were sitting cross-legged on the floor in the ancient posture when we went into the front room, talking about psychic control. More words. I wanted to say good-bye to the Martin girl, but the lights were low and in the gloom everybody looked alike. They were too interested to notice my going.

Morris shook hands effusively with me at the door and assured me I was welcome any time. I thanked him and said I'd see him before he went East. I went down the steps into the street. It was raining. It rolled over me, fresh and cool. There were pools of yellow light on the corners under the arcs. The electric signs had gone off. I walked on. A few people passed by, their faces pale as snowflakes. The Boulevard contained a few cars that splashed up ugly spray from the car tracks. They looked like moving coffins.

IX

I didn't sleep very well.

The telephone jerked me out of bed a little after eight the next morning. It was Carter reporting that the Talley woman had gone out at one-thirty in the morning and that he'd tailed her to a house on Incline Pass. He said she'd stayed in there an hour and then went back home. He said that everything was peaceful but that it was cold as hell on the mountain, that he was wet and all in and would I see he got relief.

I ordered him home to get some sleep, advising the next time he stayed out all night to take an overcoat.

I realized there was no time to lose. The house on Incline Pass where the Talley woman had gone was the Randolf Morris place.

I dressed, grabbed a bite of breakfast and went to the California Testing Laboratories near the hotel. I met a man named Batteford and showed him credentials. I asked him if it were possible to analyze dead flies and tell what killed them. He said it was and called his chief chemist, a florid-faced little man named Hauser who spoke in the diction of Weber and Fields, making his *wh's* into *v's* and his *th's* into *d's.*

"It's very important I know what killed these," I said, laying five dead flies on the table.

Hauser took the flies and went out of the office, to return fifteen minutes later.

"They were killed by formaline vapors," he said, handing them to me in a box.

"May I smell formaline vapors? I want to know what they smell like," I said.

Hauser smiled and went out. When he came back he had a small test tube which he passed under my nose. I wanted to know if formaline vapors were what I smelled in Randolf Morris' cellar. They were.

I told Batteford if he'd send the bill to the International I'd okay it, and he said there'd be no charge. I thanked him and Hauser and went out.

For two hours and a half I canvassed all the drug stores within a six-block radius of Morris' house asking for the names of formaldehyde purchasers. At one near Highland, four blocks from Morris' place, I learned they had sold a gallon of formaldehyde three weeks before, also to the same party a quantity of bitumen varnish, gum arabic and copaiba.

The purchaser was Randolf Morris.

I asked the druggist if the charges had aroused suspicion.

He said they hadn't. "Is anything wrong?" he asked.

"No, nothing's wrong," I said.

I then went to a nearby undertaking parlor and told the undertaker I'd like to satisfy myself about something.

"Can a man who possesses a knowledge of anatomy embalm a body with formaldehyde?" I asked.

He said he could. "Formaldehyde is injected into the femoral artery to sterilize the tissues," he said. "Why? Is anything wrong?"

"No, nothing's wrong," I said.

At three o'clock I went to the agency. Sara said something had happened and that Brockton had been looking all over for me. "Menefee's called your hotel a dozen times," she said.

"Get Brockton," I said, going into Menefee's office.

I appeared with the abruptness of an apparition. Menefee was chewing up his thumbs.

"— —! Where have you been?" he said, scowling heavily.

"Why?" I said mildly, to irritate him.

"Hell's busted. Brockton heard from his wife."

"That so? Where is she?"

"Well, not from her exactly, but from the kidnapers. He got a ransom letter and turned it over to the police. He fired us off the case."

"That's all right with me. That's fine," I said.

"You forget this isn't our agency," he said harshly. "We've got the Old Man to answer to. If you think he's gonna laugh when a twenty-five thousand dollar case folds up, you're nuts."

"That's still all right," I said. "They'll probably drop everything and try to trace the letter."

"That's just it. That's what I wanted to do," Menefee said.

"That's not difficult. It came from this office," I told him.

His face wore a look of complete bewilderment.

"What are you talking about?" he roared.

"I wrote it," I said.

"You wrote it?"

"Certainly I wrote it. I wanted Brockton to take it to the police," I said. "I wanted them out of the way. I didn't know then I was going to solve the case so soon."

Menefee worked his lips together. "Have you solved it?"

"I've found her," I said.

That was one on Menefee. He just sat there with his jaws hanging open.

Brockton came in, his face pale and somewhat sullen.

"I've given them the note," he said. "Why was I called here? There's nothing else you can do. Mail me your statement."

Menefee nodded complacently without saying anything. I tamped and lighted a cigarette.

"I've found your wife," I said.

"What was that?" he said, making a growling sound in his throat.

"I've found your wife," I said again.

He ran his tongue over his lips and pulled his lips back over his teeth. His eyes glittered under lowered brows. His neck bulged over the rim of his collar. His voice was low and hoarse and passionate.

"Where is she? What did she say? Who did—"

I did not say anything. Brockton searched Menefee's face but all he saw was a quivering scar as Menefee avoided his eyes. The paleness slowly left Brockton's face. There was no passion in his voice when he asked:

"Is she—"

"She's dead," I said.

"I want to see her," he said, wetting his lips.

X

Fog had descended with the twilight and the night was a mammoth moonstone with ghostly lights caught in its swimming globe.

One bulb burned in Morris' house as we went up Incline Pass. I told Menefee, Carter and Brockton to wait half a block away, standing by in case of emergency. Menefee argued that Morris was dangerous and that somebody ought to go in with me.

"I think I can handle it," I said.

They stepped back into the blackness of a giant eucalyptus.

I went on.

Morris greeted me at the door like I was a long-lost brother. There was absolutely nothing in his manner to indicate he suspected my true identity. He took my hat and sat me down. There were no traces of the party of the night before. I was beginning to believe there was one member of this mystery cast who was a finished performer.

"If you'd come fifteen minutes later you'd have missed me," Morris said.

"If you've got anything to do—"

"Oh, no. Just something about moving. I've decided to take your advice. I'm going East," he said.

I moved back into a corner of the overstuffed sofa so I could get to my guns unimpeded. I hoped I didn't have to kill him.

"It's rather sudden, isn't it?" I asked.

"Yes . . . and no. I'm anxious to arrange an exhibit."

"It's a very fine collection," I said.

"I think so. Particularly the statue of the woman I showed you last night," he said amiably.

I looked at him uncomfortably. I thought there was menace in his voice. There was something. It was entirely too amiable.

Something cold touched me in the back of the neck.

"You will please," a voice requested, "put your hands above your head!"

Morris moved towards me jerkily. His face wore a sneer.

"You delight me, sir," he said. "I don't think I have ever witnessed a more splendid performance than you gave last night." I thought that was odd, that he should think of this thing in the light of a theater. "I didn't think detectives had yet got around to abnormal psychology."

"Believe it or not, I was sincere in what I said last night," I said, still feeling that cold something at the back of my neck. "I do admire you tremendously."

"Yes, I think you do. And I admire you. I'm going to make another *Le Penseur* of you. You're nicely proportioned." He paused. "You will now stand up. I hope I need not remind you that a pistol is against your head."

I stood up, the pistol in my neck coming up with me in perfect synchronization. Morris searched me, removing a pistol from my coat pocket. He did not feel the other gun under my armpit. He took a step backward, then put all his weight behind a right to my jaw.

I saw it coming and managed to slip my head. The full force of the blow missed, but his fist slanted against my ear. He looked beyond me to the person who was holding the gun.

"We'll go below now. If he makes a move, shoot him," he commanded.

"I hope you don't think I'm fool enough to come here alone, Morris," I said.

He did not reply, gesturing for me to move along towards the stairway that led to the cellar. For a moment I debated making a break for it, risking a wound in order to have a gun explode. That would be a signal for Menefee and Carter and Brockton to come in. But I might get a bullet in my head. I decided it was too big a chance.

There was but one light in the room, a silken floor lamp covered with a huge red shade. The lamp was ten feet to my right. I figured that if I could reach this lamp, could extinguish the light, I would have a fighting chance.

I kept walking. The gun at the back of my neck didn't waver. I staggered, measuring the floor lamp out of the corner of my eye. As I straightened up, I tensed my legs for the spring. I let go, trying to arch my body to present the smallest possible target, and reaching inside my coat for my automatic.

Two hot blasts fanned by my ear and I heard the bullets whistle into the floor. I struck the lamp with my left shoulder, carrying it hard to the floor. The bulb popped apart, bringing on darkness. My shoulder stung where I had struck the lamp. It was the shoulder in which Tony Guerdalli had laid two .45 slugs six months before in Chicago. It ached like hell. I was too busy to pay any other attention to it.

I rolled over, gun in hand, and got a flash of a thick silhouette between me and the window. I squeezed the trigger twice, aiming at the center of the silhouette, and heard a series of groans. The silhouette vanished, boomed to the floor. I rolled over again, quickly, realizing that the flashes of my gun had revealed my position. I heard a hoarse cry: "Randy . . . Randy . . ." and a cold sensation ate at the roots of my hair.

I had shot a woman.

There was a lot of noise on the outside of the porch. Men were pounding and straining against the door. In a moment it gave way, erupting Menefee, Carter and Brockton into the room.

"Get down, you —damn fools," I yelled.

The rear of the dining room lighted in sharp orange-red bursts and Randolf Morris emptied his gun at the figures in front. It sounded like a Rotarian's Fourth of July. Randolf Morris was a great artist but he was a terrible marksman. One of the bullets shattered the glass in the door and the others went into the door-frame. Nobody was hit.

I heard a door open in the dining room and somebody clattered down the wooden steps.

"Turn on the lights," I yelled, getting up and running towards the cellar stairs. I poked my head around the corner of the casement and looked down. It was black. Cool air struck my face.

The powerful light came on below and I heard Morris rushing about.

I knew what he was going to do.

I went down the steps three at a time.

He was standing in the middle of the floor, shouting obscenities. He raised a bottle to his lips.

"Don't!" I yelled, firing at the same time.

My bullet caught him in the shoulder. It must have struck the bone because it spun him around and knocked him down. The bottle fell from his hand. As I charged forward he reached for it, trying to pick it up, hoping to throw the remainder of the contents into my face.

I kicked the bottle away and dropped beside him. Blue veins were standing out in his forehead. His chin was puffy. He was drooling.

"I'm glad I didn't have to kill you," I said.

When he stopped calling me filthy names Carter put some handcuffs on him.

The Homicide Squad arrived before we could get Morris upstairs. Fritz was leading them. The neighbors had put in a call.

Fritz sizzled the air with curses, and disappointment was written into every muscle of his beefy face.

We carried Morris above. When he saw the woman I had shot he screamed so lashingly Carter had to clap a hand over his mouth. Morris took a hunk of meat out of Carter's hand and cursed me for having shot his sister.

I went over and looked at his sister. It was the woman I knew as Miss Talley. She was dead.

Fritz detailed a couple of men from the Homicide Squad to look after Morris and I took the others downstairs. I led them to the statue of the woman reclining on the rock.

"Here she is," I said.

Nobody said anything. There wasn't anything anybody could say. I found a hammer and stood by one of the legs of the statue, raining blows against it. In a minute the white shining shell cracked and rolled off.

Beneath it was a leg of flesh and blood.

Brockton covered his eyes. Menefee and Carter gasped. Fritz swore prayerfully.

"Helen Brockton—the fantasy of a madman," I said. "He killed her, embalmed her, coated the body with gum arabic and copaiba, perhaps with a mixture of silicate and gypsum, or some resinous substance after the manner of the old Egyptians.

"Morris was a monomaniac obsessed with one passion—Helen Brockton. He made a gruesome death mask of her in which his sadism was restrained and which she foolishly took home. She told her servants and her husband she made it herself to avoid suspicion of seeing Morris. Even at that, he might have gone undiscovered but for these —" and I dug the box of dead flies out of my pocket.

"They're flies," Fritz said.

"Yes. They were killed by formaline vapors. Somewhere in these walls there undoubtedly is a vat in which he prepared his mixtures because the room contained enough vapor to kill these flies.

"Last night I came here. I deliberately got Morris drunk. He was easily flattered—as all egoists are. He believed me to be an erudite writer. I deliberately steered him into conversation calculated to expose him—as it subsequently did. He brought me to this cellar, I was the first outsider to see the statue. Morris not only wanted my praise, but he also wanted to see if I could recognize it as a woman of flesh and blood. I didn't, simply because at that time I didn't know what had really happened to her.

"Those flies tripped him up. He is a great genius but he momentarily forgot nature is as great a genius. The whole business was nothing more or less than a scheme to keep the woman he loved beside him."

"But—" Brockton interrupted.

"He originally planned a life figure of your wife," I said. "But when you forbade her to see him, that idea was smashed. He lured her here under some pretext or other and killed her. His sister was planted in your house—how long was Miss Talley employed there, Mr. Brockton?"

"Why—two or three years—"

"You see? She was the messenger between the two. Morris obviously got some vicarious pleasure from first-hand information regarding her —but it's impossible to try to understand such a man's mental processes," I said.

Menefee made a placatory face. Fritz swore again. Brockton looked at the statue. He climbed up on its base, staring thoughtfully at the face. When he climbed down there were tears in his eyes.

"What a horrible end," he murmured.

If you'd paid a little attention to her six months ago, this wouldn't have happened, I thought.

A couple of reporters and a cameraman came down the steps. They went to Brockton. Brockton pointed to me.

"Please stand over here," the cameraman said.

"All right, if you get Fritz in it too," I said.

Fritz and I posed. I watched the cameraman's finger tense against the flashlight trigger. I looked away as it exploded. Pictures are bad in my business. Besides, I photograph lousy.

Fritz was delighted. "By —, I thought you were a heel," he said profusely. "Say, this is pretty —damn decent of you."

"You live here. I don't," I said.

"Pretty —damn decent of you," he said again.

I told him it merely was the creed of the International.

"We swiped it from a man who used to teach nineteen hundred years ago," I said. " 'Do unto others . . . .' "

He looked puzzled. Then he caught on.

"By —, you're a case," he said boisterously.

The reporters cornered me. I gave them the story, sharing the glory with Fritz. Menefee had said he'd rather have the department with him than against him, so I was fixing that. I knew that once that story got into print the International would be back in the good graces of everybody.

I told Menefee to stick around and wash everything up, that there was a Laurel and Hardy comedy down the street and that I just had time to make the last show. I asked Fritz to see that I got back my blue-barreled gun that Morris had taken off me, saying one of the squad men who took Morris to the station probably had it.

I took a final look at Miss Talley and pushed my way through the crowd into the street.

The fog had lifted. Black armor sheathed the night. Faint, unaccountable throbs swelled out of the darkness. The moon was a pale blue bruise in the east. A lonely cloud hung crucified in midair, the cruel nails of a few stars gleaming along its edges.

© Peter McCoy and Amanda Dunn.

NOTES

[1] Material in the original typescript marked for deletion is reprinted here in full, but enclosed in square brackets. Minor spelling and punctuation errors have been silently corrected.

[2] In the typescript this line was subsequently amended to read, ". . . I could make it very unpleasant for you."

(Above) Ross Macdonald, photographed in Santa Barbara in 1973.
(Below) Macdonald explaining a point to Donald Adams.

AN INTERVIEW WITH ROSS MACDONALD

By Ralph Bruno Sipper

INTERVIEWER: There is an implicit suggestion in your books that the detective novel is or should be changing so that it depicts society as it changes. Is this a valid interpretation?

MACDONALD: It is. My own books have changed a great deal over the past twenty-five years as society has changed. I'm trying to write about contemporary life and that is a moving target.

INTERVIEWER: One reviewer has said that you use the detective novel to explore the American psyche. Is this true?

MACDONALD: Well, I'm not sure I'd put it that way, exactly. What a writer explores is life as he knows it, the people he knows and himself. If his exploration is honest and far-reaching enough and if the material that he grasps at is relevant to the experience of his time, then he could be said to be exploring the American psyche. I won't deny that that's the sort of thing I'm interested in doing. Isn't that what every serious writer is trying to do? To explore the deepest feelings and thoughts of his time through representative characters.

INTERVIEWER: Certainly, but you seem to peer down into the subterranean layers more than most writers.

MACDONALD: I do try to, of course. But then, I'm psychologically oriented. I have been all of my life. And I've devised plot structures which reflect this.

INTERVIEWER: And you're also concerned with character, aren't you?

MACDONALD: Yes, I am. The individual human being is what interests me most. The only things that interest me more are the interactions and relationships between individual human beings: family and community and their ruptures.

INTERVIEWER: In connection with that, another reviewer has said that Chandler was more interested in the individual scenes as opposed to their sum, whereas for you, the entire plot structure is what counts.

MACDONALD: That's true. Chandler considered the scene to be the essential unit of fiction. He said that it was a good plot if it produced good scenes. I disagree. I think that the overall intention of a book is very much more important than the individual scenes, and the individual scenes have to reflect that intention. In other words, I believe in the principle of narrative unity.

INTERVIEWER: Lew Archer seems to differ from other fictional private eyes in that he elicits quite a bit of voluntary information from the people he is questioning. Why do they respond so willingly?

MACDONALD: Most people are eager to tell the truth about themselves, and any stranger can elicit a life story from them just by being interested.

INTERVIEWER: But don't people sometimes tell Archer things they later regret having revealed?

MACDONALD: Yes, they do. But you must understand that Archer, as he appears in my books, is always working in a crisis. Such a situation impels people to speak more freely.

INTERVIEWER: I would assume that you have known actual private eyes.

MACDONALD: Yes, I have known several. To give you an idea of what an actual private eye thinks of Archer's methods — I was visited some time ago by a successful private detective who had the thought that he and I might collaborate on a code of ethics for California private eyes. Perhaps he recognized in my fictional private eye the kind of *modus operandi* and ethical approach that he, himself, tried to practice.

INTERVIEWER: Although six of your earlier books did not have Archer as their narrator, you have stuck with him now in your last nine or ten books.

MACDONALD: Yes, I seem to do better with Archer. The form in general, and Archer in particular, seem to fulfill my needs as a writer and enable me to get into the material that I want to write about. When that ceases to be the case, I'll cast around for something else. I admit that it is a bit unusual for a writer of serious intentions to write so many books using the same central character. But, you know, there is a sense in which Archer is not the main character at all. He is, essentially, the observer and narrator. He is not the person that everything happens to. He observes what happens to my central figures, who are always changing.

INTERVIEWER: From the statistical point of view, a disproportionate number of murderers in your books turn out to be women. Why is this?

MACDONALD: Well, the truth is I don't base my books on statistics.

INTERVIEWER: I'm certain you don't, but why is it so often that a woman turns out to be the murderer?

MACDONALD: Perhaps because, in our society, I regard women as having, essentially, been victimized. In nearly every case the women in my books who commit murders have been victims. People who have been victims tend to victimize. There is a clear illustration of this in one of my breakthrough novels (as I like to think of them), *The Doomsters*.

INTERVIEWER: What makes a murderer?

MACDONALD: I think a murderer is someone who has been very severely injured, morally and emotionally. A murderer is someone who, so to speak, has himself been murdered to the point where he strikes back blindly and self-destructively. I am not speaking of professional killers. The average murderer in the United States is a man or woman who kills somebody he knows. Often, it is his wife or husband, or some member of the family, or someone close to the family. It is very often done on the spur of the moment under the influence of severe stress. I try to write about the domestic circumstances that might produce this kind of situation.

INTERVIEWER: For the past fifteen years or so, starting with *The Doomsters* or *The Galton Case*, you have been working with themes such as the search for the lost father, and the sins of the parents being visited upon the children. These are powerful themes uncommon to detective novels. Why do you deal with them?

MACDONALD: Most writers who produce an extensive body of work do so as a result of obsessions that they have. You have named two of mine. As we grow older the meanings of our obsessions gradually change, and mature as we mature. Some of the pain goes out of them and understanding enters, perhaps. So, we return to our obsessions and we reshape them. We reshape ourselves as we write.

INTERVIEWER: At one point you said, and I paraphrase, "You have to keep saying it (what you know) over and over again, getting closer each time to what is true." How close are you?

MACDONALD: The purpose of my kind of art is only to get close. The meaning is in the process. Writing is an organic process like breathing or eating. It has to feed the writer as he is writing or it won't feed other people. It has to be a living act which you do for your own sake in your own time. You don't just do it to produce a book. You do it to struggle with demons, to get them under control. I say demons, but I mean problems, memories, or whatever else makes up one's psychic life. To put it another way, you're wrestling with your own angels.

INTERVIEWER: How do you go about writing a book? That is, from conception to conclusion?

MACDONALD: Well, invariably, I start a book with an idea and it is, generally, a plot idea. For example, the original plot idea for *The Galton Case* was that Oedipus was angry at his parents for sending him away into a foreign country. That was why he killed his father. Now this was not in the Sophoclean or mythic version. It is what might be called a Freudian dramatization of the myth, but it's my own. It comes out of my own experience. Of course, this is not exactly what happens in the book. Ideas change by the time you get them into a book. You start with an idea. I do, anyway. Then you examine its developments and you start working out characters who can embody those develop-ments, and events which show the characters developing over a period

of years. I like plots which extend over a period of two or three generations so that I can show the whole apparatus of family influence or the
lack of it.

INTERVIEWER: How much time do you spend on a book?

MACDONALD: I spend from three to six months or even longer working out in notebooks various possible developments of my initial idea,
story developments not written out as stories but as synopses of possible
events. I prepare life histories for my characters and I write them down
so I won't forget them. At the end of six months I might decide not to do
that book now but to wait for a while. Sometimes I wait as long as ten
years. I very seldom write a book I've just initiated the planning of. I
had been working on *Sleeping Beauty* for ten years before I finally finished it. In the meantime, however, I wrote other books. When I get
ready actually to write a book I sit down with about three of my main
ideas and with all the notebooks I've filled with them. Then I study the
ideas, add to them, analyze them and then decide which one is right for
me to do now, which one is going to incorporate the things I want to
talk about this time. I try to get as much into a book as there is to be
gotten into it. I try to follow out the meanings and the intentions of the
book. That takes time. The actual writing of the book might take as
long as nine months.

INTERVIEWER: The length of a pregnancy?

MACDONALD: You might say that. The actual writing of the book
might take nine months, but behind that there might be nine years.

INTERVIEWER: So you let your ideas age like a bottle of wine.

MACDONALD: Not really, because nothing happens to the bottle of
wine. I think about my books constantly, the way other people think
about, perhaps, their friends and relatives. I think about the people in
my books. They keep coming back to me.

INTERVIEWER: I can see why it takes time to do it that way.

MACDONALD: One of the two things a novelist needs is a lot of time.
The other thing he needs is the willingness to sit in a room by himself
during that time. I sit with my notebooks. These are the working habits
of a scholar, really. I write a novel the way I wrote a dissertation. I do
scholarship in the life of the present. You might call it the archaeology
of the recent past.

INTERVIEWER: You have extended the use of imagery far beyond
that of other writers of detective novels. With each succeeding book
your images integrate more with your characters and themes. To
what end?

MACDONALD: I think I am one of the few American detective story
writers who have been fortunate enough to be able to learn from the
poets how to handle imagery. Imagery is an essential feature of my

writing and, as I've said before, I think I've managed to get some symbolic depth into it. I'm not just interested in a simile for the sake of what it does in the sentence. I'm interested in what it does in terms of the whole book. Some of my similes, I think, carry the message of my book better than anything else I write. For example, on page 3 of my latest book, *Sleeping Beauty*, I have written: "The wind had changed and I began to smell the floating oil. It smelled like something that had died but would never go away." Now on the surface this merely describes how the oil in the oil spill at the beginning of the book smelled. Actually, what I have done is to relate the floating oil to the whole background of death and criminal history in my book. "Something that had died but would never go away," is the tragic background of the Lennox family. I'm using my simile to incorporate the floating oil with the past so that one becomes representative of the other. The oil, then, becomes symbolic of the whole history of the Lennox family and its moral meaning, which is the intention of the book — to make a California oil spill a physical representative of the moral life of the people who caused it.

INTERVIEWER: And that's not easy to do, is it?

MACDONALD: It takes an entire book to do it completely. Imagery is a structural element. For me, it is almost the essential element.

INTERVIEWER: You have said of the hard-boiled detective novel that, "Its distinctive ingredient is a style which tries to catch the rhythms and some of the words of the spoken language." Later, in writing about Dashiell Hammett and Raymond Chandler, you said, "Their style, terse and highly figured, seemed not quite to have reached the end of its development." Do you think that you are reaching that end?

MACDONALD: No, I don't think I'm the terminal point of the hard-boiled detective story. In fact, there are a lot of young writers carrying on in our vein right now. I do think that what I sought to accomplish, and perhaps to some extent have succeeded in doing, was to invest the imagery and the language that I inherited from Hammett and Chandler with a symbolic depth which actually belongs in the language. People speak in symbolic depth and I'm writing as I feel people really speak, expressing their deepest thoughts in a semi-unspoken way.

INTERVIEWER: What trends do you see the detective novel taking in the future?

MACDONALD: I don't see any reason why it shouldn't spread out into a form of the general novel; that is, return to its origins. I've been trying to push it in that direction. I've been trying to put into my books the same sorts of things that a reader finds in the general novel, a whole version of life in our society and in our time. Of course, my books are somewhat limited by the kind of structure and subject matter that is inherent in the contemporary detective novel. I seem to work best within such limitations. The limitations of popular art can be liberating, as the history of the drama has often shown.

INTERVIEWER: Would you like to guess at the future of the detective novel?

MACDONALD: I don't know what it will be. It depends on the kind of writers it will attract. It seems to be attracting increasingly good ones. In the twenties there was just the one Hammett and a few good writers like Paul Cain. Nowadays, there are a great many highly competent writers involved in the writing of crime fiction. So I'm optimistic about the detective novel's future.

ROSS MACDONALD: THE COMPLEXITY
OF THE MODERN QUEST FOR JUSTICE[1]

By Steven R. Carter

JUSTICE has always been a primary concern of men, and man's search for justice must be considered one of the major themes of our literature and lives. Detective fiction has centered almost exclusively on this search, and although writers in this genre often trivialize the pursuit of justice, occasionally one of them illuminates the ethical strivings and failures of our society. Certainly Ross Macdonald's outstanding contribution to literature lies in his treatment of the theme for which his form is most suited—the quest for justice in contemporary society—and in this area he is unsurpassed.

I

Nearly everything Macdonald has written contains some reference to psychoanalysis. But not until the fourth and many subsequent novels has psychoanalysis fundamentally shaped characterization, plot, and theme. On 10 October 1967, Macdonald wrote me that "Freud deepened our moral vision and rendered it forever ambivalent."[2] His novels frequently exemplify and illuminate the meaning of this statement.

Macdonald's fourth novel, *The Three Roads*, retells the Oedipus myth in a detective story format with Freudian overtones. Since the epigraph at the beginning of the book is from the play by Sophocles, the novel is a mystery only for those unacquainted with Greek drama. The protagonist, Bret Taylor, is a young naval lieutenant who develops amnesia shortly after the murder of his wife. When a psychoanalyst tries to restore the young man's memory by confronting him with the newspaper account of his wife's death, Taylor abandons analysis and attempts to find the killer. He discovers, of course, it is himself.

Interest in the book focuses on Taylor's unconscious motivations. They capture the reader's attention at first because they are the tantalizingly hidden source of his amnesia and then later because they explain how his idealism resulted in uxoricide. His father was a stern old moralist who bequeathed him an abnormally strong superego and a distrust for women, and his mother gave him something even more dangerous—his first traumatic experience. When he was four years old, he discovered his mother naked with her lover and he hit her on the breasts. The next day his father told him that she was dead (she was actually on her way to get a divorce) and the little boy thought that his tiny fists had killed her. He totally suppressed the knowledge of his imagined guilt. All he remembered of the truth was his mother in bed, but now he sees her fully clothed, with her arms folded like a woman in a coffin. Many years later, when he discovers his wife in bed with another man, the self-righteousness derived from his father and the repressed sexual fury derived from his mother's betrayal compel him to murder his wife. Afterwards, he forgets what he has done to his wife in almost the same manner that he had forgotten what he had "done" to his mother. At the conclusion of the novel, he has remembered his wife's murder, but has yet to face the truth about his mother.

Taylor is obsessed with the idea of justice, but the obsession is part of his illness. He believes that the solution to his internal problems can be found in the external world, but until he can examine and acknowledge his unconscious drives, he is completely at their mercy (and they have none). The ending of the book suggests that he is finally about to gain conscious control over himself and to live a humbled, nonpriggish existence with Paula West, a divorced woman who had remained in love with him even after he had rejected her because she had had sexual experience and he hadn't. Certainly he has learned that he is not invulnerable and that Paula's sex life hasn't made her evil. Under his former stern standards, he ought to punish himself severely for his crime, but he cannot do this without injuring Paula. She had lied to the police for his sake at a time when the truth would probably have legally acquitted him. However, if he confessed to the crime now and the authorities didn't believe him, he might be led to the gas chamber and Paula might be tried as an accomplice. The law could not be trusted, and the decision about his future must be made without resorting to it. The psychoanalytic approach has emerged predominant. Taylor is simultaneously redeemed and punished purely by his self-awareness. He must know his own guilt—and conceal it from others. Also, he must make his future life worthy enough to justify his continually required deception.

Justice is also an extralegal affair in *The Drowning Pool*. The killer is a sixteen-year-old girl, Cathy Slocum, who is tormented by the conflicts between her parents and by her mother's affair with Ralph Knudson, a local police officer. She thinks that if she murders her grandmother, her parents will gratefully divide their inheritance and separate from each other. Her mother will go off with Knudson and she and her father can live tranquilly together. She also wants to kill her grandmother for turning her father into a homosexual. (She knows

just enough psychology to understand how her grandmother has twisted her father's character so that he is unable to relate to any other
woman.) The ultimate basis for Cathy's own behavior, however, is
her Electra complex which she is partially aware of, but not completely. She knows that she loves her father and hates her mother, but she
doesn't know that there are sexual undertones in these feelings. She
definitely feels that something is forcing her to drown her grandmother. She hasn't learned enough from psychology to control herself.
She is crushed when she learns that James Slocum is her father in
name only: Knudson is her real father. The detective, Lew Archer,
decides that there is at least some hope of salvaging her and that she
ought to be given this chance rather than be turned over to the law.
Her mother has committed suicide and James Slocum has fled into the
arms of the poet Francis Marvell, thus removing from her immediate
vicinity some of the pressures that originally tore her apart, and in
their place is her true father, on the whole an honorable man, who is
willing to take care of her and raise her properly. She repents her act
and since she has enough of the right impulses in her, one day she may
become a valuable and charming human being. Legal justice would
have affected her criminally.

Psychoanalysis also enters into Archer's last conversation with
James Slocum and Francis Marvell. Archer quickly learns that the two
deaths and Cathy's discovery of the truth about her parentage have
caused Slocum to seek shelter from reality, and he advises Marvell to
take Slocum to a doctor. Later, he will advise a destructively quarreling
couple to consult a counselor or a minister, and in *Black Money*, he will
not only suggest that the fat boy, Peter Jamieson, see a psychiatrist
about his weight problem, but also imply that everyone needs psychiatric treatment at some time in his life.

In *The Way Some People Die*, Archer feels no compunction about
placing the murderess in the hands of the law. Galley Lawrence is an
intelligent woman, entirely too intelligent or too proud of her intelligence. The crime which she plans is probably the most intricate in all
of Macdonald. Part of her satisfaction with her plan lies in its demonstration of her cleverness. She is warped psychologically (her mother
has instilled in Galley both her own neurotic views on the evil of all
men and her ability to retreat into fantasy when reality becomes too
painful), but she has no major conflicts and does not appear to be
driven by an overwhelming force. In contrast to her mother's overly
moralistic view of the world, Galley's seems totally amoral. She is
highly narcissistic; she does not feel any remorse for her actions and
believes to the very end that she has been too clever to be convicted for
her crimes. Like the psychopath she is, Galley continues to proclaim
her innocence after Archer has clearly established her guilt. Psycho-

paths are typically often intelligent, cold-blooded, and perpetual liars. They are among the hardest cases to treat, possibly because no one can convince them that they need treatment. Since the only way known to curb their criminality is to lock them up or execute them, Galley will probably be executed.

The final pages of *Find a Victim* involve a search for extenuating circumstances to support a not-guilty-by-reason-of-insanity plea for Hilda Church. Mrs. Church has had an excruciating history of turmoil and illness which undoubtedly began early in her childhood. Her frequently repeated Freudian slip of calling her husband "father" suggests an early and abiding sexual fixation on her father. Her mother died when she was very young and her father attempted to raise both Hilda and her sister Anne by himself. Missing the sexual companionship of his wife, he almost certainly made unconscious advances to the girls. Anne responded by becoming sexually precocious and by running around the house naked, eventually provoking her father to have intercourse with her. (The extent to which he actually forced her is unclear.) Hilda expressed abhorrence of the act, but may have secretly envied Anne. However, shortly after this incident she married Brand Church, and together they took over the guardianship of Anne. Less than a year after her marriage, Hilda tried to commit suicide with sleeping pills because she didn't want to bring her baby into the world. She probably thought no child was safe from what had happened to her sister. She lost the baby and recovered some of her stability, although she became utterly dependent upon her husband's love. For ten years he was faithful and she felt secure. Then he began an affair with Anne, so that for the second time Anne had taken a man away from her. She went to see her sister and threatened to kill herself if Anne didn't break off the affair. Anne handed her a loaded gun and Hilda shot her. Hilda's two other murders were a direct result of the first: one was unpremeditated and the other primarily a defensive measure against a vicious man who had already forced her to take part in a robbery and who would betray her without hesitation.

Although she killed the same number of persons that Galley Lawrence did, only Hilda gains Archer's sympathy. When Sheriff Brand Church says that Hilda has had sporadic psychiatric treatment, the detective believes that Hilda's acquittal is almost certain. The fact that she didn't have a gun with her when she went to see Anne proves that her first crime sprang from a momentary impulse. She will have to be sent to a mental hospital because she is still far too unstable to be trusted by society and she might injure herself if she is left at large. Simultaneously less responsible and more dangerous than Cathy Slocum, she will probably be in the hospital a long time. A guardian isn't enough for her.

The Barbarous Coast presents Archer with a more finely delineated case for ethical judgment. Clarence Bassett is both ill *and* evil. A psychiatrist tells Archer that Bassett exhibits a death wish that may be turned against himself or others. He also has a powerful Oedipal attachment to his deceased mother and a feminine component in his nature which he may distrust and resent. Unable to achieve a satisfactory relationship with a mature woman, he must confine himself to very young girls or women who are as emotionally flawed as himself. Alone, he is harmless, but coupled to a partner with an equally powerful death wish, he is the equal of a coolheaded gangster like Carl Stern whose throat he slits because Stern is getting too close to the truth about Bassett's previous murders. The psychiatrist feels that Bassett might once have been suitable for Isobel Graff (they had planned to marry until Isobel's father matched her with Simon Graff, the movie tycoon) but that now their relationship would destroy both of them through the form of insanity called "folie à deux."

Bassett and Isobel dream about murdering Isobel's husband so that Isobel will be free to marry Bassett and to share Graff's fortune with him. They think that if Isobel can catch Graff in flagrante delicto with Gabrielle Torres, then no jury would convict her. However, the execution of this plan reflects the fundamental irrationality of the forces driving them. When the moment comes for Isobel to shoot Graff, she has a mystic vision of evil which pinpoints Gabrielle as its source. Therefore she shoots Gabrielle instead of Graff. The sexual origin of Isobel's fatal vision is evident from the fact that she tries to shoot Gabrielle in the groin. Moreover, it is possible that at the moment of the shooting, Isobel identified Graff with her father and that this identification gave her a strong awareness of the *girl's* evil. But Isobel's bullet only wounds Gabrielle, so that Bassett then feels compelled to take the gun and kill the girl himself. He had been primed for a murder and the murder hadn't taken place. He felt that he *had* to finish what he had begun. In addition, the girl's whimpering unnerved him. He *had* to silence her and he considered murder the easiest way to do it.

If Isobel had committed all the murders, Archer could handle her with the same leniency that he showed Hilda Church. He could even contemplate institutionalized treatment for Bassett as well, if Bassett's compulsive slaying of Gabrielle were his only crime. But Bassett's own statements reveal that he has *consciously* manipulated and destroyed several human beings. Furthermore, he believes so firmly in his own superiority that he will always be able to sacrifice others. Has he not already tried to frame Isobel for two of his murders, though he is supposedly in love with her? Possibly he once cared enough about his mother that he would have been willing to sacrifice himself for her, but no one else is as worthy in his eyes. He can justify anything which he does, simply because he is the one doing it. Archer, unable to accept Bassett's system of justification, makes no attempt to prevent the vengeful Tony Torres from shooting Bassett; and afterwards Archer hopes to support a justifiable homicide plea for Tony. Bassett isn't sick enough to deserve anybody's sympathy.

The case of Mildred Hallman in *The Doomsters* offers the most perplexing moral (and psychological) dilemma of all. When Archer asks Rose Parish, a psychiatric social worker, whether an insanity plea would be successful for Mildred, Rose replies:

> I doubt it. It depends on how sick she is. I'd guess, from what I've observed and what you tell me, that she's borderline schizophrenic. Probably she's been in-and-out for several years. This crisis may bring her completely out of it. I've seen it happen to patients, and she must have had considerable ego strength to have held herself together for so long. But the crisis could push her back into very deep withdrawal. Either way, there's no way out for her. The most we can do is to see that she gets decent treatment.[3]

Mildred has substantial, but by no means complete, control over her actions. She consciously wants to marry into a wealthy family and she consciously neglects to take the proper precautions during intercourse with wealthy Carl Hallman; she thinks her pregnancy will force him into marriage. However, her first murder attempt is the blind reaction to intolerable pressure when Carl's mother makes her destroy her unborn child. Mrs. Hallman actually points a gun at Mildred while her doctor performs the abortion. When Mildred becomes sufficiently conscious, she naturally smashes a bottle on Mrs. Hallman's head. Because he himself intends to kill the old woman later on, Dr. Grantland convinces Mildred that she has murdered the inert Mrs. Hallman. Then he pressures Mildred into marrying Carl and murdering Carl's father. Mildred's "second" murder is both conscious and unconscious, since she consciously plans (with the prodding of Dr. Grantland) to murder Senator Hallman to prevent him from disinheriting Carl, but she performs the deed like a sleepwalker. She has had practice at turning herself into a robot because she never enjoyed the sex act and always let her mind go blank when men slept with her. Separating the mind from the body is a means of evading both reality and responsibility. It is also a symptom of incipient schizophrenia. Yet her third murder is realistically motivated and executed, even though it is done impromptu. Her fourth and final murder is a grotesque quirk of fate. When she enters Dr. Grantland's house to stick a knife in him, she finds his mistress naked in bed and slays her out of a strange sense of embarrassment. Her mind has so separated from her actions that she feels that it is really herself she is stabbing. Her husband and a little girl still stand between her and the money she originally sought, but her mind splits into warring factions over what to do about them. She feels driven to destroy them, but she wants to refrain. She has Carl in her power for a while, but she is able to stay her hand. Eventually she might have killed him, but Archer finds out the truth in time.

Archer both pities and condemns her. He forces himself to say comforting words to her after she has confessed, but he is uneasy because his training as a policeman has left him with a residue of moral indignation. He knows that she is weak and that people have made use of her, but she is just aware enough of the consequences of her actions for him to have qualms about helping her. He talks Tom Rica into telling about Grantland's slaying of Mrs. Hallman so that Mildred will at least be freed of responsibility for this crime. However, in doing this, he is working as much for Rica's own moral benefit as for Mildred Hallman's insanity plea. He can make no final judgment about her.

Psychoanalysis with its world of sickness and treatment, and the law with its "world of crime and punishment,"[4] seem vowed to yield no quarter to each other, but Macdonald has fused them into a single moral view of great range and complexity. For him, the degree of guilt varies proportionally with the degree of consciousness in the motivation. Thus, one end of the spectrum holds Dr. Grantland, who is almost wholly rational and wholly villainous. Then it moves to Galley Lawrence and Clarence Bassett, who have disturbing undercurrents in their minds, but who also possess intelligence, superciliousness, and a genuine disregard for all human beings except themselves. In the middle is Mildred Hallman, a woman who manipulates and is manipulated; who acts sometimes cunningly, sometimes crazily. Then comes Hilda Church, who has to have a loaded gun thrust into her hand to trigger her mind into thinking about murder. She is followed by Cathy Slocum, "a harried child trying to explain the inexplicable: how one could do a murder with the best intentions in the world."[5] At the far end of the spectrum is Bret Taylor, whose unconscious motivations overpower his mind to the point where he could not consciously understand them. Each of these individuals is guilty. Every one of them has committed the ultimate outrage against life. But only a fool would place a Bret Taylor or a Cathy Slocum in the same category as Dr. Grantland and Galley Lawrence and prescribe one set punishment for them. Macdonald doesn't.

At the end of *The Doomsters*, Lew Archer vowed to trade his ex-cop's black and white picture of the world in on "one that included a few of the finer shades."[6] But on his next case he makes it clear that he has not intended to eliminate the word "evil" from his vocabulary by "lashing out" at "a world of treacherous little hustlers that wouldn't let a man believe in it."⁷ Guilt and evil loom large in this world, but they must be very carefully measured or they will only become larger —and even less distinct.

II

Knowing the social pressures upon individuals, Macdonald has always favored the disadvantaged:

> I am an attender of trials and a critic of what occurs in them. The antagonist system, combined with the professional bloodthirstiness of prosecutors, works to the disadvantage of the already disadvantaged. They are punished for being poor and stupid and sick. The courts are improving, of course, under such influences as you name, psychiatry, sociology. But I should add hastily that neither a psychiatrist nor a sociologist can be trusted with absolute power over another human being. I've known one or two psychiatrists who conceived of themselves as prosecutors, for instance. Primarily we need to go on improving our laws, including the unwritten ones, and our courts and prisons.⁸

Obviously one of the unwritten laws he would like changed is that which states the life of the rich or the important is more valuable than the life of the poor. Like Hemingway, Macdonald believes that the only essential difference between the rich and the poor is that the rich have more money, but like Fitzgerald, he is willing to examine the precise and intricate effects on the rich of their possession of money. The rich in Macdonald's novels do not merely have power through their money, they enjoy having it and enjoy using it. Money and power have dictated their way of life. Their possessions can get them what they want, but what they want is reciprocally determined by their possessions. Money seeks its own kind; power asks to be exercised, and both aspire to a prestige that is predatory. Above all, the rich can and do buy the poor. Being bought is one of the great moral dangers of our time. The buyer has already sold his own soul.

This last abuse of money is explored in *Black Money*, where there are many references to, and situations involving, the purchase of human beings.⁹ During their first meeting, Peter Jamieson remarks to Archer that he has made up his mind to buy a detective. He apologizes, but when there are conflicts between the two of them later he acts as if he thought a paid employee ought to know his place. Archer considers this a typical attitude of the rich and notes that the rich also sell people, including their own kin: debutante balls remind him of slave markets. This human merchandising by the rich is really no different from the more openly disreputable deals by gangsters and gamblers, such as Harry Hendrick's use of his wife as a stake in a card game or Leo Spillman's offer to pay for Ginny Fablon's education and to overlook Roy Fablon's debts in return for Ginny's "services" when her education is completed. Women, of course, are the most frequently purchased human beings. Kitty Hendricks asserts that her beauty enables her to pick and choose her men, but Archer replies, "You mean you get picked and chosen." [10] She is proud that she has never had to earn a living, but she is embarrassed by Leo's much-owed nurse who demands from her honest pay for honest work. Still, in her heart she despises the nurse as much as the leisure-loving rich person despises the professional man. [11]

Since the rich can buy people, it is not surprising that they can also buy justice. Policemen approach the rich more gently than they do the poor. This is true not only of a bad cop like Sheriff Ostervelt in *The Doomsters*, but also of a relatively good one like Captain Royal in *The Wycherly Woman*. One of Macdonald's favorite pejorative terms is "politician," which often describes the way any public official acts when confronted with a wealthy man. Geniality, subservience, and a touch of awe will suddenly bedeck his previously granitelike countenance. Within an instant, the pillar of law enforcement is converted into a floormat. Yet the rich man probably won't deign to notice what the official is doing for his sake. Accustomed to deference, he expects nothing else. The rich are never given the third degree.

In a few cases in Macdonald's work, crimes are actually covered up for a while through the influence of the rich. Every form of racket thrives in *Blue City* because Alonzo Sanford, the wealthiest man in town, has tacitly approved the activities of Robert Kerch, his gangster partner. Together, they put the lid on the murder of the former political boss of Blue City so that Kerch can control the new "reform" mayor who had done the killing. Simon Graff in *The Barbarous Coast* temporarily halts the investigation of his mistress's murder by putting the policeman in charge of the case on his payroll. Then he pays off two blackmailers by making them film stars at his movie studio. When the truth still begins to leak out, he thinks he can hush it up at the expense of a poor old punchdrunk ex-fighter. However, Archer is less impressed by Graff's wealth than the policeman Marfeld had been. Jerry Hallman in *The Doomsters* employs his money to buy silence for the murder of his own father which he thinks his brother has committed. Fear of scandal is sometimes a more forceful motivating factor among the rich than love for their parents. Greed motivates both the rich and those they buy.

In *The Underground Man*, the real estate agent Brian Kilpatrick finances the Canyon Estates project, which makes his own fortune, through blackmailing wealthy Elizabeth Broadhurst who shot but did not kill her husband. This project is located in a high fire-hazard area and it is ironically appropriate that a fire is started indirectly by the murderer of Mrs. Broadhurst's son, though neither she nor Kilpatrick took part in this killing. It is also significant that the fire is fought by smoke-jumpers who are "Indians and blacks and weathered whites— hard-nosed, stoic, working stiffs with nothing to lose but their bed rolls and their lives." [12]

Two scions of wealthy families go to opposite extremes. Anthony Galton in *The Galton Case* revolts against the snobbery, the mannerisms, and the wealth of his class and pictures himself as a spiritual John Brown for the working class. He hopes that his poetry can make a nonviolent contribution to the struggle of the poor for freedom and justice. Unfortunately, he couples this ideal with Rimbaud's theory of the violation of the senses. He thinks that his poetry will be valid only if he has several unusual and violent experiences. He picks up, impregnates, and marries a girl who is both a member of the lower class and a fit study for Rimbaud. Presumably with the dual intention of supporting her and his creative endeavors, he steals money and jewels from his family and then disappears. It is thus suitably ironic that he is murdered primarily for *his* money, the money that he has stolen and has so publicly disdained, and that his killer, an escaped convict, is a former lover of his wife. His Rum-bawdian wife has led him to the ultimate extreme, but it hasn't benefitted his poetry. His flight from the injustice of the inordinate wealth of the upper class is a flight to destruction because his wings are the wings of Icarus. The contradiction between his Brownian and his Rimbaudian viewpoints probably never struck him—or the man with the ax who cut off his head.

Carl Hallman in *The Doomsters* is appalled by the way his father treats his hired labor and by the way he took advantage of the Japanese Americans during World War II, buying up the land they had been forced to abandon. Carl argues with his father about this and during that night his father dies. Dr. Grantland tells Carl that the old man died from a heart attack; he later learns that the old man was murdered. If his father had suffered a heart attack as the direct result of their argument, then Carl's attack on the old man's injustice would have been responsible for the unjust act of parricide. His obsessive demand for social justice would have been the source of injustice on the individual level.

In his letter, Macdonald expressed his profound interest in Shakespeare's line, "The gods are just, and of our pleasant vices make instruments to plague us," and then continued:

Of our pleasant virtues, too. An excess of zeal in patriotism, for instance, turns into chauvinism, and then genocide is just around the corner, and finally we are killing our own people, which isn't patriotic! A passion for justice itself, unbalanced by saving graces like moral sensibility or self-questioning self-doubt, becomes hardness of heart and beckons toward sadism. Even a man with perfect moral pitch can assess some of the consequences of his own actions only in retrospect. My stories attempt in a small way to repair this deficiency in human life by writing imagined actions seen in imagined retrospect, as justly as possible.

The situations of Anthony Galton and Carl Hallman must be balanced with the problem of justice in general. This concern also carries over into the Negro's search for justice and equality. In *Trouble Follows Me*, one of Macdonald's earliest books, he shows how the hatred aroused in unfairly treated Negroes can lead them to form a hate group like Black Israel which works against their own country. Hector Land becomes a white-hater when his brother is killed during a race riot in 1943 and he himself is thrown in jail for attacking the whites who were probably responsible for his brother's death. Because he is sent to jail, his wife loses her job and becomes a prostitute. This background makes him ripe for Black Israel, which he fails to realize is a subversive organization. Out to get all white men, he thinks that this is the aim of Black Israel. When he does understand the organization's subversive intentions, he doesn't care. It still offers him a way to injure white men. With the backing of Black Israel, he sows dissension among his Negro comrades in the Navy. The narrator's attitude is that Land's background explains his actions, but does not excuse them. He can sympathize with Land's feelings, but he can't forget that Land is a traitor. Land has been hurt by extreme injustice, but what he is doing is both more extreme and more unjust. Still, the narrator is willing to help Land later because Land kills two of the subversives who not only agitated through Black Israel but also were responsible for the murder of Land's wife and two other people. However, Land chooses to commit suicide instead since his revenge has left him nothing further to live for. This enables the narrator to look on him as a figure of tragic dimensions. His moral conundrum centering on Land has passed and his distrust for extremes has been registered, so that he is now free to express his sympathy without reservation.

When Negroes are the objects of injustice, Macdonald supports them wholeheartedly. He feels that Negroes are often ready-made scapegoats for policemen seeking easy solutions. Hector Land is first accused of the murder of a white woman for no reason other than that a Southern woman suspects all Negroes of being rapists. Alex Norris in *The Ivory Grin* is accused of murder partly because he panics and partly because his race makes him a simple answer to an otherwise difficult case. Joseph Tobias in *The Barbarous Coast* is considered the most likely suspect in a murder case involving rich people because of his black skin and his poverty. When he produces an alibi, the police lose interest in the case because they have no other convenient suspect. The porter on the train in *Trouble Follows Me*, Alex Norris, and Joseph Tobias are all trying to educate themselves and possibly their studies will give them a view of the more positive aspects of justice in this country and a vision of an honorable and moderate method for obtaining them, but meanwhile social injustice will push an increasingly large number of men toward individual acts of injustice. Like Land's, these acts can't be excused, but they can be explained.

III

Human justice cannot function without administrators, but modern misuses of authority by entire regimes like Stalinist Russia and Nazi Germany have given us a heritage of mistrust for everyone in power. This heritage is reflected in all of Macdonald's work. In *The Dark Tunnel*, his first novel, the professor-hero and a Nazi spy debate the relation of morality to the state. The professor asserts that the individual conscience provides the only check on the dictates of the state and applauds the action of a German girl who tried to protect an old Jewish doctor from government authorities. Later, the professor is framed for a murder and flees, rather than trust the local government. He decides to avoid even Chet Gordon, the F.B.I. agent. Yet he eventually develops a half-trusting alliance with Gordon and almost becomes reconciled to the local police, as he reaches a balance between total acceptance and total rejection of authority.

The most interesting example of a person in authority trying to achieve balance is Howard Cross, the probation officer in *Meet Me at the Morgue*. Early in the book, when someone asks Cross if he is connected with the police, he replies: "I work with them, but under a different code. I'm a sort of middleman between the law and the lawbreaker.—The criminal is at war with society. Society fights back through cops and prisons. I try to act as a neutral arbitrator. The only way to end the war is to make some kind of peace between the two sides." [13]

Cross becomes involved in a kidnapping case because Fred Miner, a man on probation, is implicated in the crime. On the one hand, he is sympathetic toward Miner and would like to prove him innocent of involvement because the probation office has proclaimed that Miner is basically trustworthy. On the other hand, he has no sympathy for the kidnappers and would like to see every one of them punished. Thus he is willing to investigate the possibility of Miner's guilt, but he hopes that the truth will not injure Miner. His position is rendered even more delicate by the request of the missing boy's father that Cross not inform the police of the kidnapping until it is absolutely certain that the boy won't be returned. Cross understands the father's request but finds it hard to agree to it. He wants to make his own investigation, but he must do so quietly and strictly as an individual. During his investigation, he sees a patrol car and once again reflects on the nature of his job. "The anomaly of my position, halfway between policeman and civilian, hit me hard. I felt a powerful impulse to break my word to Johnson, stop the car, set off an all-points alarm. The moment passed. The prowl car drove out of hearing, dragging the impulse with it. I had to act within the limits Johnson had imposed, or not act at all." [14]

Cross's actions are primarily those of an individual, not of an authority. He locates the boy and safely returns him to his mother. But he indirectly causes the death of the innocent Miner. Like every individual, Cross is capable of doing both right and wrong, and his rescue of Jamie Johnson does both simultaneously.

Macdonald clearly recognizes that men in authority are subject to the same pressures as the rest of mankind. Both *The Drowning Pool* and *Find a Victim* show representatives of the law torn between their public duties and their private ones. Both Chief of Police Knudson and Sheriff Church have worked honestly and vigorously all their lives and both betray their professions to protect their loved ones. Knudson destroys the suicide note of his dead mistress and attempts to force Archer to leave town. He also tries to cover up the fact that his daughter has committed murder, but he has enough integrity left to resign from his job and to devote the rest of his life to raising his daughter properly. Sheriff Church lets a highjacker pass through a roadblock in order to conceal his wife's responsibility for several murders, but he also tries to lock her in their house so that she won't be able to repeat her crimes. Archer believes that both men were wrong to betray the law, but that their mistakes are understandable. Officials must be judged as flexibly as ordinary human beings.

Yet public office can be used for private ends, and the official who misapplies his authority must be condemned. Sheriff Ostervelt in *The Doomsters* is willing to hush up a murder in return for the political influence of a wealthy man. Until the murder, he has been facing exposure for his regular pay-offs from the local houses of prostitution. After the murder, he is easily re-elected to his office and no one can touch him. Later, he uses both the knowledge of this particular incident and the power of his office to force Mildred Hallman to become his mistress. Macdonald suggests that under the cover of his office Ostervelt has killed several men who might have found out too much about him. Otto Sipes in *The Far Side of the Dollar* uses his job with the police to obtain money through bribes. After he is dismissed from the force, he eventually becomes a house detective and blackmailer at a second-rate hotel. Jack Fleischer in *The Instant Enemy* waits until his retirement as deputy Sheriff before making the further investigation of a case which will enable him to collect blackmail, but he too has relied on his office for a criminal purpose. Ostervelt's power is finally undermined and both Sipes and Fleischer are murdered, but not one of the three officers deserves compassion, though they do deserve our utmost attention. Men with power can only be curbed in their excesses by ordinary men who watch them closely.

A serious challenge to all legal authority is made by a psychiatrist, Dr. Godwin, in *The Chill*. Even before he knows that Dolly McGee is guilty of murder, he decides that the police shouldn't be allowed to see her. He is convinced that the legal authorities have no proper understanding either of mental illness or of psychiatrists and regards the legal viewpoint as primitive. He doesn't want to see sick people mistreated no matter what they have done: he would rather keep them in his own hands for treatment. Lew Archer initially sympathizes with Dr. Godwin's beliefs, but he finds himself questioning them before the end of the case. Archer is hunting the solution of a series of murders, but Dr. Godwin, unconcerned about the murders, withholds vital information, thus forcing Archer to spend three unnecessary days in finding it from other sources. This delay probably causes Dean Bradshaw's death. It also costs Thomas McGee the anguish of temporarily returning to prison. Dolly's surest path back to mental health is by confronting reality and Dr. Godwin appears to be taking too slow a time even in helping her to do this. Archer's final impression of Dr. Godwin's medical authority is the same as his impression of legal authority: no individual or group should have complete control over another individual or group. This impression of medical authority is confirmed by an encounter with another psychiatrist, Dr. Smitheram, in *The Goodbye Look*. Smitheram, too, withholds information and even tries to force Archer off the case because of his interest in Larry Chalmers both as financial backer and patient, an interest so strong that he had his wife watch Chalmers while he was in the Navy which led to her affair with her husband's patient. Now, his protective concern for both Larry and Nick Chalmers enables Larry not only to commit murder but also to frame Nick for his crimes and to endanger Nick's precarious sanity. Both Dr. Godwin's and Dr. Smitheram's brand of despotism may be benevolent in intention, but it is despotic in practice. Doubtless the psychiatrists are doing strictly what they think right for their patients and for mankind, but men must ever be judged by the consequences of their actions.

Archer's own ideals are closely linked to justice; for this reason he cannot finally reject authority. In *The Zebra-Striped Hearse*, he goes to a lot of trouble to make a citizen's arrest of the suspected murderer Burke Damis, but he questions him afterwards in conjunction with the police official Captain Royal. When Damis then accuses both Captain Royal and Archer of being "storm troopers," Archer gets red in the face and feels "a growing solidarity with Royal." [15] In a later conversation with Damis, Archer tells the rebellious young painter that his cop-hater attitude is foolish and that he could have saved himself a lot of discomfort by trusting other people. Archer points to himself specifically as a person worthy of trust and states that Captain Royal also qualifies. Again he has identified himself with Captain Royal, the official representative of the law. Yet Archer more truly represents the conscience of the individual which must provide a check on the dictates of the state.

IV

In his introduction to the *Archer in Hollywood* omnibus, Macdonald reveals that his detective, though named after Sam Spade's partner, was patterned originally on Philip Marlowe. This combined reference to Spade and Marlowe is more appropriate than Macdonald indicates because there are at least some traits of both Hammett's and Chandler's detectives in Lew Archer and the ethical excitement prevalent in Macdonald's novels blends those found in the morally shifty, noble-ignoble, trickster world of Hammett and the black-and-white, chivalric world of Chandler. As a distinctively post-Freudian detective, Archer, unlike Marlowe, becomes a man of honor in spite of his instincts rather than by them or by inevitability. He is a man of "self-questioning self-doubt." He knows that he has unconscious motivations which may not only be antithetical to his conscious purposes but may also be subtly guiding his conscious actions. When a suspect accuses him of being a sadist, Archer reflects that "there was just enough truth in her accusation, enough cruelty in my will to justice, enough desire in my pity, to make the room uncomfortable for me." [16] On another occasion he admits that he is incapable of an act of "pure altruism." [17] The only thing that prevents him from comforting Mildred Hallman in *The Doomsters* is his awareness that his sympathy *might* cloak a seduction and that if he took advantage of her grief, he would be no better than Sheriff Ostervelt. Archer can nearly always be counted on to *try* to do the right thing, but as Macdonald points out in his letter, "even a man with perfect moral pitch can assess some of the consequences of his own actions only in retrospect." When Cathy Slocum in *The Drowning Pool* asks him to take her to town, Archer doesn't know that she is attempting to run away from her impulse to murder and he thinks it better to send her back to her parents. When Tom Rica in *The Doomsters* asks him for advice, he fails to comprehend how desperately Rica needs help and he brushes him off so that he can keep an "important" engagement. Thus the moral spectacle offered in the Lew Archer novels is that of a man who is perpetually striving for justice, but who may be unjust himself at times and may cause harm in ways unforeseen. One believes Archer's integrity as he believes Marlowe's, but one also has the same scepticism about the rightness of his decisions as one has about Sam Spade's and Ned Beaumont's. Archer is a more complicated man in a more complicated world: the difficulty of his decisions reflects the more sophisticated level of his perceptions. As Archer himself once said about two other people, he is a person "with enough feeling to be hurt, and enough complexity to do wrong." [18]

Archer is sharply differentiated from Marlowe even in his first novel-length appearance, *The Moving Target*. Marlowe never soiled his hands by doing divorce work, but at this moment in Archer's career his income depends upon divorce cases. (Later, in *The Chill*, he will be able to announce that he doesn't ordinarily do divorce work: his rates have doubled and the new ones are high.) Not only does he engage in divorce work for others, but he is being divorced himself. (*The Doomsters* makes evident that Archer's divorce reflects a personal moral failure.) Like Marlowe in *Farewell, My Lovely*, Archer plies a drunken old woman with liquor to make her more responsive to his questions, but he goes further than Marlowe by making her think he is sexually interested. Again like Marlowe, he regrets what he is doing—but he has done more to regret. Toward the end of the book, he uses a file to blind a hoodlum that he has tricked into fighting him barehanded. Afterwards, he drowns him. (In *The Drowning Pool* Archer comments that he had killed this man to save his own life, but that he still regrets having blood on his hands.) Thus, Archer cannot claim to be untarnished. Archer's final placing of justice above the friendship which he has felt for Albert Graves is one which Marlowe would understand (Marlowe wanted nothing further to do with Terry Lennox in *The Long Goodbye* when Lennox fell below his standards), but before this time Archer has made a speech which will forever separate his world from Marlowe's:

When I went into police work in 1935, I believed that evil was a quality some people were born with, like a harelip. A cop's job was to find those people and put them away. But evil isn't so simple. *Everybody has it in him, and whether it comes out in his actions depends on a number of things.* Environment, opportunity, economic pressure, a piece of bad luck, a wrong friend. The trouble is a cop has to go on judging people by rule of thumb, and acting on the judgment.[19] (The emphasis is my own.)

Because he is aware of the complex nature of the world, Archer knows that even a small variation in closely parallel situations may call for a large variation in his response. For this reason, his behavior often comes dangerously close to being inconsistent. In *Find a Victim*, Archer overhears Jo Summer ask Don Kerrigan to get her some marijuana cigarettes. Since Archer wants information from her that she won't give to a stranger, he takes three marijuana cigarettes from a collection he has just made during a narcotics investigation and offers them to the girl as proof that Kerrigan has sent him to her. However, in *The Doomsters*, he seizes a hypodermic needle full of heroin from the addict Tom Rica and refuses to give it back to him even when Rica offers to give him important information in return for it. Archer's reaction on this occasion is that "a few more caps in those black veins wouldn't make any difference. Except to me."[20] Heroin, of course, is far more powerful than marijuana and to abet a heroin addiction is a far more serious matter than to cater to a marijuana vice. But Archer's reactions are due to his friendship with Tom Rica and his hopes to rehabilitate him, both of which make him less ready to manipulate Rica than he would a stranger.

Another set of roughly parallel circumstances which draw forth varied responses from Archer are four requests by murderers to be allowed to commit suicide rather than be handed over to the law. Archer refuses Dr. Benning's request in *The Ivory Grin* because he dislikes and disapproves of the doctor, a man of cool reason and calculated venom: justice could be served only by punishing him to the fullest degree. On the other hand, Archer prevents the murderess in *The Doomsters* from committing suicide because he likes her. The California law no longer demands the death penalty for women guilty of murder (it did demand this penalty at the time of Galley Lawrence's murders) and it is possible that Mildred Hallman may be declared mentally ill and sent to a hospital instead of a prison. Archer can't judge the extent of her responsibility, but he wants to make sure that she receives every possible chance for recovery—or at least for continued existence. In *The Wycherly Woman*, Archer agrees to bring Carl Trevor the digitalis capsules that will end his life. Trevor is already in the hospital because of a heart ailment that might kill him at any time. He doesn't want to die for his own sake, but for the sake of a daughter who doesn't know that he is her father. Archer, too, wants to protect the girl from this knowledge which would probably loosen her precarious grip on her sanity. He demands that Trevor sign a very brief confession so that there will be no further investigation of his murders after his death and the girl can continue thinking that her father is the relatively innocent Homer Wycherly. In *The Far Side of the Dollar*, Archer doesn't have much of a choice to make. When Mrs. Hillman asks him for time to take her sleeping pills, Archer tells her that she should have taken them earlier because the police are on their way now and he couldn't help her even if he wanted to. She grabs her knitting needles and kills herself anyway, but Archer has no responsibility for her deed.

Archer is the best example of the individual conscience at work in our society because he is intelligent and conscientious without being a superman. He was a young thief who was reformed by a policeman and this gives his quest for justice the tinge of enthusiastic conversion, but his knowledge of what it was like to be a thief keeps him from being too harsh toward the lawbreakers he tracks down. He knows the complexity of man, the complexity of society, and the complexity of all systems of authority. He does not judge the representatives of the law in advance. If they are honest and reasonably intelligent, he endeavors to work with them as much as he can without hurting his clients. If they are not honest, then he will conscientiously work against them. He wants to be honest with all honest persons, but he is willing to lie when he thinks it necessary. He is not a completely "good" man, but he is the best man in his own world which is really *our* world. He is the man of balance, the man who weighs and considers and strives to avoid extremes. He offers the best *human* solutions to the problems of justice in our time, but they are not perfect solutions and his creator's vision of justice extends beyond that of this very human character, Lew Archer.

V

No matter how hard men struggle to achieve justice, they find that their efforts fail and that events are shaped in unexpected ways. Yet that unexpected and unsought for shape of events may not be opposed to a more absolute form of justice which is constantly at work in the world. In his letter, Macdonald writes:

So much for human justice, which interests me less these years than what I will call divine justice. The word "divine" is not meant to bring in theological assumptions, though it refers to a more inclusive reality than the human. I think my later novels are constructed to represent the workings of divine justice, that immensely complex causality which governs our lives and is influenced by our lives in turn, for they are a part of it, even our secret and unconscious selves. The real causal web includes everything but explains it so voluminously, in terms of its parts, that the whole can never be understood or grasped. Fiction chooses certain of these parts, elevates them into symbols, or dynamic narrative forces, and constructs a smaller and more graspable imitation of reality. In my books causality is shown in the light of irony which I try to make tragic, that is, seriously concerned with human fate. Such irony illuminates occurrences in the real world when they are studied closely e.g. the man who shot Kennedy, naval hero and commander-in-chief, learned to shoot in the U.S. Marines. From this alone it might be possible to generalize on violence. Or, shifting to the smaller and simpler world of fiction, we notice that in *Black Money* the professor kills himself with his wife's suicide gun. Death moved out of her into him.

While psychoanalysis and related disciplines have influenced my thinking, profoundly I hope, the final sources of my particular vision, an articulated vision of pity and terror, are found in traditional literature from Sophocles to Kafka. Freud deepened the grounds of our moral vision and rendered it forever ambivalent, but it was Shakespeare who wrote:
  "The gods are just, and of our pleasant vices make instruments to plague us."

In a subsequent letter (dated 23 October 1967), Macdonald elaborates on his concept of divine justice and its relation to his fictional technique:

I threw in my mention of divine justice precisely because it forces criticism to look at fiction from a supra-sociological point of view. Fictional structure has always represented divine justice, that is, the workings of it, from Aeschylus to Hardy. Modern psychology and the theology that develops out of or with it makes this structure more detailed, more conscious, and more immersed in the intricacies of human behavior. Divine justice in fiction is the same thing as poetic or prophetic justice except that it commonly sticks to the diurnally possible and refuses to look past or through causality. But this is changing, too, as psychic reality blends at the edges with Reality.—When you get down into the details of writing, justice and style, morality and technique, are the same things looked at from different points of view. Technique is poetic justice seen from below, and not only in fiction.

In Macdonald's novels, divine justice depends on the actions and decisions of Lew Archer (and occasionally other detectives), but ultimately it transcends the efforts of any individual.[21] This can best be seen in *The Doomsters* where Archer's own activities furnish us with an object lesson in the operation of divine justice. This case doesn't really begin for him when Carl Hallman comes to him for help and it doesn't end when he has performed his usual function of ferreting out and capturing the killer (i.e. Mildred Hallman). His concern for Mildred Hallman leads him to approach Tom Rica, a young man he was also concerned about at one time. Rica's confession shows Archer that the case actually began for him in his own office a long three years before when Tom Rica wanted to tell him about the murder he had seen Dr. Grantland commit. If Archer had listened to him then, he could have prevented Rica from becoming a drug addict and Mildred Hallman from becoming a murderess. He could also have preserved the lives of Senator Hallman, Jerry Hallman, and Zinnie Hallman, and he might have been able to keep Carl Hallman out of a mental institution. However, he was so wrapped up in the pain of his divorce and his plans for consolation with a young blonde that he chose to get rid of Rica quickly and not hear him out. Therefore it is ironic that his feelings of sympathy brought him at last to hear Rica's story since it was his lack of concern that kept him from hearing it originally. It is also ironic that his endeavors to discern the guilt of another person led him to discover not only that he had guilt of his own but that he must share the guilt of this other person. He has been punished for his mistake in the most appropriate way possible: his guilt arose from his refusal to accept certain information and his exceedingly painful discovery of his guilt sprang directly from his efforts to obtain the same information at a later time.

The appropriateness of the punishment to the crime is an important facet of divine justice and is hinted at in *Black Money* where it is linked to Dante's *Divine Comedy*. When Archer queries what he should do about Leo Spillman, the brain-damaged gangster he has just located, Ginny Fablon asks him: "What would be the point (of doing anything)? You say he's a sick old man, hardly more than a vegetable. It's like one of the condign punishments in Dante. A big violent man turns into a helpless cripple."[22] Similarly, in *Sleeping Beauty*, William Lennox, the head of an oil company responsible for a bad off-shore spill, dies of a heart attack while driving a bulldozer to clear the pollution off his own beach.

Another appropriate punishment occurs in "Wild Goose Chase," a short story in *The Name is Archer*. Glenway Cave's decision to murder his rich, aging wife germinates during a quarrel over a Ferrari racing car that he wants her to buy him. In her anger, she tells him that she intends to leave him for another man. He knows the identity of his rival and he knows that the man is married. Therefore he works on the jealousy of the other man's wife to get her to murder his wife. Arrested for the crime and put on trial, he is acquitted because Archer fixes the guilt on the woman who was physically responsible for the death. When Archer discovers the truth, he finds himself frustrated by the limitations of human justice: he cannot use the *legal* system to punish Cave because of the law of double jeopardy and his own hands are bound by his *moral* beliefs. The most he can do is punch Cave in the mouth, but this is woefully unsatisfying. Human justice will not fit the case of Glenway Cave. However, divine justice lies waiting down the highway where Cave is killed in an automobile accident a few months after the trial while driving the brand new Ferrari: he had ironically chosen his own instrument of death.

A second facet of divine justice is the complex nature of the "causal web" which treats the criminal as a fly. It is the irony of meaningful coincidence. The simplest illustration can be found in "The Suicide," another story in *The Name is Archer*. When their father shoots himself because he cannot bear to live without his recently deceased wife, Ethel Larrabee decides to do her best to take care of her younger sister Clare. Ethel marries a wealthy real estate man and puts Clare into college, but after three years she and her husband can no longer bear each other. When Ethel loses her settlement money on a gambling spree in Las Vegas, she persuades a dealer to pocket the housestake and run away with her. She still needs money to keep her sister in college and again she is willing to marry a man with the money. Later, she shoots her dealer-husband and conceals her crime by throwing his body in the ocean. Since he beat her up before he died, she pretends that he attacked her for the money and then ran off. When Archer tries to tell Clare the truth about her sister, Ethel is in the next room and appears in the doorway with a gun. She tries to convince them that she killed her second husband in self-defense by grabbing the gun in his hand and firing it during a struggle. The irony begins when Clare upsets her sister's story by identifying the murder weapon as the gun which her father used to commit suicide. It continues when Ethel affirms that everything she did was for Clare's sake and Clare turns her back on her because she can't bear to face what Ethel has done. The irony reaches its full conclusion when Ethel shoots herself with her father's suicide gun because Clare won't accept the sacrifices which

Ethel felt were necessitated by their father's too early abandonment of them.

Punishment and irony converge in an intricate and striking manner in *The Ferguson Affair*. While he is in his late twenties, Colonel Ferguson has an affair with a poor girl named Kate Dotery and abandons her when she gets pregnant. He spends most of his life afterwards making more and more money and finding very little love. Twenty-five years later, he sees a movie star on the screen who reminds him of Kate. The movie star calls herself Holly May. Ferguson arranges to meet her and eventually marries her. When Holly May is kidnapped by her sister and another man, Ferguson begins to find out some disturbing facts that are their own retribution. Holly May is a daughter of Kate Dotery. At first, it appears that she is Kate's eldest (and only illegitimate) daughter, and this, of course, would render Ferguson's marriage incestuous. However, such a situation would be punishing a minor sin with a major sin and would involve injuring a relatively innocent person, Holly May. Holly May is really a legitimate daughter of Kate and the man that Kate married after Ferguson ran out on her. Like Ferguson, Holly May had hoped to escape entirely from her early life but had been trapped by the coils of the past through this marriage which had promised only present love and present happiness. Ferguson ultimately confesses to her and then to her mother, the woman he had wronged such a long time ago. When both Kate Dotery and Holly May forgive him, he thinks his punishment unusually light. However, his final debt to the past is paid both by learning that his real daughter is a murderess and by watching her die in an accident while attempting to commit another murder. He knows now that the past is inescapable, and when a bystander questions him about the identity of the dead girl, he firmly replies that she is his daughter.

The most pointed examples of divine justice occur in *Find a Victim* and *The Chill*. Hilda Church in *Find a Victim* is so disturbed by her sister's affair with her husband that she contemplates suicide. Anne, her sister, seeing this as an opportunity to eliminate her competition, hands a loaded gun to Hilda so that she can kill herself; but Hilda surprises both herself and her sister by shooting Anne instead. The would-be murderess has arranged her own murder. In *The Chill*, Dean Bradshaw and Constance McGee plan to murder Bradshaw's older mistress, Tish Macready. For this reason, Constance steals her sister's revolver and gives it to Bradshaw. Bradshaw hides the gun in a lockbox in his study, but Tish finds it and uses it to shoot Constance. When Bradshaw discusses this incident with Archer, he specifically employs the term "poetic justice"[23] to describe it. There is, of course, not the slightest particle of difference between the "poetic" justice of Constance McGee's death and the "divine" justice of Anne Meyer's.

Macdonald's view of life is perfectly suited to the form which he has chosen for expressing it. For him, the coincidences and surprises inherent in detective fiction are not something alien which he employs strictly for entertainment purposes while secretly trying to insert small fragments of philosophy between large fragments of plot. Instead, the coincidences (which are not truly the products of "chance") and the surprises (which are indeed surprising) form an important part of what he wishes to communicate to the reader, just as they form part of what Lawrence Durrell hopes to communicate in *The Alexandria Quartet* and what Anthony Powell does communicate in his *Dance to the Music of Time* series. Macdonald projects his personal vision of a world in which human actions have such a powerful impact that their effect may still be felt many years after. He forcefully informs us that everything we do is important because it is part of a "causal web" that will probably catch us when we least expect it. He reminds us that we must judge our own behavior and the behavior of other men, but that we must continually be aware that our word is not the ultimate word in justice. No writer has given us a clearer picture of the complexities which have been added to man's quest for justice in our time or a better idea of how to solve them. Yet Macdonald's most important message is that no matter how complicated the human form of justice, there remains a more inclusive and more absolute justice that will always be at work in the world.

NOTES

[1] I would like to express my deep gratitude to Mr. Macdonald (Kenneth Millar in private life) for both his assistance and his encouragement. His letters gave me many new insights into his work, though he should in no way be held responsible for the conclusions of my study. I also thank Dr. Matthew J. Bruccoli for the loan of his valuable books and the gift of his valuable advice.

[2] Unless stated otherwise, all subsequent references to Macdonald's comments to me are from this letter.

[3] Ross Macdonald, *The Doomsters* (New York: Bantam, 1967), p. 170.

[4] Ross Macdonald, *The Chill* (New York: Bantam, 1965), p. 67.

[5] Ross Macdonald, *The Drowning Pool* (New York: Pocket Books, 1959), p. 192.

[6] Macdonald, *Doomsters*, p. 168.

[7] Ross Macdonald, *The Galton Case* (New York: Bantam, 1966), p. 156.

[8] Letter from author. See footnote two.

[9] Ross Macdonald, *Black Money* (New York: Bantam, 1967). The most noteworthy references are on pages 3, 19, 121, 135, and 146.

[10] Ibid., p. 166.

[11] The plot and its conclusion center on the crippling, corrupting, falsifying, and dehumanizing influence of money. Pedro Domingo felt he had to steal money and

develop a false personality in order to win the woman he loved. Ginny Fablon seemed an innocent victim trapped by a genuine, overpowering affection for him. However, the end of the novel reveals that she married him strictly for his money so that she could fleece him and flee with her older lover. Nothing more clearly indicates Macdonald's great skill as a writer than his ability to create an ending which simultaneously satisfies the mystery reader's demand for a carefully worked out but utterly surprising puzzle and the serious reader's demand for a theme that permeates an entire work.

12 Ross Macdonald, *The Underground Man* (New York: Knopf, 1971), p. 128.

13 Ross Macdonald, *Meet Me at the Morgue* (New York: Pocket Books, 1954), p. 17.

14 Ibid., p. 36.

15 Ross Macdonald, *The Zebra-Striped Hearse* (New York: Knopf, [c. 1962]), p. 164.

16 Ross Macdonald, *The Barbarous Coast*, in *Archer in Hollywood* (New York: Knopf, 1967), p. 434.

17 Ross Macdonald, "Midnight Blue," in *Best Detective Stories of the Year (17th Annual Collection)*, ed. Brett Halliday (New York: Dell, 1965), p. 67.

18 Ross Macdonald, *The Far Side of the Dollar* (New York: Knopf, [c. 1964]), p. 165.

19 Ross Macdonald, *The Moving Target*, in *Archer in Hollywood*, p. 76.

20 Macdonald, *Doomsters*, p. 94.

21 In Macdonald's earlier novels, such as *The Way Some People Die*, Lew Archer solves his cases by the fictional detective's traditionally intricate and somewhat artificial use of reason, figuring out for himself both who did the murders and why. In those later novels where Macdonald began to concentrate on divine justice, Archer tends merely to follow a train of evidence which leads him to a particular person who either tells him something that pinpoints the murderer or admits doing the murders himself and explains why. In books like *The Galton Case*, *The Chill*, and *The Far Side of the Dollar*, Archer doesn't learn the identity of the guilty person until a few pages before the end and he is as surprised by the solution as is the reader. This simplification of the detecting process enables Macdonald to focus on the irony of events and the extra-human element in justice.

22 Macdonald, *Money*, p. 171. The large number of direct and indirect references to Dante in *Black Money* suggest that the book has built allusively, particularly upon the *Inferno*. Macdonald's explicit concern with *divine* justice gives these references even greater relevance. Direct references are on pages 116, 171, and 182. Indirect references are: "Below them, like a reminder of purgatory at the gates of paradise, etc." (p. 47); "He's a very important and well-heeled man in certain circles." "The lower circles of hell?" (p. 67); "Everything that happened in Vegas seemed to be a repetition of something that had happened before" (p. 152); and "We have three eating places—The Cafeteria, the Inferno, and the Top of the North."—"The Inferno sounds interesting." "It's less interesting than it sounds" (p. 176). Macdonald also works Sartre's play *No Exit* into the plot, thus furthering the divine—and demonic—design of the work.

23 Macdonald, *Chill*, p. 212.

THE MYSTERY POEM

THE MYSTERY POEM

By Ann Stanford

Chapter One

In "The Prologue to the Mystery Poem" published in the first issue of this *Annual*, a young woman approaches her ancestral home at early evening. She is a descendant of the Gonsalvos, a family which has lived in Southern California since the earliest settlement. She moves through a garden struck by blight; the orchards around it are dying; and the dark house itself diffuses a threatening aura which keeps her from immediately knocking on the door. The heroine wonders what has happened to her brother, who should be inside. Finding the light of a candle shining through a slit in the boarded window, she looks in and discovers the body of a woman lying on the floor. Even more startling, the body seems to be that of the heroine herself. Angered by the sight, she knocks resoundingly and hears the sound reverberate through every room, every hiding place, in

THE HOUSE OF GONSALVO

When I first heard the voices
it was like a cat
mewing in the other room
the grey stalker in the grass
looked with masked eyes
into me, the mirror
of the yellow eyes
serious and intent.

It was nothing.
A sound scratching
against the window
of my thought.

I left it there
outside.
Even when the voice
first spoke my name.

Though the cat's shadow
soft with stealth
slid by the corner of the doorway
and out of sight.

I turned upon it —
Nothing.

I knew what I wanted
without voices.

Now the insistent pounding
breaks the mirror
of my silence, breaks the
peace of my resolve
shatters this moment
I have at last come to
flurries reality
back into the room.
The candle gutters down
and I walk in darkness
turn up the light
that opens up my dream
a sinewy wound.
Light wounds my eyes
severs me from the past
moments.

Holy Mother of God, I did not mean —

Now the door swings inward
and I see the entry.
The thin light drips
from a suspended lamp
casting round shadows as it turns
gently in the wind that rises in the orchards
and twists by the door
like a cat stalking.

Then he unwound
from the shadow by the staircase
his eyes — dark like mine —
turned from me to the corners of the room.

He seemed searching for an object
left behind — some clue
or trickle from a hidden deed.
He had stayed too long in that house
alone.

He was thinner than I remembered
though tall under the turning light
a hand against the oak ambry.
Behind him the light shone
dull on a shorter figure —
the empty armor
of a Gonsalvo
long dead in another country.

His right hand clenched a dagger
brown with rust
held tight
as though he broke a bird's neck
between his fingers.
He stared at me wildly.

> *Umberto!*
> Always the dense round chords
> rose from her throat
> as from a secret eden
> where the song of birds invaded
> human speech
> each note clear and separate
> those two walking out under the trees
> children of the same father
> made of each other's blood and bone
> brother and sister in that paradise.

> *Umberto.*
> But how could she be
> both here — and there?
> My eyes turned behind me
> toward the door of the second room
> where lay as I left it
> the same figure of a woman
> in a passion like
> dying.

Umberto
She said again
she stepped back
where the door
swayed
still open in the orchard wind
the breeze blowing over
this changed eden.

If I reach out to her
she will run away.
I must keep the voice
here in this room
the live note in the dusty
chamber
at the world's end.

Maybe what I did in the darkness
I only dreamed
maybe the candle lit
in the early evening
called forth shadows
into my mind.
Maybe what I felt
was no real flesh
falling beneath the pressure
of my hands.

I looked down at them
and saw the dagger.
As I looked down
she eased softly toward the doorway.
I pulled her into the room.
The door snarled closed on rusty hinges.

The anger that had made her eyes
bright as the bronze wings
of Michael in the morning sun
holding his sword — the archangel —

dimmed as I held her
captive — a bird
in my hand.
I set the dagger
gently on the ambry
whence I had snatched it
at the furious pounding on the door.
I spoke her name gently
pushed her into the high backed chair
beside Gonsalvo's armor.
The black slits of the visor
gazed down at us
a father looking on his children.

Had I not seen that light of anger
had I not felt her pulsing
against my body
I would have called her *ghost*.
But her voice vibrated in my ears
as the silver clapper of a bell
resounding louder than the pounding
of the heavy knocker on the door.

What have you done, Umberto?

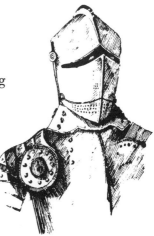

In truth I did not know.
How could my soul
divided
lie in the second room
beneath the portrait
sit here beside the armor

pulse in my throat as the
clapper of a slow bell
tolling some end or beginning.

As my sister moved upward
from the ancestral chair
I heard the wind rising
it rattled the windows
a loose board somewhere
banged twice
and was silent
the owl cried nearby
and a small sharp breaking
as though a tile dropped from the upper storey
the wind entered somewhere
breathed along the passage
which led to the other room.

My brother heard the sound
as soon as I did
turned his head, listening.
My fear vanished.
I rose and flung myself
into the passage.
I heard his steps behind me
but I reached the room
of the portrait of Gonsalvo
threw upon the door
as he caught hold of me.

Together we fell into the dimness
beside the oak table.
The candle threw
its circle of light
on the table's edge
on the floor beside it
on the square red tiles
the rug I remembered —
its tan field and green labyrinth —
from childhood.
The light barely reached
the chairs by the fireplace
where the fire's single eye

glowed dully
looked at the far reaches of the room.
Nothing had moved there
since we were children.

The eyes of Gonsalvo followed mine
into dim corners
the candle flared
collapsed on itself and died.
But in its last flickering
I could see we were alone.

No stranger lay upon the floor
beneath the portrait of Gonsalvo
nothing had changed here
for generations.
What I saw through the slit
in the boards
had been my own reflection.

My brother turned up the lights
yellow in their iron brackets
they cast long shadows in the room.

And why the candle?
Though I remembered Umberto
the romantic
reading by candlelight.

Was I mad to imagine a terror
in this old house?
in my brother
bracing himself against the onslaught
of the dragon
that breathed destruction?
Poor Umberto
losing himself in a crazy dream!

But, in the light, red glistened
among the green scrollwork of the carpet
made a small wet rose
on the brown field.

There was wine on the table.
Had it spilled as he hurried
to the door?

And by my shoe
lay a small bright object.
While he poured wine
from the carafe
I picked it up
a thin chain
a small gold cross
set with a diamond
the chain broken.
What had I seen then through the window
that left so solid a reflection?

My brother stared at me
over his glass.
Did he know that I suspected
that a woman had been lying
dead perhaps beside the table
beneath the portrait of Gonsalvo?

Where was she now
if she existed?
The room was empty

save for us two
the windows boarded shut
my brother standing
between me and the door.
His eyes met mine
with a strange excitement.

Outside the moon dissolves above the landscape
settles like silver over the rising mist
making a pavement above us bright as day.
But here in the earthbound fog we listen to voices.
The three of us waiting in the doomed house
the three of us waiting in the doomed house
for the wrenching that throws down the heavy beams
the old mortar of our generations
three of us, a trinity, and one a ghost.
Which one, which one, incorporeal,
bodiless as the voices. Does she stand
before me now waiting to be clasped
held fast in my fingers like the bird, the phoenix
that sings more glorious after resurrection?

JAMES HOGG'S
CONFESSIONS OF A JUSTIFIED SINNER:
AN ANATOMY OF TERROR

By Robert L. Chianese

NOT MANY READERS of mystery and detection fiction will be familiar with James Hogg's *The Private Memoirs and Confessions of a Justified Sinner*, a curiously titled book, written in 1824 by a Scottish friend of Wordsworth, Southey and Byron. It deserves a wider readership,[1] since its strange theme and odd form make it an intriguing and remarkable work, especially considering its early date.

The Confessions of a Justified Sinner is a book of assembled parts. There is, first, the anonymous editor's chronicle of the life and times of the "justified sinner," Robert (Wringhim) Colwan, whose supposed parents are seventeenth-century Scottish gentry, Laird and Lady Dalcastle. George Sr. is a hearty country rake, while Rabina is a crabbed, though beautiful, religious fanatic. Their legitimate son, George Jr., resembles his raucous father in temperament; but Robert is more akin to Rabina and her intimate spiritual advisor, Reverend Robert Wringhim, his actual father.

Guided by the lurid light of Rev. Wringhim's aberrant Calvinism (in which the absolute conviction of being one of God's chosen is paramount), Robert becomes a firm believer in antinomianism. This creed allows one to reject moral law for divine right and consider predestined election and not one's "works" as the sole means to salvation. In Robert's case, adherence to the creed leads to apparent murder, insanity and suicide, and his victims include his brother and mother. In reporting these events, the editor uses a number of recognizable literary forms, such as the comical history of the early Colwans, replete with stock, humorous characters, and the mystery and detection story of Robert's exploits, which culminates in a court scene.

Following the editor's account is Robert (Wringhim) Colwan's "pamphlet" called *The Confessions*, supposedly written in 1711, though not previously published. It, along with the manuscript of his *Private Memoirs* of 1712, is allegedly exhumed with his body in 1824. This section constitutes the bulk of the novel and presents from Robert's point of view many of the incidents described by the editor as well as "the sinner's" own account of his exemplary religious life. Here we find a collage of other literary forms: the gothic horror story of Robert's criminal acts; the autobiographical narrative of his conversion to absolute belief in his salvation and mission; the "case-history" aspect of Robert's confessions; the parable of Robin Ruthven and the two crows, told in Scots dialect by Robert's servant, Scrape; and finally, the realistic portraits of exterior landscapes and interior states of mind. Following this is a stroke of Hitchcockian humor as Hogg has the editor reprint an actual letter from "James Hogg" in *Blackwood's Magazine* of 1823, attesting to the facts of Robert's exhumation. The novel concludes with the editor's own report of his investigation of the grave. The variety of modes and styles used in these various sections makes the book a literary anatomy.

One other unusual and interesting factor is Robert's mysterious friend, Gil-Martin, whom we soon recognize as the Devil, though Robert never does. Gil-Martin transforms himself into Robert's double and assures him that Robert's treacherous deeds are "justified" whenever he begins to doubt that God sanctions them. This psychological element makes the book fertile territory for Freudians and Jungians alike: simple incidents, such as Robert's delight in being "humbled" by his *doppelgänger*, Gil-Martin, have fascinating psychological implications. When, in 1947, he praised Hogg's book as "astounding" and "an extraordinary achievement," André Gide apparently felt that the combination of its theme and its psychological insight into deviant behavior was peculiarly attractive: "One of the major interests of the book is the figurative portrayal of states of subjective consciousness and the slow exposition of the something possibly flattering in this progressive acquaintanceship with the Prince of Darkness."

Robert's initial ambivalence about Gil-Martin, which gradually gives way to perverse dependency and zealous hero-worship, is indeed well done, especially when we view the book psychologically. Robert's religious justification for his murders is an unconscious self-justification for his alien and loveless life. Antinomian doctrine becomes a psychotic's nightmarish logic, just as Gil-Martin becomes a projection or "shadow" of Robert's own repressed and distorted desires. We at once fear the forces that drive Robert to such desperation, and we pity someone who feels anxiously compelled to measure up to the grandiose expectations of the worst side of his psyche. Remembering him as the author of *The Immoralist, Strait is the Gate* and *Lafcadio's Adventures*, we need not wonder at Gide's admiration for a story dealing with unresolved homosexual desires, religious sanctions for human suffering and gratuitous acts of crime.

However, there is a problem in reading the book that way, and Gide points it out: we know the Devil is the Devil and not a psychic projection; and the whole mystery and intrigue of the story is explained through the diabolic *deus ex machina*. For Gide—and, one imagines, many other readers—this spoils the book, and he must, as he says, judge the last quarter of the "memoir" a regrettable failure. Nonetheless, the reader can readily accept its supernaturalism, or what Hogg himself called "superstition," as native to the rich Scottish tradition of folk tales from which Hogg consciously drew. Indeed, Louis Simpson implies that the literary achievement of *The Confessions of a Justified Sinner* depends upon its supernatural subject matter, which, he contends, led Hogg to devise careful, intricate plots: "the power of the novel derives from its action."[2] However, subject matter and well-wrought plots do not in themselves make great books. They may characterize special, second-class genres, such as utopian, science-fiction, horror, crime and mystery stories. If all these genres turn on the plot or situation, and it turns on "hocus-pocus," then Gide's criticism is surely appropriate.

The book's genius begins to appear in Hogg's deliberate blending of the natural and the supernatural. Gil-Martin is made anything but an hallucination, and the actuality of diabolical forces is demonstrated through realistic description.[3] But Hogg does more than make the ordinarily unreal frighteningly real: he orchestrates a whole range of narrative styles to create terror. It is the blending of not only the natural and the supernatural that creates the terror in his book. Hogg's work is an anatomy of various styles, which, when brought together in differing relationships, generate the anxiety we as readers feel.[4] This, I contend, is Hogg's purpose—to manipulate the reader's sympathies through style, by portraying Robert's dilemma as more and more human and therefore more pitiable as he sinks deeper and deeper into the fantastic control of the Devil. Thus the book depicts Robert both as a dull and two-dimensional tool of standard devilry and as a genuinely sympathetic victim of forces beyond all human control. Hogg does blend the natural and the supernatural; more important, he employs careful stylistic variation and juxtaposition to stretch our credulity and engage our sympathy.

The novel begins with the editor's biography of Robert, which echoes *Tristram Shandy* in that the wedding-night difficulties of the "hero's" parents are seen as an appropriate starting point:

> The laird went up to caress her; but she turned away her head, and spoke of the follies of aged men, and something of the broad way that leadeth to destruction. The laird did not thoroughly comprehend this allusion; but being considerably flustered by drinking, and disposed to take all in good part, he only remarked, as he took off his shoes and stockings, "that whether the way was broad or narrow, it was time that they were in their bed."

"Sure, Mr. Colwan, you won't go to bed to-night, at such an important period of your life, without first saying prayers for yourself and me." (p. 4)

To delay her inevitable deflowerment, Rabina delivers a harangue on the need for family prayers before retiring, using argument after argument of her intimate spiritual advisor, the Reverend Robert Wringhim. Frustrated and defeated, the laird falls asleep:

> He began, in truth, to sound a nasal bugle of no ordinary calibre, —the notes being little inferior to those of a military trumpet. The lady tried to proceed, but every returning note from the bed burst on her ear with a louder twang, and a longer peal, till the concord of sweet sounds became so truly pathetic, that the meek spirit of the dame was quite overcome; and after shedding a flood of tears, she arose from her knees, and retired to the chimney-corner with her Bible in her lap, there to spend the hours in holy meditation till such time as the inebriated trumpeter should awaken to a sense of propriety. (pp. 5-6)

Simpson feels that these characters are "convincing gentry," but this is true only if our idea of the gentry has been shaped by the literary conventions of Fielding, Smollett and Sterne. Hogg, like those writers, but unlike Scott whom he befriended, admired and often imitated, describes the nobility here as stock comic characters.

The purpose of such low comedy is to remove us as far as possible from the world of horror and diabolism. The Devil never rears his head in such a fictive universe. If there is terror in a laird's country castle, it is usually explained away comically: the ghost is really the escaping schoolmaster, entangled in the sheets of the laird's unfaithful wife. The same farce is nearly replayed here, since Rev. Wringhim's intimacy with Rabina is more than divine and Robert is the presumed result. Hogg even employs the comic sexual punning, characteristic of this kind of writing, in a description of Reverend Wringhim's and Rabina's late-night debate over a fine point of antinomian doctrine: ". . . it was their custom, on each visit, to sit up a night in the same apartment, for the sake of sweet spiritual converse; but that time, in the course of the night, they differed so materially on a small point, somewhere between justification and final election, that the minister, in the heat of his zeal, sprung from his seat, paced the floor, and maintained his point with such ardour, that [the maid] Martha was alarmed. . ." (p. 16). So the editor tells the whole history of the Colwans in this burlesque manner. We hiss the obvious villains, Reverend

Wringhim and Robert Jr., and we cheer the young hero, George Jr., the laird's first (and only) son.

Such comedy depends on the invulnerability of the characters to real pain. Hogg allows us to enjoy this comic mode only long enough to shock us out of it; the comedy leaves us totally unprepared for the appearance of the Devil's agent. The half-brothers, separated and unknown to each other, meet on a tennis court, and Robert's inexplicable taunting of George earns him a bloody nose. The incident in itself has comic potential: the strange picture of Robert condemning the players for their sinful tennis game is somewhat ludicrous, and there is the possibility of a happy reunion. But the brothers, once they discover each other, turn up as enemies instead, and Robert's injury is described too graphically to be taken as the result of adolescent horseplay:

> In the meantime, young Wringhim was an object to all of the uttermost disgust. The blood flowing from his mouth and nose he took no pains to stem, neither did he so much as wipe it away; so that it spread over all his cheeks, and breast, even off at his toes. In that state did he take up his station in the middle of the competitors; and he did not now keep his place, but ran about, impeding every one who attempted to make at the ball. They loaded him with execrations, but it availed nothing; he seemed courting persecution and buffetings, keeping stedfastly to his old joke of damnation.... (pp. 23-24)

The anonymous editor who describes this scene purports to be recording historical facts, but the language Hogg makes him employ hints at the way we should begin to read this book. As Robert is described as "courting persecution and buffetings," we attend to the Christian implications of his suffering, which is obviously not comic. Although at this point in the story we have no way of knowing that Robert is a sado-masochistic disciple of the Anti-Christ, we should sense an abrupt shift from the world of comedy to a world of bloody wounds and ominous Biblical implications. It is the style of this passage that accomplishes the dislocation. The elegant formality of "They loaded him with execrations, but it availed nothing" imparts a strange seriousness as well as an unaccountable heroism to Robert's predicament. For all we know here, Robert's passivity amidst affliction sincerely imitates Christ's "passion." Hogg's ostensibly impartial editor prevents our seeing Robert's inactivity as premeditated vengeance. Yet the stylistic shift creates uneasiness, since the description of the blood is too real and Robert's behavior too bizarre to be amusing. If earlier we could respond in simple fashion by hissing the villain and cheering the hero, we are now no longer allowed the comfort of such a simplistic response. We soon discover that the world of this book is fraught with traps and illusions. We become accustomed to one mode of reality, only to have it dissolve into another, and thus our own experience of the book resembles Robert's experience of reality—a reality controlled by the Devil. Primed for such radical shifts, which occur frequently, we may become immune to shock, but Hogg has achieved his desired end: the creation through style of suspense and tension, which make us susceptible to terror.

Hogg evokes the same kind of terror in another manner, when the editor tries to account scientifically for the mysterious events that take place on the top of Arthur's Seat. Since this ridge juts above the early morning clouds, one sees during sunrise blended hues and rainbows refracted in the mist below. This, the editor assures us, explains the disarming experience of strange lights that George sees as he perches there in anxious meditation. Furthermore, the floating vision of Robert approaching him is no devil, or satanic hallucination, but merely the reflection on the clouds of the real Robert, enraged in an all too human fashion, attacking his brother from the rear. The apparent work of the Devil is the actual viciousness of Robert—or so the editor would have us believe. But his scientific objectivity and his wish to demonstrate the ordinary causes of the fabulous lead him to the following description of George's ascent:

> He was still involved in a blue haze, like a dense smoke, but yet in the midst of it the respiration was the most refreshing and delicious. The grass and the flowers were loaden with dew; and, on taking off his hat to wipe his forehead, he perceived that the black glossy fur of which his chaperon was wrought, was all covered with a tissue of the most delicate silver—a fairy web, composed of little spheres, so minute that no eye could discern any one of them; yet there they were shining in lovely millions. Afraid of defacing so beautiful and so delicate a garnish, he replaced his hat with the greatest caution, and went on his way light of heart. (p. 39)

The florid style and light tone of the passage are intended to assuage our fears about the presence of the Devil or evil forces in nature's enchanted world. But the description of George's pause to examine the fragile beauty of the dew-covered spider's web, and the editor's obvious delight in painting a healthy boy's encounter with nature's wonders, have the opposite effect. The symbolic implications of George's entangling his hat in the web make us suspicious of his freedom from the taint of diabolic evil and put us on the alert to watch for further trickery.

When the enlarged cloud-vision of Robert appears to George, we do not know how to interpret it. It could be a psychological projection of George's own guilt, evidence of his possession, or straight devil-work. The plausible meteorological explanation of the editor, for all his objectivity and desire to defend George's sanity and honesty, clearly will not do. It is this very editor who unconsciously raises our suspicions: we no longer trust him as a reliable source of information—even about such a simple thing as the narration of an event. Hogg achieves something fine here: from this moment on, we are not able to trust anyone's account of what happens in the book.

Despite his "unreliability," the anonymous editor is an altogether interesting character. He is not a mechanical device, created solely to meet the demands of the narrative. While confidently dismissing the Devil with science, he relies upon God to clear up all mysteries. He even delivers a sermon on the detective powers of God[5] when he reaches the critical stage of his narrative. George has been killed, and his friend Drummond legally found guilty of the murder; Laird Dalcastle has died of grief; and Robert is in possession of the estate, now occupied by him, his fanatical mother and Reverend Wringhim. To the editor, who throughout the story wishes to exonerate George and condemn Robert as the villain, it is clear that Satan, Sin and Death have temporarily gotten the upper hand. He then sermonizes:

> But the ways of heaven are altogether inscrutable, and soar as far above and beyond the works and the comprehensions of man, as the sun, flaming in majesty, is above the tiny boy's evening rocket. It is the controller of Nature alone, that can bring light out of darkness, and order out of confusion. Who is he that causeth the mole, from his secret path of darkness, to throw up the gem, the gold, and the precious ore? The same, that from the mouths of babes and sucklings can extract the perfection of praise, and who can make the most abject of his creatures instrumental in bringing the most hidden truths to light. (p. 56)

This passage is not a confusing parody, however comic and daring it may be. The editor is a good Christian who fears God, takes no stock in the Devil, and has a scientist's curiosity about the world. His metaphor of the toy rocket is silly, but it is appropriate to his character.

Furthermore, the editor has a difficult task. Miss Logan, the old laird's mistress and George's surrogate mother, is the source of Robert's inevitable demise. She becomes a detective, tracing the clues that lead to the disclosure of the strange events at the brothel where George was killed and persuading the prostitute, Bel Calvert, to confess all she knows about George's murder and to accompany her in tracking Robert down. Directly after the sermon, the editor begins to relate Miss Logan's heroic exploits that lead to George's vindication. Obviously the sermon references to the "mole" and to "the most abject" of God's "creatures" that He uses as "instruments" to bring about the truth are the editor's awkward attempts to allude as discreetly as possible to Miss Logan, a woman of dubious moral character but one who sets the official record straight.

Indeed, this sermon reveals the crux of the novel. The Devil not only exists and in the name of God urges Robert to commit all kinds of evil acts, or commits them for him: he also wishes Robert to be finally caught. The reader's understanding of this terrible plan is truly "instrumental in bringing the most hidden truths to light." Ironically, then, the good but "fallen" Miss Logan is of the Devil's party without knowing it, for she puts in motion the forces that lead to Robert's flight and eventual suicide. The sermon contains a grotesque but central irony: no one in the book understands the Devil's ultimate purpose— neither the editor, nor Miss Logan, nor Robert. The "order out of confusion" which the editor mentions is never reached; the "light out of darkness" is never discerned. The editor's sermon tragically demonstrates that an earnest, simple man, armed with whatever pithy truisms, cannot fathom diabolic forces. In his awkward expression of faith in God's ultimate purpose, he inadvertently confirms the Devil's craftiness and shares with Robert the dangerous, unquestioning confidence in what he takes to be God's plan for justice and retribution.

This Devil of Hogg's is much too complex to be viewed as a projection or "shadow" of Robert's rather dull though distorted personality. Robert is either morbidly serious, anxious or vain. The Devil, chameleon-like, adapts his personality to mirror that of each victim, so in Robert's presence the Devil acts grim, fretful and imperious. But in setting Robert up for damnation, the Devil displays a lighter side, the character of a confident jester, thoroughly amused by his own cunning and the alarm and confusion it causes. We detect the Devil's jaunty brazenness in the incident that Bel relates. A man in tartans, looking exactly like Drummond, beckoned to her from below to watch George's murder from an upstairs window:

> I thought all this while I was closely concealed from them, and wondered not a little when he in tartans gave me a sly nod, as much as to say, "What do you think of this?" or, "Take note of what you see," something to that effect, from which I perceived,

that whatever he was about, he did not wish it to be kept a secret. For all that, I was impressed with a terror and anxiety that I could not overcome, but it only made me mark every event with the more intense curiosity. The Highlander, whom I still could not help regarding as the evil genius of Thomas Drummond, performed every action, as with the quickness of thought. (p. 75)

The "evil genius" in tartans who secures a witness to George's murder is, of course, the Devil, accomplishing three things at once: first, he is about to have Robert kill his brother George; second, he is about to have an innocent man, Drummond, charged for it; third, he is assuring that Robert will eventually be sought out as the murderer.

Since Bel must tell her story to Miss Logan in order for Robert to be implicated, we conclude that the Devil engineers their "coincidental" meeting. It is more than likely the Devil, transformed once again, who leads Bel to rob Miss Logan, who then turns "king's evidence" against her so she is jailed for it, and whom finally the sheriff describes as the "accomplished villain" who planned the crime. The Devil, then, maneuvers Bel into a predicament where she can give her account of George's murder in exchange for her own freedom.

This background is necessary if we are to fathom the bizarre trial-testimony of Miss Logan's maid, which might otherwise be deemed inappropriate or mistaken as low comedy. If we see the Devil directing or delivering this testimony in disguise, then the maid's seemingly inane wit becomes satanic satire, leveled at the inadequacy of human justice and knowledge by the mocking power of darkness itself. We suspect the Devil's influence here because of his wish to have Bel go free and because of the nature of the testimony itself. When asked by the deputy-advocate to give some "particulars" of the burglary, the maid puns on the word: "O, sir, the thieves didna stand upon particulars: they were halesale dealers in a' our best wares." The Devil, too, does not "stand upon particulars" but seeks to corrupt all that is best in human nature. Mispronouncing the name Wringhims as "Ringans," the maid is asked to explain what Miss Logan meant by the "Ringans": "I fancy they are some creatures that she has dreamed about, for I think there canna be as ill folks living as she ca's them." Through this banter can again be heard the Devil's mockery of his intended victim. When the maid is questioned about the resemblance of some recovered goods to those stolen from Miss Logan, she plays verbal games with the notion of resemblance itself by reiterating the inconclusive connection between things that are just "very like." The Devil too appears to be "very like" other people, but that does not mean he can be identified or that they are identical to him. The prosecutor tires of these quibbles and sees that the maid's reluctance to answer truthfully is really deliberate scrupulousness:

> "Perhaps you are not aware, girl, that this scrupulousness of yours is likely to thwart the purposes of justice, and bereave your mistress of property to the amount of a thousand merks?" (*From the Judge.*)
>
> "I canna help that, my lord: that's her lookout. For my part, I am resolved to keep a clear conscience, till I be married, at any rate." (pp. 67-68)

It is Robert's sin of "scrupulousness" that thwarts "the purposes of justice" and makes him a prime victim for the Devil. That the maid finally turns the idea of a "clear conscience" into sexual ignorance further reveals the perversity of diabolic logic.

If the Devil has possessed or replaced the maid in this court scene, then Hogg's Devil is a very clever rhetorician. But our suspicions can never be confirmed, and Bel's conclusion about the limits of human knowledge characterizes not only the sources of her fear, but the tension we feel as we puzzle whether the Devil is laughing at us through this simple girl: "We have nothing on earth but our senses to depend upon: if these deceive us, what are we to do."

We are not confused, however, when the Devil finally arranges the snare in which Robert catches himself. Walking and disputing with him, the Devil motions to Miss Logan and Bel, hidden in the woods, to listen carefully to Robert's confession of murder. When the two ladies, likened to two "harpies" by the editor, easily subdue the reputedly vicious sinner, we are invited to laugh at the scene, related once again in low style. But our laughter now cannot be comfortable: we know that the Devil is in complete control—our laughter is at the expense of desperate human beings, not ridiculous fops. Hogg's comedy evokes tragic pity and fear.

Turning from the editor's narrative to the very beginning of Robert's *Confessions* themselves, we experience another unsettling dislocation, once again accomplished through style:

> My life has been a life of trouble and turmoil; of change and vicissitude; of anger and exultation; of sorrow and of vengeance. My sorrows have all been for a slighted gospel, and my vengeance has been wreaked on its adversaries. Therefore, in the might of heaven I will sit down and write: I will let the wicked of this world know what I have done in the faith of the promises, and justification by grace, that they may read and tremble, and

bless their gods of silver and of gold, that the minister of heaven was removed from their sphere before their blood was mingled with their sacrifices. (p. 97)

Hogg makes Robert sound less a seventeenth-century divine than a latter day Jeremiah, introducing his *Lamentations*. But these tales of anguish are expressly written to make the "wicked" "tremble" and not to record the humility that often accompanies the suffering of a genuine Jeremiah. Robert wishes his *Confessions* to reveal how he discovered his absolute justification and to trace the course of his purposeful vengeance upon the wicked. Instead, they expose his total possession by the Devil and his pointless crimes and suffering. Unable to maintain his arrogant piety throughout the *Confessions*, Robert gives way to confused fear about the motives of his friend, Gil-Martin. His unshaken confidence in the doctrine of justification, however, is the final, technical snare that allows the Devil to capture his soul. These very human fears might have otherwise allowed him to elude the Devil's grasp. It is both the conscious and unconscious expression of this fear by Robert that makes us sympathize with an arrogant and vicious man. Our discovery that the Devil (and not some internal, psychological aberration) finally controls Robert's fate does not detract from our capacity to pity him. Throughout this section, Hogg builds sympathy for the victim, while exposing more and more the diabolical nature of his victimizer.

When, as a young man, Robert learns that Rev. Wringhim has doubts about Robert's salvation, he is in real terror. The Devil has not yet entered upon the scene, but the anxiety Robert feels is intense and genuine:

> My heart quaked with terror, when I thought of being still living in a state of reprobation, subjected to the awful issues of death, judgment, and eternal misery, by the slightest accident or casualty.... (pp. 99-100)
>
> It was about this time that my reverend father preached a sermon, one sentence of which affected me most disagreeably: It was to the purport, that every unrepented sin was productive of a new sin with each breath that a man drew; and every one of these new sins added to the catalogue in the same manner. I was utterly confounded at the multitude of my transgressions.... (p. 107)

The emotional effects of such apprehension, induced by one's ("spiritual") father, become all too clear to us as Robert's *Confessions* continue. But Hogg allows us even at this point to measure the extent of

Robert's fanaticism through the frank and comic estimate of Robert's character by John Barnet, Reverend Wringhim's servant:

> "What a wonderful boy he is!" said my mother.
> "I'm feared he turn out to be a conceited gowk," said old Barnet, the minister's man. (p. 99)

Aside from mocking Robert, Barnet's comment reflects the opinion of a normal, honest man. We see the depth of Robert's ignorance of his own strangeness when he rejects Barnet as a worthless sinner. Hogg's careful juxtaposition of Barnet's terse and earthy wit with Robert's elaborate meditations upon sin highlights Robert's frightening unnaturalness.

One obvious effect of Robert's upbringing is his dreaded fear of sexuality:

> In particular, I brought myself to despise, if not to abhor, the beauty of women, looking on it as the greatest snare to which mankind are subjected, and though young men and maidens, and even old women, (my mother among the rest,) taxed me with being an unnatural wretch, I gloried in my acquisition; and to this day, am thankful for having escaped the most dangerous of all snares. (p. 113)

These statements directly precede his first meeting with Gil-Martin, whom Robert immediately describes as having "a sort of invisible power" of attraction, a "force of enchantment" that evoked "strange sensations that thrilled through my whole frame." Diabolic powers acquire sexual significance. This becomes nearly explicit as Robert describes how, later, Gil-Martin completely conquered his soul:

> I rejoiced in him, was proud of him, and soon could not live without him; yet, though resolved everyday to disclose the whole history of my connection with him, I had it not in my power: Something always prevented me, till at length I thought no more of it, but resolved to enjoy his fascinating company in private, and by all means to keep my own with him. The resolution was vain: I set a bold face to it, but my powers were inadequate to the task; my adherent, with all the suavity imaginable, was sure to carry his point. (p. 127)

The style of Biblical jubilation, which Robert employs to celebrate his intimacy with Gil-Martin, reveals through its perverse application

how the Devil distorts normal forms of worship. Robert's lyrical ex-
postulations to Gil-Martin suggest how praise of God becomes idolatry
and how spiritual love becomes homosexual hero-worship. Robert's
language, latent with sexual implications of which he is unaware,
makes this clear. Thus precisely where the novel moves into the realm
of the supernatural, Robert is made to exhibit a most human weakness
—sexual ignorance and confusion. This blindness leads to his very
understandable but dangerous wooing of the Devil.

This illicit love-affair with the Prince of Darkness arouses the suspicions of Robert's mother and Rev. Wringhim, who, like apprehensive
parents, "examine" Robert as to his mysterious behavior and his
rejection of them for new-found interests. The scene could be viewed
as domestic comedy, except that we realize Robert is maturing from
one level of fanatical behavior to another, through an unconscious
sexual initiation into diabolic "delights," which are really frustrations.
Later, when the Devil has Robert fairly well under control, he toys
with his captive by having him charged with the seduction of an innocent girl, whose mother demands he marry her to restore her honor.
The farcical incident once again shows Hogg's mastery in mixing
bathos with pathos, since Robert's undeniably comic disclaimer of
knowledge of, or interest in, the girl is based on a long period of unconsciousness and illness, induced by the Devil. Brutality mixes with
comedy when Gil-Martin later explains to Robert that he is wanted for
the murder of this girl as well as that of his own mother.

We might reject Robert as a serious character here, if Hogg did not
continue to endow the comical and grotesque portrait of him with a
human dimension. Directly after this horribly whimsical seduction-
and-betrayal episode, concocted by the drollest melodramatist, Robert
becomes gravely disturbed about just exactly what is happening to
him. His realistic cry of uneasiness is entirely credible:

But from this time forth I began to be sick at times of my existence. I had heart-burnings, longings, and yearnings, that would
not be satisfied; and I seemed hardly to be an accountable creature; being thus in the habit of executing transactions of the utmost moment, without being sensible that I did them. I was a
being incomprehensible to myself. Either I had a second self, who
transacted business in my likeness, or else my body was at times
possessed by a spirit over which I had no controul, and of whose
actions my own soul was wholly unconscious. This was an
anomaly not to be accounted for by any philosophy of mine, and
I was many times, in contemplating it, excited to terrors and
mental torments hardly describable. To be in a state of conscious-

ness and unconsciousness, at the same time, in the same body and same spirit, was impossible. (p. 182)

A plainly confused man tries to fathom a nearly incomprehensible mystery in natural language. His logic evidences his sanity; his inevitable confusion becomes pathetic. Hogg permits us to watch Robert's tortured self-questioning about the appropriateness of what the Devil urges him to do, so that when Robert begins to discover the Devil's delight in his suffering and is on the verge of renouncing his friend and reasserting his own free will, we see how "normal" he really is (though, of course, in his own eyes he potentially has damned himself through such a renunciation): "There was I doomed to remain in misery, subjugated, soul and body, to one whose presence was become more intolerable to me than ought on earth could compensate: And at that moment, when he beheld the anguish of my soul, he could not conceal that he enjoyed it" (pp. 189-90).

Such an insight, however, has no power to free Robert from the arguments of the Devil, who takes advantage of Robert's intense loneliness and weariness and appeals to his resolute vanity and uncompromising faith in the doctrine of justification.

The balance between our awareness of the Devil and our sympathy for Robert is maintained to the very end of the *Private Memoirs*. Now completely secure in our knowledge that Robert has sealed his fate in a suicide pact with the Devil, we are still asked to respond sympathetically to his dilemma. Robert's farewell to the world and his description of the Devil's final approach could have been a trite and hollow conclusion well befitting a scoundrel, except that Hogg has followed the internal mental workings of this destitute man and has suggested to us, through language and stylistic juxtaposition, the extent and terror of all human delusion:

Farewell, world, with all thy miseries; for comforts or enjoyments hast thou none! Farewell, woman, whom I have despised and shunned; and man, whom I have hated; whom, nevertheless, I desire to leave in charity! And thou, sun, bright emblem of a far brighter effulgence, I bid farewell to thee also! I do not now take my last look of thee, for to thy glorious orb shall a poor suicide's last earthly look be raised. But, ah! who is yon that I see approaching furiously—his stern face blackened with horrid despair! My hour is at hand.—Almighty God, what is this that I am about to do! The hour of repentance is past, and now my fate is inevitable.—*Amen, for ever!* (pp. 239-40)

After Robert delivers this pathetic farewell at the end of his "memoir," we learn about his fate through the editor, who tries to assemble the evidence surrounding his death. The editor's attempt to resolve what actually happened to Robert only leads to further, supernatural mysteries, about which he seems unwilling to comment. The plain, almost drab style he uses to report his gruesome examination of Robert's corpse and its miraculously preserved clothing suggests that the editor has changed from the confident defender of George Colwan Jr.'s character to a man deeply troubled by the essential ambiguities of George's brother. The editor's ultimate confusion, which the reader is meant to share, and the frequent, undetected evidence of diabolic influence upon the lives of almost every character in the book, all suggest a world in which human knowledge and faith are imperfect instruments for discovering the truth. Hogg has created a book that has the appearance of being itself manipulated by the Devil. What might surprise us is that the Devil is willing to reveal so much.

NOTES

1 The two recent editions of Hogg's novel listed here may provide that readership. James Hogg, *The Private Memoirs and Confessions of a Justified Sinner*, edited with an introduction by John Carey (London: Oxford University Press, 1969). All references to the text of the novel are made from this edition. A paperback edition of the book (New York: W. W. Norton Company, 1970) has an introduction by Robert M. Adams and reprints André Gide's comments on the work as an "Afterword." It is from this text and translation (by Dorothy Bussy) of the "Afterword" that my quotations from Gide are taken.

2 Louis Simpson, *James Hogg: A Critical Study* (New York: St. Martin's, 1962), p. 186.

3 Simpson, op. cit. makes the point neatly: "Gil-Martin is seen by several people; his appearances astonish Robert Colwan; and above all, Hogg has no reason to deny the supernatural" (p. 188). Still, C. F. Keppler wants it both ways. In his study, *The Literature of the Second Self* (Tucson: University of Arizona Press, 1972), Keppler contends that the Devil is the Devil *and* a psychological projection of "that particular evil which lies in Robert's own being" (p. 69). Keppler views Hogg's book in the great tradition of the literature of the "second self," but his central thesis leads him to some confusing and inevitably illogical statements, such as, "Thus though in this story we have the very complicated situation of a protagonist who plays the role of second self to one character and first self to another, actually the central dichotomy is between Robert Wringhim as first self and his diabolical visitant as second" (p. 68). We cannot have it both ways, since Robert alone cannot "play" his "second self" to his "first self," while at the same time his "second self" is off creating havoc. L. L. Lee, in "The Devil's Figure: James Hogg's *Justified Sinner*," *Studies in Scottish Literature*, III, 230-239, argues that Hogg's Devil remains to the last an ambiguous figure. He is an indefinable mixture of both Satan and Robert's own projected evil, demonology and psychology. Though Lee admits that other characters in the novel

claim to have seen Gil-Martin, he explains that the editor who reports their claims is simply recording the traditional version of the story and not necessarily the facts. While this is true, Lee's major thesis about the ambiguous devil figure leads him to judge Robert morally responsible for his crimes: "Robert, then, fails to understand himself, and there are times when the reader may almost feel pity for him but not as one would feel it for Ivan [Karamazov]. For Robert's failure of self-understanding is a failure of the moral sense, a chosen failure on his part, not just a failure in belief of a weakness imposed upon him by God or society" (p. 236). Lee's judgment and consequent refusal to view Robert as a pitiful man seem inconsistent with his major thesis, for if we cannot tell whether Gil-Martin is Satan or Robert's psychological shadow, then how can we condemn Robert? Further, Lee ends his argument with the statement that "the novel insists that evil exists but we can never be sure of its form" (p. 239). If this is true, then Robert cannot be held morally responsible for his decision to serve Gil-Martin. Lee obviously wishes to demonstrate that our response to the book must be complex, but he equates complexity with ambiguity. I contend that Hogg wants us to accept the Devil as real *and* to pity Robert as a human being; this is a complexity Lee does not discern.

4 Robert M. Adams, in the "Introduction" to the Norton edition, mentions a few of the styles adopted by Hogg to tell his amazing tale, but for Adams such virtuosity is a mere curiosity. He finds the major interest in the book to be its depiction of the sinner himself, who "takes his honored place (truly supralapsarian at last!) amid a large throng of impressively schizoid heroes . . ." (p. xiv). We are back to a purely psychological appreciation of the novel, one that will not stand close scrutiny.

5 Adams finds the sermon to be an unaccountable burlesque and evidence of Hogg's daring if pointless willingness to take a stylistic "gamble" (p. xii).

THE POET'S PURLOINED LETTER

By Martin Roth

IT IS NOW well over a century since Poe challenged his readers to identify the purloined letter as the letter "o"—the vocalic power in the name of God. The challenge was published as an item in his marginalia series shortly after the tale was written:[1]

> Here is an edition [*Camöens—Genoa*—II.32], which, so far as microscopical excellence and absolute accuracy of typography are concerned, might well be prefaced with the phrase of the Koran— "There is *no* error in this book." We cannot call a single inverted *o* an error—*can* we? But I am really as glad of having found that inverted *o*, as ever was a Columbus or an Archimedes. What, after all, are continents discovered, or silversmiths exposed? Give us a good *o* turned upside-down, and a whole herd of bibliomanic Arguses overlooking it for years.[2]

The item is obviously ironic, but is it anything more than a typically overt *jeu d'esprit?* The letter "o" is one of several that cannot be inverted; in type it is usually the only letter which cannot be. Put another way, it is the letter whose inversion *cannot be detected* by "Argus eyes" and "microscopical excellence," phrases which should remind us of the prefect's unsuccessful search for the missing letter, which the poet as critic is announcing here that he has found. The allusion to the *Koran* is too heavy for this apparently trivial content, yet the *Koran* is the source for the title of Poe's first experiment in cosmography, "Al Aaraaf." And the allusion to the exposed silversmith is, I believe, Poe's earliest reference to the title of his late cosmographic fable, *Eureka*. Columbus translated the world into an "o" and can be said to have inverted it by sailing from Europe to America, whereas Archimedes' exclamation of triumph occurred when he discovered how to detect misrepresentation in the asserted perfection of a crown, that royal O. The unscrupulous minister did not merely hide the letter, he also inverted it: he had "refolded [it] in a reversed direction, in the same creases or edges which had formed the original fold. . . . the letter had been turned . . . inside out" (VI, 50).[3] Now the minister can leave his cosmic letter in plain view, for there is no eye so keen, no microscope so fine, that can detect it.

To entertain the suggestion that Poe is punning in the title of his tale should lead to a further observation: apart from C. Auguste Dupin (whose name contains every vowel except "o"; whose last name points to the absence of "o" in two reverse directions—vocalically ["u"—"i"] and consonantally ["p"—"n"]) only two characters in the tale are given names—names, moreover, which are indicated only by an initial consonant; and these consonants are G and D.

Poe's strategy for meaning in the tale is not a mere game played with his readers, it is a legitimate artistic gesture; and, until we accept this, we will continue to be puzzled at the importance that Poe holds for writers like Mallarmé, Borges, and Nabokov, who are also devoted to the value of word play as art. In a recent book on Poe, Daniel Hoffman suggests that the literary act is by nature an act of secret writing: "There's something about creating or using a secret language which appeals to all mankind. To poets especially. And particularly to poets who know themselves the discoverers of secret knowledge, of truths as yet unrevealed to others. A poet can use a secret language to conceal such a truth. Even more exciting is the prospect that by his being the only man capable of cracking a code in which the truth he seeks is hidden, he may become the possessor of that truth."[4]

Cryptography and Biblical scholarship and criticism were among the innumerable arts and skills of which Poe claimed total (and often unrivalled) mastery. Poe's obsession with codes and ciphers is too well known to need extensive comment here. His public career as a master cryptographer began on 18 December 1839, and on 25 March of the following year he announced:

> We *can* decypher any thing of the kind, or of any other kind. What is said about a key being necessary for the solution is based upon a misconception. It does not follow that, because cyphers are put together by laborious or intricate processes . . . that we must go through the same intricate process in unriddling them. We assert roundly, and in general terms, that human ingenuity cannot concoct a proper cypher which we cannot resolve.[5]

Poe's knowledge of the Bible and Biblical scholarship and criticism may have come to him at second hand, but he presented himself as an expert in matters Biblical, withheld his sources, and offered his opinions with an air of infallibility. Most of these appeared in the *Pinakidia* of 1836 and in a review of John Lloyd Stephens' *Arabia Petraea* in 1837. In the latter review Poe wrote, "It is essential, however, that these prophesies be literally rendered; and it is a matter for regret as well as surprise, that Dr. Keith should have failed to determine so important a point as the exactness or falsity of the version of his text. This we will now briefly examine" (X, 17). Poe then proceeded to emend the text in question, but neither the tone of his introduction here quoted nor his emendation indicated that it was all printed verbatim from a letter to Poe by Charles Anthon, professor of Greek and Latin at Columbia College.

But Poe claimed to possess an even more esoteric familiarity with Biblical lore. Two of Poe's *Pinakidia* items, for example, announced his discovery of unsuspected word-play in the Bible:

The standard of Judas Maccabaeus displayed the words "Mi camoca baelim Jehovah"—Who is like unto thee, O Lord, among the Gods? This being afterwards intimated by the first letter of each word, in the manner of the S. P. Q. R., gave rise to the surname Maccabaeus—for the initials in Hebrew form "Maccabi." (XIV, 55)

The "Lamentations" of Jeremiah are written, with the exception of the last chapter, in acrostic verse; that is to say, every line or couplet begins, in alphabetical order, with some letter in the Hebrew alphabet. In the third chapter each letter is repeated three times successively. (XIV, 42)

It is hard to believe that Poe would not have been familiar with the mystery of the Tetragrammaton, the consonantal form of the divine name (J H V H), and behind this the belief, common to many early cultures, that the virtues of the divinity are contained in the vowels of his name and that the power, and even the existence, of the divinity depends upon those vowels remaining the secret possession of the priesthood. The Talmud tells us that Rabbis communicated the true pronunciation to their disciples only once every seven years.

Poe did not refer directly to the Tetragrammaton in his writing, but he alluded to it in a *Pinakidia* piece which begins: "The word Jehovah is not Hebrew" (XIV, 49). He went on to claim that the Hebrew had no such letters as J or V; but, when the piece was reprinted in his *Marginalia* almost a decade later, it consisted of that first sentence alone. Poe referred twice to the Massoretic vocalization of the Hebrew scriptures, which occurred in the ninth or tenth century A.D. when a guild of trained scholars provided the scriptural text with a set of vowel points and accents. He implied that the Massoretes *deliberately* falsified the vowels to keep them from profane eyes: "The Hebrew language has lain now for two thousand years mute and incapable of utterance. The 'Masoretical punctuation' which professes to supply the vowels was formed a thousand years after the language had ceased to be spoken, and disagrees in many instances with the Seventy, Origen and other writers" (XIV, 53-54).[6]

Our regard for "The Purloined Letter" as an early example of detective fiction is an act of condescension. It is not a good detective tale, because it is not a detective tale in any ordinary sense of that term. It is a cosmographic fable (Richard Wilbur has suggested that all Poe's tales are[7]), although the cosmic fiction intersects the surface of the tale. I am referring particularly to that barely discernible backdrop of a court scandal. Like Hawthorne, Poe deliberately thinned this fiction in order to prevent the reader from anchoring his sense of the tale in Parisian time and space.

The prefect had resorted to "the cant of diplomacy" as he recounted the circumstances of the crime, presumably to keep the identities of the principals a secret from Dupin. He tells Dupin that "this is an affair demanding the greatest secrecy, and . . . I should most probably lose the position I now hold, were it known that I confided it to any one" (30). Yet he mentions the word "royal," and he might as well have gone on and said the king and queen, *if he is referring to them*. Dupin must know immediately to whom he refers, for he tells the narrator later in the tale that he is a partisan of the lady in question, and there are hints in the tale that he is to be identified as the lady's secret lover, the author of the purloined letter. Moreover, what could the immensely valuable power that results from the minister's possession of the letter be? He may be in a position to blackmail the queen, but to what end? Can the queen persuade or coerce the king to turn all policy decisions in the state over to the minister, declare war at his bidding . . . or what? The fiction of immense power cannot be understood in national terms.

If, however, the "cant of diplomacy" refers to Poe's God and angelic creatures on the order of Nesace or Ligeia in "Al Aaraaf," the phrases cease to be melodramatic and inflated; they become quite literal: "I have received personal information from *a very high quarter*, that a certain document *of the last importance*, has been purloined from the royal apartments. . . . the paper gives its holder a certain power in a certain quarter where such power is immensely valuable. . . . the disclosure of the document to a third person, *who shall be nameless*, would bring in question the honor of a personage *of most exalted station*; and this fact gives the holder of the document an *ascendancy* over *the illustrious personage*" (30-31; italics mine).

Dupin knows who the lady is, yet he claims that he cannot understand the prefect's language. Later, however, he uses the "cant of diplomacy" himself, without any trace of self-consciousness: "the superscription, to a certain royal personage, was . . . bold" (49). One can talk of these personages only in cant terms; that is, in language which has no particular reference. Supernal being and supernal truth are outside the limits of human language. They are indefinite and that is why poetry, the highest human art form touching most directly upon supernal beauty, "is opposed to . . . romance, by having for its object an *indefinite* instead of a *definite* pleasure, being a poem only so far as this object is attained."[8]

If the surface fiction of the tale corresponds to Poe's cosmic fiction, we may identify the royal lady's lover with the poet in his youth.[9] While he is still able to remember the universe in its original simplicity, he sends her a letter of immense power (it is also a poem) which a bold and unscrupulous minister intercepts and subverts. The ideal love which exists between Ligeia and the narrator of that tale is, as Wilbur has argued, a fiction for that early state of poetic wholeness: "In the superficial story, this happy period belongs to his adult life, but there are strong hints of another chronology. . . . It is, in fact, as a child that the hero dwells with Ligeia and the heavenly harmony she confers . . . and the passing of Ligeia is the passing of childhood and its 'visionary gleam.' "[10]

The minister D——— is Dupin's double. He is Dupin's dark counterpart, the "bold" Promethean man who "dares all things, those unbecoming as well as those becoming a man" (31). He has come into the possession of the power that once was God's—later recreated by the poet—and has dedicated himself to keeping that power hidden. His "ascendancy" depends upon the letter's remaining undiscoverable: the "possession, and not any employment of the letter . . . bestows the power. With the employment the power departs" (32).

Such a reading of "The Purloined Letter" is at least in keeping with Poe's sense of the created universe and its destiny, as indicated in *Eureka.* In rewriting *Genesis* Poe found it unthinkable that something could be created out of nothing. The world obviously had a material source and that was the simple and unparticled materiality of God Himself. God gave Himself to the creation of the universe. He willingly allowed Himself to be translated into the diverse particles of the universe of space. And as the universe expands in terms of its physical laws, God is diminished; He will ultimately be annihilated and absorbed into His own creation. This original act, however, has its limit, its own "barrier and ban," and that is a point of maximum diffusion in which space is filled with a distribution of matter which corresponds spatially to the will of God Himself, the volition of the initial act of creation. Poe believed that the universe was soon to enter into its retrograde phase or had already done so. This would involve a concentration of matter into itself, annihilating itself and reconstituting God. But the energy for that retrograde phase is not available, since the power of God has totally exhausted itself by that point in cosmic time.

The role of the poet in this second half of universal history is not explicit in *Eureka*, but I tend to agree with Wilbur's formulation of it:

> Since God in creating the universe, fragmented Himself into His
> creatures, and now exists only in those "infinite individualizations
> of Himself," it is they who must, by some counterimpulse, restore
> the original oneness of things.
>
> What must this counterimpulse be? Since "the source of all
> motion is thought," it must be intellectual or spiritual in charac-
> ter. And since the creation is a work of art, the counterimpulse
> which can reunify it must be imaginative. In short, the duty of
> God's creatures is to think God together again by discovering,
> through the fusing power of poetic imagination, the primal unity
> in the present diversity.
>
> . . . In [the poet] . . . alone, of all the inhabitants of Earth, the
> divine spark of imagination still burns brightly; his soul alone
> vaguely remembers, from a previous existence, a divine harmony
> and beauty, and yearns to return thither.[11]

II

Richard Wilbur characterizes Dupin as a man who possesses "pure
poetic intuition bordering on omniscience," a man of "preterhuman
powers," unlimited "power of divination," "godlike genius." Yet he
accepts that reading of the tale which merely has Dupin reconstruct
the minister's thought processes at the time he originally concealed the
letter. His phrases for Dupin, however, are appropriate if Dupin is
acting for an absent God and restoring to the universe some of its
original harmony and simplicity. And if this is the case, his recovery
of the letter is the result of an act of poetic creativity, not ratiocination.
He does not find a hidden letter but dreams a new letter into the world
of time and space. And if this is the case, then the prefect could not find
the letter when he searched the apartment because it was not there to
be found.

I realize that I am contradicting many of the statements made in the
first part of this article, but I believe that this confusion is not of my
making but Poe's. Art surfaces can hold a number of meanings in sus-
pension, and art serves greater ends than the anal satisfaction of consistency. There is a tendency in writers like Poe, who have dreamed a
total and closed vision of ultimate reality, to treat it (as it serves their
purpose) in at least two modes—the cosmogonic and the cosmographic, the world as narrative and the world as model. Are the angelic
and the divine realms images of a reality that existed prior to the creation of the universe and will exist again after its annihilation, as

Eureka suggests, or do they coexist transcendentally with the world of space and time, as it is dramatized in "Al Aaraaf"? The two parts of this article treat "The Purloined Letter" respectively as a cosmogonic and as a cosmographic fable.

The formulaic element in the tale which Poe has been praised for— the concealment of an object in a place so obvious that the searcher is psychologically unable to discover it—is far more intellectually respectable in a tale like G. K. Chesterton's "The Invisible Man," than in this one. If the prefect is limited by his assumption that criminals invariably hide their secrets in minuscule or *recherché* nooks, he is easily outwitted by a more comprehensive mind. If the prefect is blind to what lies under his nose, and the minister has placed the letter under his nose for that very reason, then the minister is acting only in opposition to the prefect, and that is hardly a fair match. Dupin's solution, also, seems to be an obvious inference based on the limitations of the prefect's mind: if the police cannot find the letter, it must be under their noses.

Yet the minister knows Dupin; they had crossed swords once before in Vienna. He should respect his intelligence. Does it never occur to him that the prefect might go to Dupin for advice? (He anticipates all the other moves of the police.) Does he know nothing of the previous cases of Marie Roget and the Rue Morgue? (Dupin and the narrator had been discussing both at dinner, and the narrator is meditating upon them when the prefect rushes in.)

If the minister were matching wits with Dupin, where would he have hidden the letter? Dupin and the prefect need merely search together: if the hiding place is subtle, the prefect will eventually find it; if it is obvious, Dupin will march directly to the spot. The minister's vaunted perspicacity seems sadly wanting in another instance as well. He knows why he has been waylaid by footpads; he knows that he is under constant surveillance by the police; he knows that his apartment has been repeatedly searched (he absents himself in the evening for the convenience of the police). He knows that Dupin has a grudge against him and is a political partisan of the lady in question. Dupin visits him twice; once, the minister has to turn his back on Dupin because of the distraction of a musket going off under his window. Yet Dupin has to give the minister a clue in his own substitute letter, because "he would feel some curiosity in regard to the identity of the person who had outwitted him" (52). Fifty years later, Irene Adler sees through a similar ruse by Holmes immediately.

I would ask the reader to entertain the possibility that Dupin, in his explanation of how he determined the letter's hiding place, may not be giving us the earliest version of the "too obvious" formula. The most contrary piece of evidence, however, is Dupin's statement: "But this is

a point, it appears, somewhat *above or beneath* the understanding of
the Prefect. He never once thought it probable, or possible, that the
Minister had deposited the letter immediately beneath the nose *of the
whole world, by way of best preventing any portion of that world from
perceiving it*" (48, italics mine). That would seem to settle the matter.
Yet the elements I have italicized are either imprecisely or curiously
phrased; they introduce meanings that cannot be accommodated to
the apparent meaning of Dupin's explanation.[12] Dupin also tells the
narrator that he "saw, in fine, that . . . [the minister] would be driven,
as a matter of course, to *simplicity*" (46). I will comment on this term
shortly, but *simple* need not mean *obvious*.

The epigraph to the tale ("*Nil sapientiae odiosius acumine nimio*")
seems to support the "too obvious" formula, even to support it when
translated "nothing is more distasteful to good sense than too much
cunning," as one editor has it. I believe that Poe would have translated
it to read, "nothing is more odious to wisdom than excessive acumen."
"Odious" and "acumen" are recurring terms in Poe's vocabulary. Poe
is much more precise in his use of language than most of his critics
implicitly give him credit for. Their attitude is a little surprising since
the verbal imprecision of others is one of the most frequent grounds of
attack in Poe's own reviews and articles. He also tends, like Thoreau,
to work through the radical meaning of words.[13] "Acumen" means
sharpness, pointedness, and when it is applied to the intellect, it is used
in that radical sense, as in the following discussion of faulty method in
"The Murders in the Rue Morgue":

> The Parisian police, so much extolled for *acumen*, are cunning,
> but no more. . . . Vidocq, for example . . . erred continually by the
> very intensity of his investigations. He impaired his vision by
> holding the object too close. . . . Thus there is such a thing as being
> too profound. Truth is not always in a well. . . . The modes and
> sources of this kind of error are well typified in the contemplation
> of the heavenly bodies. To look at a star by glances—to view it in
> a side-long way . . . is to behold the star distinctly—is to have the
> best appreciation of its lustre—a lustre which grows dim just in
> proportion as we turn our vision *fully* upon it. . . . By undue pro-
> fundity we perplex and enfeeble thought; and it is possible to
> make even Venus herself vanish from the firmament by a scrutiny
> too sustained, too concentrated, or too direct. (IV, 165-66)

The distinction here is not between the subtle and the obvious but
between the harsh focus upon particulars which robs us of "useful"
beauty and a lateral view of the whole which confirms true "distinction." If I may move from one tale to another, Poe further compounds

the epistemology of "The Purloined Letter" by suggesting that even if the letter had been in the room when the prefect was searching for it, the search itself would have caused the letter to disappear. The method of mathematical analysis literally destroys truth and beauty; it causes Venus to vanish from the firmament!

III

It would be a grave weakness in "The Purloined Letter" to identify the prefect with the operation of methodical or mathematical reasoning and then use him in the tale as an inept practitioner of that method. On the contrary, Dupin tells us twice that the police are as competent a body of investigators as one could find: "The measures adopted were not only the best of their kind, but carried out to absolute perfection. Had the letter been deposited within the *range* of their search, these fellows would, beyond a question, have found it [39-40; italics mine]. . . . where the case is of importance—or, what amounts to the same thing in the policial eyes, when the reward is of magnitude,—the qualities in question have *never* been known to fail" (43).

The Cartesian analysis which the prefect's search exemplifies is absolutely adequate for the location of any object in whatever place it is hidden. The prefect's method involves the total exhaustion of space. If an object is known or presumed to be concealed, that is, locatable, within a finite body of space, then it must occupy a place on the Cartesian graph of that space. If an investigator methodically examines (or exhausts) in sequence all the coordinate cubes that describe that space, then he simply must find his object. And this is what the prefect did: "We divided . . . [the] entire surface [of the house] into compartments, which we numbered, so that none might be missed; then we scrutinized each individual square inch throughout the premises, including the two houses immediately adjoining" (36).

The prefect's description of his search is one of the many set pieces in the tale, and it spreads over three pages. The narrator formally opens this dissertation by asking the prefect to detail the particulars of his search, and the prefect answers, "Why the fact is, we took our time, and we searched *everywhere*. I have had long experience in these affairs. I took the entire building, room by room; devoting the nights of a whole week to each" (34). The narrator interrupts the prefect ten times. He objects that the prefect could not possibly have searched as exhaustively as his description of method indicates; he points out areas that the prefect might have overlooked. Here is the sequence of phrases that introduce the prefect's replies: "by no means," "certainly not; but we did better," "that of course," "certainly," "beyond doubt." And the narrator concludes: "Then . . . you have been making a miscalculation, and the letter is *not* upon the premises, as you suppose" (37).

One of the narrator's questions is particularly relevant to this discussion: "You looked among D———'s papers, of course"? And the prefect answers, "Certainly; we opened every package and parcel" (36). Yet among those papers is a letter which, along with five or six visiting cards, occupies a card rack with three or four compartments. The prefect may not have been able to recognize the letter he was seeking by its surface appearance, but he certainly would have found it had he opened it, as he explicitly claims he did. Must we then conclude that he is a liar as well as a fool? [14]

IV

In the opening of the tale, Dupin does not solve the mystery of the purloined letter, but he does tell the prefect that he will not find the letter in the minister's apartment; and he does this by defining what a mystery is: it is too simple, too plain, and too self-evident. To this the prefect laughingly replies, "Who ever heard of such an idea?" (29). When Dupin explains the mystery after the fact, he drops the middle term and refers to the minister being driven to *simplicity* and the prefect being troubled by the mystery "on account of its being so *very* self-evident" (46).

Dupin was attempting to remind the prefect that if his problem involves a mystery—that is, a truth—then it is by definition simple and self-evident. It is, therefore, unresolvable, since it is not subject to the only "resolving" processes that, according to Poe, we may claim to possess: the methods of deduction and induction. The simple is that which cannot be analyzed—that is, it cannot be broken into component parts. But analysis of this kind is essential to the operation of the deductive method. The self-evident fact or truth is that which cannot be arrived at by any evidence other than itself, but external evidence is essential for the operation of the inductive method.

I must admit that I find it easier to understand the prefect's failure in epistemological terms. If the minister's apartment is an image of the mind, then the purloined letter can represent a truth that is not yet grasped, not yet part of the mind's contents; and the prefect's method is incapable of generating it. Nonetheless, I believe that we approach Poe's vision of reality more closely if we can accept the prefect's failure in ontological or cosmological terms. The letter does not exist in the world of time and space as truth or beauty until Dupin dreams it into material existence. If Wilbur is correct in his understanding of *Eureka,* the poet in the "latter days" of the universe has the awful responsibility of dreaming God back into existence and thereby dreaming the world back into its original state of simplicity.

Such an understanding would give more point to the exchange that follows the prefect's lengthy account of his search. The narrator concludes that the prefect has been making a *"miscalculation"* in supposing the letter to be on the premises. The prefect agrees and asks Dupin's advice, and he is told to "make a thorough re-search of the premises" (37). The advice is absurd on the face of it. If Dupin condemns the prefect's method of searching because he invariably overlooks objects in plain sight, he would hardly advise him to go through those futile motions again. He must, therefore, be understood to tell the prefect to "re-search," or "research," his own premises as to the nature of truth. On another level, however, the method of mathematical reason, the thorough exhaustion of time and space, is only invalid *a priori* but perfectly adequate to the discovery or location of a truth once it does exist in time and space. (After Kepler guessed his laws, Newton was then able to draw deductions from them.) Dupin's advice, then, is also literally sound: if looked for *now*, the letter will be found.

The human mind, for Poe, is incapable of generating truth methodically, either through the analysis of its own contents or through inferences based upon the sense data of the external world. These are the two roads of Aries Tottle and Hog in *Eureka*. In that work the anonymous letter writer of 2848 A.D. informs his correspondent that "it is scarcely more than eight or nine hundred years ago since the metaphysicians first consented to relieve the people of the singular fancy that there exist *but two practicable roads to Truth*" (XVI, 188).

The road of the Hog-ites should remind us of the errors of Vidocq and the prefect: "The error of our progenitors was quite analogous with that of the wiseacre who fancies he must necessarily see an object the more distinctly, the more closely he holds it to his eyes. They blinded themselves . . . with the impalpable, titillating Scotch snuff of *detail*" (XVI, 190). The other road is equally useless: "Nor had our forefathers any better right to talk about *certainty*, when pursuing, in blind confidence, the *a priori* path of axioms, or of the Ram [Aries]. . . . The simple truth is, that the Aristotelians erected their castles upon a basis far less reliable than air; *for no such things as axioms ever existed or can possibly exist at all*" (XVI, 192). Poe cannot offer his readers any road to truth, for, alas, there is none. Truth is accessible to man but not as a result of method:

> would it not have given these bigots some trouble to determine by which of their two roads was reached the most momentous and sublime of *all* their truths—the truth—the fact of *gravitation?* . . . Kepler admitted that these laws he *guessed* . . . Yes!—these

vital laws Kepler *guessed*—that is to say, he *imagined* them. Had
he been asked to point out either the *de*ductive or *in*ductive route
by which he attained them, his reply might have been—"I know
nothing about *routes*—but I *do* know the machinery of the Universe. Here it is. I grasped it with *my soul*—I reached it through
mere dint of *intuition.*" (XVI, 196-97)

The minister defeats the prefect because he is a poet as well as a
mathematician, a Kepler as well as a Newton, while the prefect is only
a mathematician. The narrator attempts at one point to separate these
two orders of mind: " 'But is [the minister] . . . really the poet?' I
asked. 'There are two brothers, I know; and both have attained reputation in letters. The Minister I believe has written learnedly on the
Differential Calculus. He is a mathematician and no poet.' " Dupin
answers: "You are mistaken; I know him well; he is both. As poet *and*
mathematician, he would reason well; as mere mathematician, he
could not have reasoned at all, and thus would have been at the mercy
of the Prefect" (43). Following this exchange, Dupin launches into a
discussion of the limitations of mathematical reasoning which is particularly relevant to my argument:

> I dispute, in particular, the reason educed by mathematical study.
> The mathematics are the science of form and quantity; mathe-
> matical reasoning is merely logic applied to observation upon
> form and quantity. The great error lies in supposing that even the
> truths of what is called *pure* algebra, are abstract or general truths.
> . . . Mathematical axioms are *not* axioms of general truth. What
> is true of *relation*—of form and quantity—is often grossly false
> in regard to morals, for example. In this latter science it is very
> *un*true that the aggregated parts are equal to the whole. (44)

The prefect's search fails because he assumes that *the parts are equal
to the whole*, an axiom true in the world of space, but not true in the
"spirit's outer world" (XVI, 89).

Kepler imagined "the fact of *gravitation*," and Newton was then
able to subject that unanalyzable truth into mathematical equations
which were true for the universe of space. The poet of "The Poetic
Principle," "inspired by an ecstatic prescience of the glories beyond
the grave, 'struggles' to attain a portion of that loveliness whose very
elements, perhaps, appertain to eternity." It is he who dreams "The
Raven," after which the poet in "The Philosophy of Composition" can
"truly" explain that the poem was engineered with the cold precision
of a mathematical calculator. Dupin dreams a letter into existence in
the material world and then explains its existence in terms of that

world alone. The second and third cases are no more contradictory than the first which Poe asserts to be a true paradox.

It is one thing to glimpse supernal beauty, but in order to extend that ecstasy into poetic structure; or to explain how that poem was written; or to explain how an unscrupulous minister hid a letter so that it could not be found by the police—for these processes the poet must be his own mathematical brother.[15]

V

Since I have made the assertion that it is Dupin who dreams the purloined letter into existence (in the first and second place), I might as well commit myself to locating this poetic act in the tale. I believe that it takes place on the occasion of Dupin's first visit to the minister's apartment. The letter, we are told, is contained in a "trumpery fillagree card-rack of pasteboard, that hung dangling by a dirty blue ribbon, from a little brass knob just beneath the middle of the mantelpiece." And there is some reason to believe that the card rack is rotating.[16] This is another instance of the "chandelier" image which occurs in most of Poe's tales. Wilbur has isolated and identified this image, particularly in "Ligeia": "Ligeia [first] appears . . . in the pool of light beneath the censer . . . which hangs on its golden chain in the center of the chamber. . . . Poe plainly found it in *Paradise Lost* . . . where the created universe depends from heaven by a golden chain which serves also as the pathway of angels. . . . The golden chain reappears, as a chandelier, in a number of Poe interiors, signifying always the linkage between poetic imagination and the divine mind."[17] I would associate with these the chimney in "The Murders in the Rue Morgue" and the pendulum in "The Pit and the Pendulum." In the latter story it more clearly symbolizes the path along which supernal truth enters the material world.

Dupin only discovers the letter because his eyes have made a "circuit of the room." The effect of such visual activity must be read in the context of the following passage from the opening of *Eureka* (which also explains, I believe, Dupin's curious statement that he feared for his life on that first visit):

He who from the top of Ætna casts his eyes leisurely around, is affected chiefly by the *extent* and *diversity* of the scene. Only by a rapid whirling on his heel could he hope to comprehend the panorama in the sublimity of its *oneness*. But as, on the summit of Ætna, *no* man has thought of whirling on his heel, so no man has ever taken into his brain the full uniqueness of the prospect; and so, again, whatever considerations lie involved in this uniqueness, have as yet no practical existence for mankind. (XVI, 186)

NOTES

1 "The Purloined Letter" was written and as yet unpublished on 28 May 1844; *The Letters of Edgar Allan Poe*, ed. John Ward Ostrom (Cambridge, Mass.: Harvard University Press, 1948), I, 253.

2 *The Complete Works of Edgar Allan Poe*, ed. James A. Harrison (New York: Crowell, 1902), XVI, 41-42. All my Poe citations are to this edition.

3 All further citations to "The Purloined Letter" are to this volume.

4 Daniel Hoffman, POE POE POE POE POE POE POE (Garden City and New York: Doubleday, 1972), p. 99. The only possible hint in "The Purloined Letter" that Poe was deliberately encoding his tale is the repeated reference to the "D—— cipher." How extensive was Poe's tendency toward literary encoding has yet to be demonstrated or ascertained. I can only assert in this article that the missing vowel in the title of Poe's detective hoax "Thou Art the Man" is the true identity of the criminal, the artist as criminal. I also believe that Poe encoded "The Murders in the Rue Morgue"; the tag Poe chose for the tale—"What song the Syrens sang, or what name Achilles assumed when he hid himself among women, although puzzling questions, are not beyond *all* conjecture"—should mean that the act of resolving a mystery, which Dupin performs, is analogous in some way to the discovery of a sacred and esoteric song and name. I believe that the discovery of the cobbler's name before he assumed that of Chantilly will provide us with a key to a new level of meaning in the tale. The shift from that earlier name to Chantilly involved only a change in the initial letter, but that change, Dupin tells us, destroyed the ancient sound.

5 Clarence S. Brigham, *Edgar Allan Poe's Contributions to Alexander's Weekly Messenger* (Worcester, Mass.: American Antiquarian Society, 1943), pp. 61-62.

6 Sidney Kaplan, in his introduction to *The Narrative of Arthur Gordon Pym* (New York: Hill and Wang, 1960), pp. xvii-xix, argues that the names of persons and places on the island of Tsalal, as well as the language spoken there, are barely distinguishable Hebrew words, and he asks, "Why then invent names in the Biblical tongue? Was it simply play—another experiment in cryptography, of which he was so fond?"

7 Throughout this article I am working more or less within the context of Wilbur's work on Poe, particularly his discussion of "The Purloined Letter" in the introduction to Poe which he wrote for Perry Miller's anthology, *Major Writers of America* (New York: Harcourt, 1962), pp. 378-80; and all citations to Wilbur, unless otherwise specified, are to this piece.

I feel that it is no more than just to say that Poe's reputation in the future will be largely the result of Wilbur's suggestions. He has sketched the outlines of that cosmic myth which encompasses Poe's writings, and, more importantly, he has shown or suggested how many of the individual pieces can be seen either as integral expressions of certain key moments in that myth or as fictive and poetic processes that imitate his world's truth.

8 "Letter to Mr. ——" (1831), in *Introduction to Poe: A Thematic Reader*, ed. Eric W. Carlson (Glenview, Ill.: Scott Foresman, 1967), pp. 473-74.

9 If, however, D—— is Dupin's double, then he also is the royal lady's lover. Hoffman (p. 131) argues that the incident in Vienna involved the minister's purloining the lady's love from Dupin, so that his theft of Dupin's love letter in addition is a double insult which cannot be borne. I would object to this explanation if only on the grounds that it literalizes the surface tale and lends weight to plot elements that Poe deliberately left as vague as possible. I would also wonder why Dupin is still

writing letters to the lady after he has lost her affection. The structure is much more complicated, however, for there are indications in the tale that the minister is also *the author of the original letter*. In the original, "the superscription, to a certain royal personage, was markedly bold and decided" (49). The word "bold" is repeatedly applied to the minister. Even more confusing is the fact that the disguised letter is not only addressed to the minister, but it was also sent by the minister: "here the seal was large and black, with the D—— cipher" (49). There must be some explanation for this; it is much too large a point for Poe to have overlooked.

10 Wilbur, pp. 376-77.

11 Wilbur, pp. 373-74. Wilbur is, I think, mistaken in identifying God with spirit. In "Mesmeric Revelation" the "unparticled matter, or God, in quiescence, is (as nearly as we can conceive it) what men call mind. And the power of self-movement (equivalent in effect to human volition) is, in the unprincipled matter, the result of its unity and omniprevalence" (V, 246).

12 Poe has a tendency to parody his own serious meanings; support for the extravagant claim that the letter is physically dreamed into the world of time and space may be found in a tale, "The Angel of the Odd," published in 1844, after "The Purloined Letter" had been written. In that tale, the narrator, who is quite drunk, flies into a rage at the account of an odd accident (an accident for which there is no explanation) which he reads in a newspaper. He denies the possibility of such occurrences and intends "to believe nothing henceforward that has anything of the 'singular' about it" (VI, 104). At this, a voice calls him a fool. The narrator is drunk enough to feel "nothing of trepidation, but merely uplifted my eyes with a leisurely movement, and looked carefully around the room for the intruder. I could not, however, perceive any one at all. . . ." The narrator continues, "Hereupon I bethought me of looking immediately before my nose, and there, sure enough, confronting me at the table sat a personage nondescript, although not altogether undescribable" (VI, 105). The narrator is eventually brought to admit that he believes in the "odd" and the "Angel of the Odd."

The word "odd" dominates the opening of "The Purloined Letter." It is associated with the mystery in that tale and anything else that lies outside the limits of the prefect's comprehension: "and [he] thus lived amid an absolute legion of 'oddities' " (29). The prefect may not be able to find the letter because it is under his nose, but the Angel of the Odd is no less supernatural for being under the nose of his drunken narrator.

13 Dupin is himself aware of the confusion that results from the generalization or diversion of the original meaning of words. He accuses the mathematicians of having deceptively made the term "analysis" part of the vocabulary of algebra: "but if a term is of any importance—if words derive any value from applicability—then 'analysis' conveys 'algebra' about as much as, in Latin, *'ambitus'* conveys 'ambition,' *'religio'* 'religion' or *'homines honesti,'* 'a set of *honorable* men' " (44). In "The Colloquy of Monos and Una," Poe added two footnotes to his text to indicate to the reader that his terms "history" and "purification" must be understood in their radical sense: to the phrase, "In history of these regions," he noted that "history" was from the Greek for "to contemplate"; and, in reference to the purification of the Earth, he noted that "the word, *'purification'* seems here to be used with reference to its root in the Greek . . . fire" (IV, 205). *Pinakidia* and *Marginalia* testify amply to Poe's absorbing interest in etymology, and one item in the former reads as follows: "Albert, in his Hebrew Dictionary, pretends to discover in each word, in its root, in its letters, and in the manner of pronouncing them, the reason of its signification. Leescher in his treatise De causis Linguae Hebreae, carries the matter even farther" (XIV, 70).

14 Poe has the prefect use the term, *recherché*, to describe both the places in which he presumes criminals hide things and the manner in which he presumes they hide them. I would suggest that Poe is punning very economically, and his pun allows a reader to identify the term as the French adjective, rare, uncommon, which supports the surface meaning of the tale. It may also be the participial form of the verb and thus mean "searchable." The prefect does indeed assume that criminals hide objects in searchable places, places that may be searched.

15 Poe's strongest statement on the necessity of combining mathematics and imagination occurs in 1842 in a review, "Mr. Griswold and the Poets": "It may be demonstrated that the two divisions of mental power are never to be found in perfection apart. The *highest* order of the imaginative intellect is always preeminently mathematical; and the converse."

A very curious addition to the tale occurred in the text published in *The Gift* for 1845; the italicized portion of the following quotation did not appear in the text published in Poe's *Tales* of the same year: "if the Minister had been no more than a mathematician, the Prefect would have been under no necessity of giving me this check. *Had he been no more than poet, I think it probable he would have foiled us all.*" (45, 278). The addition makes sense on the analogy of the letter to a poem: had the poet been gifted with intense Ideality but lacked the faculties of Causality and Comparison, he might have glimpsed supernal beauty, but he could never have brought it into the world as a poem. It does, however, raise problems in the tale, for it identifies the minister as an alternate, or as the *only*, dreamer of the letter. Dupin could never have found the letter if the minister had not posssssed powers of analysis, and, indeed, Dupin's explanation, or analysis, is merely a reconstruction of the minister's earlier analysis. This possibility, however, gives Dupin nothing to do as a poet himself. There may be a coherent explanation for all of this, but I suspect that Poe saw himself getting tangled up in the implications of identifying Dupin and the minister as doubles and excised the entangling sentence from his volume text.

16 Like his other tales of ratiocination, "The Purloined Letter" has been taken to task in studies of detective fiction for errors of fact:

> The flaw here, noted by several writers, is not seriously damaging to the story. It lies in the fact that Dupin could have seen only the front or the back of the envelope containing the letter, and therefore could not possibly have observed at the same time the "large black seal" (on the back) and the address "in a diminutive female hand" (on the front) [Julian Symons, *Mortal Consequences* (New York: Harper, 1972), p. 35].

17 Wilbur, p. 378.

POE IN THE SEVENTIES:
THE POET AMONG THE CRITICS

By Benjamin Franklin Fisher IV

I

Books about Edgar Allan Poe and his work have been proliferating in recent years, and perhaps the seventies will appear to future generations as a watershed in Poe criticism. Appropriately, 1973 is a good year for surveying Poe in the current decade, for in May came the announcement that the Mabbott-Harvard edition of Poe, intended to supersede the long standard Harrison text and halted by Professor Mabbott's untimely death in 1968, would continue under the able, energetic hand of Burton R. Pollin. The books considered below fall chiefly into two groups, the first those that contain "papers on Poe," to borrow from the title of one of them, by diverse hands, the second considerations of Poe and his work by one writer alone. In *New Approaches to Poe* ([Hartford, Conn.: Transcendental Books, 1970]. $10.00), Richard P. Benton, after briefly surveying old and new Poe scholarship, asks: "What will the '70's reveal? I hope a fuller understanding of Poe's art and greatness, which, although defying complete assessment, still can challenge perceptive readers . . ." (p. 3). The books reviewed below all present varying responses to Poe, and they prove indeed that his art and greatness are not so easily encompassed in casual reading.

Benton's own book provides us with a series of papers which approach Poe from various critical angles of vision, not all of them so "new" as the title implies. This mixture of traditional with recent guides for reading Poe is fitting, however, for Benton himself has furnished us both traditional and more modern studies of his subject. His bibliographical knowledge of Poe is demonstrated in his meticulous checklists of useful materials in both the *Emerson Society Quarterly* and *Poe Studies* (he is a member of the editorial boards of both journals). He has also written good critical articles, assessing his author's sources and his more subtle literary artistry.[1] Other essays in the book, such as those by H. Allen Greer, Burton R. Pollin, and Gerald E. Gerber, adhere closely to one long familiar method in Poe scholarship, i.e., they get at their subject by means of source studies. A fourth such essay is Harriet Holman's "Longfellow in the 'Rue Morgue,' " which verges on the absurd in its attempt to project Poe's personal life into this fine detective tale, a hoax of another sort more surely, as an essay, "Blackwood Articles À La Poe: How to Make a False Start Pay," forthcoming in the 1973 *Revue des Langues Vivantes* (Bruxelles) will demonstrate. A "newer" approach is that to some of Poe's early tales by G. R. Thompson, in which Thompson attempts to illuminate the satiric thrust in those tales originally intended as parts of "Tales of the Folio Club," a volume that never did see print, and published subsequently in the Philadelphia *Saturday Courier* in 1832. More will be said on the subject of these early tales in a section below dealing with Thompson's more recent book on Poe's fiction.

Poe's fiction is the focus for all but three of the other eleven essays in the Benton volume. The short tales properly receive the lion's share of study, and Sidney Moss provides an essay on Poe as a probabilist, using E. D. Forgues' 1846 critique of Poe as a text (he translates fair portions of it) by means of which he can show how frequently critics fail to see their subject entire. Irony in "Ligeia," that much-scrutinized tale, is the subject of Joseph M. Garrison's study. Here we are allowed to see Poe having some fun at the expense of his readers and critics. James Gargano's near companion study, "Art and Irony in 'William Wilson,' " continues his own excellent series of close readings of Poe's tales and careful examinations of the narrators in particular.

David M. La Guardia's "Poe, *Pym*, and Initiation" links Poe with the American folk imagination and by this means suggests a still greater area for approaches to Poe, Constance Rourke notwithstanding. Of the essays on the poetry, Lasley Dameron's on Poe and Stephen Crane stands out as a perceptive probing of Crane's affinities with American Gothic and dark Romanticism, as opposed to the view of him as an American literary eccentric (the same goes for Poe himself, as an essay in the 1970 *Revue des Langues Vivantes*, by Roger Forclaz, indicates). A final study for our notice is Alice Chandler's " 'The Visionary Race': Poe's Attitude toward his Dreamers." Poe's ideas about the worth of art, as they altered from the tales of the thirties into those of the late years, are illuminated here. Particularly commendable is the analysis of "The Assignation," a tale little studied and meriting greater attention (I am editing the original appearance, as "The Visionary," in *Godey's Lady's Book*, 1834, for reprinting with commentary).

A second collection of essays from various hands is Richard P. Veler (ed.), *Papers on Poe: Essays in Honor of John Ward Ostrom* ([Springfield, Ohio: Chantrey Music Press, Inc. at Wittenberg University, 1972].$5.95). Opening with Richard Beale Davis' splendid tribute to Ostrom as both Poe scholar and friend, these essays continue through several hundred pages to form a significant contribution to Poe studies. The first essay in Poe studies proper, Eric W. Carlson's "Poe's Vision of Man," (which dates back to 1969) sets out to correct those critics who see only death and destruction in the Poe canon. Carlson convincingly argues that Poe's vision of man was a threefold one: "the Neoplatonic or Paradisiacal, the Existential, and the Psycho-Transcendental, which see life in terms of the Past, the Present, and the Present-Future, respectively" (p.8). In Poe's tales, particularly in "Ligeia" and "Usher," are apparent man's conflicts in attempting to draw upon his inner, psycho-transcendental substance, conflicts resulting from too much yielding to his intellectually rational side. In Poe's attempts to dramatize transcendentalism within the self, says Carlson, we see a theory that goes beyond just the Emersonian-Bostonian theories, balderdash in Poe's mind, but which is, nevertheless, thoroughly within the greater stream of transcendental visions of the self current in Poe's own day. Corroborating the theories set forth in Robert D. Jacobs's *Poe as Journalist and Critic*, Carlson views Poe as embodying popular "isms" and "ologies" of his day rather than as being a *rara avis*, an astonishingly "horrific" exception to the complacent-Emersonian-idealistic thought of the nineteenth century. In this respect Poe is strikingly similar to his younger brother-poet, Swinburne, who was often more in than out of touch with the thought of his own times.

Further essays in Veler's assemblage continue to view Poe in relation to nineteenth-century familiar trends. Clark Griffith's all-too-brief "Poe and the Gothic" suggests a host of possibilities still to be explored in this much touched upon—but generally only touched upon—subject. The approach followed by G. R. Thompson, detailed below, is but one of several keys to the Gothic house of Poe.[2] Following the pioneer lead of Robert E. Spiller, Griffith emphasizes Poe's "internalization" of the Gothic and his modifications of traditional Gothic trappings and techniques, a subject that invites numerous further interpretations. Two additional critiques linking Poe to other popular modes of his day are G. R. Thompson's "Poe and 'Romantic Irony'" and Donald Barlow Stauffer's "Poe as Phrenologist: The Example of Monsieur Dupin." Stauffer's study supplements the old but still valuable work on Poe and Phrenology by Edward Hungerford in the 1930 *American Literature*.

Other papers illuminate still more aspects of Poe. Beginning in a fashion akin to those essays already scanned, Burton Pollin's lively "Poe's Tale of Psyche Zenobia: A Reading for Humor and Ingenious Construction" may well face Carlson's to form the finest parts of this collection. Building upon, and correcting at times, the earlier studies of Thomas H. McNeal and Gerald E. Gerber, Pollin's modern Blackwood article, if I may call it so, throws much new light upon "How to Write a Blackwood Article" and its pendent sequel "A Predicament." Poe himself would probably approve Pollin's careful attention to his texts, and the latter-day Professor's researches, from Chinese Literature to Liberty Hyde Bailey's *Cyclopedia of Horticulture*, would delight the omnivorous nineteenth-century creative plagiarist. Besides being a survey *in petto* of Poe's knowledge of the fads and foibles of his times, Pollin's paper indicates *how* Poe worked his materials into piquant satire, something studied also in the recent essays of G. R. Thompson and Alexander Hammond, particularly in the opening paragraphs of Hammond's 1972 *Poe Studies* "A Reconstruction of Poe's 1833 'Tales of the Folio Club.' " Like Pollin's essay, those concerning *Pym*, by William Peden and J. V. Ridgley, amplify views about the opening and the closing portions of Poe's novel.

Three attempts to emphasize Poe's modernity or "relevance" to today's world are Sidney P. Moss's "Poe's Apocalyptic Vision," William Goldhurst's "Poe-esque Themes," and James Roy King's "Richmond in Tokyo: The Fortunes of Edgar Allan Poe in Contemporary Japan." Moving from Greek Drama to Brecht in order to establish an apocalyptic context, Moss attempts to place Poe therein—although he refers rather slightingly to Poe's Gothicism in so doing. King's essay is an intriguing excursion into Japanese detective fiction à la Edgar Allan Poe, and it shows with greater certainty than usual in this sort of study some ramifications of Poe's "influence."

Other than King's essay, those which close the volume stress biographical materials. John E. Reilly adds to our knowledge of Poe's relationship with Mrs. Jane Ermina Locke, while William Coyle and William Gravely show Poe in conflict with the artists John Frankenstein and Thomas Dunn English respectively. Arlin Turner's "Poe and Simms: Friendly Critics, Sometimes Friends" adds dimension to biographical portraiture of Poe, while simultaneously providing more evidence about Poe's critical principles, theories of fiction, and—in a broader context—Southern literature in the early nineteenth century.

A third volume of "papers on Poe" to appear in 1970 ([Notre Dame, Ind.: University of Notre Dame Press]. $12.50) is Burton R. Pollin's *New Discoveries in Poe*. Here the "papers" have the unity of a single author's pen, and a further note of similarity is struck in that they all examine Poe's relationships with literary and biographical inspirations. Some of the chapters are recast from previously printed articles in scholarly journals (chs. I, II, VI, VIII, X, and XI), others are original contributions for the volume. All are thorough studies of how Poe creatively plagiarized from other writings or drew upon incidents in his own life and artistically fired them into new and interesting "shapes," that is, tales and poems. The links with Hugo, Godwin, Byron, Shelley, to mention only readily familiar names, indicate how essential is wide literary knowledge for full appreciation of Poe. A problem in this respect is that too often a reader conversant with the Poe canon quails before the large shelves of Bulwer, De Quincey, Disraeli, Scott—(not to mention foreign authors) whose works Poe may or may not have read in the originals (particularly in the case of German writers). Not so Burton Pollin! Like Richard Altick in *The Scholar Adventurers*, Pollin indicates a tone of enthusiasm for his source detection, and his results are interesting enough to warrant his enthusiasm. To take but one example in "The Motto of 'Eleonora': Its Source and Significance," we are led through a maze of literary and unprinted manuscript sources toward greater knowledge of Poe's relationship with Mrs. Whitman. Her name, Helen, is a variant of Ellen and Eleonora—or Lenore—and so we move through Pollin's volume as through that long-admired detective story of Coleridge's imagination and its ways, *The Road to Xanadu*. As Poe's own Mr. Blackwood advises Miss Psyche Zenobia to do, Pollin manages to provide us with "piquant" and little-known facts.

II

To move from the gatherings on Poe to books that are more thematic wholes is no great journey, and, since all of them have appeared during 1972 and 1973, no rigid approach to chronological appearance will be necessary. As we opened Part I by centering on Professor Benton's book, it is proper here to review the book by his editorial colleague for *Poe Studies*, G. R. Thompson. *Poe's Fiction: Romantic Irony in the Gothic Tales* ([Madison, Wisc.: University of Wisconsin Press, 1973]. $12.50) is a revision of his Ph.D. Dissertation (University of Southern California, 1966), which has appeared in large part previously as a series of articles, some in Benton's and Veler's volumes, others in various journals. The title of Thompson's book may mislead some readers, because not all of Poe's fiction is surveyed by Thompson. In his attempts to "cite evidence that his [Poe's] Gothic mode was not supernaturalistic but the psychologically realistic, into which he insinuated an element of burlesque (p. xii), Thompson does not include substantial enough evidence for his scant attention to such pieces as "The Masque of the Red Death" (analyzed at length in just three pages: 120-22), "How to Write a Blackwood Article" and "A Predicament," or "The System of Dr. Tarr and Professor Fether," this last surely a fine text for illustrating Thompson's theories (but not mentioned at all in the book).[3]

Such caveats are minor, however. Thompson's book will doubtless stimulate further Poe studies of this sort, either in agreement with or in rebuttal of his own work. Like Griffith's essay mentioned above, it suggests a number of possibilities for approaching Poe from the Gothic point of view, and it impresses one with what remains yet to be done. It synthesizes a great amount of secondary material (though at times in too thesis-like format), drawing mightily from, supplementing, and acknowledging fully and graciously the previous studies of Benton, Griffith, Abel, and others.

After a first chapter linking Poe to the popular "Germanism" in the early nineteenth century, Thompson systematically details the ironic and the "flawed Gothic" qualities of the mode that especially appealed to Poe. Hoaxer, amateur detective, solver of puzzles and cryptographer that he was, says Thompson, Poe frequently fooled his contemporary readers (and, by implication, twentieth-century readers) into thinking they were reading "straight" horror stories. Beneath the surface, however, Poe deliberately inserted puns and practical jokes, to delight the elitist audience for whom he really wished to write, to put down those readers who, like the Prefect or Minister D— in the Dupin tales, too eagerly apprehended only the surfaces of what they beheld. It might be argued that Thompson's reading of "Metzengerstein" as most emphatically satiric is too thesis-ridden, and that he is unduly severe on David Carson's opinion that Poe's hoaxing in "The Duc de L'Omelette" draws on details from Poe's career at West Point. Otherwise, the chapter illuminates many aspects in the early tales. In a subsequent chapter, with a particularly fine analysis of "Ligeia" to illustrate his opinions, Thompson treats "Explained Gothic" to show how Poe outdistanced many of his cruder predecessors and contemporaries in this vein. In Chapter 5 Thompson comes to grips with those ubiquitous terms in Poe criticism, "Grotesque" and "Arabesque," indicating how they throw into relief Poe's romantic irony, how they are nearly interchangeable, and how they imply the psychological in fiction. In Chapter 6, "The Nightside," such tales as "Eleonora," "A Tale of the Ragged Mountains," and "Mesmeric Revelation" are considered as Poe's ironic responses to the pseudo-sciences of his day. A final chapter, "Romantic Skepticism," expatiates upon several of the later tales and *Pym*, showing Poe's increasing uncertainty about his Romantic world and many of the too-easily idealistic assumptions in it.

Thompson's Poe is, then, a "dark" Poe, opposed to Carlson's Poe. This dark Poe is a writer who, as a literary craftsman, is quick to seize on popular literary trends and adapt (or, more precisely, invert) them to carry his personal brand of Romanticism, that of irony and skepticism. The book also draws attention to Poe's revisions in his tales. "Eleonora," "The Oval Portrait," and "Mesmeric Revelation" are particularly mentioned as undergoing significant change, but the tantalizingly cursory treatment of this vital element of Poe's craftsmanship only paves the way for future, concentrated studies of the subject. (A forthcoming issue of *American Transcendental Quarterly*, a symposium about the short story in the American Renaissance, will provide several such studies.) One might—after careful examination of this matter—conclude that the true method of how to write a Blackwood Article is to revise, revise, revise, as Poe's own work so tellingly shows. Taken whole, Thompson's work opens up exciting new directions for Poe studies.

Stuart Levine's previous researches in the Poe field have borne substantial fruit in *Edgar Poe: Seer and Craftsman* ([Deland, Fla.: Everett/Edwards, Inc., 1972]. $13.00). More of the Poe canon is assayed by Levine than by Thompson, for instance, and while Levine's informal tone may initially put off fastidious readers, his insights into Poe's methods are worth pursuing. Like Michael Allen, he pays close attention to Poe's building upon contemporaneous magazine fashions and to his adhering to mainstream thought of the day. Yet Levine does not err factually so often as Allen does and he faces squarely some of the speculative issues so popular with recent critics. Levine's treatment of Poe's occultism—his employment of the pseudo-sciences such as animal magnetism and mesmerism, is more sympathetic than Thompson's, and consequently his studies of tales like "The Facts in the Case of M. Valdemar" or "A Tale of the Ragged Mountains" allow for greater diversity of approach. In his "Preface" Levine stresses this diversity over the similarity in Poe's work, and so Mooney's theory of Poe's "grand design" and those readers who conceive a Poe whose overriding aim is horror are dealt a sharp blow. Levine states bluntly: "A better explanation is that Poe's attitude toward the tale of terror was largely professional" (p. 43). Following Levine's principles, one may interpret "A Tale of the Ragged Mountains" as an example of the American tall tale, something not frequently considered by readers of that tale. The turning of horrors into art was what distinguished Poe from his numerous, now-forgotten, contemporaries. Levine also synthesizes, or perhaps arrives independently from, the work of Mabbott, Griffith, and Carlson, to conclude that Poe's transcendentalism is much closer to that of Emerson and Whitman than Poe himself—or many subsequent commentators—would willingly admit. According to Levine, Dupin's intuitive perceptions bracket him more securely with Whitman's "I" or the narrator in *Walden*, than might at first glance appear to be the case, thus making him a thoroughgoing "Transcendentalist Hero" (a hypothesis which will, doubtless, elicit challenges from many quarters!). Levine's book is refreshing in its admissions, blunt or tacit, that its author is not an authoritarian interpreter of Poe. He readily admits his puzzlement about the serious versus the comic in "Ligeia," and he allows no space to issues so uncertainly speculative as which of Poe's tales may or may not have been numbered among the projected "Tales of the Folio Club," a guessing game that has engaged students from the time of Mabbott's 1928 *Sewanee Review* conjectures to the recent, more earnest endeavors of Alexander Hammond in the *Emerson Society Quarterly* and *Poe Studies*. Many of these conjectures forget that Mabbott's assignments of tales to tellers were playful, that Poe's letter to Harrison Hall emphasizes that criticism, as much as the fiction itself, was to be the target for burlesque, and, finally, that we simply do not *know*, but can only theorize, about the make-up of the Folio Club.

In delineating Poe as seer, Levine is quick to show the frequent de-emphasis of "plot" to enhance the elements of "perception" or "vision" in many of the tales, a characteristic which often fails to grip casual readers. Thus "William Wilson" becomes more of a "plot" tale and perhaps more immediately compelling than "The Masque of the Red Death," in which latter work Poe's planning for "effect" combines with morality to demand a sophisticated response from readers. Levine sees "The Masque" as Poe's flawed effort to transmute operative effect into musical magazine prose. Such a view bypasses a host of suggestions of Poe's debt to De Quincey, still another area for fruitful investigation, whose lasting fame rests upon the dream-engendering cadences of the *Confessions*. Levine's book closes with extended analyses of "The Man of the Crowd," *Pym*, and *Julius Rodman*. The first is ineffective because, the irony notwithstanding, Poe really did not know what he was talking about. *Pym* is just as displeasing, but here Levine attacks Poe's slipshod craftsmanship instead of his muddled vision. *Julius Rodman* also fails because of Poe's feeble craftsmanship and shameless plagiarizing from other writers. The pressure for magazine copy is at fault in this case, and so we come full circle from Levine's early commentary about Poe's ambivalence toward the magazine world, to a telling illustration of how it could dominate him in a negative fashion.

Two recent books that survey the entire Poe canon from a single, critical perspective are Daniel Hoffman's *Poe Poe Poe Poe Poe Poe Poe* ([Garden City and New York: Doubleday and Co., Inc., 1972]. $7.95) and David Halliburton's *Edgar Allan Poe: A Phenomenological View* ([Princeton, New Jersey: Princeton University Press, 1973]. $15.00). Hoffman's book has already been the subject of controversy among reviewers, and those whose specialities are Poe studies have ably laid bare the deficiencies of the volume, pointing out its stylistic limitations and factual errors. Masquerading in a tricksy-cutesy style (who cares about Hoffman's personal life, obtruded in a cloying manner? Who cares how assiduously Hoffman has attempted to resemble Poe, as the dustjacket photos so oppressively suggest?) this book is a lamentable display of vulgar narcissism from a once fine scholar and critic. The chapters on "Usher" and *Pym* might have made two valuable articles. The recurring errors about "The Assignation" (Mentoni is the Marchesa's old *husband*, not her passionate lover or a Byronic browed personage, for instance) are but one aspect of what "will make Poe scholars wince," to cite but one reviewer (in the March, 1973 *Nineteenth-Century Fiction*, p. 484).

A sounder attempt at surveying all of Poe, David Halliburton's *Edgar Allan Poe: A Phenomenological View*, will probably attract readers who are initially taken by what sounds like the new or the "in." Attentive perusal, nevertheless, will reward those who proceed beyond the survey of phenomenology into the chapters analyzing specific writings. Halliburton has most evidently read widely (he teaches comparative literature), and he skillfully combines his intelligent synthesis of many modern philosophical and critical viewpoints with Poe criticism, old and new, to expand our horizons.

Surveying what previous critics have accomplished, Halliburton states how he will go beyond their results, taking a much less bellicose tone toward his predecessors than is so often fashionable in Poe criticism. He continues by stating that his own aim is "to explain, not to explain away" (p. 11), and his explanations are surely worthwhile for anyone interested in Poe. Suggesting that the principle underlying Poe's works most inclusively is a "will to power"—that is "a transcendence or 'going beyond,' the making of a bad situation into a good one, the reworking of an adequate poem into a better one, the conquest of decay and death through a theory of indestructible life"—Halliburton goes on to provide helpful readings, first of the poems, then the tales, and finally the dialogues and *Eureka*.

Halliburton tells us early that the phenomenologist's chief concern is with the text itself, and he takes pains to demonstrate the relation between the physical and the psychical in a literary creation, specifically those of Poe (because, as Halliburton writes, "he is an important writer who poses some interesting challenges"). His critiques of the works resemble those of J. Hillis Miller—particularly in his books on Dickens and other nineteenth-century writers. Greater light of all hues is thus thrown on Poe's works, and any number of critical insights come our way, the revelations reminding one so often of his own half-formulated theories about an individual work or passage. In "Tamerlane," to consider one example, Halliburton charts the gradual loss of narrative interest in the revisions toward a lyric mode that attracts decided admirers and vehement detractors. The split between essence and existence in the hero makes him, according to Haliburton, a combination to be viewed as existentialist hero or platonic idealist (admirers and detractors can find something here!).

Going beyond source-study-for-source-study's-sake, Halliburton adds to our knowledge about Poe's affinities with other Romantics, especially Byron and Shelley. Because of Shelley's and Poe's lyrical impulse, it is no far move to an exceptionally perceptive section on Poe's own lyricism. That Poe derives from the old bardic and ballad types of "singing" poetry, through Romantic literature and his classical knowledge, is made clearer in Halliburton's concluding remarks on the poems. Poe's combinations of lyric with narrative and dramatic features, increasing as the years passed, as analyzed here, remind us of the continuing of those traits in the verse of Swinburne and Rossetti in the later years of the nineteenth century. Halliburton also stresses an affirmative note (recognizing that it is not the only note) in Poe's verse, particularly in that of his last years.

The tales, too, yield up new treasures under the penetrating reading of this critic. Stressing the experimental nature of Poe's prose (a feature frequently overlooked by those who attempt Poe only as *the* great derivative writer, the combiner of and the plagiarist from the works of others), Halliburton contributes significantly in explicating the tales. Centering on the well-known tales, such as "Masque," "William Wilson," and "Usher," particularly the last, these pages remind us how subtly Poe employed phenomena—in "Usher" the biological is most apparent—as literary symbols. In the midst of the "Usher" explication is the only attempt I have seen to come to grips with the briefly-presented, mysterious doctor, whose tendencies toward grave-robbing are what occupy Halliburton. A more questionable statement (p. 316) is that Prospero dies upon his own blade, but this is a small flaw in the otherwise excellent analyses of the tales. The idea of "Rhythm" in the tales, akin to that in verse and also to the idea of natural flux, simultaneously adds dimension to theories linking Poe's prose to his poetic techniques, and to the previous discussions, mentioned above, of Poe's transcendentalism. Other valuable information, on subjects ranging from Poe's supernaturalism to his use of italics, may be had for those willing to read this rather long (but by no means padded) book.

III

Three books with some differences from those already considered—one a reputation study, two anthologies of (a) critiques and (b) translations of some tales—conclude our survey. Carl Anderson's *Poe in Northlight: The Scandinavian Response to His Life and Work* ([Durham, N. C.: Duke University Press, 1973]. $5.75) is self-explanatory in its title. Taking an overview of Scandinavian knowledge of Poe, Anderson then surveys the Danish response to Poe in a second chapter, moves through the Norwegian and Swedish views, and devotes a chapter apiece to Poe's impact on Ola Hansson, the Swedish poet and critic, and on Strindberg. A final chapter scans Poe's Scandinavian fortunes since the 1890's. In an appendix Anderson translates Hansson's long essay on Poe, thus making readily available this important critique. Anderson's thoroughness is evident everywhere, although the style of the volume may deter the general reader. Notwithstanding the typical manner of a reputation study, Anderson's study, particularly in the sections on Hansson and Strindberg, will attract students of literary history. Hansson's essay was intended to counter the influence of Georg Brandes although his main thrust was Poe's dark romanticism. Poe, to Hansson, was a psychological and conscious artist—precisely what Hansson himself wished to be. A personal friend, Hansson first urged Strindberg to acquaint himself with Poe, an acquaintance that was intensified by Strindberg's familiarity with psychiatric literature. "The Gold Bug" in translation most delighted Strindberg, and Poe's peculiar appeal accorded with the dramatist's interest in metempsychosis and hypnotism. Poe's impact on Strindberg's writings, such as *Tschandala*, are also treated in Anderson's pages.

Anthologists are never at a loss for subjects, and Poe as material for anthologists would make the subject of a revealing study. Stuart Levine's forthcoming volumes of the tales, with their copious annotation, are eagerly awaited from the Bobbs-Merrill Press. Two anthologies of a different type are with us now, however, two which deepen the features on the "French Face" of Edgar Allan Poe. W. T. Bandy (ed.), *Edgar Allan Poe: Seven Tales* ([New York: Schocken Books, 1971]. $10.00) provides a bilingual anthology. Using the Baudelaire translations, from the Redfield edition of 1850, which he keeps for his English texts, Bandy adds his own translation of Baudelaire's essay on Poe's life and works. A personal collection, the anthology reflects the individual tastes of editor Bandy, although his introduction is valuable. Bandy fails to reveal, however, that Baudelaire's 1852 essay was largely plagiarized from two *Southern Literary Messenger* articles by John M. Daniel and John R. Thompson—a fact revealed by Bandy himself in 1953!

Another kind of gathering, entirely different from Bandy's, is Jean Alexander (ed.) *Affidavits of Genius: Edgar Allan Poe and The French Critics, 1847-1924* ([Port Washington, New York: Kennikat Press, Inc., 1971]. $12.50). This book might be used as a companion volume to Patrick Quinn's *The French Face of Edgar Poe*, for it gathers texts of many of the critiques mentioned by Quinn. Despite Levine's caution about placing too much trust in foreign views of Poe, French criticism cannot be ignored. Miss Alexander assembles essays from such critics as E. D. Forgues, to whose essay on the tales we have already paid respects. Several of Baudelaire's essays are translated here.

Most of the articles are by writers who were themselves not just professional critics but authors of imaginative works. The facts and the psychology of Poe's life were fascinating to many of these writers, who
felt themselves attracted to his darker, tormented side. The poems and
tales received the lion's share of attention, however, and Valéry's essay
on *Eureka*, fittingly, closes the collection. A useful introduction by
editor Alexander attends Poe under categories such as "The Outlaw,"
"The American," and "The Poet," adding a further piece, as Anderson's study does, to that great mosaic of Poe studies.

IV

One unifying factor among these diverse studies, be they concerned
with Poe's unity, his traditions, his diversity, or his experimentation,
is their agreement on his general greatness as a literary artist. All of
them attempt to illuminate his successes and the positive qualities of
his work. Gone are the days of the Griswold trend of calumniation or
vituperative denunciation.[4] Finally, in replying to Professor Benton's
query, quoted in my opening section, I can say that his expectations
about varied approaches to Poe have been well met in the books
reviewed here. Let us hope that the quality generally existing among
them will continue to infuse Poe studies till the end of—and beyond—
the seventies.

NOTES

* My friends and former students, Mr. and Mrs. Dayton Duncan, of Munsonville,
N.H., deserve particular thanks for facilitating the major portion of this essay.

[1] Benton's traditional studies include "The Works of N. P. Willis as a Catalyst of
Poe's Criticism," *AL*, 39 (1967), 315-24 and " 'The Masque of the Red Death': The
Primary Source," *ATQ*, 1 (1969), 12-13. A "newer" approach appears in "Is Poe's
'The Assignation' a Hoax?," *NCF*, 18 (1963), 193-97. Benton's most recent publication of length, "The Gothic Tradition in Nineteenth-Century American Literature,"
ESQ, 18 (1972), 5-123, features Poe's work as staples of that tradition.
    Like Benton, most of the writers of work reviewed here have concentrated on Poe's
short fiction. The tales emerge ever more clearly as his chief contribution to American literary artistry.
[2] Controversial confusion has arisen in recent years about the comic versus the
serious Gothic "keys" to Poe's tales. My own "Poe's 'Metzengerstein': Not a Hoax,"
AL, 42 (1971), 487-94, attempts to balance some of the more extreme assays upon
that tale as a hoax on traditional Gothicism. Benton's introduction to his symposium,
mentioned above, is a penetrating survey of "problems" of the American Gothicism
in Poe's time and on into the twentieth century.
[3] Two perceptive studies of "Tarr & Fether" are Richard P. Benton's, in *PN*, 1

(1968), 7-9, and Bernard A. Drabeck's, in *ATQ*, 14 (1973), 177-84. I have also prepared a study of this tale showing that it can also be read as a burlesque of Poe's own earlier tales. It is also curious to find "A Tale of Jerusalem" among "Gothic" tales, for its thrust is not nearly so Gothic as that of "The Duc de L'Omelette" or "Bon-Bon."

4 Twentieth-Century studies of Poe have, at times, notes like those staccato attacks in Poe's own criticism—the sort that earned him the epithet of the "Tomahawk Man." The reprinting of John W. Robertson's *Edgar A. Poe: A Psychopathic Study* ([New York: Haskell House, 1970]. $14.95—originally published, 1921) allows its inclusion here. But Robertson's condescension to such predecessors as Woodberry and Harrison, combined with a self-aggrandizing, pompous tone about his own ideas about Poe, makes one wonder why this book was thought to merit reprinting. Halliburton, in his otherwise fine book, seems all too ready to belittle the work of that late dean of all Poe scholars, Thomas Ollive Mabbott. John Wesley Arnold's "The Poe Perplex: A Guide to the Tales" (Ph.D. diss., U. of Mass., 1967) sounds notes like those some critics attribute to Poe's own Mr. Snap, but his no-nonsense handling of the "Folio Club" matter is refreshing. Arnold argues that much too much ink has been spilled over that matter, one which he clearly points out continues to defy certainty in interpretation.

RECALLED AND AWAKENED:
THE ROMANTIC FICTION OF
WILLIAM GODWIN, JR.

by Donald K. Adams

WHEN THE PUPIL first becomes master of his own actions, and chooses his avocations and his associates, he will necessarily be acquainted with many things of which before he had very slender notions. At this time the follies of the world wear their most alluring face. He can scarcely avoid imagining that he has hitherto laboured under some species of delusion. Delusion, when detected, causes him upon whom it was practised to be indignant and restive. The only chance which remains, is that, after a time, he should be recalled and awakened: and against this chance there are the progressive inticements of society; sensuality, ambition, sordid interest, false ridicule, and the incessant decay of that unblemished purity which attended him in his outset.

William Godwin, *Enquiry
Concerning Political Justice*
(3rd ed. I, iv, 51)

William Godwin is familiar to political philosophers as the author of *Enquiry Concerning Political Justice* (1793) and to students of English literature as the creator of *Things As They Are,* better known by its subtitle, *The Adventures of Caleb Williams* (1794). With its themes of despotic crime, consuming guilt and remorseless pursuit, *Caleb Williams* may well be regarded as the first detective novel and its author the first practitioner of the form soon to be made whole and vital by Edgar Allan Poe. Poe himself, well aware of *Caleb Williams,* paid special attention to its construction and theme.

But students of the mystery novel need not cross the Atlantic to discern the influence of *Caleb Williams* and such other Godwinian works as *St. Leon* (1799), *Fleetwood* (1805), and *Mandeville* (1817), novels all freighted with persecution, guilt, isolation and misanthropy. The influence could be found in Godwin's own home. His children were quick to learn their father's philosophical and literary lessons. Mary Shelley modelled her *Frankenstein, or the Modern Prometheus* (1818) on Godwinian precepts, and truly surpassed the expertise of the master. Another of William Godwin's children, his son and namesake, also wrote fiction—several novellas and one full-length novel—but it has gone as unremembered as *Frankenstein* has been notorious. However, no work done under the influence of William Godwin, and to a lesser extent of Mary Shelley, can be totally unremarkable. The fiction of the younger William Godwin has its modest attractions and should be recalled and awakened.

I

William Godwin's first wife, Mary Wollstonecraft, died in childbirth on the morning of 10 September 1797, leaving her sorrowing husband the legacy not only of their own daughter, Mary (later, in 1814, to elope with Percy Bysshe Shelley), but also of her child by Gilbert Imlay, Fanny (who committed suicide in 1816, driven—some said—by frustrated love for Shelley). Whatever his philosophical attitudes to the tyranny of contracts and legal obligations, Godwin was deeply anxious to remarry, partly for his own comfort and partly to provide a mother for his children. Twice after Mary's death he proposed to such other women as he considered sufficiently refined and intelligent. But when, one day in 1801, his next-door neighbor called from her open window, "Is it possible that I behold the immortal Godwin?" he eagerly recorded the fact in his journal, "Meet Mrs. Clairmont."

Mrs. Clairmont was herself the mother of two children: Charles (Gaulis) Clairmont and Mary Jane (Claire) Clairmont, both of whose paternity remains in some doubt. Claire Clairmont, years later, was said to have made overtures to Shelley and been rebuffed. She became Byron's mistress and outlived them all until her death in 1879, aged 91, leaving behind (some assert) her ghostly presence in the faded Miss Bordereau of *The Aspern Papers*.

Godwin proposed to Mrs. Clairmont, was accepted, and married her on 21 December 1801. Their sole child—and thus Godwin's only son—was born fifteen months later on 28 March 1803.

Although William Godwin was primarily interested in his own literary career, in the success of his various money-making schemes (such as operating a book store), and in the harmonious progress of his marriage, he welcomed the five children with placid equanimity, making no distinction in his affections between his own children and those by his wives. And he took their education seriously. William Jr., being his father's male heir, received particular attention. Godwin acknowledged that his son had a quick mind and a precise understanding, qualities that revealed themselves early: "What he set himself to learn scarcely cost him any labour in acquiring."

Young William did have his tempestuous moments. But he also possessed a lively sense of humor and a gift for teasing and mimicry.

In February, 1812, Aaron Burr remarked in amusement of young William Godwin's "weekly lecture" in imitation of Coleridge. The boy, now eight, occasionally accompanied his father and sisters to hear Coleridge speak, and "having heard how Coleridge and others lectured, he would also lecture; and one of his sisters (Mary, I think) writes a lecture, which he reads from a little pulpit which they have erected for him. He went through it with great gravity and decorum. The subject was 'The Influence of Government on the Character of the People.' "[1] (Burr, completing a tour of the Continent that stretched from 1809 until 1811, had reached England in October 1811 and, upon arriving in London, had gone at once to call upon the Godwins. From then until his departure for America in March, 1812, he repeated his visits many times. Burr was much affected by the cheerful warmth of Godwin's household—so much in contrast to his own vagrant life of the past three years—and encouraged by Godwin's small money loans and his assistance in arranging return passage to America.)

Godwin determined to spare no expense and expend every effort to give the boy the best education possible. At eight, he was sent as a day-scholar to the Charterhouse where he stayed for three or four years until, exhibiting the first signs of a restless and impatient nature, he asked to be taken away. Godwin acknowledged that the regular boarders at the school treated the day-boys with condescension and disdain. The young William was angered by this attitude, and so was sent (in September 1814) to a private school in Greenwich run by Dr. Charles Burney, a respected scholar and teacher, and brother of Fanny Burney. Godwin hoped that Burney would provide the boy with more polish than the Charterhouse achieved, and this wish seems to have been realized. The boy remained at the school for three or four years more, coming away in 1817 "decidedly improved" (as his father felt) and with what Dr. Burney called "good looks, and . . . an excellent character."[2] Not everyone shared William Godwin's optimism about his son's character and manner. As late as 1824 Henry Crabb Robinson (no great lover of youth, to be sure) was calling him "ill-bred" and complaining about his noisy habit of pounding loudly on the table when playing whist. Mrs. Godwin herself (according to Crabb Robinson) said the young man was "very clever, but . . . indolent and will settle to nothing that requires permanent labour."[3]

Young William was now on the threshold of manhood. William Godwin was aware of his son's intellectual potentialities and limitations. In a letter written in 1818, Godwin spoke of his sixteen-year-old son this way: "He has . . . had nearly every advantage of education. His proficiency in the Latin, Greek, and French languages is considerable. He has been initiated in algebra, geometry, chemistry, etc. He has begun Spanish. My own opinion of his intellectual abilities is, that he is not an original thinker; but he has a remarkably clear head, and retentive memory."⁴ Like all fathers, William Godwin began to cast about for a trade or profession for his son, one that would appeal to the boy. But young William was unsure of his interests. Literature, as a permanent profession, seemed of small value to him, "and I am glad of it" his father wrote, doubtless reflecting on his own lifelong struggle as a man of letters. Godwin decided to place the boy in commerce, in some mercantile or mechanical way. Early in 1818 young William went to a commercial school in Woodford and a year later went on to study mathematics with Peter Nicholson, in London Street, Fitzroy Square. Two years later, the young man was expressing great interest in engineering, and his attentive father hurried to consult such eminent authorities as John Rennie (who had once worked with Boulton and Watt) and Bryan Donkin, the inventor of early high-speed printing machinery. On their advice, Godwin placed his son early in 1820 with Maudslay, Sons and Field, marine engineers, headed by the distinguished mechanical engineer Henry Maudslay. This promising apprenticeship was soon checked by the young man's accidental loss of a finger, a circumstance that cooled his further enthusiasm for engineering.

Young William Godwin then evinced an interest in architecture, and his attentive father was quick to call upon the great John Nash. Nash confessed that he usually charged five hundred guineas for taking a pupil, but such was his respect and admiration for William Godwin that he would accept young Godwin without fee of any kind.

Alas, the young man's "unsteady and roving disposition" prevented this offer from ever being accepted. Just why, we do not know. But certain it is that young William Godwin reached his twenty-first year still without any settled choice of vocation and without exhibiting any detectable interest in literature. But at this point, in 1823, he surprised his relieved father by presenting him with two essays, "Country Church-yards" and "The Cottage," both undeniably modest familiar essays of the sentimental school, but both undeniably published. They are to be found in the November and December issues, 1823, of the *Literary Examiner* (and they were published just in time, for the *Examiner* collapsed with the issuance of the December number).

At least these two sketches were a start. Young William Godwin seemingly had stumbled on his profession, and his father was eager to help him into a job that paid a living salary. He became a reporter for *The Morning Chronicle*, a post he held until his death on 9 September 1832. During these nine years the younger Godwin worked faithfully for his newspaper, earning the admiration and respect of all who knew him. But he earnestly wanted to emulate his father and step-sister in the writing of more serious literature, both essays and fiction. Two of his essays, "On Shakspeare's Knowledge of his own Greatness" and a "Dissertation on the Dramatic Unities," were written for a club which he founded and named "The Mulberries." The members of the group were instructed to write original essays which were to be presented, in rotation, before fellow members. The essays had to relate to Shakespeare, in whose honor and memory the club had been established. William Godwin asserts that both his son's essays posthumously found their way into print in the pages of the "Court Magazine."

Young Godwin admired his father's fiction and had attempted several brief fictional sketches and a longer novel which he subsequently destroyed. On the authority of his father, we know that he also "wrote a slight piece in the nature of an opera on the story of Robin Hood, and even attempted a tragedy on the fate of Regulus."[5] These early attempts have not survived, and probably with good reason: "It was his propensity to engage with fervour and an eager impatience in what he thus projected, and, being little satisfied with what he had done, then to throw it aside, and seemingly to forget that it had ever existed."[6]

But he succeeded in finishing one full novel a year or two before his death. This is *Transfusion, or The Orphans of Unwalden*. At his death the manuscript was left unpublished and it was eventually issued in 1835 by J. Macrone in London and (in the same year) by Baudry in Paris.

William Godwin, Jr., died of cholera, leaving a wife but no children. In the "Memoir of the Author" which the young man's father affixed to the published version of the novel, William Godwin the elder said farewell to his only son in these words:

"William Godwin, the subject of these pages, was of a somewhat fiery disposition, but easily disposed to listen to reason when it was duly presented to him. He was inclined to be somewhat reserved and self-concentrated, where he apprehended an opposition which came to him in the shape of authority. But if you could once show that there was sound sense and sobriety in what was alleged in opposition to his views, he instantly became attentive and tractable. He was a being of the warmest affections and the most entire generosity of temper. He had great powers of conversation, and could easily pass through all its humours, 'from grave to gay, from lively to severe.' And accordingly, all his chosen associates felt a very earnest attachment to him, and a strong sense of his extraordinary gifts. In the last two years of his life, he in a striking degree shook off the errors that occasionally clouded his earlier years, and would infallibly have distinguished himself with honour in any career in which he had engaged."[7]

And of what value to the student of literature is young William Godwin's *Transfusion* and what relevance does it have to historians of mystery fiction? The answer lies in the title, *Transfusion*, which in the Paris edition of Baudry's European Library, published later in 1835, is adjusted to read *The Orphans of Unwalden, or the Soul's Transfusion*. "The original conception is not a little extraordinary; and it will perhaps be admitted that a very considerable fervour and mastery are displayed in the development."[8] Such were his father's words, partial praise no doubt. But in fact the basic conception, akin to Mary Shelley's notion of the spark of synthetic vitality, is of the ability of a soul, when its possessor is worked up to a paroxysm of ecstatic love or sympathy, to leave its body and flow into that of another person. Contemporary reviewers spoke diplomatically of *Transfusion*, recognizing the author's untimely death several years earlier. "The tale itself is one of Swiss construction, in which seduction, love, and other villainies are involved; and ends in a most tragical conclusion." Thus the reviewer in *The Literary Gazette*, who seems not to have had a high regard for love. And the notice in the *London Gentleman's Magazine* (June, 1836) stated that "It partakes of the family wildness and irregularity of genius."

Modern interest in *Transfusion* will naturally be partly historical and biographical and partly artistic. The novel is at times extravagant in diction and style and the denouement is long delayed. But it possesses considerable power and is indeed (as the reviewer in *The Literary Gazette* observed) "a work of sufficient interest to chain the attention of readers." *Transfusion* is a strange combination of Gothic novel, philosophical tale, romantic tragedy, pseudo-Italian revenge story, and doctrinaire tract. At its heart is a long-sustained mystery dealing (apparently) only with the identity of the hero and heroine but ultimately with the secret of "the soul's transfusion." It is with this central and ultra-Romantic conception that the novel can claim a kinship with such similar works as *Frankenstein*, Dr. Polidori's *The Vampyre*, and John Moore's *Zeluco*.

II

In two issues of *Blackwood's Edinburgh Magazine*, those of February and March 1832, appeared a curious novella entitled "The Executioner" and signed "Syphax."[9] The plot of this modest Gothic tale employed, as will be seen, a number of familiar Romantic themes: the corruption of simple innocence both by the parent and by society; the fruitless search for the father; the Byronic self-discovery—"I am my own accuser"; the awareness of sin and the acceptance of pen-

ance and expiation—the marked man; the relentless, even supernatural, pursuit that drives a helpless soul to madness; the discovery
of secrets, like Adam's in Eden, whose knowledge curses the new
owner; and the assurance that, whatever the corruption of the world
and its laws, simple love will triumph in the end. The tale hints at
more disturbing moral lessons: that in this inhumane world it is the
mad who are sane and the sane mad; that money, property and institutional power corrupt utterly; and that the sentient creator ultimately
rejects his creation.

Familiar themes indeed. Their presence in many Gothic tales and
novels during the early decades of the nineteenth century need not
excite comment. But in this case perhaps they should be discussed. For
the author was unmistakably the son of the author of *Political Justice*
and *Caleb Williams*. We need only remember the similar themes in
Caleb Williams: Williams's discovery of Falkland's guilty secret, his
merciless pursuit by Falkland (who had treated him as indeed a foster
son), and his eventual survival, after Falkland's fall, as a troubled,
self-accusatory and melancholy member of a debased humanity. In
those early pages of *Caleb Williams* are the anticipations of young
William Godwin's later Gothic fiction. *Caleb Williams* was published
in 1794. It is appropriate to see its influence reappearing thirty-eight
years later in the first published fiction from the pen of the younger
Godwin.

The curious reader will also be pardoned for seeing in "The Executioner" some influence of *Frankenstein*, the novel completed in 1817
by young William's half-sister, Mary Shelley. Victor Frankenstein's
scientific curiosity gets the better of his humanity to create a being
whom he abandons and grows to hate. The monster's sad education in
the selfish ways of the world leads to self-torture, anguish, and a form
of Byronic audacity, where the created turns in mingled love and hate
on the creator. These themes, too, are to be found in "The Executioner," suggestive evidence that the young William Godwin read his
sister's novel with care.

Born to a father who appears to have abandoned him to a dull and
rude upbringing in the gloomy fens of Lincolnshire, the hero of "The
Executioner" matures in vacant loneliness, attended only by a weak,
dumb and aged woman. His very name—Ambrose—evokes ambiguous echoes: St. Ambrose, the music-loving Early Church Father, and
Ambrosio, the depraved hero of Lewis's *Monk*. The boy's only touch
with the outside world occurs with the monthly visits by his strange
and troubled father, who flies into rages when begged to take his son
with him into the world.

At length, in his 23rd year, the youth gains release. His aged housekeeper dies. Now wholly alone, and totally unprepared by education

or companionship, Ambrose sets off to find his father (to us, in the twentieth century, significant quest!). But instead of comfort and direction, insults and rejection greet him. "Go on, and prosper," is his motto. He wanders for days, chilled and starving, until he stumbles into a village whose inhabitants when he beseeches them for food and shelter drive him from their doors: "hark ye, youngster, did you never hear of rent and taxes, and poor-rates to boot?" The well-fed lord of the manor even breaks out against the Church: "Heyday, why the chap is a Methodist parson in disguise, after all!—Harkye, Mr. Parson-pauper, please to turn out.—Once a-week is quite enough for that sort of thing."

From village to town Ambrose treads his rapidly souring Pilgrim's Progress. Work or charity are as scarce as friendship or compassion. Even his father appears to be beyond finding: " 'Oh, father, father!' cried I, with bitterness in my accent . . . 'Where am I to seek you? How am I to find you?' " Resentment and hatred soon corrupt his native humanity: "What now had become of my fancy-decked picture of the all-receiving brotherhood of mankind? Whither had flown the friendship, the kindness, the heart-in-hand welcome that I had so fondly dreamt waited my arrival in the abodes of the world? Fictions! empty, deceitful fictions, that had betrayed me to myself, and that . . . had taken the place of the withering, frightful truth, that for the houseless, penniless wanderer there was no sympathy, no hospitable tendering to his necessities! . . . As I laboured along in solitude, misery, and neglect, I demanded of myself a thousand times, 'Why am I to have love for man, when mankind has none for me?' "

Ambrose is eventually arrested for vagrancy by the constable in another village, despite the offer of shelter by "a thin, sickly-looking youth about eighteen or nineteen years of age" on whose face "sorrow, and well-nigh despair, were seated." Ambrose is sentenced by the village magistrate to a fortnight's hard labor in the local jail. After a few days he is joined by a man named Edward Foster, committed for horse-stealing, and by one Stephen Lockwood, companion in crime to Foster, who has turned king's evidence against his friend. To Ambrose's astonishment, Lockwood proves to be his father!

Lockwood soon reveals himself a demon in earthly disguise. Practising on his son's newly-developed misanthropy, Lockwood uncovers his master plan for vengeance, a plan meant to repay "the unkind treatment of that world that has used your father so bitterly." Lockwood now reveals to his son his own life's history and the justification for his harsh revenge on mankind. Born of humble parents, he had been adopted by the leading citizen of his village as a companion to that man's only son, Edward. The two boys grew up bosom friends. But Lockwood was eventually sent out on business to his patron's East

Indies estates; after a two-year absence he returned and was horrified to discover his true love—"my Ellen—mine—she whom I had deemed to be the truest, the faithfullest of her sex"—living with Edward as "his avowed mistress—acknowledged, brazen, bare-faced." Worse, Edward and his mistress had kept as their own the male infant, Lockwood's own child, whom Ellen was carrying when Lockwood had left on his journey.

Ambrose is then revealed as the betrayed child, carried off secretly by Lockwood after he has confronted Ellen with her infidelity and driven her to suicide. Since that tragic event, Lockwood has kept Ambrose hidden away in obscurity while he, for twenty years, has plotted revenge against the devilish Edward, whom he blames for the death of Ellen and for the attempted theft of her child. Such is Lockwood's own story. The Edward of his tale is of course the same Edward Foster imprisoned in this very jail.

Lockwood can now reveal his full subtle strategy, twenty years amellowing. After Ellen's death Foster had married, had had a son of his own, but had eventually fallen into the unsteady life of a compulsive gambler (led into this fate, indeed, by Lockwood's own paid spies). Now, after enough years have passed that he cannot possibly be recognized by his victim, Lockwood has fastened upon Foster. He has proposed an irresistible and sure-fire gambling scheme for the Newmarket races. Foster grows excited. They decide to hurry at once to Newmarket, though aware they will probably arrive after the start of the meet. Lockwood soon persuades Foster to join him in stealing a pair of horses to speed up their arrival at the race course. And this once done, Lockwood betrays Foster to the authorities and volunteers to turn king's evidence to secure a quick conviction.

At last Lockwood's triumph approaches. Through threats and appeals to filial loyalty he persuades his son to volunteer for the vacant post of hangman. Inflamed by his father's violent words, the youth does as he is told, is appointed, and soon finds himself preparing to draw the bolt that will plunge Edward Foster into eternity. At the last moment Foster whispers to Ambrose: "Young man, I know not how this bitter duty fell to your lot—yours is no countenance for the office; and yet it comes upon my vision as a reproach. God bless you, sir! This is my world-farewelling word; and I use it to say—I forgive you, as I hope to be forgiven."

Ambrose's humane soul rises up within him in self-reproach. He cannot join the priest in prayer: "Each holy word that was uttered seemed not for Foster, but for me—stabbing, not soothing." But there is no time for repentance or refusal. Ambrose must perform his job. The signal is given, the bolt withdrawn, and Foster is dead, "swinging to the play of the winds—the living soul rudely dismissed, the body a lifeless mass of obliterated sensations." At once a deep hoarse groan surges through the multitude watching the spectacle, a groan not of sympathy for the criminal but of sorrow for Ambrose himself: "It gave token of an eternal line of separation drawn between me and the boundaries of humanity."

The remainder of the Gothic tale is quickly told. For many months the distraught Ambrose wanders alone across the face of England, tortured by his own act and driven by the angry cries of "wretch," "villain," and "hangman" that pursue him into the remotest country towns. "I was the marked of men," he laments. In some mysterious fashion, no matter where he settles, whispering gossip about his inhumane act poisons his waking moments. "What could it mean? Was I pursued through all my winding paths and labyrinth of ways by some treacherous spy, that only tracked me to betray, and hold me up to the detestation of mankind?" Now he sinks to the lowest levels of society, brutalizes his body and mind, and Faust-like tries every experience that might promise novelty and forgetfulness. But all to no purpose.

At length he discovers his pursuer and betrayer, and from this moment his regeneration commences. The villain is—himself! To lose himself he had taken to drink, each night trying to escape from truth and responsibility; and each night, while his conscious mind slumbers, his unconscious self babbles forth the dark secret to anyone in the tavern who will listen. Like a latter-day Ancient Mariner he must pour forth his guilt and meekly accept the punishment that follows.

But with this insight Ambrose is forearmed against the return of his horrific father. Lockwood, with mirthless smile, appears and offers Ambrose the sweet taste of ultimate revenge. Edward Foster's son, who had escaped his father's ruin and thwarted Lockwood's attempts at discovery these twenty years, has been found in (for Lockwood) the happiest of places: in prison and, like his father before him, condemned to be hanged. Lockwood commands his son to fulfill one final filial obligation: Ambrose must once again volunteer as hangman. He must dispatch the son as he did the father, to gratify his own father's twisted sense of justice.

Ambrose is horrified at the suggestion and refuses, in spite of all his father's entreaties, commands and threats. His blank refusals finally drive Lockwood to use his ultimate argument: he tells Ambrose that they are not father and son. Ambrose is, in deed and in fact, son to Edward Foster, and thus his father's murderer and soon to be his brother's executioner.

"I could endure it no longer. I was mad—mad—mad! And, unwitting what influence ruled me, I rushed from the room, while he roared after me—'Stay, good father-killer, your brother Charles lies waiting for your further practice!' "

Escaped at last from Lockwood's obscene gibes, Ambrose slowly returns to his senses. He devises a plan of escape for the imprisoned Edward. As Lockwood had demanded he do, he offers himself as volunteer hangman in the nearby town, manages to arrange a few moments alone with his new-found brother, and reveals everything to the prisoner. He tells Edward to obey him implicitly, up to the final moments on the scaffold, and then he arranges a scheme by which, at a whispered signal, Edward's bonds would be cut and he must jump into the sympathetic crowd, make his way to the nearby stream, and there swim out to a waiting boat and row to the opposite shore, from which escape is sure.

Everything goes as planned. Edward makes his escape from the gallows and runs to the river, but on the bank is almost captured by a man who leaps out from behind a shed. It is Lockwood. Ambrose, who is pretending to pursue the fugitive, falls on Lockwood and drags him down into the mire of the river bank. Edward escapes, Ambrose loses consciousness in the struggle, and the hate-filled Lockwood drowns.

The final scene shows us Ambrose, confined in a madhouse and still haunted by the dreadful taunts of Lockwood "by which he has made my own thoughts my own hell." Ambrose, though marked as insane by the world of men, now has a degree of inner peace in the knowledge that in freeing Edward, his brother, he has partly expiated the murder of his own real father. The only troubling thought in his mind is the fear that Edward may someday be recaptured. It is "as though the ghost of Lockwood, yet unsatiated, was still employed in hunting him into its toils."

III

William Godwin, Jr., evidently inherited the family ability of spinning out elaborate and compelling plots. In his preface to the "Standard Novels" edition (1832) of *Fleetwood* William Godwin the elder explained how he had created the plot of *Caleb Williams* backward, working from the denouement back to the events that had produced it: "I invented first the third volume of my tale, then the second, and last of all the first. I bent myself to the conception of a series of adventures of flight and pursuit; the fugitive in perpetual apprehension of being overwhelmed with the worst calamities, and the pursuer, by his ingenuity and resources, keeping his victim in a state of the most fearful alarm. This was the project of my third volume." [10] Thus he clearly was fulfilling Aristotle's dictum that plot, the soul of the tragedy, lies in the careful choice and arrangement of incidents.

Simply stated, plot in a detective or mystery story becomes the creation in the reader of a nervous insistence upon knowing what happens next. And as will be demonstrated, awkward and preposterous as the plots of William Godwin, Jr., could sometimes be, they show no deficiency on their creator's part in the ingenious ability to create this essentially suspenseful structure. In his case, having first invented a sensational denouement dealing with liberating the soul from its body (a circumstance obviously influenced by the plot of his sister's *Frankenstein* and those plots invented by his father) the young William Godwin, like his father before him, worked backward to create a concatenation of compelling incidents.

The plot of *Transfusion* turns upon two mysteries, one conventional and the other strange. The former is the familiar Godwinian (and Romantic) search for a father, who goes about in disguise and, when ultimately discovered, proves to be quite different from what was expected. The latter plot deals with "the soul's transfusion," the ultimate capacity of the human soul, profoundly excited by the most intense passions, to free itself from the body. Some call this death. But perhaps, the author asks, it can be achieved in life, though with who knows what disastrous results.

Transfusion is indeed a novel of passion, in both the baser and the more elevated forms. "There are two sorts of love," the author writes, "one—pure, exquisite, and lovely; founded on affection for a single and invaluable object, and resting its whole hope on that object's happiness: the other is single and insidious, built only on self-gratification and the desire for indulging at all hazards an unsharing principle. But both the one and the other—the good and the bad—summon ardour to their aid...."[11]

The plot focuses on the ambivalent relationship between a brother and sister who have been raised in the retired Swiss lowland valley of "sweet Unwalden." The young people, Albert and Madeline, 15 and 17 years of age respectively, are dissimilar in character yet bound together by the strongest affections. Albert is a serious-minded youth whose wondering joy in nature and deep love for his sister are the psychological results of a serious physiological defect: he is deaf. Because of his sheltered upbringing and the silence in which his childhood and youth have been spent, Albert clings to his sister and her guidance. Madeline is not the wisest of mentors, however. Though beautiful and quite as carefully and modestly raised by her apparently widowed mother as is her brother, she suffers from pride, vanity and self-will. Charged with arrogant behavior toward her bucolic lover, a local youth, she bursts out: "Be assured that ... I am, and ever will be, my own free agent. I know no bound but that of inclination, and all else must be fruitless of management. I would rather fly to earth's confines than submit . . ." (I, 52). No wonder her guardian remarks: "So young, and already so in love with sophistry!" (I, 50). Only by her affection for her brother—the dominant drive in her life, it seems—is her headstrong impetuosity controlled.

The love Albert and Madeline feel for each other and the power it exerts over their subsequent destinies significantly resembles the relationship between Victor Frankenstein and his foster-sister, Elizabeth, the orphaned child of an Italian patriot. Raised "in the majestic and wondrous scenes" which surrounded their Swiss home, Victor and Elizabeth developed a deep affection for each other, a love too soon to be destroyed by the engine of Victor's own scientific curiosity. While Elizabeth remained content with her emotional responses to life, Victor hungered to master the secrets of the universe: "While my companion contemplated with a serious and satisfied spirit the magnificent appearances of things, I delighted in investigating their causes. The world was to me a secret which I desired to divine. Curiosity, earnest research to learn the hidden laws of nature, gladness akin to rapture, as they were unfolded to me, are among the earliest sensations I can remember." [12] Thus Victor Frankenstein.

In *Transfusion* the relationship between the brother and sister is adjusted so that Madeline assumes the mundane—and dominant—role and her brother the spiritual and poetical—and thus recessive—role. Madeline becomes the cold spirit who, denying her capacity for humane love, is determined to shape the world to her own selfish and calculating ends. Albert, locked in total silence, remains the passive spellbound observer of the world's natural mysteries. Only at the end of the novel does Albert call upon that profound self-command latent within himself to attempt the rescue and stay the approaching death of his sister. Both novels teach that deep feeling will ultimately overcome egotistic reason, and both suggest (as we learn from the "Ode to a Nightingale") that exalted emotion may be the highroad to easeful death.

Albert and Madeline begin their slow awakening to the perils of the outside world at the time of the final illness of their mother, Agnes, long (as far as they are aware) a widow. The old woman's last moments are observed by one of those mysterious strangers dear to Gothic fiction. He has coincidentally turned up in Unwalden in time to witness the mother's declining hours and death, to introduce himself to the children as their uncle, and to consent, after the funeral, to stay with them as guardian.

A year now intervenes in the plot, twelve months during which the uncle, careful of his new role as mentor and guardian, observes Albert and Madeline closely. Madeline's behavior is deeply troubling, since she treats her infatuated rural lover, Wahrend, with a mixture of teasing coquetry and callous indifference. The uncle eventually despairs of ever seeing in Madeline any signs of genuine feeling: only impetuousness, boredom and self-indulgence. Deciding that his moral guidance is of little value, the uncle slips away one night as mysteriously as he had come a year earlier, leaving behind a lengthy letter summarizing his own history and categorically forbidding Albert and Madeline from attempting to follow him, under pain of losing the annuity which he has set up for them.

The story of his life is one of those tales-within-a-tale common to eighteenth-century novels and often used by William Godwin, Sr. In this inset narrative is introduced one of the two principal villains of the novel (*Transfusion* has not only two youthful characters making their naive way into the wicked world, but also two malevolent individuals, one of whom has been taught to be evil by a misanthropic parent and the other of whom is innately corrupt).

The letter left by the departed uncle, whose name is Henry Seaton, frankly confesses that he and the children's late mother were not in fact brother and sister. They had been the children of neighboring gentry families dwelling quietly in the English countryside; the two young people had been promised to each other by their parents and they themselves had fallen in love and looked forward eagerly to marriage. But this happy destiny is frustrated. Henry is sent one day to London to conduct business pertaining to his father's West Indian estates. His father's family agent, having been called unexpectedly to Paris, deputizes his own son, Stephen Warner, to conduct the financial affairs with Henry Seaton. The two young men soon become close friends. And Stephen, a deep and practiced schemer, on learning from Henry the beauty and charm of his rural fiancée, determines to seduce Agnes. Stephen's motivations arise from some inherent evil, for part of his joy in the project will follow from the ruin of Henry Seaton's benign trust and innocence.

Stephen Warner's strategem creates the dramatic action. First he introduces Henry to all the vices of London and easily persuades him to stay behind enjoying the sinful pleasures while he, Stephen, travels to Agnes's home. There he practices on her affections with such success that he wins her trusting love, elopes with her, marries her, and only then reveals his diabolical self. Forcing Agnes to accompany him to the Continent he wanders in a sort of Byronic frenzy across Europe, from city to city, rejoicing both in the humiliations and brutality he has inflicted on his wife (no longer an innocent being) and in the helpless frustrations of Agnes's parents (who soon sink into the grave) and of Henry Seaton.

Henry's alarm at learning of Agnes's fate drives him into a nervous breakdown. After two months of oblivion and wild Romantic ravings, he arises from the sickbed with a cold thirst for "Revenge! Revenge!" and sets out to track Stephen and his suffering bride wherever they may turn. Years of remorseless pursuit ensue: all across the Continent, and through Russian winters and Sicilian summers. But the pursuit is fruitless. After six years Henry returns home in despair to brood alone over his disappointment.

Then, unexpectedly, a letter arrives from Agnes herself, confirming that her life these many years has been a hell, her husband, a very "fiend incarnate." But, in Florence, she and her two children have managed to escape their master and flee to a friend in Geneva, a certain Madame Lalande, who in turn sends the helpless fugitives into hiding under assumed names. Stephen Warner, Agnes writes, was reported to have moved on to Rome and Naples and there probably to have died in a drunken attempt to join the "famous Abruzzi bandit Latroni."

Henry concludes his valedictory letter to Albert and Madeline by explaining that it took him a few more years to identify the exact location of their hiding place; indeed, it was only Agnes's approaching death that persuaded Madame Lalande to reveal to Henry the name Unwalden. And thus it was that Henry Seaton, the mysterious stranger, had turned up on the very evening of Agnes's death.

This inset tale, unremarkable as it may seem to the reader of Romantic fiction, contains several points of interest. Stephen Warner, who is clearly related to Stephen Lockwood, the villain of "The Executioner," has a number of characteristics that we can hardly doubt must have been based on Lord Byron's less attractive features. (William Godwin, Jr., had heard a good deal about Byron in Switzerland and Italy from Mary Shelley and Claire Clairmont, both of whom had become generously disillusioned with Byron, especially during his eccentric life in Venice in 1818.) Stephen's almost motiveless malignance and his appetite for wandering gypsy-like all over civilized Europe and less civilized Russia may well be young William Godwin's version of the myth of the Byronic hero.

In addition, Henry Seaton's monomaniacal six-year pursuit of Stephen Warner bears significant resemblances to Falkland's tireless pursuit of Caleb Williams. The double moral that underlies Henry's letter is of course meant to be clear to Albert and Madeline: one must never be deceived by false love nor deflected from true affection by any of the pretty baubles of the world's vanity fair; and (as a corollary) those who give themselves in marriage on the basis of any emotion other than true love shall pay a bitter price.

Henry concludes his letter with a specific warning to Madeline, in whom he sees "the first buddings" of her father's violent temperament:

"a sacrifice of the sense of what is right at the shrine of passion and impulse." The letter strikes to her heart, although whether in remorse at her past wilfullness or in indignation at having been so frankly and truthfully summed up by her guardian (to whom she is indebted for her livelihood) it is hard to say. In any event, Madeline is not content to be told off as cold-hearted and calculating. She determines to disobey Seaton's injunction and to follow him, begging his pardon and coaxing him into sympathy. She soon gains Albert's agreement to their own search and pursuit. Thus *Transfusion*, like so many other Romantic novels, is built around a search for identities and a series of errors, contretemps and final revelations. There is even some suggestion in *Transfusion* (as is made so much clearer in *Caleb Williams*) that some secrets are best left unsolved. To search, and find, is to lose the innocence and virtue of Eden.

Albert and Madeline set off for Geneva, resolving to locate their mother's sometime friend, Madame Lalande, the only one who might direct them after Henry Seaton. The travellers break their journey the first night at a roadside inn, and it is here that Madeline meets her match for willfulness and determination in a young French playboy, Count De Mara. Spoiled, handsome, vain and daring, he catches a glimpse of Madeline and bets his drinking companions that he can capture her affections within the night. De Mara manages an introduction to Madeline and shrewdly pretends an acquaintance with Madame Lalande. Even during these first minutes with Madeline, De Mara becomes aware of her innocent but wayward personality, and he begins —almost unconsciously—to enlarge his initial casual flirtation with the girl. Something in him, and in Madeline as well, impels him to a more serious intimacy. Madeline, too, is insensibly drawn to the Count.

Under the hasty excuse of introducing Madeline and her brother to Madame Lalande, De Mara arranges to call upon the young people at their Geneva hotel. He then hurries back through the night to Geneva, there to wait upon an old crony, a Madame Deboos. Madame Deboos is a middle-aged lady of firm opinions and outspoken manners, whose experience of life is obviously extensive and not always polite. "She, in her worst moments, had a deep-seated, intellectual expression spread over her countenance," which gave some hint of what she might have been "had not ill passions and swerving temper been predominant" (I, 165). (In Madame Deboos the curious reader may trace many of the characteristics of Mary Wollstonecraft; the portrait of Deboos is by no means uncomplimentary and often testifies to a masculine intellectuality: "She still was what she had ever been—a most commanding creature, something within human nature indeed, but far beyond what we understand as definitely applicable to feminine human nature" [I, 157].)

Count De Mara, having rescued Madame Deboos from a black-mailer, now claims repayment. Madame Deboos is to impersonate Madame Lalande and thus assist the Count in his seduction of Madeline. De Mara is intelligent enough to recognize that he is attracted to Madeline not only sexually and emotionally, but also intellectually. Much in her character is the mirror of his own. Her conquest, which he can engineer with all the ingenious strategy of a general mapping a battle, becomes a secondary end. This love of the game of love has been the most tangible bequest of his late mother, who had cynically taught him, when only a youth, to treat women as inferior beings unworthy of deep love and lasting commitment. Count De Mara's mind "was indelibly stamped with the imperfectibility of women." But as Madeline is destined to be shaken out of her petulant self-will by her deepening infatuation with the Count, so he is to fall genuinely in love in spite of all his treacherous scheming. Both characters come to ruin through unruly passions which take revenge on excessive and calculating reason.

Young Godwin thus prepared for Madeline a deceiver who is yet a lover, and a lover incapable of trust; a sensualist concerned with only his own gratification; a man entrapped by an unsentimental education imposed on him by a worldly parent. Like Stephen Warner, though in a more human fashion, De Mara is another Byronic figure, a fit companion for Madeline who shares many of his egotistical passions. Plainly the two are meant for each other. It is their tragedy that they are too suspicious and too blind to recognize their twin identities.

Madame Deboos acts at once to have the real Madame Lalande called away from Geneva, and the Count, having settled Albert and Madeline in comfortable quarters, begins his assault. His campaign meets with encouragement. Madeline grows visibly interested in De Mara and is only too willing to be conducted by him into all the worldly delights of social Geneva. She shows little reluctance to the idea of becoming the Count's mistress.

Still, Albert remains a stumbling block. Though deaf to the honeyed words De Mara addresses to Madeline, Albert can observe very sharply indeed. He instinctively dislikes and distrusts De Mara. But the Count relies on Madame Deboos to distract Albert from this constant attention to his sister. De Mara's careful plan suffers a grave setback with the sudden, unexpected, and mysterious death of Madame Deboos. She has been strangled by a murderer whom the police are unable to identify or apprehend, although De Mara (like the reader) guesses that Deboos's blackmailer is the likely suspect. (The murder anticipates *Transfusion*'s denouement, but the reader is unable to guess how.)

With Madame Deboos dead and Albert threatening De Mara's designs on Madeline, the Count must act. The solution to his problem has been in front of him all the time: residing in Geneva is one of Europe's foremost physicians, a man famous for having pioneered innovative surgery to restore hearing. De Mara easily persuades Madeline to have her brother examined by him. The surgery succeeds beyond their wildest hope; after a childhood and youth spent in complete silence, Albert can now hear! And the first sounds are words uttered by his sister.

" 'Can it be?' said he . . . 'My sister speaks, and I am able to track her soft, silky sounds stealing on some new sensation within my brain; it is human music, and tells me I am no longer an outcast from my fellows of the creation!'

"Before a moment elapsed, the Orphans of Unwalden were fast locked in each other's arms; and Albert declared a thousand times that day, that if aught could have enhanced his joy at having his faculties established in their full rights, it was that the first information of that establishment was told in the sweet tones of his sister's voice" (II, 31).

The successful surgery gains De Mara time and advantage. Albert has no interest now in guarding his sister's innocence; he is too preoccupied with the dizzy sensations newly open to him. Too, Albert is understandably ready to think more charitably about his sister's suitor since it was the Count who arranged and paid for the operation. Madeline herself, her egotism touched in spite of itself, is much more sympathetic to the Count's addresses. In fact, De Mara's charitable act, though arising out of self-interest, refines his own and Madeline's character. Both characters have learned a lesson about the unselfish nature of true affection.

As for Albert, his introduction to this new sensation triggers an outburst of extravagant emotion. The sounds of a voice, especially that of his sister, and the intoxicating experience of music are more than enough to occupy Albert's whole attention for many weeks to come, leaving De Mara to less noble activities. But the reader recognizes that Albert's transports of almost uncontrollable vigor are subtly directed to some artistic end in the novel, an end that will eventually—and ironically—prove to be the undoing of De Mara's careful plans and, more sadly, the overthrow of Madeline and De Mara themselves: proof, it would seem, that just as excessive reason makes men inhuman, overpowering emotion makes them gods. And gods have no place in a mundane and debased world.

De Mara suffers yet another setback in his campaign for Madeline. Madeline's former lover of Unwalden days, Wahrend, turns up in Geneva. In some manner that the author fails to clarify, Wahrend materializes stylishly dressed and elegantly spoken, a far cry from the humble country swain Madeline had known earlier. Wahrend represents a clear challenge to the Count's plans. And it is with De Mara's attempts to get rid of Wahrend, along with the appearance of another (and more sinister) stranger, that the plot of *Transfusion* hurries to its catastrophe.

The ominous stranger is Urfort, a gaunt and sullen Englishman who has recently come from southern Italy. This is the very man who had been blackmailing the late Madame Deboos and is her probable murderer. Urfort, in apparent despair at the hopelessness of his own life, attempts suicide in Lake Geneva but is rescued by De Mara who is fortuitously wandering along the shore. There is of course the hint that Urfort, who does nothing without malevolent design, has waited for an opportunity to force De Mara into such a generous act. Urfort well knows the meaning of the old proverb that to rescue a drowning man is to enslave oneself to him forever. In any event, De Mara does indeed rescue Urfort, helps him to shelter and food, and offers him employment as a kind of pandarus and spy in Madeline's house of love. This is exactly what Urfort has hoped would happen. He is paid to spy on Madeline's private life and to unfold to De Mara her thoughts and movements. And Urfort shrewdly sells his services to Madeline in turn, offering to provide her (for a price) with every detail of the Count's thoughts and movements. The reader will by now have recognized the diabolical Urfort as the long-missing father, Stephen Warner, reappeared in a much care-worn and damaged form.

For the best working of his scheme Urfort must separate Madeline not only from De Mara but also from Albert and from Wahrend. It is a further irony of the plot that it is Urfort's evil attempt to alienate Albert and Madeline that brings to light the great and humane secret of the novel, the secret that Albert, through all his years of passive obedience to his sister's will, has hidden even from her: his secret ability to effect the transfusion of souls. Albert is so pained by his sister's enigmatic coldness towards him (for she imagines that Albert is standing in the way of her love for De Mara) that he contemplates, by an act of supreme emotion, projecting his consciousness into hers in order to fathom her thoughts and motivations. But Madeline artfully guesses that he is holding something from her, and she is strong enough to force its revelation.

" 'Oh, Madeline, I am not the creature that I was! . . . I was gentle, and of habits formed:—now, though I trust no ungentleness marks my course, my habits have passed into air—they are non-existent. I am a creature fitful in mood, and made up of strange and overwhelming thoughts, that feel their power, but find it of such vast and unwieldy nature that they know not how to exercise it.'

" 'But though you are altered, I am the same,' exclaimed Madeline. 'A moment past, I invoked the secret in your mother's name: now I invoke it in my own—in yours.'

"Suddenly he paused.—'Sister, you have conquered, . . . I, ignorant and untutored as I am, have grasped one of the most hidden mysteries of nature, and discovered the SOUL'S TRANSFUSION' " (III, 27-28, 30).

Albert tells his astonished sister that the revelation came to him mysteriously: "Ask not where the secret lies! be content to know that I have it fast locked in the cells of my brain. The vast and incessant whirl that music's magic force instituted in my soul stirred me almost to madness. Like Columbus, I knew that there was a new world awaiting my discovery, but, like him, too, I was driven desperately from sea to sea, and my whole faculty and power of perception was threatened shipwreck. . . . But it came—at length it came. Like some sudden and momentary meteor it flashed in my mind's eye: I was dazzled with the glare, and well nigh overburdened by its magnitude; but, the first shock weathered, and the reality of the wondrous power that enlightened me recurred again and again, till my soul became accustomed to the conviction, and was capable of feeding on the unutterable thoughts that it begat" (III, 31).

In a kind of Byronic self-certitude, Albert knows, he says, that the petty world turns on its most imaginative men. "What got Socrates for his wisdom?" "What Galileo? . . . What Columbus?" No, he says, the hatred of the world means nothing to him:

"Why then should I not be called visionary, and be subjected to persecution? Welcome, welcome either, both, or anything, as long as I can lay my finger on my forehead and say, 'Here stands the man that possesses the secret of the soul's transfusion—that can change his own mind with that of any other—or can pour that which is one man's brain into another's, and reverse the operation as long as life endures.' "

Madeline at once recognizes that she can use Albert's discovery— not to further their own self-discovery but rather to penetrate the secrets of De Mara's mind. To Albert the power of the soul's transfusion had meant the union of sympathetic minds—the ultimate aim of all lovers through the world's history and of all Romantics, an aim never hitherto realized: "Henceforth," Albert says to his sister, "we will be one, single and indissoluble, even as though we had practiced this great mystery on ourselves, and each had received the other's soul transfused" (III, 53-54). Alas, Madeline in her self-absorption rejects the noble experiment. She cares only to discover the petty vascillations of her lover's mind. But Albert refuses to gratify Madeline in this ignoble end.

The novel now hurries to its sad conclusion. De Mara is enraged by Urfort's carefully inflammatory reports of Wahrend's love for Madeline. Blinded with jealousy, he challenges the youth to a duel. As a hot-blooded French gentleman, De Mara is of course an accomplished swordsman. But Wahrend, in spite of his bucolic upbringing, is provided by the author (somewhat unconvincingly) with equal skill. Evenly matched, the duellists fight to a draw, and it is only when Urfort treacherously trips Wahrend that De Mara runs him through. Shock at what he has done, contempt for Urfort, fear of apprehension by the police, and alarm at this check to his pursuit of Madeline, all jostle in the Count's mind and he prepares to flee Geneva. Although he cannot fathom Urfort's elaborate and subtle game of revenge, De Mara nevertheless recognizes in Urfort's treachery some horrifying evil: "Devil in disguise of man!" De Mara shouts at Urfort, "You were my evil genius . . . and, by the act, more deeply wounded my honour than yon body was pierced by my sword. Oh, Wahrend! I was your enemy and deadly foe; but, if ever there was faith in man, there is faith in me, when I declare, that ten thousand times rather would I have knelt—ay, knelt to your mercy,—than be the instrument of so foul a construction as this" (III, 152-53).

Wahrend's death and De Mara's flight throw Madeline into confusion. Albert, seeing the intensity of his sister's anguish, determines that he should at last use his great secret and possess full knowledge of Madeline's intentions. "Her soul his, and his soul hers—and then indeed he might hope to counteract the fatal design that was hovering o'er her brain, waiting still more fatal execution,—yes! Transfusion of the Soul should pass between them" (III, 176).

But Urfort, the disguised Stephen Warner, is determined to push his diabolical scheme to its appropriate end. Drafting a false letter which he signs, "Henry Seaton," Urfort directs Albert and Madeline to return to Unwalden. And in his own name, Urfort tells Madeline that De Mara, fleeing from Geneva, will pass through the remote valley and will be reunited with her there. He whispers the same news to De Mara: that Madeline awaits him in Unwalden. Urfort, whom we should now call by his true name, himself travels to Unwalden in order to savor the enactment of his ingenious plan.

When Albert and Madeline arrive at the Single Cottage, their former home, Madeline is hysterical and unable to focus on anything save the appearance of the Count. Fearing for her sanity, Albert decides immediately to make Madeline the subject of his first experiment in transfusion of souls.

Poor Albert! His courageous and dangerous experiment is checked once more, though now for the last time. He is interrupted by the surprising, and somewhat unconvincing, arrival of the long-missing Henry Seaton, who, guilty at having abandoned his charges many months ago, has now returned to Unwalden to resume his guardianship. Seaton has been driven to return by the news that "Warner, whom we had so long supposed dead, was still alive, and . . . had, beyond all doubt, been at Geneva lately" (III, 263). Albert relates to Seaton all the events of the past months, particularly the actions of Count De Mara and the death of Wahrend. Seaton hurries off to the local inn to confront De Mara and his mysterious travelling companion. There, at the inn, Stephen Warner has succeeded in urging De Mara, now apprehensive of being discovered either by the Genevese police or by Wahrend's relatives, to venture forth to his long-awaited rendezvous with Madeline. But Seaton arrives before he can leave. There is a moment of classical recognition: Seaton instantly knows Urfort as the villanous Stephen Warner, and Warner realizes that, as the suspected murderer of Madame Deboos, his own hours of freedom are few.

The moment that Albert, following his guardian, learns of the discovery and of De Mara's intention to hurry to Madeline, he himself returns to effect the transfusion of his soul into Madeline's and to achieve that union of their identities, so long postponed. By an act of immense concentration and exhausting will, he achieves the act (upon which young Godwin draws "the veil of obscurity," thus frustrating our desire for details). But Albert has delayed the experiment too long:

"Never, never would he have dared the enterprise, had he for a moment dived into the real condition of his sister's intellect. Had it once been whispered to him that her erst majestic mind had been fast crumbling into decay, and was now within her a scathed and blighted ruin, . . . he would have found no occasion to resort to so violent a method of discovering the meaning of what had baffled his best skill to interpret" (III, 286-87). Madeline has gone mad. Even her physical body, worn out by her febrile activity of the past weeks, has weakened. She has become, indeed, too feeble a vessel to support the violent passions of not one but two souls.

"But it is accomplished! The mystery is performed,—Transfusion! His soul—moved by a mighty spell, recedes from its natural mansion, and is forced into the shattered and crazed abode . . ." (III, 288). And as Albert's soul flows into her mind, Madeline's exhausted soul escapes. She dies, leaving Albert a confused prisoner in a dying body. " 'Where am I? . . . ah! Madeline, where art thou? . . . What is the spell? Why is my recollection so halt? . . . my limbs sink beneath me, and a strange sickness is at my heart! Oh!—what have I done? Where am I?' and the miserable youth sank down, and covered his eyes with his hands, and strove to collect his scattered, incapable intellects" (III, 290-91).

Thus Albert has thrown away his strength, his identity, his very life. Driven, it is true, by the most laudable motives, he has performed an experiment forbidden to man. He has attempted that which has always been prohibited, the ultimate union of souls and minds within a single body.

Struggling for escape from Madeline's body, Albert now stumbles in the direction of the village inn, where he hopes Seaton or someone else may be able to help him reverse his strange experiment. He reaches the inn only to witness the ruin and the confessions of the other actors in the drama: De Mara, enraged by his confederate's attempt to steal off with the Count's wealth, shoots Warner. Mortally wounded, the unmasked Warner has time maliciously to accuse De Mara before witnesses of the murder of Wahrend and of the attempted seduction of Madeline, his own daughter. In his dying ravings Warner implicates himself in Deboos's murder, yet dies unrepentant with curses on his lips, curses not only on his own children but for all mankind as well.

The form of Madeline appears before De Mara, Seaton, and the local authorities. De Mara appeals to her, but is stunned to hear only reproaches. He has to suffer hearing from Madeline's lips the full catalogue of his own stratagems, deceits, and crimes.

Madeline's physical form now sinks to the floor and Albert, helpless within, must find his living spirit extinguished before its time. De Mara, heedless of the charges Albert (in Madeline's voice) has thrown at him, tries pathetically to reawaken her love for him. But it is all in vain. Madeline dies before their eyes, De Mara is led away by the authorities, and a distraught Seaton hurries back to the Single Cottage, there to find the cold shell of Albert's body.

The reader will recognize that *Transfusion*'s plot has many similarities to that of "The Executioner" and no doubt grew out of it. The features common to Romantic fiction—the false and deceiving father, the inhumanity of thoughtless men, the affirmation of the fellowship of man more common among the humble than the great, the corruptive power of money and rank, remorseless revenge, and the unwisdom of scientific experiments that attempt to frustrate God's natural processes—all these features are present in *Transfusion*.

But unusual ones are here too. Young Godwin's insistence that heightened emotion is both ennobling and dangerous explains the sense of pathos which both Madeline (in her whimsical passions) and De Mara (in his scheming) command from the reader. That intense emotion may produce madness, or that sometimes such intensity is itself mad, is an idea common to the Romantic poets; young Godwin must have discussed it with Mary Shelley and with his father. It also accounts for the catastrophe of the novel, in which the innocent and well-meaning Albert must die for having indulged himself in a naturally unnatural act. It is not his fault that his mind is too highly strung and too intense for his body to bear. But his fate is that of Victor Frankenstein: God sometimes gives men powers that can be used to their benefit or their destruction. It is up to those favored men to decide at what moment to refuse the apple of proscribed knowledge.

The tragedy of *Transfusion* is thus carefully explained; the tragedy of young William Godwin's youthful life can only be guessed at. The only son of a strong-willed father determined that his namesake should live up to family expectations, petted and indulged and encouraged while a child and adolescent boy, well aware of the strange and imaginative lives led by his sisters, Mary Shelley and Claire Clairmont, young Godwin doubtless felt a sense of extreme pressure on himself to excel in some intellectual endeavor. Perhaps he could create a novel, sensational in plot and bearing a philosophical message as arresting as that of *Frankenstein*, of *Caleb Williams*, or of any of his father's other tales. Though probably unfinished at its author's death, *Transfusion*— over-long and excessively dependent on coincidence—yet bears the unmistakable mark of that family genius for carefully structured philosophical and supernatural fiction. Unfortunately, young Godwin died before he might have refined and developed that genius in a unique fashion. *Transfusion* is his earnest attempt to answer the chilling remark once made by Claire Clairmont:

> . . . in our family, if you cannot write an epic poem or novel that by its originality knocks all other novels on the head, you are a despicable creature, not worth acknowledging.[13]

NOTES

[1] Aaron Burr's *Journal*, quoted in *Shelley and His Circle*, ed. Kenneth Neill Cameron (Cambridge: Harvard, 1970), III, 76.

[2] C. Kegan Paul, *William Godwin: His Friends and Contemporaries* (Boston: Roberts Bros., 1876), II, 251.

[3] *Henry Crabb Robinson on Books and Their Writers*, ed. Edith J. Morley (London: Dent, 1938), I, 307 and 299.

[4] Kegan Paul, *Godwin*, II, 258.

[5] "Memoir of the Author, By His Father," in William Godwin, Jr., *Transfusion* (London: J. Macrone, 1835), I, xi.

[6] "Memoir," I, xi.

[7] "Memoir," I, xvii-xix.

[8] "Memoir," I, xv.

[9] The historical Syphax was a Numidian chieftain who, to gain political allies, expediently married Sophonisba, daughter of a powerful Cartheginian general; but the Nubian prince to whom the girl had long been betrothed threw his support to Scipio's Roman expeditionary force, which overran Syphax's kingdom, captured him, and sent him off disgraced to imprisonment and death in Rome. Syphax was a man helplessly trapped between powerful forces—Carthage and Rome—and driven into tragic circumstances which destroyed him: fit matter for the drama, as Addison recognized when he wrote *Cato*. The hero of "The Executioner" suffers a similar fate.

William Godwin, Jr., published one other work in *Blackwood's Edinburgh Magazine:* a pair of related essays, "Who Is Born?" and "Who is Dead?" These appear in *Blackwood's* for October, 1833, pp. 469-84. Both are pseudo-philosophical essays, the former dealing with the mystery of birth and the promise of genius, and the latter presenting a disquisition on all the world as a prison and men helpless victims of a death that may come today or ten years from now. These two essays contain brief fictional sketches, but they are not themselves novellas.

10 "Godwin's Account of the Composition of *Caleb Williams*," Appendix II to William Godwin, *Caleb Williams*, ed. David McCracken (London: Oxford, 1970), p. 337.

11 *Transfusion*, I, 172. Subsequent references to *Transfusion* will be incorporated in the text.

12 Mary Shelley, *Frankenstein, or The Modern Prometheus*, ed. M. K. Joseph (London: Oxford, 1969), p. 36.

13 Quoted in R. Glynn Grylls, *Claire Clairmont, Mother of Byron's Allegra* (London: John Murray, 1939), p. 193.

EDITIONS OF *TRANSFUSION*

Transfusion (London: J. Macrone, 1835), 3 vols. (Includes the "Memoir of the Author, By His Father.")

The Orphans of Unwalden, or The Soul's Transfusion (Paris: Baudry's European Library, 1835), vol. XCIV of Baudry's Collection of Ancient and Modern British Authors. (Includes the "Memoir of the Author, By His Father.")

Transfusion; or, the Orphans of Unwalden (New York: Wallis and Newell, 1836), the Franklin Library Edition.

Transfusion; or, The Orphans of Unwalden (New York: G. Dearborn and Co., 1837), "G. Dearborn & Co.'s Stereotype Edition."

Transfusion; or, the Orphans of Unwalden (Hartford: Silas Andrus & Son, 1846). (All three American editions were printed from the same plates. None includes the "Memoir.")

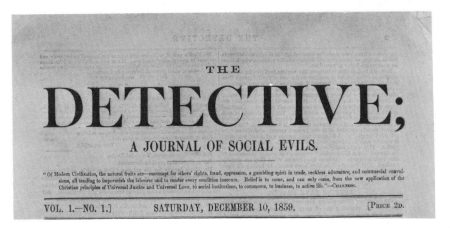

THE

DETECTIVE;

A JOURNAL OF SOCIAL EVILS.

" Of Modern Civilization, the natural fruits are—contempt for others' rights, fraud, oppression, a gambling spirit in trade, reckless adventure, and commercial convulsions, all tending to impoverish the labourer and to render every condition insecure. Relief is to come, and can only come, from the new application of the Christian principles of Universal Justice and Universal Love, to social institutions, to commerce, to business, to active life."—Channing.

VOL. 1.—NO. 1.]   SATURDAY, DECEMBER 10, 1859.   [Price 2d.

"WHO CAN BE TRUSTED?":
THE DETECTIVE,
AN EARLY JOURNAL OF DETECTION

By *Albert D. Hutter and Mary W. Miller*

THE FOLLOWING ADDRESS opens *The Detective* (1859-60), the earliest English journal we have seen based on the new nineteenth-century science of detection:[1]

ADDRESS

The amount of Fraud and Crime prevalent in society is a disgrace to it. . . . Every kind of Institution established for the benefit or protection of society becomes more or less tainted and corrupted by fraud. Banks, Railway and Assurance Companies, Monetary Institutions of all kinds, Benevolent Societies, Charitable Institutions—invaluable boons to society when governed with honesty and integrity, betray at intervals a fearful aspect of rottenness. We ask—Who can be trusted?

But systematic fraud is not limited to these institutions of high pretensions; it descends to the lowest grades of society; and even the pauper's and the beggar's meal is shorn of its due weight, and vitiated in quality by the fraudulent tradesman.

Bubble Companies, Loan Societies, Quack Doctors, and a host

of Disinterested Advertisers, spread their nets to catch the unwary, borrowing for their nefarious purposes the guise and speech of honest men. It requires a special Detective Agency to cope with this legion of knaves, and to discover and expose their ingenious designs upon public faith and credulity. We have elected ourselves to this office, and propose, through the columns of this Journal, to place the public in a position to protect itself against the host of vermin who exist only by preying upon honest men's goods and labours.

. . . .

It cannot be for the good of society that so much Crime, as daily shocks the public sense, should exist. But we must not expect it to diminish greatly while we occupy ourselves so much with its punishment and so little with its prevention. Means for the repression of crime do, it is admitted, already exist, and its amount might, undoubtedly, be greatly reduced if measures were generally taken to that end. Our columns will be open to the details of successful efforts in this direction, and to suggestions for others that are practicable. We shall endeavour to trace the causes of crime to their source, and thence be enabled to apply the preventive measures. The insidious agencies at work to produce crime, although they baffle all calculation, may be reduced in number if they are boldly investigated.

Social Evils!—they are many; but there is one, lately pronounced the greatest, from which every virtuous man shrinks with horror. But the depths of this evil have not been sounded. Yet we must not shrink from the truth, if we seek earnestly to mitigate its horrors. This subject will receive full development in our columns, to the result, we hope, of ameliorating its condition.

Our Journal has a mission peculiarly its own. The subjects to which it is devoted are only partially considered by the press, while from their deep importance to the well-being of society, they demand earnest and concentrated attention. Be it our task to give it.

The rhetoric of this new journal may be exaggerated, but its claim to have "a mission peculiarly its own" is well justified. Accounts of crime in broadsheet, ballad, trial pamphlets, criminal "Calendars," and police gazettes had been published for centuries. But detection was a new interest. The first detective story, Poe's "Murders in the Rue Morgue," did not appear until 1841, and London's first Detective Police were not created until 1842. These police aroused immediate public

interest and were the subject of highly popular articles in the newspapers and journals over the next twenty years; in fiction they gave
rise to Inspector Bucket of *Bleak House* (1852-53) and to the *Recollec-
tions of a Detective Police-Officer* (by "Waters") which led in turn to
a run of detective yellowbacks by the early 1860's. But no magazine
was entirely devoted to the detection of crime, the new methods of
criminal investigation, and reports about the new Detective Police
themselves. In fact, no full-length detective novel had been written; in
1859 the entire field was barely eighteen years old.

The Detective seems to have reprinted many of its pieces from these
other sources, without acknowledgment. Apparently factual accounts
of trials and crimes were altered or fabricated from the start. *The
Detective's* main value for us is not so much in the originality of its
pieces as in the collection of such a wide range of news items and stories
under the organizing principle—at times, almost a public obsession—
of a new idea. In one sense, a journal dedicated to the new concept of
detection marked the formal acceptance of the Detective Police and
detective fiction. As Michael Wolff writes: "One might almost claim
that an attitude, an opinion, an idea, did not exist until it had registered
itself in the press, and that an interest group, a sect, a profession, came
of age when it inaugurated its journal."[2] In a final page of advertising
attached to its first issue, *The Detective* proclaims: "Such is the corrupt
state of society, that the scope of the labours of THE DETECTIVE has
become almost unlimited. His presence is required everywhere; his aid
is sought by every one. THE DETECTIVE will let light into dark places,
and discomfit the vermin who prey and fatten upon other men's goods
and labours." The detective is here something very close to God, and
The Detective is designed to broadcast His Truth to the masses.

I

The journal's opening address places "Fraud" before "Crime," and
throughout this editorial there is a constant emphasis on political,
personal, and consumer fraud (with a special paragraph, in hushed
tones, reserved for prostitution). Subsequent issues show much more
range than this address would lead us to expect; but its overriding concern with "Monetary Institutions," "Charitable Institutions," "Bubble
Companies," and "Quack Doctors" reflects, far more accurately than
the recent flood of books on Victorian sensational crime, the dominant
concerns of this period. Dickens raged against the begging-letter
writer, whom he classed with the murderers, robbers, "preventible

diseases," or, most directly, "the scum of the Earth"³; and Tennyson linked defrauding the poor with murder:

> And chalk and alum and plaster are sold to the poor for bread,
> And the spirit of murder works in the very means of life.
>
> (*Maud*, I, 39-40)

The homicidal doings of William Palmer or Madeleine Smith affected the Victorians far less directly than betting frauds, bank frauds, and the sort of consumer fraud still very much an issue today. When Dickens invited Inspector Field and his associates of the Detective Police for an evening of cigars and drink, he was not struck by the problems of tracking down sensational murderers, but rather those of tracing men like "Tally-ho Thompson," the famous horse-stealer, "couper" and "magsman" (fence and confidence man); or "Fikey, the man accused of forging the Sou' Western Railway debentures"; or the gang involved in "extensive robberies of lawns and silks."⁴ Such were the stories he later recounted in *Household Words*.

The Detective writes of London merchants with particular scorn, especially in their abuse of the poor. False weights, false change, and adulterated products were part of the undramatic procedure which robbed the poor of their already meager income. In the absence of any effective government control, such practice was commonplace: "There is scarcely a trade in this wealth-seeking age which could not furnish an example of some dishonest and fraudulent trade mark" (4:41). In such an article as "Adulterations, and the Means of Detecting Them" (3:28), *The Detective* tries to prevent crime by consumer education and an argument for legislative reform. Its list of common fraudulent foodstuffs is striking, but the principle is familiar: bread filled with alum and ground bones; butter, with lard; milk, with water; pickles colored with copper sulfate; and cayenne, with red lead. The average Victorian's tobacco—an unappetizing mixture of stalks, ground-up vegetables, rotten wood, and sawdust—would scarcely have qualified for listing among Sherlock Holmes's "140 Forms of Cigar, Cigarette, and Pipe Tobacco."

The feature on "Coffee and Crime" (2:13-14; 4:37-38) is perhaps the most interesting of *The Detective*'s consumer articles. It begins by condemning adulteration with chicory and cries out against the English habit of boiling coffee. It goes on to argue that, since coffee is a more wholesome stimulant than alcohol, and since alcohol is responsible for a large number of crimes, the cheap sale of unadulterated, unboiled coffee would markedly reduce crime in the British Isles. This enthusiasm for coffee leads the writers into excesses which run through the journal, as they do through the age:

> Coffee ... does not enervate the system ... is eminently nutritive, and also aids nutrition by preventing the loss of nutritive materials taken as food, to the extent of one-third. Thus, a working man who takes a pint of real Coffee and milk for his breakfast can labour and maintain his strength upon one-third less of his usual supply of food without the coffee.
>
> . . . .
>
> Coffee is an excellent tonic, it increases the circulation of the blood, it assists digestion, it excites the functions of the brain, it dissipates lowness of spirits and disposes the mind to cheerfulness, it removes head-ache. It counteracts the narcotic effects of opium, it has been given with salutary effect in hooping cough, and in intermittent fevers, and if applied to gangrenous sores, acts as an astringent. Of its restorative effects we lately observed two remarkable instances. One, of a robust man suffering under all the painful symptoms of strangulated hernia, and so depressed, that he appeared unable to endure an operation, but upon a pint of very strong infusion of Coffee being administered to him, to the great astonishment of the surgeon, the patient's face immediately afterwards exhibited less anxiety, and the reduction of the hernia was effected without the least difficulty. The other case was that of a middle-aged woman, who, through some internal obstruction, was sinking rapidly, and when the surgeon left her in the evening he did not expect to see her alive next morning. Fully aware that medicine could afford her no relief, he prescribed half-a-pint of strong Coffee to be taken every hour. Upon his visit next morning, in the full expectation of finding her dead, he, to his great surprise saw her up and about attending to her domestic duties. (2:13)

Coffee begins to sound like a cure-all. In a later issue *The Detective* ironically attacks quack doctors and their false claims, and then itself advertises patent medicines (see page 172).

With fewer and less obvious contradictions, *The Detective* touches on virtually every variety of fraud that was catalogued by Mayhew in *London Labour and the London Poor*: begging letter imposters (6:9), charity subscription frauds (6), counterfeiting (8), counterfeit loan societies (7), employment fraud (7), bankruptcy fraud (3, 7, 8), deed fraud (7), gaming (betting bank) fraud (1-5), newspaper fraud (1,

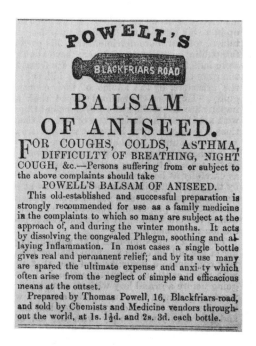

POWELL'S

BLACKFRIARS ROAD

BALSAM
OF ANISEED.

FOR COUGHS, COLDS, ASTHMA,
DIFFICULTY OF BREATHING, NIGHT
COUGH, &c.—Persons suffering from or subject to
the above complaints should take
POWELL'S BALSAM OF ANISEED.
This old-established and successful preparation is
strongly recommended for use as a family medicine
in the complaints to which so many are subject at the
approach of, and during the winter months. It acts
by dissolving the congealed Phlegm, soothing and al-
laying Inflammation. In most cases a single bottle
gives real and permanent relief; and by its use many
are spared the ultimate expense and anxi-ty which
often arise from the neglect of simple and efficacious
means at the outset.
Prepared by Thomas Powell, 16, Blackfriars-road,
and sold by Chemists and Medicine vendors throughout the world, at 1s. 1½d. and 2s. 3d. each bottle.

7), and Marine-Store Dealers (receivers of stolen goods) (4). Another
major category, called "Domestic Fraud," involved fraudulent mar-
riages, fortune-hunting—every possible confidence game practiced by
one sex upon the other (1, 7, 9). Although women were denied access
to much of the commercial and gaming worlds and consequently lost
the opportunity to distinguish themselves in related fraud, they apparently found full scope for their talents in domestic fraud. We read of
male domestic frauds, but the majority of cases feature female swind-
lers, including the spectacular "Marchioness Païva" ("A Very Woman," 1:10-11). A Russian Jewess, she began her career with beauty,
knowledge, intelligence, and no money whatever. She was taken to
Paris by a "great pianist" who "had the weakness to present her as his
legitimate wife in society, and even at a court ball."[5] She took up with
a member of the Orleans family, ruined the pianist, and went to London with "Lord ——, known . . . for his conquests of this kind." The
Englishman could not afford to keep her long, and she was obliged to
focus her attentions on the "young Marquis of Païva, brother of the
Portuguese ambassador, whom she so fascinated, that he espoused her
legally and religiously, promising her a million of francs in case they
should separate from incompatibility of temper." They married, her
temper took a sudden turn for the worse, and her fortunes radically im-

proved. She went through the million in a year, sold all her goods "to the last penny," and vowed "that she would soon be a millionaire or drowned." She rapidly turned the head of a young Prussian noble. "He followed his tempter to Paris, and surrendered himself to her with such abandonment, that I have heard that young man, endowed nobly in body and mind, who knew all the antecedents of her who had seduced him, express his regret that she was not a widow, so that he could bestow upon her his name as he had his fortune. He was hardly twenty-eight years old, while she was over forty!" As is the case with so many articles in this journal, the revelation of underlying social attitudes and psychological prejudices is more interesting than the questionable "factual" reporting. "A Very Woman" descends directly from the tradition of the picaresque heroine and most immediately from *Vanity Fair*; the charm and intelligence of the Marchioness, as well as her considerable linguistic skill ("She spoke seven languages perfectly"), remind us of Becky Sharp, who also operated in Paris, London, and Germany.[6]

II

One of the most interesting detective concerns, repeated throughout the journal, is the relationship between technology and crime. In the first issue we are told: "The criminal has ever shown himself prompt to seize upon the resources of science, and turn them into instruments and weapons of fraud and crime" (1:1). *The Detective* begins its articles with "The Electric Telegraph as Criminal Agent," a discussion of the ways in which criminals are able to manipulate the newly instituted telegraph system. Unlike the Post Office, which could only postmark a letter from its true point of origin, the telegraph agencies could and did print any point of origin desired by the sender. Criminals were quick to use this system to lure victims away from their homes (*Liverpool. Aunt Agnes dying. Come immediately.*) and either rob the traveler or his vacated home; to cast suspicion on an innocent party; or to create a false alibi. The police, however, were quick to turn the telegraph to their own advantage. In the article on "Police Telegraphs," all British police stations are urged to set up telegraphic communication with each other. "We have resided in a city where . . . these kinds of communication have been established, and have witnessed the best results arising from them" (5:53). Escaping criminals would be more easily apprehended, large fires more quickly extinguished, and missing persons readily identified. The article goes on to describe two lost children who were finally brought into a London police station just after noon:

The police telegraph was brought into requisition, and at 12:15 every police station throughout the great city knew that two little children, whose age and appearance were briefly described, were awaiting recognition at the police headquarters in Bridge Street. At 12:20 p.m. the intelligence was communicated to the mother, whose state of mind can be more easily imagined than described. At 12:30 p.m. they were in her arms.

The little creatures had wandered a mile away from home. But for the police telegraph who knows whether their mother would ever have seen them again? (5:53)

Five issues later, the most unextraordinary part of the "Extraordinary Escape and Recapture of Two Prisoners" is the routine use of the telegraph in communicating news of an escape to surrounding police stations (10:111).

The development of the electric telegraph and its incorporation into police detection reflects a more general relationship between technology and detection. A growing fear of technology accompanied the rapid progress of industry and science in the nineteenth century; in the 1850's that fear was most powerfully reflected in fictional works like *Hard Times* and Mrs. Gaskell's *North and South*, where the new technology and its accompanying ideology threaten to mechanize humanity instead of serve it. To label the electric telegraph a "criminal agent" and describe its unlawful uses hints at a similar fear of any scientific advance. Technology is itself perceived as criminal until it can be tamed. And through the course of the article we do see it gradually tamed, literally made "lawful" as it becomes a weapon for the detective police. It is no accident that so many early detectives, including Holmes himself, were amateur scientists; and today stories of police method and police science seem, if anything, to have increased in popularity. Throughout detective literature readers have been encouraged to feel a sense of control over a frightening technology. In identifying with the detective, particularly the detective-scientist, readers experience science as an ally rather than an oppressor.

In July of 1839 a telegraph line first connected Paddington with West Drayton. By 1845 this new mode of communication was crucial to the solution of the Salt Hill murder case. John Tawell was seen hurrying from the cottage of his mistress, Sarah Hart, who was heard screaming. A neighbor, finding her dying, called a doctor, who in turn sent someone to the railway station after Tawell. A telegraph clerk was alerted, and a message sent to Paddington:

A murder has just been committed at Salt Hill, and the suspected murderer was seen to take a first class ticket for London by the train which left Slough at 7h. 42m. p.m. He is in the garb of a Quaker, with a brown greatcoat on which reaches nearly down to his feet; he is in the last compartment of the second first-class carriage.[7]

Over the next few years, each use of the telegraph to trap a criminal received special comment in the press, such as: "The following instance of speedy justice, through the medium of the electric telegraph, speaks more for the efficiency of that invention, as applied to the purposes of detecting crime, than volumes."[8] Thus, instead of being overwhelmed by the complex technology of modern urban life, the Victorians were able to feel—in detective fiction and in trial reports—that they had conquered a labyrinthine world which, in real life, usually defeated them. In 1856 the *Quarterly Review* described the current mode of distributing intelligence of murders or thefts by "route-papers, or papers of particulars of the offence, on the backs of which are marked the hour at which they were received at the different divisions through which they passed." The route-papers were carried by hand, and could be distributed in two hours' time. But a better mode of communication was possible: "We understand . . . that the electric telegraph is now shooting its nerve-like threads to all the divisional stations in the metropolis, and, when the new agent is brought to bear, the communication will be almost instantaneous."[9] This striking image literally humanizes technology and the city, describing the metropolis as an organism and attributing to the telegraph the ability to unify spatially and temporally the vast distances and to order the confusion of the city as human nerves unify the body. If we follow the metaphor to its logical conclusion, then the equivalent of the brain, at the center of the vast network of nerves, is the figure of the detective—reading the city, locating crime, and organizing the means of controlling criminal activity.

An 1856 article on "Murder and the Microscope" shows how another advance in modern technology may be used to track criminals and correct wrong-doing; but the piece betrays a fear of this potent instrument and takes care to remind us that the microscope is itself dependent on human interpretation:

It ought, however, to be borne in mind, that the microscope, and similar scientific instruments, do not in any way enable us to dispense with the testimony of learned men in criminal cases, but rather serve to render such evidence more valuable; for although it is very true that the revelations made by so simple an instrument as a piece of tube some nine or ten inches long, with a few glasses at either end, are sufficient in many cases to send a man to the gallows; yet the tale such an instrument tells, can be understood only by those who, by long observation and experience, have learned the "language" in which it is told.[10]

Of course, these "learned men" are also capable of perverting the powerful but dangerous possibilities of scientific knowledge—as Professor Moriarty makes only too clear. In the highly moral world of most detective fiction, science must ultimately be brought under the domain of the detective.

"On the Means by which Criminals are Detected" (3) uses science principally to disguise sensationalism. It begins with some heavy-handed moralizing: ". . . the criminal is one who dares to break the chain by which we are mysteriously bound together; and everything conspires to bring retribution on his head." Such statements are consonant with the journal's opening *Address* and the aim of preventing crime by showing its inevitable exposure, its vulnerability to detection. But the moral is overstated: the criminal in this case is in fact acquitted of murder. The moral preface seems designed instead to justify the retelling of a sensational case of infanticide in gruesome detail. A newborn infant, found mummified two years after its death, had been placed in a chimney, "in a confined space entirely free from access of moisture, where there was no circulation of air." Its exterior was well-preserved, but "The principal organs, as the lungs, heart, and brain, had completely disappeared. The cavities they had occupied contained a great number of small bodies about the size of a grain of wheat, dry, brittle, hollow, open at one end, and of a deep mahogany colour. These were the shells of the grubs, from whence the insects, the larvae of which had devoured the missing organs, had escaped. These same grubs were found in large numbers in the mouth and on the neck of the infant. . . . The cavities of the eyes were also filled; it was through them that the larvae had penetrated to the brain." As each part of the child is verbally measured, dissected, and analyzed, the account reads increasingly like a tale of horror:

The navel-string formed a ribbon of eight inches in length by one-third of an inch in breadth. Its colour was yellow brown.

·   ·   ·   ·   ·   ·   ·   ·   ·   ·   ·

The interior of the belly contained black dried foliaceous plates, which were the abdominal organs, arrived at the last stage of dessication.

The interior of the limbs was filled with larvae or white worms, full of life, which had hollowed out long galleries in the flesh upon which they had fed. The thick part of the thighs and of the buttocks presented a great number. The fleshy part of these regions was only partially destroyed. In some places there was a thin layer of adipocere. The skin had become like parchment; it was black, and formed a hard shell or crust over the cavities in which the larvae existed.

The linen in which the body was enveloped measured 40 inches by 20. Three of its corners were sound, and without mark; but at the fourth corner a piece about 5 inches square had been torn or cut out, evidently with the object of removing the mark by which it could be identified.

The descriptions, however, are interrupted by lists of questions which concern the conditions of the child's birth and death. Inductive reasoning proves from medical and entomological evidence that the infant was born alive, at full term, and died shortly after birth. The varieties of living and dead insects found in the body are classified, and we are given a brief lesson in entomology: "This transformation requires a whole year for its completion. The female lays its eggs during the summer, and the latter become larvae, preserving this form during the winter, to be transformed into grubs in the spring, and into the perfect insect at the beginning of the summer." This background in "entomological physiology" prepares us for an ingenious process of reasoning:

These facts enable us to solve the problem before us. The eggs producing the larvae found in the body of the infant in March, 1850, must have been deposited in the middle of the summer of 1849. Therefore it becomes certain that the infant must have been placed there at least prior to that date. But the body, besides the living *larvae*, contained a great number of shells from which the insects had escaped. These shells were preceded by larvae which had passed the winter of 1848-49 in the body, and originated from eggs deposited in the course of the summer of 1848. We are thus carried back another year, with the certainty that the child must have been dead at least that period. But may it not have died at a still more distant period? We conclude it did not for the following reasons. The shells found in the cavities of the body belong to the *carnivorous* or flesh-eating fly; an insect that deposits its larvae in soft flesh before it becomes dried; so we may be sure that the larvae which produced the grubs were hatched a short time after the death of the infant. On the other hand, the larvae found in the limbs did not belong to the fly family, but to small night-moths, the larvae of which, under the name of *ticks*, are the plague of natural history museums, and the destruction of woollen articles, and which generally attack dried animal matters. These larvae, or rather these caterpillars—for so the larvae of butter-flies and moths are called, are also transformed into chrysalids before changing to butterflies. If the date of concealing the infant was further back than the summer of 1848—if, for instance, it had been in 1846 and 1847—the first deposit of eggs would have had time to give birth to chrysalids, the sheaths of which were found in the body of the infant. But not the least vestige of any was discovered; so that the larvae found must have come from the first and only laying that had taken place in the body; and this laying could only have taken place in 1849, as the larvae had not yet had time to be converted into chrysalids.

Therefore, two generations of insects, representing the revolu-tion of two years, had existed in the body of this infant: the flesh-fly deposited its larva in the fresh body in 1848, and the butterfly laid its eggs that became ticks, in 1849.

From these facts the police identify a woman who at the time of the baby's death had occupied the room where the baby was found. They then learn of other circumstances, from her illicit pregnancy to the suspiciously bloody linen seen by her laundress, which seem to clinch the case. But the jury is not convinced that the child's death is un-natural, and they convict the mother only on charges of "concealment of birth and unlawful burial."

The scientific reasoning in this case, and particularly the use of entomology, is unique. *The Detective* calls it a "singular case . . . prob-ably the first in which the light of entomological physiology was brought to bear on the discovery of a murder." Unfortunately, the entomological material is completely inaccurate. The "flesh-eating fly" referred to seems to be the *sarcophagidae*, closely related to the house fly, whose eggs can go through a complete cycle to maturity in four to five days under optimal conditions.[11] Even making allowance for the English climate, a slower development in another form of flesh-eating fly, and generally unfavorable conditions, Professor Walter Ebeling of UCLA's Department of Entomology insists that the fly de-scribed in *The Detective* must have gone through at least ten to fifteen generations within a single year; otherwise, it would not have survived at all.[12] The misapplication of other terms, such as "grubs" and "ticks," indicates an attempt at a show of scientific accuracy in what must be—at least in part—a work of fiction. The article claims that "The woman was . . . tried at the sessions in June, 1850." No such trial is reported in the *London Times*, the *London Guardian*, or the *Manchester Guardian* for that month, nor for May or July of that year, but the newspapers are full of other cases much like the account in *The Detective*. A twenty-two year old "spinster," Elizabeth Mary Marshall, was indicted for concealing the birth of a female child, but her character and "the medical testimony not supporting the indictment she was *Acquitted*." [13] "Mitigating circumstances" also help secure the release of Mary Jane Frew, "21, spinster, . . . indicted for endeavouring to conceal the birth of her female child." [14] A more spectacular case involved three women: Elizabeth Barker "and her paramour, a woman named Cook, and Harriet Campbell, a midwife, . . . in custody on suspicion of being concerned in the murder of the child [Barker's illegitimate daughter], and also with unfairly disposing of another child . . . buried . . . by the woman Cook as a still-born babe, although it lived two days." [15] Infanticide was obviously common, and the story in *The Detective* appears to have condensed the most interesting features of several cases. The following report, which did occur in June of 1850, most closely resembles the detached, mathematically precise tone of *The Detective* article, although many of its material details, from the measurements to the sexual mutilation of the child, are significantly different:

> Yesterday Mr. H. M. Wakley held an inquest at the Lord Hill, North-wharf-road, Paddington, on the body of a child about 18 months old, which was so horribly mutilated that its sex could not be discovered. It appeared that on the 29th of October, 1848, a deal box, about 14 inches square and 10½ inches deep, sewn up in a piece of canvas, and which had the direction on it, "Mrs. Watson, passenger, Exeter, Devon," was found on the platform of the Slough station by one of the porters. . . . It was there till Saturday last, the 1st of June. . . . Mr. Bailey . . . opened the box, and then discovered the body of the deceased, which was carefully folded up in a piece of calico. It had all the appearance of a mummy, having been evidently pressed down in the box. A cambric handkerchief was tied tightly round its throat. The sexual structure was entirely removed, as if by some sharp instrument. There were cuts about the arms and legs, showing that there had been attempts to sever the limbs from the body. [16]

If the article in *The Detective* is indeed fictional, its use of scientific reasoning and entomological evidence to recreate the infanticide and its subsequent solution is strikingly original. In this piece the morality of the article's opening statement is replaced by the new moralities of science and scientific investigation, which distance horror and create the impression of rational control and detachment.

III

Detective reasoning and scientific investigation also occur in many of the journal's serialized detective tales, particularly in *Leaves From A Detective's Note Book*,[17] a series of short tales emphasizing different aspects of detective work.

In "The Button" the policeman-narrator offers one of the earliest references to what modern police call an "M.O.": "We can often tell what 'school' of thieves to suspect by the way the work has been done. In the 'Hatters' Bank' case, for instance, as soon as we saw how neatly the job had been done, we had our suspicions at once." In this case of a wholesale furnishing store robbery, the police trace three criminals by means of a button which one of them had lost. "That button's the only c[l]ue we've got to 'em, and it's my opinion we can get 'em by that." The logic is simple and effective; and the rest of the story details the legwork in tracking down the thieves. As in so many early detective stories, the police must devote great ingenuity to apprehending the criminal in a neutral area, where a crowd, hostile to the authorities, would not interfere. In England and the United States, as well as in France, the police were widely regarded with suspicion, and were linked to criminals, bribery, and even political spying. Thus in "The Button," when the three thieves are traced to a theater, we are told: "It wouldn't do to try to arrest them there, for there were more birds of that feather in the place, and they would have turned to and made a row...."

"The Forger's Cipher" presents us with two different types of code to unravel, one intentional, the other unintentional: the first is a simple but interesting cipher, which is thoroughly analyzed; the second is a series of accents which run through the narration. The narrator himself, presumably a New York policeman, refers, in his own peculiar vernacular, to that favorite beverage of *The Detective*: "Speaking of 'hot tod,' though, I'd rather have hot *coffee* anytime—and that brings me back to the story, with a short turn, and 'sarve me right.' " The thieves are heard shouting "something in Dutch or French" which is understood as *"Current wheat!"*—obviously French for forty-eight. The Frenchman, however, sounds more like a depraved German: "Bien! but you will smoke the *cigar* vit me." While the other characters' accents are degenerating, the narrator's command of English keeps improving: "The more I looked at it the more I feared that its evident age would make it worthless; and yet I knew I should not rest satisfied. . . ." By comparison, the cipher is easy to break:

"3 — k1bh — m45 — h4 — r3bq — r4f — y2 — 1 — s44q — t4fg2
— q21x2f, ht2 — f3sth — y1b.=3 — k1bh — 1 — c13f,& — 1 —
x21q2f, h4 — y1w2 — 1 — h21y — 4r — *htf22*=114 — qf3j2 —
3b — 5xgh2fP45bhm.=3 — gt1xx — n2 — 3b — h4kb — 3b —
htf22 — k22wg.=Kf3h2 — h4 — y2 — kt2f2 — h4 — y22h
— t3y.
  "1qqf2gg — T2bfm — X1b32f, X1bg3bsn5fst." (2, 23)

The numbers correspond to vowels, and the narrator's explanation clearly recalls the still-recent "Gold-Bug" (1843). Poe's Legrand says "Now, in English, the letter which most frequently occurs is *e*. . . . Now, of all *words* in the language, 'the' is most usual."[18] The narrator in "The Forger's Cipher" tells us:

> Printers say that *e* is the commonest letter in the language. Now look through and see how many 2's there are. Don't that help to prove that my first guess about the vowels was a good one?
>   Now, in the next place, *the* is the commonest *word* in the language. . . . (2:23)[19]

Forty years later Holmes uses similar reasoning to break the cipher in "The Dancing Men."

"The Absconding Debtor—A Skating Story" must surely be the first—and perhaps the only—detective case on ice skates. The escaping criminal is that most heinous of all Victorian types, a "dishonest bankrupt," while the detective, one Tomson, is an engaging narrator with the technical and physical expertise of a nineteenth-century James Bond. The story is set in the winter of 1854, "in the middle of one of the most slippery portions of that rigorous season . . . with one of the most slippery customers I ever met. . . ." That customer, having accumulated and profited from a vast amount of unpaid merchandise, plans to slip through a network of police guarding his home, street, and neighboring railway stations by skating at night some twenty-five miles along the frozen river. Tomson, impersonating an accomplice of the criminal, discovers the plan. The rest is easy: "for skating being a 'specialty' of mine, I made no doubt that . . . I could overhaul him on the river." The fugitive is "a great, rough, black-whiskered bully," but this, too, hardly fazes Tomson: "some risks must be taken, and with my training in the fistic art, I did not, on the whole, fear for the result of a single combat." The description of the high-speed chase is well paced and vividly mixes technical detail with a sharply etched setting:

> I hurried down the high precipitous bank to the river, slid out upon the gray, glassy ice, and, kneeling down, proceeded to put on the skates. Deliberately—for in such a business the more haste the less speed—and carefully I fitted them, jammed the heel-pins home, passed and buckled the straps, straining them until my feet felt as if compressed in iron shoes, replaced my mittens, grasped my stick, one hand at each end, holding it athwart me—a most excellent plan, by-the-way, in skating long distances—and wheeling about in a few small circuits to feel the ice, and the skates, and the elasticity of my muscles, I turned northward, bent low, headed diagonally across the river to round the next point above, and struck out across the glimmering silent ice with long, steady, rapid, sweeping strokes.

After a long pursuit, Tomson comes on his man, Tapling, as the river approaches the County Prison. Tapling hears "the ringing of . . . skate-irons" and redoubles speed. "Away we flew for nearly a mile in perfect silence, except for the scoring and ringing skate-strokes." Tapling tries unsuccessfully to fire at the hero with a revolver when suddenly "the gray ice over which we had been gliding disappeared, and I seemed to be skating on water. It was dead black ice. *An air hole!*" By a combination of instant thinking and gymnastic prowess, Tomson uses his momentum for a "terrific leap . . . over ten feet of black, open water." Tapling is not so fortunate. Before Tomson will save him, he must promise to return the stolen money. Once he complies, Tomson rescues him and allows him to continue his escape. What obviously counts is the money, although Tomson does tell us at the close that "no money would buy me to experience again the one quick, deadly pang of fright that thrilled through me at the sight of the black ice of the air-hole."

"The Ebony Box" is a confused narrative, with more complexity and forced coincidence than a Gaboriau novel. It does explain rationally the apparently supernatural appearance of a woman in white, although, unlike those in a well-constructed detective story, the supernatural events and the naturalistic explanation are tangential. There is a glimmer of handwriting analysis, equally tangential. The story is the weakest narrative in this generally excellent series.

"The Stolen Watch" makes use of what has since become a cliché: "Upon examining the broken glass carefully, I found that it had been pushed *outwards*, showing that the thief must have been on the inside when he broke the pane." The circumstances of the story are elaborately contrived: the scene of the burglary, for example, is preserved untouched for two years with the expectation that it will be reexamined by a proper detective. The setting, however, is of particular historical interest. The story begins in 1829, the year in which the Metropolitan Police replace the Bow Street Runners, and that transition is discussed extensively. The more efficient Metropolitan Police created their own detective branch in 1842. In 1850 Dickens wrote an article on the detective branch which favorably contrasted it with the old Bow Street Runners, and "The Stolen Watch" recalls Dickens's criticism of the Runners. Dickens wrote: "We are not by any means devout believers in the old Bow Street Police. To say the truth, we think there was a vast amount of humbug about those worthies. . . . they never lost a public occasion of jobbing and trading in mystery and making the most of themselves. . . . they became a sort of superstition. . . . they remain with some people a superstition to the present day."[20] The narrator of "The Stolen Watch," himself a member of the Metropolitan Police, also disparaged the Bow Street Officers and the persistent public superstition about them: "They had for many years monopolized the 'detective' business all to themselves. By most of the common people they were supposed to possess supernatural powers, and were looked upon as the (infernal) gods of the metropolis." Later in the story the thief hides out in Rats' Castle, "one of the lowest of low dens." This area was described in Dickens's article "On Duty with Inspector Field" and served as a model for Tom-All-Alone's in *Bleak House*: "How many people . . . in London . . . would know it [Rats' Castle] for a not remote part of the city in which their lives are passed? How many, who amidst this compound of sickening smells, these heaps of filth, these tumbling houses, with all their vile contents, animate, and inanimate, slimily overflowing into the black road, would believe that they breathe *this* air?"[21]

"My First Charge," like "The Stolen Watch," also begins in 1829. The story contains several references to the Metropolitan Police, some of them possibly tongue-in-cheek: "Evidently frightened at my authoritative manner, she became silent, and surveyed me from head to foot, with a sort of awe. For at that time people had a great dread of the mysterious powers of the New Police, and both old and young were terribly afraid of coming under the displeasure of one of the 'Peel brigade,' as they commonly called us." The "evidently frightened" woman is meanwhile trying to bribe the narrator with two pence and assailing the taxation levied on the public to support "a parcel of fellows in fine clothes" like the new Police. The narrator proceeds to arrest a respectable mother and daughter who had been reduced to pawning the articles of their rented room. The mother is committed to the workhouse and the well-intentioned narrator gives her money; later, when she dies, he pays the parish for her to have a proper funeral. The daughter becomes a "fortunate unfortunate lady": she is transported to New South Wales, makes an excellent marriage, and returns to England twenty years later to reward the narrator with an "elegant diamond ring" and five hundred pounds—another detective story with a financial moral.

"Vidocq: The French Thief Catcher" claims to be an account of "His last act as a Private Detective." The famous French thief and chief of the *Sûreté* is now in private practice; he helps a wealthy French merchant try to recover 150,000 francs from his employee (with the unusual French name of Arthur), who is having an affair with the merchant's young wife. Vidocq deports the employee-lover, teaches the wife a moral lesson, returns all the unspent money, and keeps the merchant in blissful ignorance of his wife's character.

"The Ex-Policeman's Story" is more a melodramatic tale of misplaced love than a detective story. Hallett, the ex-policeman, rescues a beautiful woman half his age and marries her knowing nothing of her background. She eases the considerable burdens of an ordinary policeman's life:

> "We lived very much alone. I never had time to make any very large number of friends. I don't know as how I wanted to—for friends in our walk—policeman's friends, that is—are, a precious sight too often, these smooth-faced fellows who would get you off your beat to drink with 'em, and then report you to headquarters to get your place. So I was civil to every body, and intimate with hardly a soul. Mary was enough for me."

One evening he finds Mary with another man, and she subsequently disappears. Hallett collapses and recovers only when he is offered an opportunity to join the new Detective Police. After some time, he traces a female thief to her lodgings and sees a man emerge carrying the stolen goods. Only a Victorian writer could have contrived the climactic scene in which Hallett struggles with the man, sees a pistol suddenly pointed in his direction, twists the criminal to take the shot, and witnesses the man's dying curse: Mary, aiming at her husband, has unintentionally killed her lover. Still very much in love with his wife, Hallett later helps her to escape from prison; he is dismissed from the force and goes insane. The tale is surprisingly moving despite not only its strained coincidences but the jarring textual inconsistencies which suggest clumsy revisions from an American source. For example, the narrator's comment about a colleague reads like a mixture of exaggerated American speech with a little Irish thrown in: "For ye

see I wanted to help him on a bit, bein' he hadn't much book larnin'."
Indeed, the diction in several stories is a combination of Fenimore
Cooper, Dan'l Boone, County Cork, and Cockney. Elsewhere in *Leaves
From A Detective's Note Book*, however, the writer or editor is careful
to set off and explain American criminal slang: "Well, there seemed a
poor show for making much in this case, and our plan seemed to be to
watch round for the next attempt, and meanwhile to 'turn up' (search)
some of the 'fences' (receivers of stolen goods) to see if we could find
any of the property; though it's only by chance that you ever make
any thing that way, the 'fences' are too fly (smart)" ("The Button,"
1:9).

In "The Ex-Policeman's Story" the editor does not distinguish so
carefully between British and American locations: the New York
Police are organized by "Scotland-yard" and St. Paul's Cathedral turns
up disconcertingly as a New York landmark. "The Forger's Cipher"
has a similarly miraculous geography, in which the detective can grab
the next train to Dublin—from New York. The inconsistencies in some
of the stories in *Leaves From A Detective's Note Book* probably stem
from several sources, including careless typesetting. But the geographical confusions suggest a hurried editorial job in an attempt to
transpose the stories from one side of the Atlantic to the other. *The
Detective's Note Book*, a yellowback first published in 1860, reprints
several of these stories, but with much more editorial consistency.[22] It
is unclear whether the yellowback takes the stories from *The Detective*
or, more probably, from an earlier source which *The Detective* used
independently. (More work will have to be done to establish American
and British variants for these stories, and we would welcome any additional information from interested readers.)

Other fiction in *The Detective* includes "Caught in his own Trap,"
the last story in *Leaves From A Detective's Note Book*, and "Betting
Bank Frauds" (1:2; 2:14-15; 3:26-27; 4:38-39; 5:51-52). "Caught in
his own Trap" begins with two detectives chasing a noted forger and
then awkwardly shifts to the tale of a Captain Hawser who, through a
false marriage, has duped a beautiful French woman into living with
him. The narrator-detective manages to prove the false marriage binding, which, strangely enough, seems to earn him the gratitude of all
parties. The woman "must have forgotten or changed her resolution
never to live again with Captain Hawser"; while the captain "never
failed to admit that he had been very nicely, through my instrumental-
ity, CAUGHT IN HIS OWN TRAP." "Betting Bank Frauds" is an epistolary
detective tale which exposes a clever scheme for obtaining money from
gullible investors.

Contemporary crime cases are scrupulously covered during the
short life of *The Detective*, particularly "The Rev. John Henry Hatch's

A typical page of advertisements in *The Detective*.

Case" (6:67-71; 7:73, 80-82; 8:90-94; 9:103, 104-05; 10:116; 11:127-28; 13:152), about which the *London Times* gives only a sketchy report. Hatch was accused of molesting two young girls whom he was instructing and was sentenced to four years in prison. When information favorable to Hatch, but suppressed during the trial, was brought to light, the jury was not allowed to reverse its findings. *The Detective* discusses not only the case and all relevant evidence, but also editorializes for related judicial reform. In neither its fictional nor its factual accounts, did *The Detective* forget its avowed ethical purpose.

IV

We cannot cover the journal's poetry nor all the other articles of interest, but the advertisements deserve special attention because of their historical and social value. Our reproduction of a full page of advertisements (facing page) contains three notices from the office of Charles Frederick Field, former chief of the Detective Police. Field had appeared in several articles written by Dickens in the 1850's, and he served as a model for Inspector Bucket in *Bleak House*. He went into private practice in 1852 while his reputation continued to grow. Field's advertisements may be found in other contemporary journals and newspapers, but this set of advertisements in *The Detective* is especially extensive and revealing. It begins with a plea for help for a convict's wife, subscriptions to be sent to C. F. Field; the following two advertisements turn directly to the business of his agency. Such public relations helped to create an image of Field—and consequently an important early prototype for the detective—as both kindly and business-like, charitable whenever possible but always committed to his trade. His fictional counterpart, Inspector Bucket, is obliged to take in George Rouncewell, but refuses to disturb the party Rouncewell is attending or be unnecessarily cruel when he must later handcuff his victim: "Mr. Bucket adjusts them [the handcuffs] in a moment. 'How do you find them? Are they comfortable? If not, say so, for I wish to make things as pleasant as is consistent with my duty, and I've got another pair in my pocket.' This remark he offers like a most respectable tradesman, anxious to execute an order neatly, and to the perfect satisfaction of his customer."[23] Dickens's description is at once comic and accurate: commerce and crime are linked throughout the period, and it is only fitting that the perfect detective should behave like a perfect tradesman.

Field placed many advertisements in *The Detective*, and some of his cases spill over into the journal itself. On 21 January 1860, he ran the following notice:

ONE HUNDRED POUNDS REWARD.—Whereas Mons. GEORGES
HIRSCH, native of Paris, did, on the 6th day of December last,
arrive in Southampton from Rio Janeiro, having with him a large
sum of money in Bills of Exchange on Liverpool and London,
amounting to upwards of 30,000 francs; and whereas the said
George Hirsch left Southampton, and came and resided for one
night only, namely, on the 7th of December last, in the neighbour-
hood of Red Lion square, and on the following morning left his
habitation, and has since mysteriously DISAPPEARED, causing
considerable anxiety and alarm to his friends and relatives:—
Notice is hereby given, that £100 reward will be paid by the
friends of the said George Hirsch for information as to his where-
abouts and recovery of the said sum of 30,000 francs, or a propor-
tionate part thereof. And, in the event of the death of the said
George Hirsch, the sum of £50 will be paid to any person or persons who shall give information as to his decease. Description:—
Age 22 years, 5 feet 8 or 9 inches, black hair inclined to curl, high
forehead, eyes brown, aquiline nose, dark complexion, very thick
eyebrows and lips; inclined to stoop. Information to Charles
Frederick Field, late Chief Inspector of the Detective Police of the
Metropolis, Private Inquiry-office, 20, Devereux-court, Strand.
(7:84)

The notice had previously appeared in the *Times*, and it aroused a
reaction in other papers. In two later issues (8, 10), *The Detective*
reprinted a piece from the *Globe* which described the handling of the
Hirsch case by a Mr. Pollaky, Field's "foreign superintendent." Pollaky determined that, far from meeting with foul play, Hirsch had
committed fraud; his disappearance coincided with the assumption of
a false name. The article concludes with some irony and a reference to
the telegraph, now fully under Field's control:

> What could have induced Mr. Hirsch to have acted in the manner
> described will no doubt have hereafter to be explained. It is almost
> needless to say Mr. Hirsch never paid Mr. Rimmel for the goods,
> nor did he return to this gentleman after he had obtained discount
> of the bills. The Home Office was set to work to cause inquiries to
> be made about the missing Mr. Hirsch; but a telegraphic message
> from Mr. Field to Paris soon put out of the question further trouble
> on the part of the Government. (10:117)

Hirsch, Sr., replies briefly and indignantly to the *Globe* that its statements "are singularly inaccurate; many being greatly exaggerated,

and others entirely false"; Field himself answered: "To these sweeping remarks no reply can be made, excepting that such general terms go very little way in an enlightened country like England." He urged the elder Hirsch to read more accurately and concludes:

> We never disputed, nor do we care whether the 30,000 francs are legally Mr. Hirsch's or any one else's; our point was to ascertain (as represented to the highest authority in Paris) whether Mr. Hirsch, jun., *was* or was *not* murdered in *this* country.
>
> All our researches, and they are most remarkable ones, go to prove that up to the 7th inst., Mr. Hirsch was in a perfect state of convalescence, which, according to Mr. Hirsch, sen.'s shewing, Mr. Hirsch, jun., had forgotten to inform his doubtless anxious parents.

The Detective adds a note to this reprinted correspondence, urging that the £100 reward offered for accurate information about Hirsch be given to Field, who had certainly earned it (10:117-18). Field must have been the ideal customer for *The Detective*, placing frequent advertisements and providing exciting copy to increase sales.

The whole page of advertising is a delight to read, including the "medical" ads which have already been mentioned. But, as a closing reminder of the rich possibilities of this journal, we would call your attention to the following personal, which appeared over three successive weeks in issues 8, 9 and 10:

> THE CABMAN who TOOK UP A LADY and CHILD, about three years old—the latter dressed in a dark blue French merino pelisse and black felt hat, at the Crystal Palace station, London Bridge, at about 12:30 p.m., will be handsomely Rewarded by applying at 2, Weymouth Street, Portland Place.

It is not difficult to imagine a prototypical Holmes and Watson reading this personal:

"You've no doubt noticed," Holmes says to his slow but necessary companion, "the striking fact about the date."

"But there is no date."

"Precisely, my dear fellow. Given its extreme exactness, particularly an estimated time of day, we may draw only two conclusions from the curious omission of a date: either a misprint, or a code. And since the repetition of this notice, without change, for three successive weeks, excludes the possibility of a misprint . . ."

ACKNOWLEDGMENT

The authors wish to acknowledge the courteous assistance provided by Mr. Brooke Whiting and the staff of the Department of Special Collections, University Research Library, University of California, Los Angeles; Mr. Wilbur Smith and Professor Ada Nisbet, who got us started; and Susan Crow, who helped us through.

[1] Mr. Wilbur Smith, retired head of Special Collections, Research Library, University of California, Los Angeles, recently unearthed *The Detective* in a group of obscure, unbound Victorian periodicals he bought twenty years ago to add as background material to UCLA's Sadleir Collection of nineteenth-century fiction. Other items in this group of periodicals contain manuscript notes by Sadleir, and there is good reason to believe that *The Detective* was Sadleir's own copy of a work he found to be a rarity of considerable interest. *The Detective* is in folio format (13¼" x 9¼" or 33.5cm x 24cm); numbers 1-11 contain four sheets or sixteen pages, number 13 contains three sheets or twelve pages. There are no signatures to indicate collation; instead, the pages in the issues are numbered consecutively, starting in issue 1 with page one. Through issue 13 there are 156 pages. The journal was published by Thomas Danks, No. 9, Crane Court, Fleet Street. The dates from No. 1 to No. 13 are 10 December 1859 to 3 March 1860. Of the fourteen copyrighted issues listed by the British Museum, UCLA owns original copies of issues 1-11 and 13—the only known copies outside of the British Museum. The two missing issues, No's. 12 and 14, are being added to the file in Xerox copies. The journal has no illustrations. Each page is divided into two columns, double-ruled at the top, with the running title THE DETECTIVE. The masthead for the first ten issues is identical with that at the beginning of this article. Starting with issue 11, the masthead reads:

THE
DETECTIVE
AND
PUBLIC PROTECTOR:
A JOURNAL OF SOCIAL EVILS.

A note in issue 11 explains this change:

TO OUR READERS

THE scope of this Journal having taken a wider extension than was at first contemplated, we have thought it advisable to add to the original title of Detective, which was thought by many to be ambiguous, that of PUBLIC PROTECTOR,

—this term more clearly expressing the mere object of the Journal,—that of protecting the Public against the constant invasions of Fraud and Crime to which it is daily subjected. (11:126)

Beginning with issue 7, the back page is divided into three columns of general advertising and personals—a radical increase in advertising, and perhaps in circulation. Articles reprinted from other British periodicals are so noted, although other pieces—either because of their early date or on the basis of contradictions within the texts, as we describe in the article—seem to be unacknowledged reprints.

All subsequent references to articles in *The Detective* will be carried in parenthesis in the text, with the issue number followed by pages; as the journal existed for only four months, we shall omit the date of publication from subsequent citations. Misleading or awkward inconsistencies in punctuation in the text of the journal have been regularized.

2 Michael Wolff in *Editing Nineteenth Century Texts*, ed. John M. Robson (Toronto: University of Toronto Press, 1967), p. 42.

3 "The Begging Letter Writers," in *Reprinted Pieces* (Bloomsbury: The Nonesuch Press, 1938), pp. 20-21.

4 "The Detective Police," in *Reprinted Pieces*, p. 153.

5 "A Very Woman" may well be based on the career of Lola Montez, as this detail in particular seems to suggest. She met Liszt in Dresden and had a brief affair with him which terminated after he had taken her to Paris. Her main conquest was Ludwig I of Bavaria, and she herself took the title of Countess of Landsfeld.

6 Social and sexual prejudice is nowhere more apparent in this journal than in the related series of articles on prostitution (1-11). However, this broad topic requires a fuller treatment than we can give it here; it also leads us away from detective interests.

7 Geoffrey Hubbard, *Cooke and Wheatstone and the Invention of the Electric Telegraph* (London: Routledge & Kegan Paul, 1965), p. 107. The material is taken from the Tawell murder trial of 13 March 1845.

8 *London Times*, 15 Oct. 1846, p. 4, col. d. A lengthy account of the case follows. For other direct references to the miraculous use of the electric telegraph as detective agent see: *London Times*, 13 Oct. 1846, p. 7, col. c; *London Times*, 30 June 1847, p. 5, col. c; *London Times*, 16 July 1846, p. 6, col. b; *London Times*, 3 Aug. 1852, p. 6, col. c.

9 "The Police and the Thieves," *Quarterly Review*, 99 (1856), 166.

10 "Murder and the Microscope," *Chambers's Journal of Popular Literature, Science and Arts* (London: Chambers), No. 150 (15 November 1856), p. 307.

11 See E. O. Essig, *College Entomology* (New York: Macmillan, 1942), pp. 800-08, and M. T. James & R. F. Harwood, *Medical Entomology*, 6th ed. (New York: Macmillan, 1971), p. 259.

12 Professor Ebeling also assures us that no respectable mid-nineteenth century entomologist would have supported the entomological assertions in *The Detective*. The mistakes are those of the author of the article, not of nineteenth-century science.

13 *London Times*, 8 March 1850, p. 7, col. e.

14 *London Times*, 13 May 1850, p. 7, col. f.

15 *London Times*, 20 May 1850, p. 7, col. f.

16 *London Times*, 5 June 1850, p. 8, col. e.

17 *Leaves From A Detective's Note Book* consists of the following short stories:

	issue	pages
The Button	1	9-10
The Forger's Cipher	2	22-24
The Absconding Debtor—A Skating Story	3	33-35
The Ebony Box	4, 5	39-41; 56-58
The Stolen Watch	6	61-62
Vidocq: The French Thief Catcher	7	73-74
My First Charge	8, 9	85-86; 98-99
The Ex-Policeman's Story	10, 11	111-13; 122-24
Caught in his own Trap	13	146-47

18 Edgar Allan Poe, "The Gold Bug," in *The Complete Works of Edgar Allan Poe*, ed. James A. Harrison (New York: Crowell, 1902), V, 133.

19 Poe himself presumably took his information from Abraham Rees, *Cyclopaedia or Universal Dictionary of Arts, Sciences, and Literature* (London: Longman, 1819), VIII, Bb 8; the language in "The Forger's Cipher," however, most clearly resembles Poe's.

20 Charles Dickens, "The Detective Police," in *Reprinted Pieces*, p. 149.

21 Charles Dickens, "On Duty with Inspector Field," in *Reprinted Pieces*, p. 178.

22 *The Detective's Note Book*, ed. "Charles Martel" (London: Ward and Lock, 1860). The changes made in the stories deal with money (the journal refers to dollars; the book, to pounds); cities; locations within the cities; proper names; common spelling ("gray" to "grey"); and vernacular (a "store" in the journal is a "shop" in the book). The book contains six of the nine stories in *The Detective*: "The Button," "The Forger's Cipher," "The Absconding Debtor," "The Ebony Box," "The Ex-Policeman's Story," and "Caught in his own Trap"; "The Stolen Watch," "Vidocq: The French Thief Catcher," and "My First Charge" are not included.

23 Charles Dickens, *Bleak House* (London: Oxford University Press, 1948), Chapter XLIX, pp. 678-79. See also "On Duty with Inspector Field," *Reprinted Pieces*, pp. 177-89, and Philip Collins, *Dickens and Crime* (London: Macmillan & Co., 1965), pp. 210-13.

MYSTERY FICTION
IN THE
NINETEENTH CENTURY

By Wilbur Jordan Smith

IN THE 1972 issue of *The Mystery & Detection Annual,* during the course of a review of Ordean Hagen's *Who Done It? A Guide to Detective, Mystery, and Suspense Fiction,* I made the guess that "a complete listing of nineteenth-century mystery fiction would probably run to six thousand titles." Several readers have challenged that estimate, most notably the editor of *The Armchair Detective* who writes: ". . . I should be delighted (nay, ecstatic) if Mr. Smith would supply me with full bibliographic details (as well as the criteria of thematic judgment applied) for the 6000 titles of 19th century mystery fiction he says were probably published" (6, No. 2 [Feb. 1973], 115). Here, then, is the data on which I based my claim. I will leave it to the reader to judge whether or not my estimate is a reasonable one.

Though Hagen's bibliography advertised the comprehensiveness of its coverage, it actually listed (by my count) only 302 nineteenth-century titles. Included in Hagen's overall checklist (as its subtitle suggested) were mysteries, tales of suspense, and detective stories. Thus I felt the Gothic novel to be an important ingredient in any listing of mystery books. And Gothic novels became the first large figure in my estimate of nineteenth-century mystery production. Montague Summers's *A Gothic Bibliography* (London: Fortune Press, 1941) lists about 4,800 titles, of which, by my reckoning, 78 percent were published between the years 1801-1900. The proportion gives us 3,750 Gothic novels, English and American. To that number I added 1,400 mystery and detective titles of the period 1886-1900. Such a number is surprisingly large, I will admit, but was arrived at by the following steps.

In the remoter storage areas of the Department of Special Collections of the Research Library at the University of California, Los Angeles, is a collection of four thousand American paperback novels of the late nineteenth century. These were acquired in 1959 and have remained untouched during the intervening years, largely because of their extreme fragility. Most of them are "storage copies" from the Library of Congress; that is, they are the second copies of the two which are required by law to be deposited in order to secure copyright.

PLATE 1. Yellowback detective fiction from the Michael Sadleir Collection of 19th century novels. The entire collection, described in Sadleir's *XIX Century Fiction*, was bought by UCLA in 1951. It is housed in the University Research Library's Bradford A. Booth Room, Department of Special Collections.

The Library of Congress, no doubt in an effort to ease its space problems, declared these to be surplus — they are so stamped — and disposed of them. UCLA bought them from a bookseller and, after opening a few hundred of the individually wrapped copies, consigned them to storage to await a time when they might be rendered usable by future innovative conservation techniques.

A word should perhaps be said about the background of these obscure publications. The United States Postal laws of 1879 provided publishers with the opportunity of shipping novels anywhere in the country at the rate of a penny a pound, if such novels could be shown to be published as periodicals. They had to be sold as subscription series and, among other specifications, must be "formed of printed paper sheets, without board, cloth, leather, or other substantial binding, such as distinguish printed books for preservation from periodical publications."

One may judge that among other factors involved, the profits made possible by this masquerade (a saving of seven cents a pound over the previous postal rate for books) brought about an enormous output of paperback fiction during the years 1880-1900. In his research at the Library of Congress, Lyle Wright says that he came across 195 different series. Because they were technically serial publications, they did not qualify for inclusion in his *American Fiction, 1876-1900* (San Marino: Huntington Library, 1966), excepting the relatively few which were issued simultaneously in hard covers and not as part of subscription series. The majority of copies seems to have disappeared from the scene, if one may judge from the rarity with which they appear in the National Union Catalog. When they do show up there at all it is usually as one copy only — the Library of Congress depository copy.

The UCLA paperbacks are entirely of this category. Most are first editions. In my original sampling of two hundred titles, made at the time of purchase, I was interested to discover that seventy-one were detective or mystery stories. That is about 35 percent, and so by applying that percentage to the remainder of the collection I have arrived at a total of 1,400 volumes. As I have only recently recommenced unwrapping and examining the collection I cannot yet provide an exact count. But if the percentage of mystery books to other titles continues to hold, as I anticipate it will, I can increase my grand total of nineteenth-century mystery and detective titles to 5,150.

That leaves 850 titles to account for. Mid-nineteenth-century English detective novels of the yellowback variety, a representative group of which is here illustrated, ought at a conservative guess to account for another three hundred titles. The final balance of 550 I conjecture would have been published in England during the fifteen years following the enormous success of Fergus Hume's *The Mystery of the Han-*

som Cab (1887). The Sherlock Holmes stories appeared during those years, of course, and undoubtedly gave the genre its greatest boost. I put this modest estimate of 550 volumes as only a conjecture, since I can find little evidence of an English outpouring of such novels to match in volume that which took place in America during the years from 1885 to 1900. Cheap paperbacks there certainly were, many of them original editions and not just reprints. But except for the "penny bloods" directed by their authors at a juvenile audience, I cannot cite mystery and detection series, published in London, in anything like the quantity of American publication. Michael Sadleir saved from oblivion those of the mid-century but was less interested in books of the latter years. But if I am allowed my reasonable guess I can complete my estimate of six thousand volumes of mystery and detection published in Britain and American throughout the last century.

In the accompanying illustrations are shown some examples of detective yellowbacks, chiefly of the 1850's and 1860's, from the Michael Sadleir Collection of Nineteenth-Century English Fiction at the University of California, Los Angeles, Research Library. This is said to be the largest and finest such collection in existence. The books illustrated are mostly first editions and, except for the translations of Gaboriau and Du Boisgobey, are of English origin.

In the other plates are illustrated a number of samples from the subscription series. Excepting, once again, a few translations from the French, all are American and are the first, and presumably only, editions. None appears in Wright. The examples are taken from the following series:

The Choice Series (N.Y.: Robert Bonner's Sons)
Pinkerton Detective Series (Chicago: Laird & Lee)
Good Company Series (Boston: Lee and Shepard)
The Railway Series (N.Y.: The National Book Co.)
Lovell's Detective Series (N.Y.: John Lovell Co.)
The Champion Detective Series (N.Y.: J. S. Ogilvie & Co.)
The Melbourne Series (Chicago: E. A. Weeks & Co.)
The Echo Series (N.Y.: Pollard & Moss)
The Sunnyside Series (N.Y.: J. S. Ogilvie & Co.)
Neely's Universal Library (N.Y.: F. Tennyson Neely)
The Manhattan Series of Popular American Novels (N.Y.: A. L. Burt)
The Princess Series (N.Y.: Street & Smith)

Finally, I reproduce an assortment of titles from the Street and Smith *Secret Service Series*. This series commenced publication in late 1887. A new title appeared each month. At the present state of my un-

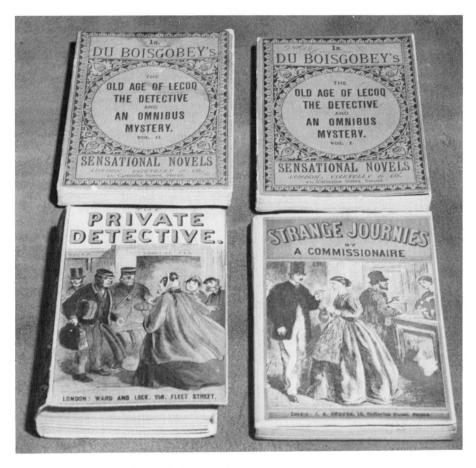

PLATE 2. More ephemeral detective fiction from the Sadleir Collection. Vizetelly published 32 of the tales of Du Boisgobey, all but two of which are present in the collection in original wrappers.

PLATE 3. The above and all other English books shown in the illustrations are described in Volume 2 of Michael Sadleir's *XIX Century Fiction*.

PLATE 4. Of these Sadleir items, two are not yellowbacks, but as in the case of others illustrated, are original editions. *Held in Thrall* is in gaudy colored wrappers. *A Mystery Still* is an exception to Vizetelly's publication of Du Boisgobey, the others being issued in wrappers.

PLATE 5. A few of the many hundreds of American paperback mysteries in subscription series, published in the last twenty years of the 19th century. None of these titles appears in Wright's *American Fiction, 1876-1900*.

PLATE 6. Additional American detective stories issued in subscription series. None of these titles appears in Wright, excepting the one at the top left, which, in non-series form, is in an edition of three years later. The "Wall Street Man" was David L. Proudfit.

PLATE 7. An example of a series which was not numbered nor sold by subscription, and is therefore admitted into Lyle Wright's bibliography. The camera angle makes the book appear dumpier than it actually is.

PLATE 8. The Secret Service Series, published by Street & Smith. The portrait of Gaboriau, shown on the book at the lower left, is an enlarged and glamorized copy of the woodcut used by Vizetelly in the English edition of 1885, which is described by Haycraft as the only known surviving likeness of the French writer. The translation is that of the Vizetelly edition, which was, however, entitled *The Gilded Clique*.

wrapping the long-dormant collection of American paperback novels the latest numbered title in the *Secret Service Series* which I have found is No. 62, dated December, 1892. If the series continued in that fashion throughout 1900, as it seems likely it did, it should have reached 158 titles. Readers of *The Mystery & Detection Annual* may be interested in a catalogue of those first sixty-two titles in the series. Only sixteen of the sixty-two have been located thus far in the UCLA collection (the remainder of the titles are taken from the lists printed in the sixteen books found so far). I expect most, if not all, of the remaining titles will turn up. None of the sixty-two titles which follow is in the Wright bibliography and, as I recall, none (excepting a few French titles) appears in Hagen's *Who Done It?*. Most of these books have a frontispiece illustration — a black-and-white line sketch — and a few have additional illustrations. They average about 220 pages in length (barely complying with Dorothy Sayers's dictum about size). It should be noted that Street and Smith published other subscription series devoted exclusively to detective fiction. At least 165 titles in its Magnet Detective Series appeared prior to 1901.

The Secret Service Series, New York: Street & Smith

1. [Halsey, Harlan Page]. Brant Adams, the Emperor of Detectives. By "Old Sleuth" (pseud.). c 1887.
2. ———. Bruce Angelo, the City Detective. By "Old Sleuth" (pseud.). c 1887.
3. ———. Van, the Government Detective; or, The Base Metal Coiners. By "Old Sleuth" (pseud.). 1888.
4. Hill, K. F. The Twin Detectives; or, The Robbers of the Tomb. 1888.
5. [Halsey, Harlan Page]. The Masked Detective. A Tale of Strange Mysteries. By Judson R. Taylor (Pseud.). 1888.
6. ———. Old Stonewall, the Colorado Detective. By Judson R. Taylor (pseud.). 1888.
7. ———. The Chosen Man; or, The Mystery of the Secret Service. By Judson R. Taylor (pseud.). 1888.
8. James, Police Captain. Little Lightning, the Shadow Detective; or, The Twenty-third Street Mystery. 1888.
9. Baxter, Young. Old Mortality. 1888.
10. Goode, George W. The Post-Office Detective. 1888.
11. Sawyer, Eugene T. The Maltese Cross. 1888.
12. Murray, Lieutenant. The Dog Detective. 1888.
13. Stauffer, Frank H. Darke Darrell. 1888.

14. "Old Hutch." The Detective's Clew. 1888.
15. [Halsey, Harlan Page]. Tom and Jerry; or, The Double Detectives. By Tony Pastor (pseud.). 1889.
16. [Patten, J. A.]., The Mountaineer Detective. By Clayton W. Cobb (pseud.). 1889.
17. [Coryell, John Russell]. The Old Detective's Pupil; or, The Mysterious Crime of Madison Square. By Nick Carter (pseud.). 1889.
18. ———. The Wall Street Haul; or, A Bold Stroke for a Fortune. By Nick Carter (pseud.). 1889.
19. [Halsey, Harlan Page]. The Swordsman of Warsaw; or, Ralph of the Iron Arm. By Tony Pastor (pseud.). 1889.
20. Hill, K. F. The Mystery of a Madstone; or, The Commercial Traveler Detective. 1889.
21. [Coryell, John Russell]. The American Marquis; or, Detective for Vengeance, a Story of a Masked Bride and a Husband's Quest. By Nick Carter (pseud.). 1889.
22. Maitland, Oscar. The Society Detective. 1889.
23. Hill, K. F. A Mysterious Case; or, Tracing a Crime. 1889.
24. Richardson, Leander Pease. The Prairie Detective. 1889.
25. [Judson, Edward Zane Carroll]. The Naval Detective's Chase; or, Nick, the Steeple-Climber. By Ned Buntline (pseud.). 1889.
26. McKenzie, Donald J. Under his Thumb; or, The Rival Detective's Clews. 1889.
27. James, Police Captain. The Revenue Detective. 1890.
28. Deane, Edwin S. Bob Younger's Fate. 1890.
29. Manly, Marline. The Poker King; or, A Cool Million at Stake. A Story of the Traps and Snares of New York. 1890.
30. [Urner, Nathan D.]. Gold-dust Darrell. By Burke Brentford (pseud.). 1890.
31. Weir, Mariposa. A Chase Round the World; or, A Detective By Chance. 1890.
32. Dale, Henry. Adventures and Exploits of the Younger Brothers, Missouri's Most Daring Outlaws. 1890.
33. Robertson, Alexander, M.D. Old Specie, the Treasury Detective; or, The Harbor Lights of New York. 1890.
34. Taylor, R. M. Detective Bob Bridger. 1890.
35. [Van Rensselaer, Frederick]. Muertalma; or, The Poisoned Pin. A Detective Story. By Marmaduke Dey (pseud.). 1890.
36. Merrick, Doctor Mark. The Great Travers Case. A Wonderful Story of a Most Remarkable Mystery. 1890.
37. Coryell, John R. A Woman's Hand; or, Detective Wit Against Lawyer's Wiles. 1890.
38. Sawyer, Eugene Taylor. The Los Huecos Mystery. 1890.

39. Robertson, Alexander. The Vestibule Limited Mystery. 1891.
40. Manly, Marline. Rube Burrow's League. 1891.
41. Matthew, Charles. Mabel Seymour. 1891.
42. Gaboriau, Emile. Caught in the Net. 1891.
43. ———. The Champdoce Mystery. 1891.
44. Du Boisgobey, Fortuné. The Red Lottery Ticket. 1891.
45. Gaboriau, Emile. The Detective's Dilemma. 1891.
46. ———. The Detective's Triumph. 1891.
47. Du Boisgobey, Fortuné. The Steel Necklace. 1891.
48. ———. The Convict Colonel. 1891.
49. Gaboriau, Emile. The Widow Lerouge. 1891.
50. ———. The Clique of Gold. 1891.
51. Du Boisgobey, Fortuné. The Crime of the Opera House. Two volumes. 1892.
52. Gaboriau, Emile. File 113. 1892.
53. [Jones, Clara Augusta]. Found Dead; or, The Charles River Mystery. By Hero Strong (pseud.). 1892.
54. [Coryell, John Russell]. The Crime of a Countess; or, The American Detective and the Russian Nihilist. By Nick Carter (pseud.). 1892.
55. McKenzie, Donald J. Face to Face. 1892.
56. [Coryell, John Russell]. A Titled Counterfeiter. By Nick Carter (pseud.). 1892.
57. ———. Fighting Against Millions. By Nick Carter (pseud.). 1892.
58. Lawson, W. B. The Dalton Boys in California. 1892.
59. [Coryell, John Russell]. The Piano Box Mystery. By Nick Carter (pseud.). 1892.
60. ———. A Stolen Identity. By Nick Carter (pseud.). 1892.
61. ———. The Great Enigma; or, Nick Carter's Triple Puzzle. By Nick Carter (pseud.). 1892.
62. ———. The Gamblers' Syndicate. The Story of a Great Swindle. By Nick Carter (pseud.). 1892.

So critical is the condition of these paperback novels that it may be some time before they are available for study and use.

The student of nineteenth-century mystery, crime and detective novels should have at hand, besides Summers's *Gothic Bibliography* and Wright's *American Fiction, 1876-1900* (both mentioned earlier), such valuable reference works as Dorothy Blakey's *The Minerva Press, 1790-1820* (London: Bibliographical Society, 1939 [for 1935]), Andrew Block's *The English Novel, 1740-1850* (London: Dawsons, 1962), the third volumes of *The Cambridge Bibliography of English Literature* (1940), and *The New Cambridge Bibliography of English*

Literature (1969), Edmund Miller's *Australian Literature* (Sydney: Angus and Robertson, 1956, rev. ed. [the original edition of 1940 is also of great value]), Michael Sadleir's *XIX Century Fiction* (London: Constable, 1951), and Wright's other volumes, *American Fiction, 1774-1850* and *American Fiction, 1851-1875* (San Marino: Huntington Library, 1969 and 1965).

From these bibliographies Hagen, in his *Who Done It?*, might have added an additional forty-eight titles to the three he assigned to the prolific Fergus Hume.

The opening of nineteenth-century paperback detective novels at UCLA continues slowly. But I hope to complete the job this next year and will provide a final report on the collection in the 1974 *Mystery & Detection Annual*.

AT THE BOTTOM OF THE POOL

By Mark McCloskey

THERE IS something white at the bottom of the pool
the weather is still open, there are no doors
tonight, only glass, cushions like bubbles,
fruit wine in white tureens, hashish-
confetti in the terrace shadows

there is something white at the bottom of the pool

there is bubble-music behind the wall,
the girl I saw at the party last weekend on the star-hill across from this one
is wearing the same panvelvet hair,
but there are flywheels between her lips
this time, my hands are iron gloves
before the greed of her breasts

something white at the bottom of the pool

it's not pink enough to go swimming,
the city fizzes below me and up the hills
like a stopped movie of the Milky Way,
I go to the other side of the house to the pool
and put my hand in, a ripple goes out from me —
snowflake, eyelid, fingernail of a baby

there is something white at the bottom of the pool

I am falling beneath it.

CLUES (FOR SUKEY)

By Mark McCloskey

THE DESCRIPTION of her is sketchy. Witnesses
say her hair is so pale it can't be real,
or there are false eyelashes in her purse,
or her small grin swindles magistrates
into valets, her uncertain voice
nightclubs into thickets where the moon shivers.
For they are partial who say these things—
the gamblers, the landladies with bum ankles,
the lawyers who can't sleep in their tufty beds
wanting her, the sopranos who want her secret.
And there are others, the Nazi types
—ski bums and chorus boys in musicals—
who play so hard at mirrors and amnesia
what she looks like underneath escaped them.
Even her parents contradict each other,
and her best friend is so devoted to music
he talks in notes about her as I do,
insisting it is impossible to find her
except in the mazes of my own craft,
as though the detective and magician were the same.

Ngaio Marsh. Green & Hahn Photography Ltd., Christchurch, New Zealand.

STARTING WITH PEOPLE

By Ngaio Marsh

IN HIS ADMIRABLE and astute probe into the origins and growth of detective fiction,[1] Julian Symons says that I "take refuge from real emotional problems in the official investigation and interrogation of suspects." This is almost a definition of one of the major limitations of the genre. I would question only the "take refuge" bit. The introduction of police procedure is not, I think, an attempt to avoid a further exploration of character but arises out of an unwilling and sometimes maladroit observance of the rules of the game. And it is at this point that the two main streams of crime fiction can be distinguished.

The classic form, originating in Poe, developed in varying degrees of excellence or banality by Conan Doyle and his followers and sustained with superb mastery by Agatha Christie, presents a puzzle and its solution. Characterization, however lively, is two-dimensional. Each person is given certain traits by which he or she can be readily distinguished. The characters perform after the manner of puppets and it is upon the manipulative skill of their creator that the success of the offering depends. This is detective fiction in its pure form and to say that the persons are silhouettes is not to belittle them. What three-dimensional figure has attained a wider fictional reality than the profile of a deerstalker, a hooked nose and a meerschaum pipe, or inspired as enduring an affection as the plump, natty, egg-headed, moustached marionette who for over fifty years has performed under the name of Hercule Poirot?

The second stream, to which I think I belong, is impure. It treats, or attempts to treat, of persons in the round and is obliged, constantly, to come to terms with the limitations of the genre. The purists, being wholly concerned with the posing of a conundrum, start—as I guess—with an articulate and severely defined plot, to which all else must be subservient. Whereas I, and I can speak only for myself, invariably start with people. With two or three or more people about whom I feel I would like to write. Because I am a maker of detective fiction I must involve one of them in a crime of violence. So I have to ask myself which of these persons is capable of such a crime, what form it would take and under what circumstances would he or she commit it. Very often I begin to write about these people in their immediate situation with no more than the scantiest framework for a plot and its denouement. This is a cockeyed method of setting about a strictly conventional form and it lands one with a great deal of re-writing. But it's the only way I can work and I fancy it illustrates one of the occupational hazards of the second stream of crime-writing.

Authors of this "impure" or denser type of whodunit are beset with pitfalls. Dorothy Sayers, for instance, toppled into one from which she never escaped: she fell in love with her own sleuth and from having started him off as a pretty tiresome two-dimensional Wodehouse pastiche, allowed him to grow into a sort of romantic monster. In the process her great gift for inventive plot-material became overlaid and enfeebled by novelistic embellishments. This unfortunate development was perhaps due as much to an error of taste as to the awkward transition from one form to another and could have been avoided if Miss Sayers had not so embarrassingly lost her head as well as her heart. The basic predicament that confronts every "novelistic" crime writer is this: the more deeply and honestly he examines his characters, the more disquieting becomes the skulduggery that he is obliged to practice in respect to the guilty party. And however bold he may be in the exploration of the party's inner motivation, there is at last one thought and its outcome, about which, if he is to maintain the puzzlement, he is obliged to be dumb.

Again, Julian Symons's point about police procedure is well taken. This problem, too, is endemic in the "impure" form of the crime novel. There is a certain, sometimes a formidable, amount of factual evidence, valid or misleading, that must be brought out. To avoid the outdated post-mortem-after-the-denouement technique, the author tries to introduce this material before the gaff is blown, tries to keep it as crisp as possible, tries to enliven and sustain it by maintaining atmosphere and characterization in the round. Only too often the result is an unhappy change of style and a disjointed book.

That this tightrope is not unwalkable has been proved by — for example — Symons himself, by Marjory Allingham and by an author who wrote long before detective fiction had been analyzed as a craft or restrained within a convention: Wilkie Collins.

And I am absolutely certain that if Charles Dickens had lived to complete *The Mystery of Edwin Drood* these difficulties would have been dealt with and we would have had the greatest of all detective-novels-in-the-round.

NOTES

[1] *Mortal Consequences* (New York: Harper and Row, 1972).

MICHEL BUTOR'S *PASSING TIME* AND
THE DETECTIVE HERO

By Thomas D. O'Donnell

As EARLY as *Passage de Milan*, and as recently as *Où*, Michel Butor
has evidenced in his works a view of reality that distinguishes him
from other practitioners of the French New Novel, and notably Robbe-
Grillet. Reality, in Butor's eyes, is a code system waiting to be de-
ciphered. The artist, or novelist, initially decodes the world around
him; he then re-codes his discoveries, by creating his work of art, which
the spectator-reader must in turn decode.

Butor's second novel, *Passing Time*, is no exception to this general
rule. The novel deals with Jacques Revel, a French clerk who has come
to the English industrial city of Bleston to work for a year in a rather
drab office. Starting in October, he passes his spare time in dubious
attempts to reconnoiter the city with the aid of a map purchased from
Ann Bailey, a store clerk with whom he will eventually become emotionally involved. These attempts lead him to visit Bleston's two cathedrals and its museum, all three of which contain works of art which
will help Revel to decipher his own situation. The nature of the city of
Bleston itself is partly elucidated by a detective story, *The Bleston
Murder*, which Revel purchases after about one month in the city.

In the course of his year's stay in Bleston, Revel develops a very
hostile relationship with the city. This hostility is counterbalanced by
his interest in Ann Bailey, which is in turn counterbalanced, and
finally replaced, by a fascination with Ann's sister, Rose. Having
rejected Ann, Revel purchases from her a ream of paper and begins to
record, in May, the events of his stay in Bleston beginning with his
arrival the previous October. As his recording task becomes increasingly complex and time-consuming, Revel sacrifices his already paltry
social life to it, and in so doing loses Rose Bailey to Lucien Blaise, another homesick Frenchman whom Revel had "adopted." Shortly after
Revel's attention is predictably redirected to Ann, he discovers that
Ann is engaged to James Jenkins, the only Blestonian Revel had been
able to call his friend. Revel returns to his native soil accompanied
neither by Ann nor by Rose, but rather by the manuscript journal of
his experience in Bleston.

Revel's ennuis in Bleston are aggravated by his lack of familiarity
with the English language: like the reader, he must constantly decode
the reality he encounters. His task will be facilitated to some extent by

the presence of clues scattered throughout the city; that of the reader by clues scattered throughout the book. One clue available to both Revel and reader is the detective story, *The Bleston Murder*. This title is, of course, ambiguous, in that it may refer to a crime committed against the city of Bleston, by the city, or merely within the city limits. Written under the pseudonym of J. C. Hamilton, by a novelist named Burton, *The Bleston Murder* involves a murder and the ultimate punishment of the criminal. By taking advantage of the presence of this author and work within *Passing Time*, Butor is able to point out a number of striking parallels between the artist, the detective and the heroes of classical myth.

Burton's novel is linked, in Revel's mind, to Bleston's Old and New Cathedrals: "Through a newspaper poster I had discovered J. C. Hamilton's detective story *The Bleston Murder*; through reading this I had discovered the Murderer's Window, which in its turn had given rise to this conversation with its closing words of advice to visit the New Cathedral. It was as though a trail had been laid for me, at each stage of which I was allowed to see the end of the next stage, a trail which was to lead me hopelessly astray."[1]

In fact, Burton's negative comments on the New Cathedral in *The Bleston Murder* have a strong effect not only on Revel but on James Jenkins as well. Jenkins, we discover, is the grandson of the sculptor who created the "particularly insipid" statuary of the New Cathedral, and is therefore a logical suspect when Burton becomes the victim of a murder attempt. Revel's suspicions, and our own, shift, however when it is discovered that Richard Tenn, attached to the Bailey family, may have been a model for the criminal in *The Bleston Murder*. As *Revel* has *revealed* the true identity of the author to each suspect, his concern over his probable responsibility leads him to do a certain amount of "detective work" during the frantic last months of his visit to Bleston. However, because he is so overwhelmed with his job, his journal and his interest in Ann and/or Rose Bailey, his investigation is token and superficial. Revel's investigation of the crime committed in Bleston is in fact only a reflection of his attempt to understand Bleston, "the city of Cain," and to grasp his own role as artist/detective.

George Burton's comments in *The Bleston Murder* provide a number of indications which clarify *Passing Time* and Butor's idea of the artist's role in society. In *The Bleston Murder*, the cricket player Johny Winn, murdered by his brother, is found lying on the "X" formed by intersecting shadows in the New Cathedral. His brother, killed by the detective, falls and bleeds in the red light projected by the Murderer's Window in the Old Cathedral. As Revel points out, "the book thus produced an optical illusion which was deliberately intended by the author" (p. 125). The superimposition of two murders in two cathedrals in *The Bleston Murder* has, in fact, the same effect as the non-chronological construction of *Passing Time*: the reader must choose between an impressionistic reaction to the book or a more careful reconstruction of the events it contains: "the narrative is not merely the projection on a flat surface of a series of events, it rebuilds these, as it were, spatially, since they appear differently according to the position occupied by the detective or the narrator . . ." (p. 168).

The phenomenon occurring in *Passing Time* is quite similar. A chronological approach to the events of Jacques Revel's year in Bleston not only would be boring but also would fail to raise the very questions that Revel must answer to keep his sanity: what made me betray George Burton? why was I so blind about Rose and Lucien? why was I so blind about Ann and Jenkins? The different presentations of "the architecture of events" in *Passing Time* vary, not according to the narrator's position or the detective's, but according to the stage of development Revel has reached in understanding these events, and according to the other events which have since occurred and which have colored his perception of them.

Because the detective story, and *Passing Time*, are written as architectural reconstructions rather than as plane projections, there is no reason why normal chronological order may not be reversed at times: "in detective fiction the story goes against the stream, beginning with the crime, the climax of all the dramatic events which the detective has to rediscover gradually; . . . this is in many respects more natural than the narrative proceeding without a backward look . . ." (p. 178). Thus, the simple chronological narration of October is abandoned at the end of one month, since only the most primitive of minds operates in a strictly chronological fashion. Because the formal elements of a novel must correspond to the reality they will convey, the narration almost *must* go backward: "the narrative gradually explores events anterior to the event with which it begins, and this, though it may disconcert some readers, is quite natural . . ." (p. 178). It is for this reason that Revel must work backward to discover the events leading up to his betrayal of Burton and to the loss of Ann Bailey.

To construct a diagram of the five monthly narrative sequences in *Passing Time*, noting the dates on which narrative patterns begin and the terminal dates towards which they tend, is to clarify the structural importance of certain key dates. If the numbers I through V represent the sequences begun in each of the novel's five parts, then patterns II, III and IV all are seen to begin with the weekend of May 31-June 1, the date of Revel's betrayal of the identity of the author of *The Bleston Murder*; patterns IV and V converge on the engagement of Rose Bailey and Lucien Blaise, and patterns I and III converge on February 29, the extra day of leap year, whose events are doomed to remain unrecorded. The rationale behind the patterns which emerge from such a structure diagram becomes clearer if *Passing Time* is treated as a detective story: "in detective fiction the story goes against the stream, or more exactly . . . superimposes two temporal sequences, the days of the inquiry which start at the crime, and the days of the drama which lead up to it, and . . . this is quite natural . . ." (p. 178). These two series may, in fact, overlap, if the future victim experiences threats or forebodings and asks the detective for protection.

These, then, are some of George Burton's ideas on the theory of the detective story, and their applications to *Passing Time*. Is *Passing Time* therefore a kind of estheticized detective story, a self-conscious Agatha Christie mystery? It is not, no more than *Passage de Milan*, with its discussion of the theory of science fiction, is Butor's answer to Jules Verne. On the contrary, it is a highly self-conscious novel, one whose main subject is the composition of a novel, and Burton (Butor + n = Burton) describes his ideal detective in much the same way that Butor thinks of the modern novelist, or artist in general.

Burton-Butor makes three main points about the role of the detective in society; each statement clarifies the role of the artist in society. First, all detective stories are based on two murders: that of the victim by the assassin, and that of the assassin by the detective. The first murder is the cause and the prefiguration of the second. The second murder, the pure and unpunishable murder of the assassin by the detective, is brought about through *truth*. Likewise, the corrupt elements of society, in this case, the modern industrial city, will be destroyed by the artist, who will use as his weapon the truth about that society and what it does to those who live within it.

The second point is that the detective is the real executor. Scotland Yard and the Federal Bureau of Investigation do not like the detective, because they are charged with preserving order in a dangerous situation, whereas the detective wishes to "disturb and probe, to expose and alter things" (p. 153). The detective's whole life is directed toward that moment of *truth* when he kills the assassin, "that moment when reality is transformed and purified by the sole power of his keen and accurate vision" (p. 153). He cleanses the world not only of the death of the victim, but also of the accompanying stain, and so in fact restores the harmony whose façade Scotland Yard and the Federal Bureau of Investigation are attempting to maintain. Similarly, the role of the artist in modern society is to transform reality, through the power and truth of his vision. In so doing, he may well produce art whose subject matter is irritating to the Establishment and whose formal qualities are condemned by the Académie Française. He will continue to be an artist, however, because he needs the truth of his art, just as Butor continues to write, stating that literature is a spinal column for him.

Third, Burton points out that the detective has much in common with Oedipus: each solves a puzzle, each kills the man to whom he owes his title. That each does so is predicted at his birth, or predictable by his nature, and each becomes "king" by this murder. The artist also solves a puzzle, that of fitting reality to form and form to reality. As a murderer, he is defined by his victim, society, and so needs society for his survival as an artist; on the other hand, to attack society is the natural thing for him to do. The regal nature of the artist is a reflection of his "privileged" position in society; society's ambivalent attitude toward the artist is reflected in turn by the inevitability of the fall of the Oedipal monarch.

The New Cathedral, which is the epitome of all things Blestonian, just as Bleston is the epitome of the modern industrial city, is a work of art, and yet is criticized by George Burton for its lack of artistic qualities. Jacques Revel ultimately takes issue with Burton's judgment, but Burton's judgment seems to be born out by Revel's own description of the Cathedral. While the New Cathedral may have a number of artistic qualities, it has very little art. There are no stained glass windows, and the interior of the building resembles the skeleton of a whale. The columns are covered with decorative statuary, representing appropriate floral and animal classifications: indeed, the church is not really very different from the University museum. The statue of the Virgin, "particularly insipid," is protected by a frieze of flies, emblematic of the city of Bleston (p. 159). The meaning of the New Cathedral will become clearer after an examination of the Old Cathedral.

The Old Cathedral is at least as Blestonian as the new one: just as the apartment house of *Passage de Milan* is built above the ruins of an abandoned church, the Old Cathedral was built on the ruins of a temple of war dating back at least to Roman times, and possibly further. This is the origin of the city's name, according to some: Belli Civitas, city of war. The name "Bleston" is also explained by the cathedral bells (Bells Town) which had cracked the walls of the building. Inside the Old Cathedral, Revel's eyes are continually drawn to the red lamp in the sanctuary, suggesting the fires which have always been part of Bleston's history. Most of Revel's description, however, is devoted to the stained glass windows, imported from France in the sixteenth century.

The apse of the Cathedral was to have contained a large window depicting the Lord presiding at the Last Judgment. On his immediate left were smaller windows depicting Imperial Rome, Babylon, Sodom and Babel. In the south transept, immediately adjoining, was a large

window showing the story of Cain. On the right-hand side, receiving
the Lord's benediction, were the cities of the blessed, starting with
papal Rome. In the north transept was a large window showing the
story of Abel.

As a result of a riot and over-zealous ringing of the bells, however,
the picture was very much changed. The Last Judgment was never
installed, and the other windows were all more or less destroyed with
the conspicuous exception of Cain's window, "the Murderer's Window." Moreover, Cain, the reprobate, is seen on the right as one approaches the altar, giving Revel the impression that the entire edifice
is dedicated to Cain.

Bleston is, in fact, Cain's city. Renaissance artists honored Cain, we
are told, as the father of the arts (p. 75); consequently, included with
images of Cain are smaller sections of the window dedicated to his
three sons, Jabal, Jubal and Tubalcain, the fathers of weaving, music
and metallurgy, respectively. Bleston has incorporated from this tradition all that belongs to modern industry and rejected the rest:

> Bleston, city of weavers and metal workers, what
> has become of your musicians?
> I hear the hoarse rattle of a lorry. (p. 75)

Even more striking is the scene in the window depicting Cain as a
bricklayer. The artist chose sixteenth-century Bleston as a model for
Cain's city, and so Cain became the symbolic founder of the industrial
city. The mark burned into Cain's forehead, protecting him from his
enemies, subsists in the penitentiary in the ninth district of the city.

The Old Cathedral is associated with a tradition of violence. Because
of the ambiguity of its relationship to the figure of Cain, its windows
were partially destroyed. The New Cathedral, on the other hand, represents an entirely different spirit. Every effort has been made to
avoid the ambiguity and the structural weaknesses of the Old Cathedral, but at the cost of erecting a building that is more museum than
cathedral, a building with few, if any, religious characteristics. The
role of the artist, we are led to suspect, is to create *his own* cathedral:
a work of art and a renewed society.

The Harvey tapestries, depicting eighteen incidents in the life of
Theseus, are noteworthy both in their role as a key to aid decoding and
in their mythological content. Like the Murderer's Window, they are
of French origin. They are arranged in five interconnecting rooms in
the Bleston Museum of Fine Arts, forcing Revel to zig-zag from panel
to panel in an imitation of the non-chronological structure of the novel
itself. The tapestries are also suggestive of the novel in that a single
panel may show events lasting for a duration of time rather than simp-

ly for a single instant. Each one may show several scenes in succession. Thus, Theseus appears three times in the fifteenth panel, showing his descent into Hades with Pirithoüs. This overlapping is once again an imitation of the structure of *Passing Time*, in which several of Revel's actions may be presented on a single page or in a single chapter. Revel's effort to decipher the city of Bleston is paralleled by his patient, personal approach to the Harvey tapestries, in which he initially recognizes only the common denominator of Theseus:

> If I had been spared this preliminary work, if I had had at my disposal a catalogue such as the one which has since taught me the names of these men and women and places, the tapestries would not have played so important a role in my life.
>
> What would I have learned, in that case, from these few printed lines? Far from giving me a desire to penetrate into the realm to which these tapestries are the gates, I think they would forever have prevented me from entering it, for even without appreciating their value I should have been satisfied, I should have made no further search, perhaps I should never have returned to these museum rooms. But being already involved in exploration of these enigmas when the guidebook came into my hands, I was able to assess its merits as well as its deficiencies and to extract all possible information from it. (p. 162)

Because Theseus, too, escaped from a labyrinth, Jacques Revel identifies with Theseus, and associates those about him with the other characters in the Theseus legend. Ariadne represents Ann Bailey, her sister Phaedra becomes Ann's sister Rose, Pirithoüs is Revel's fellow exile, Lucien Blaise, as is Dionysos consoling Ariadne. A conscious effort has obviously been made by the author to write his novel in conformity with certain elements of the story of Theseus. On many occasions, nonetheless, he departs from his pre-established mythological pattern. It must be emphasized here that Butor's purpose is not to rewrite the story of Theseus, in the manner of a seventeenth-century French tragedian. *Passing Time* is not simply an attempt to examine anew an old tradition in the light of industrial society. Rather, Butor has seen in the myth of Theseus and the labyrinth a parable for modern man and for the artist. We are all trapped in a labyrinth, and we must all find our own way out. For the artist, the way out is through his art. For the rest of us, Butor hopes that *Passing Time* will serve as "Ariadne's thread."

The legend of Theseus is not the only myth involved in *Passing Time*, however, and because of the overlapping of these other myths, characters overlap as well. We have already seen that Lucien Blaise corresponds to both Dionysos and Pirithoüs, at different times in the career of Theseus. Though Revel does not openly confirm our suspicions, there is ample evidence to attach Lucien's name to that of Hippolytus as well. Likewise, Rose Bailey is both Phaedra and Persephone. Most of the melding of characters that exists, however, has to do with Jacques Revel himself.

Revel is, first of all, Theseus. He never ceases to be Theseus throughout the entire novel. However, just as there are many similarities between the detective and Oedipus (p. 154), so too there exist similarities between Oedipus and Theseus:

> Their destinies indeed had much in common; each was brought up in ignorance of his birth and race, far from his native city; each slew the monsters threatening that city, cleared a road, solved riddles; and each killed his father . . . , and each by this means won a precarious throne, each at last was driven from that throne, each beheld his city in flames and died far away, powerless to help her. (p. 181)

Revel, like Oedipus, is a detective trying to solve a crime, the attempted murder of his father-figure, George Burton. Like Oedipus, he is finally forced to admit that he must be held personally responsible, and like Oedipus's, his punishment will be blindness, figurative if not real. The equation of Theseus and Oedipus serves to underline George Burton's earlier contention that the detective is himself a murderer.

Because he too is a "murderer" and an "artisan," Jacques Revel clearly participates in the tradition of Cain. Trapped under the soot of Bleston, Revel could hardly fail to see a brother in Cain offering his sacrifice to God: "The smoke rising from his altar has spread all over the sky above him and dropped down again to cover him" (p. 73). The similarities are emphasized by the fact that Cain, in the window, is wearing "a close-fitting cuirass with ribbons floating over his thighs, almost in the same attitude as Theseus at grips with the Minotaur, bending forward like him . . ." (p. 71). The closeness of the relationship between Revel and Cain is revealed later in the novel, as Revel describes another visit to the Old Cathedral:

> The effort strained my eyes so that the leaden lines began to quiver and dissolve, the red blood began to stream thickly down from Abel's wounds to Cain's red tunic in the light below, where the Almighty brands him on the forehead.
>
> The red blood streamed like a slow downpour through the red sky above the city, behind Jabal's looms, behind Jubal's orchestra, behind the forge of Tubalcain; then it spilled out from the Win-

dow over the walls and paving stones, even over the pews, even over my hands, most of all over my hands which were covered and steeped in thick, luminous redness, like a murderer's hands, as if I were condemned to murder, my hands in the center of the pool of blood, my hands in the center of the bloodstain spilled from the scene above, in the silence. (p. 205)

Revel is not only Cain, but also his father, Adam. During his first visit to the Old Cathedral, a girl, tentatively identified as Rose Bailey, bumps into him, causing him to fall, dirty his face and stain his raincoat. He cleans himself off with the handkerchief he had bought the previous day as a talisman for protection in the city of Bleston. Less than three weeks after his arrival in England he re-enacts Adam's fall through the influence of Eve, is stained by original sin, and is cleansed, all of this in front of the sculpted prophets of the Old Testament (pp. 52-53). Completing the cycle of the Old Testament, the detective-artist also plays the role of the Messiah:

> He cleanses this small fraction of the world from its offense, which was not so much the mere fact that one man has killed another . . . but rather the defilement that murder brings with it, the bloodstained shadows that it casts about it, and at the same time that deep-seated, age-old discord which becomes incarnate in the criminal from the moment when, by his act, he revealed its presence and aroused those vast buried forces which now disturb the hitherto accepted order of things and betray its fragility. (p. 153)

Passing Time is a detective story, certainly, but goes well beyond the traditional limitations of the genre. The most basic form of the detective story contained within *Passing Time* is *The Bleston Murder*. Not too surprisingly, this detective-story-within-a-detective-story reflects many of the elements of *Passing Time*; moreover, *The Bleston Murder* actually precipitates much of the intrigue of *Passing Time*, encouraging Jacques Revel to visit both cathedrals and causing him to become involved in an attempt on the life of the author. Revel's efforts to unravel the attempt on Burton's life (an attempt for which Revel must accept partial blame) parallel his efforts to understand, with benefit of hindsight, his loss of Rose and Ann. Thus, all basic elements of the novel's plot reinforce each other within the general framework of the detective story.

Butor, however, is not satisfied to examine the personal problems of a single French clerk exiled in Bleston; in order to broaden the scope of his novel, he obligingly points out the mythic qualities of his detective-hero. Revel participates in the myth of Oedipus, probably Western literature's original detective, and in the myth of Theseus, related to that of Oedipus. Moreover, the inevitable comparison of myth to complex makes Revel the image of us all; this extension is reinforced by the introduction of Adam's fall and the murder of Abel by Cain, clear biblical parallels to the Oedipus myth (cf. Dumézil).

Finally, the guilt of Revel/reader as Adam/Cain/Oedipus is to be cleansed by the artist/Messiah. Revel's work of art, his diary, is written in order to punish a criminal, in this case the city of Bleston itself. Bleston objects to this punishment by fire, literal and otherwise, and yet needs it in order to be reborn. Likewise, society accords only marginal tolerance to the detective, who must first lay bare society's wounds in order to heal them. The artist, then, will follow the detective's example: he is necessary to society, and grudgingly accepted, but will continue to play Sherlock Holmes to society's Inspector Lestrade.

NOTES

[1] Michel Butor, *Passing Time* (New York: Simon and Schuster, 1960), p. 82. All references are to this edition.

SIMENON: THE SHADOW AND THE SELF

AN INTERVIEW WITH GEORGES SIMENON

By J. Stuart Whiteley

THE INTERVIEW *which follows was broadcast as "The Mirror of Maigret" on 28 September 1971 over the ATV Television Network Ltd. London and is reproduced here through the courtesy of the Network. M. Simenon was interviewed over two days, 7 and 8 May 1971, by two distinguished British medical experts: Professor Francis Camps and Dr. J. Stuart Whiteley. Dr. Whiteley has subsequently written the introduction and other comments that accompany the interview. In printing the following material the editors of* The Mystery & Detection Annual *gratefully acknowledge the cooperation of Dr. Whiteley; that of the Administrators of the Estate of the late Professor Camps and of his widow, Dr. Ann Camps; and of course that of M. Georges Simenon himself.*

THE HOUSE at Epalinges above Lausanne is a white rectangular block built around three sides of a tarmac forecourt. There is no garden as such but the house sits at the head of a grass paddock delineated from the surrounding fields by a simple post and rail fence. The house is cleverly sited on the crown of a hill, with the ground sloping away all around. The main road is tucked out of sight under the brow of the hill so that from the patio in front of the house one can see only fields, the tops of trees and distant mountains, with the intervening landscape hidden below the line of sight.

Professor Francis Camps, the forensic pathologist, and I, a psychiatrist who works with psychopaths and criminals, came to the house on May 7th, 1971 to interview Simenon for a television film. We were both Simenon fans although neither of us had read all the four-hundred-or-so books that Simenon had written. We knew that Simenon was the most widely published author of this century and that, through this success, he had become a millionaire. We knew too that, at 68, Simenon lived in relative isolation with his twelve-year-old son in a house that he had designed himself. To run this house of forty-four rooms he had a staff of twelve including two private secretaries. What we did not know was how this man had been able to write over four hundred volumes in his lifetime and still continue to turn out books at the rate of four a year. We knew very little of Simenon the man as distinct from his work, and now had our chance to study for ourselves this literary giant.

The house is in an area where there are no other large or expensive residences. On the other side of the track leading up to the gate are the small holdings, sheds and humble cottages of several peasant farmers.

It is not the luxurious mansion of a millionaire but looks more like a sanatorium or seminary. Although the air is full of the sound of cowbells, within the house it is silent—because of the double glazing. To the left is the office accommodation, and a small undistinguished room which is really a book warehouse and holds shelf upon shelf of Simenon's works in all imaginable translations. The books are not set out as in an exhibition or assembled systematically as in a collection. Several volumes of the same book in, say, Russian may be next to a totally different story in an unrelated tongue. The books seem to be there simply because they exist. In the right-hand wing of the building are the kitchen and domestic quarters while in the center is the entrance lobby, a magnificently appointed and spacious reception room, and above that the living quarters. The house is functional, both as a place of business and as a domicile. In the grounds there is a separate building which contains a well equipped and fitted swimming bath such as any provincial town or college might envy. It is not the patio pool to unwind by and its still waters give off that special chlorinated smell of municipal swimming baths; one's footsteps echo from the high arched roof and tiled walls.

The silence of the house too is striking; the orderliness makes one feel at once untidy. The maid seems to move quietly and swiftly on tip-toe like a ballerina and always to be there when an ash tray is absent-mindedly reached for. One catches occasional glimpses of one of the secretaries hurrying expressionless down a corridor.

Once inside we were directed into the study which rather resembles a stage set: the desk with its row of pipes, the ornamental golden "think" ball beside the note-pad, the large wing-chair and the occasional table with the newspapers neat and fresh from the shop meticulously arranged upon it. One dare not touch.

Professor Camps and I made forced observations and halting conversation about the room as the cameras rolled. And then Simenon entered.

By now I am quite unsure of myself, over-awed by the occasion and lost for any form of real contact with the small but stocky, oldish man who clearly holds the house and occupants in a somewhat tense control.

My companion, the extroverted and genial Professor of Forensic

Medicine, is not so affected. He steps straight through the psychological barriers about Simenon and at once almost naively and intuitively makes contact.

Professor Camps (picking up the golden ball from Simenon's desk): Tell me, what is the significance of this?
Simenon: When I am working on a novel, and thinking about the next chapter, I like to walk around my office here and to play with something. (Simenon fingers the golden ball.) Or when I am sitting at the desk I do this. (He spins the ball on the leather top of the desk, making a high-pitched squeaking sound.) Little tricks, nothing else.
Prof. Camps: Did you have it especially made for you?
Simenon: Yes. It helps me to concentrate.
Dr. Stuart Whiteley: We were talking about your medical books before you came in. You have a comprehensive collection of technical books here. Do you use them when you are writing? Or do you just collect them?
Simenon: No, not at all. Collecting them is just a hobby for me. I like medicine. I like doctors, too; all my friends are doctors—about nine or ten of them. I think that medical men have the same interest in man—in mankind—as the writer does. I read medicine because if I were not a writer I would like to be, or probably would be, a doctor.
Prof. Camps: Of course you know that your Maigret ideology contains a basic principle that most of us who practice legal medicine teach: the resultant outcome of a case in the courtroom is not our concern. Our duty is to produce the scientific facts of the case.
Simenon: Yes, exactly. There is no morality or immorality in Maigret. Maigret is a civil servant; he does what he has to do. I wrote the first Maigret in 1928 at a time when I knew many police officers and officials in Liège. I was a reporter in those days. In fact, from the time I was sixteen to twenty I went to police headquarters every day, and of course I met a lot of policemen. When I came to Paris I decided to earn my living by writing pulp novels. I think you say pulp novels in England? Just cheap, cheap novels. I did it for three or four years, and doing so was not too bad. I began to learn how to have a character entering from this door and why another character should leave through that door. Just the material backgrounds of my novels. Then one day I decided that I was ready to try a second step, to go a little higher. I still didn't feel strong enough to attempt a plain novel, a straight one; I needed support. And this support was Maigret. Since then I never start with an idea. I start with a character. In fact, at the beginning of a novel I know two things: the main characters and the locale. Then I write down the names of my characters, their ages, even their phone

numbers and the names of their grandfathers. I know if the action will take place in a small provincial town, or in Paris, or in New York. I do need to know the characters and to believe in them.

I had to learn my trade little by little. I knew at the age of twenty that I wouldn't write my first true novel before the age of forty. When I was forty I decided, Oh, it's too early, maybe it will be fifty. And at fifty I said sixty. And now I say maybe eighty.

All the time I am writing a novel I must believe in my characters more completely than I do in the people I see out on the street or those who enter my home. Always I am interested in one very simple question: what can happen to this man? Who would push him to the end of himself? As soon as I name my main character I become him. It is not my intelligence which writes the novel, but my impulses. I believe in my characters more than in myself.

Prof. Camps: Once you have started you have to go on?

Simenon: Once I begin I have to write very fast. I write a novel now in about seven days because physically I can't stay longer in such a nervous state of being something or somebody else. It is not easy to be somebody else for a long time. When I get into this state my children remark, "I suppose your novel is about a very old man?" "Why?" "The way you walk and speak and behave right now." They say this because all day I continue to play the character. You know, what interests me in police novels, and the reason I sometimes have the temptation of being a police inspector, is the fact that I have a man inside of myself and I have to discover everything possible about him. It is like the doctor trying to make a diagnosis. My job is not as physical as the doctor's, however.

Prof. Camps: But it is in fact great art.

Simenon: Yes.

Prof. Camps: Putting yourself in another person's position, getting under his skin, seeing what he is looking at—it is a very difficult thing to do?

Simenon: Yes, it's difficult and it's also very tiring.

Prof. Camps: It is?

Simenon: And sometimes it is, perhaps, disgusting, because you discover that you yourself have a little—not much—but a little of the same tendencies as the man within. You begin to say, "But in the same situation maybe I would do the same." And soon you are not really quiet about yourself.

Prof. Camps: This is a familiar response. Inbau, from Northwestern University in Chicago, wrote a book on interrogation and described interviewing a young sex killer. Just at the moment of the completion of the interview the father came in and said to the boy, "You didn't do it." And the boy answered, "Yes, I did, Dad. And Doctor Inbau almost did it too." (General laughter)

> I feel even more out of place as they yarn, about places and people mutually known, but at the same time I begin to be conscious that Simenon is watching me.
>
> From time to time I put in a question about this or that aspect of the writer's life and antecedents and little by little Simenon answers more fully. Then the chat goes off course again as the Professor, enjoyably puffing the pipe-full of special tobacco that Simenon has proffered him, launches into another anecdote. I await the opportunity to intervene, more confident now for I am in my accustomed role as a psychotherapist. My colleague is the co-therapist or catalyst in our triad and Simenon has accepted the role of patient.

Simenon: That's marvelous. But I remember a conversation we had here two years ago when Charlie Chaplin was dining with us. After dinner the discussion turned to psychotherapy and sociology, and I said that in fact both of us are psychopaths. And Chaplin agreed: "Sure, but the difference between us and other psychopaths is that they pay to be cured and we are paid to cure ourselves."

Dr. Whiteley: Do you think you are curing yourself through your books?

Simenon: Yes.

Dr. Whiteley: I remember that in your "Notebook" you talked about an uncle—I think you called him a tramp—who was the black sheep of the family. What were the things you liked about him? Why were you attracted to him?

Simenon: It is complicated to explain. I have always been tempted by what I call complete liberty. To be completely free a man must be a tramp because only then does he cut himself off from the rest of the world. The tramp is alone. He doesn't depend on anybody or anything. He's just a tramp. I used to think sometimes—and I find myself doing it even now—that maybe I could finish as a tramp under a bridge in Paris.

Dr. Whiteley: Unhappily as a tramp.

Simenon: No, happily.

Dr. Whiteley: Happily? Do you feel that tramps are happy, then?

Simenon: Yes, it's their superiority. It is superiority not to need all those gadgets, not to need a house, a woman, anything. You just sleep on the stones. You eat some bread with a piece of sausage and a bottle of wine. That's all. I consider that superiority.

Dr. Whiteley: But you're cold and hungry and you have no human contacts. Wouldn't this be a very unhappy life, then?

Simenon: I don't think so.

Dr. Whiteley: My experience of tramps has been that they are very much the sort of people who have been unable to fit into society because they have been mentally ill. Some kind of disintegration has led them to this situation.

Simenon: Yes, but it is a voluntary disintegration, and that's the difference. Once in Paris, under a bridge, I met an old tramp who had been a doctor in Strasbourg for thirty years and who one day said, "Enough of it. I will be a tramp." And he became a tramp. I also met a Professor of Psychology—this one in Grenoble—and he had become a tramp too.

Dr. Whiteley: But in a much more comfortable way you have been a tramp, haven't you, if I may say so? You have voyaged around the world, for example?

Simenon: I went to Africa in 1928 when it was still very wild. I went to visit a tribe where there were still cannibals. Oh yes, I play the tramp. But I am not a true one, you know. It's too easy to play the tramp!

Prof. Camps: What do you think of Van Gogh?

Simenon: He was a real man, but he was also crazy. Like many painters and, maybe, many writers.

Dr. Whiteley: It seems to me that you see Maigret as all good. He is a very stable, incorruptible, moral person. Whereas the main character of most of your books (who, incidentally, is usually a man; I cannot remember one where the main character is a woman) is a man who is perhaps an immoral character; certainly a bad person. There is a strange contradiction here. You live Maigret part of your time and the bad character other parts of your time.

Simenon: Yes, that's true. But maybe you shouldn't call these men "bad." I know them well. Somebody said—I cannot remember who— "We are all criminals but we don't all have the opportunities." I mean that there is the question of responsibility. I don't believe in total responsibility. Even a criminal is not wholly responsible. Even if the psychiatrist says he is responsible, I say no.

Dr. Whiteley: But surely one acquires conscience, either through the influence of parents or through the influence of one's fellow beings, or perhaps through the thing one is taught at school? Surely one does acquire responsibility?

Simenon: My youngest son is only twelve years old. Sometimes I am sad about the fact because he will not have his father very long. But on the other hand I feel younger myself because of him and because of my daughter who is 17 or 18 now.

Prof. Camps: Is she married?

Simenon: No. Unfortunately, she is in a psychiatric hospital, though not for very long. She is under the care of a neuro-surgeon, you know. But what can I do? I have not taught my children any kind of morality; morality changes from one country to another. In one country you can have ten wives, in another one, or sometimes half a one. Divorce is permitted in some countries, not in others. The poor Italians, for example, cannot divorce. Morality seems to change everywhere every thirty or forty years; so why believe in it?

Dr. Whiteley: But surely you teach your children some rules of social conduct?

Simenon: Yes. If they can look at themselves in the mirror without being disgusted, they are all right.

Dr. Whiteley: In your early life, when you felt free, like the youth of today who are often rebellious and anti-authoritarian, did you conform to the law and order of society. Or were you something of an anarchist?

Simenon: I was anti-conformist. I was never a conformist. Always against, never for.

Dr. Whiteley: And yet there is so much conformity in your life; I seem to find evidence of it all the time. There are obviously two sides to the coin.

Simenon: Well, I know what you mean and it's true that at the age of twenty I was against everything—society, parents, teachers, everybody.

Dr. Whiteley: Against both parents?

Simenon: Not against my father. On the contrary, he was always a kind of god for me. But my mother, no. She died three months ago at the age of ninety-one, and I must confess that at the end I was not very moved. We never had any relationship.

Dr. Whiteley: You had a feeling of real compatibility with your father, something that is very important for a son to possess?

Simenon: Yes, certainly. But now I think we had better continue tomorrow morning.

After the first day's interview the production crew, myself and Professor Camps mulled over the proceedings in a hotel bedroom in Lausanne. Even the luxury hotel at the lakeside seemed to fit into the atmosphere created by the Simenon meeting. It was built on gracious lines, sumptuously furnished yet largely deserted, and the rooms and corridors had the mysterious air of the hotel in *Last Year at Marienbad*. It had become quite clear and accepted by us all that the encounter had become a psychiatric interview, therefore I was pressed for my opinion on the further development.

At the time I commented on camera: "He began to talk about

his family and about his daughter who is mentally ill and I think this must have been the time when he decided that he could talk more freely. The other thing that was so striking today was his obsessionality—the rigid almost ritualistic way in which he conducts his life.

"Obsessional people are usually keeping something under lock and key—they're guarding their own emotions—they're keeping something under control—they're keeping something inside them which they fear may get out, be out of control and do something dreadful—and one wonders what it is that Simenon—this million-aire—fears even at this stage. What is it that he fears is going to get out and somehow wreck him—somehow wreak destruction? One thing of course that is inside him is this preoccupation with crime, his preoccupation with the bad aspects of life, and with what he fears as an awful force within from which he has constantly to guard himself. He gave us glimpses of it and presumably he got glimpses of this himself: violence, criminality, sexuality, mental illness—all of these things are somehow moving about in the back of his mind. He tired, or said he tired, and rather abruptly brought the shutters down again on his life. I just wonder what will happen tomorrow?"

I felt that I would have liked to have been able to continue the first day's interview without a break and that we had now reached a crucial stage. Facts and feelings were being expressed by Simenon in a way that had not hitherto been expressed in his autobiography, *When I Was Old*, for instance. I feared that the break would allow him to reinstate his defenses, even to contradict or deny his previous statement, and thus to summarily dismiss us.

This would not have been unreasonable, for in all honesty we were intruding into an individual's personal life in a public situation through the use of professional skills which ethically should be devoted to the private well-being of the individual rather than to the satisfaction of public curiosity. At the same time I felt I must go on even more single-mindedly with the psychiatric case-taking, so fascinating was the story that was unfolding, and that the decision to make public or not the results should be taken by Simenon and John Goldschmidt, the film's director. I remained a technician just as much as were the camera men and the sound recordist.

The next day we presented ourselves at Epalinges punctually and were shown to our chairs of the previous day. The room was as before. Only the newspapers had been changed.

Simenon entered. He sat down, arms on the chair sides and faced me as I sat expectantly in my side-chair. Professor Camps at the desk took in the situation, filled up his pipe and sat back. Simenon *was* going to talk on.

Dr. Whiteley: Yesterday we had reached the very interesting point where you'd begun to tell us about your childhood and your life with your parents. I feel that this information is very important, particularly in relation to your observations about raising your children, about not imposing any moral discipline on them.

Simenon: Yes, because my mother was very religious. She went to mass every morning at six o'clock. I was sent to Catholic school, where everything was very severe, everything was taboo. I hate taboos. I had the impression of living in a world where everything was forbidden, you understand? And so very early I set myself against such a world. I remember when my mother said, "You have to respect your parents," I said, "It's a word I don't understand." "Which word?" "Respect." Why respect? What is respectable and what is not respectable is very difficult for a young boy to understand. Everything I heard in my youth was to respect my home, respect the neighbors, respect old people, respect pregnant women. And so I started to be against everything. And during the first war, around 1916, I almost became a delinquent. In fact, I *was* a delinquent. My father was a very quiet and happy man. He had been a clerk in Liège. Maigret looks more like my father than anybody else. My mother, on the contrary, was a very complicated woman and a very ambitious one. She came from a family who twenty years before had been rich. But in my time we didn't have much money; we always had five or six lodgers in the house. My father didn't even have the right to sit in his own armchair because of the student lodgers. My mother was always saying about the writing he was doing, "What do you do with all this writing? It has no value. You don't earn your living with it?" At the end my wife was the winner—

Dr. Whiteley: You said your wife. You meant your mother?

Simenon: Yes, I meant my mother. All those women I mix together. Anyway, my mother won the game because my father died at the age of forty-two and two years later my mother married a civil servant.

Dr. Whiteley: Do you feel that in fact you draw female characters as well as you do male?

Simenon: Some people tell me I am too severe and unjust with women. It is possible that I am expressing experience, not just my own, but the experience of all the people I know and of all my friends. I think that usually the man believes he is head of the family. But in fact he is almost nothing; it is the woman who is the chief of the family.

Dr. Whiteley: Could you possibly tell us of your experience with other women?

Simenon: Yes. My first wife I divorced in America. When we got divorced I discovered that she was as interested in money as my mother was. Then I took a second wife; but that is another case. I never saw my mother for thirty years. But last December I found myself sitting on her bed seeing her sink lower and lower. And then she died. Now something characteristic has happened to me. I never thought about her when she was alive but now that she is dead I have the feeling that I have missed something.

Dr. Whiteley: Perhaps you miss the feeling of her constant reproach?

Simenon: Maybe. Or perhaps just the feeling of having a mother. But to return to the point, I don't think I am too severe with women. For example, I wrote two or three books recently about young girls—seventeen, eighteen or nineteen years old—and I believe I have been very kind with them.

Dr. Whiteley: But these are young girls?

Simenon: Young girls, yes.

Dr. Whiteley: The age of your daughter, in fact?

Simenon: Yes, the age of my daughter.

Dr. Whiteley: You mentioned her illness briefly. Is it something that worries you a great deal, something that troubles you?

Simenon: Yes, a great deal. She is in a psychiatric ward and she is losing one year or maybe two from her life; I don't know when she will be free. But she isn't keeping up with her friends and her class, she isn't working, she does almost nothing. You know what happens in psychiatric wards: they make dolls or do some little work of that sort. It is very sad. It was only last month that she came back home for a week. Otherwise, for the remainder of the year I don't see her at all.

Dr. Whiteley: Don't you go to visit her?

Simenon: No, no. I don't have the right.

Dr. Whiteley: How do you feel about that?

Simenon: I feel terrible. I only have the right to one telephone call a week.

Dr. Whiteley: And whose discipline is this, then?

Simenon: I don't know. I do have complete confidence in the doctor, Professor Duronne; perhaps you know his name? For twenty years he has been one of my best friends. With one patient he conducts psychotherapy, with another he administers drugs, with a third he undertakes a long psychoanalysis. My wife, you know, is in another psychiatric ward in the same hospital.

Dr. Whiteley: What are your feelings about that? You must be—

Simenon: I am alone. Loneliness, I suppose, must be the case with everybody. I think man is always alone.

Dr. Whiteley: Your relationship with your second wife was a much closer and more intimate one than that with your first wife? A much happier one?

Simenon: Well, yes and no. When I met her in the United States—she is Canadian and was working in New York—she struck me the very first day as what in France we call a bird for the cat. She was so unstable—she had no stability at all. One day she was gay and foolish, another day she would be on her bed. So I said, maybe I will cure her. I will give her security and pride in herself. And I tried and tried, very hard, to give her everything I can. She has a life that is as easy as possible. From the first day we met she knew I was seeing other women, and she didn't care at all.

Dr. Whiteley: She didn't care at all?

Simenon: Not at all.

Dr. Whiteley: And did you feel any sense of guilt for what you were doing?

Simenon: Not at all, not at all. I never have the idea that making love can cause guilt. I must say that I very seldom make love to the wife of a friend or what you would call an honest woman. Most of the time the women are on the fringe of honesty and dishonesty. They're not whores exactly. Sometimes dancers, who have much better bodies generally than the honest women. And they are always beautiful, otherwise they wouldn't be dancers. I am always satisfied with these women. I never feel resentment afterwards, never any kind of disgust, as so many men do. On the contrary, I feel that making love is a beautiful thing. I just cannot understand why it must happen with only one woman in a man's life. A life with just one woman I do not understand.

Dr. Whiteley: But most people follow this pattern?

Simenon: No, they say they follow it, but they don't. I have often talked to women about this matter, and they are perfectly honest in what they say. If you knew the stories of all the men who go to bed with them, or try to, you would understand that very few men sleep only with their wives.

Dr. Whiteley: Were any of your relationships lasting, or were they brief and purely sexual encounters?

Simenon: I never spent two or three hours with a woman without feeling a kind of—I can't say *sensibilité* or sensuality, but friendship—yes, friendship for three hours or for a day. I do respect every one of those women, even the last whore. I respect such women and treat them with as much respect as I do any other woman. There is a very pleasant kind of rapport. In fact, when I finish a novel I have to go and see one or two women, maybe three. It's a necessity. It is "The End," you know. I have said that when I write "The End" to a novel I am very happy. But the happiness comes when I can go and see a woman.

Dr. Whiteley: In many of your stories you present a character who is well controlled and leading a relatively normal life. Then an incident happens and his life changes completely. It is as if his subconscious self comes to the surface. Is there an incident like this in your own life?

Simenon: Yes and no. My divorce from my first wife took less than five minutes to decide. In five minutes everything was done. It was a day like any other at three o'clock in the afternoon. I remember we were in the garden and I realized I wanted a divorce. She said, "Why?" "I don't know, but we will get divorced." And we did.

Dr. Whiteley: And did your life change then?

Simenon: My life changed.

Dr. Whiteley: In what way?

Simenon: I took another wife, completely different. So life became different too.

Dr. Whiteley: Well, was it different, or—?

Simenon: Oh yes, it was different. My first wife was very jealous, so I had to tell stories every time I went to see another woman. A man never forgets how a wife humiliates him. It's a humiliation to invent a story. So the first question I asked my second wife before we married was, "Are you jealous?" And I told her that almost every day I would be seeing other women. She said, "Okay; if you don't fall in love with them I don't care." So you see it was a different life.

Dr. Whiteley: And so in fact you were then able to be free and to live out all the fantasies you had repressed?

Simenon: That's it.

Dr. Whiteley: This is very much like many of your characters.

Simenon: Yes, that is true.

Dr. Whiteley: One thing I wonder about: your mother had a very repressive attitude about sexuality?

Simenon: Yes, and I remember when I was sixteen and had already had sex with many girls my mother was still praying in church every morning that I remain a virgin until my marriage. A funny idea. We can't understand it any more.

Dr. Whiteley: A little while ago, when you talked about your family and then very intimately about your daughter, I felt that from that moment on our interview changed and we were able to talk much more freely.

Simenon: Yes, and I am not ashamed about anything I said. I am just a man, so why try to show myself better than I am?

*   *   *   *   *

AT THE END *of the television interview Simenon, still before the cameras, talked about his views with his friend and former agent, Therese de Saint Phalle, who had just joined him.*

Simenon: I am a kind of public man, since my income comes from the public. And so the public has a kind of claim on me. There are things they want to know, and must know, and I consider I must explain. It is my duty.

I have a theory that I have in myself the worst and the best, and I am afraid that the worst will be more important than the best. I am not basically a writer, a novelist. I am a businessman. I have all my rights —literary rights, movie rights, publishing rights. We sign more contracts here than do most of the publishers in Paris.

One of the Professors asked me if I liked Van Gogh. I said yes. But I didn't think right away about the reason for the question. Later I thought, Oh God, I understand now! I remember the whole life of Van Gogh and I realized maybe they were comparing me with Van Gogh. Because Van Gogh was completely unconscious of what he was doing. It was the same with me. We are both the same. Perhaps I am not completely crazy but I am anyway a psychopath, and the Professors know it, I am sure.

* * * * *

It seemed to me then that what Simenon was trying to work out in this interview was just how far he could go in his discovery of himself. Could he come to grips with the things within? If he faced up to himself, what would happen? I thought that the outcome might well be a complete breakdown and he would be a mentally ill person himself. And therefore he kept acting out the problems and conflicts, and avoiding the real issues. He gets a little further towards understanding himself, but he continues to write, to put his problems down on paper rather than facing them in real life.

If Simenon ever were to reach a solution, and to come to know himself, perhaps he would stop writing. I commented that there would be no further need to try and probe for discovery of the secrets within. But I am sure he will never achieve this solution.

During the course of this interview, which took two days to conduct, I felt that something important happened: the general conversation became a psychiatric interview. The exchange of polite words became an exchange of information in a psychiatric interview. There was also an exploration of feelings and the working out of something between the three of us, and I think that this was very meaningful. I think, too, that Simenon saw it as a psychiatric interview with all that that implies—in other words that he was the patient and that there was something wrong with him.

WINDING UP

When it was all over we spoke a few non-committal words among ourselves. Simenon conducted us into the reception room and simultaneously a quiet maidservant arrived bearing champagne in a silver wine cooler.

Simenon spoke freely with the Professor, a little less so with me (or me with him) now that our roles were changed and the film technicians were clearly posted to an outer situation in the two-tier circle that we formed. Nevertheless Simenon indicated that they should be given a drink. He did not converse with them. Striving for some conversational gambit I expressed a genuine liking for his paintings, and asked if he was a collector. Not really a collector, he repeated, but friends like Bernard Buffet or Picasso would give him pictures from time to time! I asked if it were possible to see these and Simenon delightedly acquiesced. Suddenly the atmosphere was liberated from the formality of the day's interviewing. The camera men abandoned their champagne and reached for their equipment. In a small but otherwise bare room in the "office" corridor were some twenty or thirty paintings arranged as if in a gallery. Simenon stopped before a Picasso and jocularly compared it with the adjacent picture which, he said, was painted by a schizophrenic in the local psychiatric hospital.

"There is no difference you see" he chuckled, metaphorically digging me in the ribs. Certainly the pictures were equally well framed, lit and hung.

"But there are differences" I countered. The disorganization, the splitting and fragmentation of the schizophrenic's picture, the typical breaking up into many parts which then covered the canvas could be contrasted with the organized, indeed draughtsmanlike, break up and juxtaposition of parts in the Picasso painting. There was, too, a clear and uncluttered background in the master's painting against which the object was set.

"Then look at these," went on Simenon. Across the room were a series of sketches of stick-like figures resembling those in an Egyptian frieze, which he said were painted by another mental patient using a twig and sump-oil from a car (there being no other materials available).

"And they have been sold for thousands of dollars in New York," proclaimed the beaming Simenon.

AFTER THOUGHTS

Reading the transcript of the interviews and watching the film again and again, one struggles to produce a justifiable summary or evaluation of Simenon, the man.

It seemed to me that in Simenon we had a living, working model of Jung's conception of the Shadow and the Self. Contrasting yet balancing parts, the Self in the conscious and the Shadow in the unconscious, each influencing the other to produce the individual as we know him. In all that Simenon did these two halves were accorded their outlet. We had the obsessional orderliness of his household, his timetable and his professional work; but the chaos of his personal life. There was the uprightness of Maigret but the dark and sinister goings-on in the non-Maigret books.

It is trite, of course, to say that a writer lives out his fantasies on paper. Yet Simenon does this so patently that it has to be said. Which, one may ask, is the real Simenon? Is he the correct and controlled individual who plunges singularly into the swimming pool on the stroke of six o'clock each morning, has total charge of all his international business, and allows no interference with his set course of actions? Maigret—the loved, accepted and successful image—would be the persona of this aspect of Simenon's life. Or is the restless individual playing out those different life-styles—the Middle West rancher, the Montmartre bohemian, the alcoholic writer, the African explorer, the off-shore yachtsman—nearer the true Simenon? Are the identities portrayed in turn no more than defenses against the deep, dark and fearful person that Simenon *might* be should the Shadow be unleashed and depose the Self?

In the non-Maigret books—which are the ones that Simenon prefers and which certainly have the more genuine and authentic feeling to the reader—the Shadow figures play out the innermost fantasies.

Are the characters mad or bad to be as they are? It seems to be a recurring question for Simenon and one which he as the writer seldom answers but leaves for us, as readers, to decide. Are madness and badness anyway no more than facets of the normality that encompasses us all, asks Simenon.

Is there really a difference between the emotional and artistic expression of the professional artist and that of the schizophrenic? Simenon seems to urge us to say there is no difference. But if there is no difference and we are all mad or bad in parts, then what happens if control is lost? Somehow Simenon seems to vacillate between control and uncontrol, between freedom and restraint, without striking a satisfactory balance.

Simenon is discreet and difficult to contact or meet, yet he almost impulsively puts himself forward to be interviewed—often by journalists whom he despises for their lack of perception and skill. Doctors on the other hand he seems to venerate in an equally unjustifiable way.

The autobiography *When I Was Old* is a series of day-to-day jottings, haphazard and without form or continuity. The happenings of the day, thoughts from the past, trivial or important viewpoints and occasional insights, jostle each other on the pages. The book has always struck me as being the notes of a psychoanalysis. The origin of the book was in fact rooted in the despair that Simenon experienced as a direct consequence of his second wife's mental illness. When deeply troubled he would take himself off to a tower room in the château that they then shared and work out his feelings in the diary. Thus it became something of a self-analysis and it ceased at a point when the ultimate crisis passed and "D," his wife, finally had to leave the household.

Simenon seems to have little need of people. The emotional relationships he has made have often been disastrous, leaving him a rather lonely man as the years pass by. The contacts he makes, as exemplified by the sexual ones, are unemotional and cursory. He is self-sufficient and independent of others but maintains this emotional aloofness uneasily. His youngest son was the one person we met with whom Simenon still has some obvious bond of feeling. Pierre, an orderly and serious looking school-boy, appeared from time to time as sessions ended and the business was relaxed. He and his father could simply touch and grin at each other or joke familiarly. It was good to see.

Simenon's greatest fear, he said, was to be incapacitated, to suffer a stroke and be paralyzed, thus finding himself in the care of others and lacking control over his body and perhaps, too, over his own mind. The fear of illness and what that may imply is referred to in his interview published in the Swiss journal *Médecine et Hygiène* (1968). In the house at Epalinges there is even a fully equipped but as yet unused operating theatre.

It was with sadness therefore that I read in an English newspaper in Spring, 1973, that Simenon had left the big house at Epalinges and was living in a small flat in Lausanne because he had been suffering from dizzy spells. The talk of dizzy spells and being knocked off balance, in reality and figuratively, recurs in the *Médicine et Hygiène* interview and perhaps again points to the precarious balance that Simenon perceives in his own personality as he proceeds through life.

Simenon is like the anti-hero of the non-Maigret books, a person about whom we know a great deal of intimate information and yet who remains an enigmatic figure glimpsed briefly, as through a mist, sitting alone on a quay-side as one's boat glides out into the busy sealanes.

CONSIDER, SIR,
THE HYACINTH HAIR

By John Robertson

consider, sir, the hyacinth hair
freshly plucked from yonder head
do notice how the thick tresses
—stone grey
lie across the hearth, alien

hair cleaved there
curls on the stone

and do notice what remains . . .
— the roots
clotted with fragments of scalp, shear

force weeded
a few dappled with blood

a few spartan roots for planting

fleshy hands
may transplant those tubers
in particularly cruel dirt

unaware of morbid
death-beds (stirring
in time)

indifferent to the gravity

April
will ponder those stems
(single and double)
perhaps grey
perhaps white

and sanguine blooms

237

PROGRESS OF A CRIME WRITER

By Julian Symons

I SUPPOSE I must have been eight or nine years old when I began to read crime stories. The large box-like Victorian house in Clapham where I grew up did not contain many books. One not very large case held them all, and they were an odd lot, ranging from something called *Jack's Encyclopaedia*, through a comic novel named *My Friend— Bilhooley* and several volumes of crime stories, to George Moore's *Celibate Lives* and a couple of novels by F. Marion Crawford. I consulted *Jack's Encyclopaedia* frequently, and read all the other books, although *Celibate Lives* was taken away from me, I suppose on the ground that George Moore was an unsuitable author for a child. The crime stories were the books I liked best.

They included Guy Boothby's *Dr. Nikola*, Richard Marsh's *The Beetle*, a collection of Sherlock Holmes stories, and *Paul Beck* and its successor *Young Beck*, by F. McDonnell Bodkin. I read the Beck stories even more often than those about Holmes, and they made a great impression on me, particularly a tale about two card cheats who operated through a verbal code, and a story about a sweepstake on the length of a ship's daily run. *Young Beck* is a scarce book, and I suppose must be worth something today, but my mother got rid of it in the course of a clearing-out process before the War.

The appetite grew. A couple of years later I had developed a passion for Edgar Wallace, and used to go to the public library and hang around the returns trolley, ready to pounce on any Wallace book. I read *The Crimson Circle* when it was serialized in the *Daily Express*, and was amazed when the villain turned out to be the brilliant private detective who was helping the police, indignant when one of my brothers said that this had been obvious from the start, more indignant yet to be told by my eldest brother AJ that I ought to stop reading such trash. But a couple of years later I suppose I was expressing tacit agreement with him. A process of self-education in relation to fiction, which began with the work of Aldous Huxley and James Branch Cabell, widened very rapidly. I moved on from Huxley and Cabell to writers as varied as Joyce, Wyndham Lewis, Mary Butts, decided that no middlebrow fiction was of any interest at all, and turned away from fiction altogether to reading poetry and criticism.

Yet I never lost interest in detective stories. It is difficult to remember exactly one's reading habits, but certainly during the early Thirties

I read a great many detective stories as they were published — J. J. Connington, Freeman Wills Crofts, Christie and Sayers, as well as congenial Americans like Van Dine and Ellery Queen. I read *The Maltese Falcon* and *The Glass Key* very soon after they appeared with the minimum of publicity in England, and was one of the English readers of *Black Mask*, which was at that time a cult paper for a few young intellectuals. The best current writing in America, we used to say, was not that of turgid Wolfe, dull Sinclair Lewis, or clodhopping James T. Farrell, but the direct stories of action found in *Black Mask*. Hemingway? Yes, he had learned something from Hammett. Faulkner? *Sanctuary* was undoubtedly a good thriller. About all this there was obviously some affectation, and it wasn't meant quite seriously, but I am far from admitting that we were altogether wrong. I would still much rather read the best of Hammett than Wolfe, Lewis or Farrell.

Another member of this little *Black Mask* admiration society was my friend, the Scottish poet Ruthven Todd — indeed, I think it was Ruthven who introduced me to the magazine. My first crime story was written as a result of our friendship. We lived opposite each other in a Pimlico square, and met three or four times a week to drink and talk. In 1936 Ruthven had some sort of job working at the Surrealist Exhibition which amused or shocked London in that year. He knew a good many of the Surrealists and I had met one or two of them, and in the course of some drinking sessions long after the Exhibition was over, we planned a book that should have a similar exhibition as a background, and in which friends should be introduced, libelled, and either killed off or appear as particularly nasty suspects. Ruthven buzzed with bizarrely ingenious ideas, but never got down to any actual writing. He used some of the ideas, or others equally ingenious, years later in 1945, when under the name of R. T. Campbell he wrote ten detective stories in six months to pay off some debts. Did he write ten books or twelve, were ten published or eight? This is a nice minor literary problem. *Death Is Not Particular, Death Is Our Physician, No Man Lives Forever*, and *The Hungry Worms Are Waiting* were announced, but did they ever appear? The publisher, John Westhouse, is long since defunct and cannot be consulted. The British Museum catalogue is uninformative. Ruthven himself now writes from his home in Majorca that these four books were "probably written but not published." I like that "probably": it is very much in the spirit of *The Immaterial Murder Case*, the book that in the end I wrote alone, although the original inspiration of it came from Ruthven. Indeed, inspiration carried further, for the most recognizable figure in the story was a caricature of him. When the book was finished I did not show it to Ruthven, or send it to a publisher, but put it away in a drawer. The whole thing had been a joke, and the joke was now over.

The typescript lay in its drawer, or perhaps in two or three different drawers, for six years in which I shifted flats more than once, got married, was invalided out of the Army. One day in 1944 my wife took out the typescript, read it, said that parts of it were quite funny, and suggested that I should send it to a publisher. I sent it to Victor Gollancz, probably the only English publisher who would have considered such a zany detective story, and he accepted it.

The Immaterial Murder Case is an appallingly bad detective story. I got into such a tangle with the plot that at one point I included a four-page chart showing the movements of the characters, done for my own benefit rather than that of readers. The style is like *Black Mask* with the violence removed, and the result filtered through an English high-brow sensibility — very odd. I've forgotten now who most of the grotesques in the story were meant to be, but I do remember that Ruthven was justifiably angered and upset by the caricature of himself, and not noticeably mollified by the dedication which said in part:

> Dear murderer, see without too much rage
> Your name set here, not on the title page.

The book was an in-joke, to the point that one reviewer wrote: "For those who know any of the characters, the best clue is in the dedication." Parts of it still seem to me funny — the invention of an art movement called Immaterialism in which you paint what is not there, the discovery of an art critic murdered inside a sort of Brancusi egg — but I made up my mind a few years ago not to let it be reprinted. An American edition appeared, without much success, in 1957.

This book was followed by *A Man Called Jones* and that by *Bland Beginning*, the first of my crime stories to appear in America. Some people have liked this book, which was based on the Thomas J. Wise literary forgeries, although I don't think much of it myself. The first crime story I can look back on with anything like satisfaction is *The Thirty-first of February*, which appeared in 1950.

Crime stories are written, first of all, to make money. They have been for me the basis of a comfortable, not luxurious, way of life. From *The Immaterial Murder Case* in the first couple of years after its publication I made around £200. Add a Penguin paperback published a long while after, and the American edition, and I suppose the book earned altogether about £500, certainly not much more. That perhaps represents treble the sum today, if one allows for inflation, but even so I certainly do a great deal better now. Without considering film options and sales, those distant stars in the sky, but including translations and paperbacks, I suppose I make rather more than £5000 from each book, with an unfortunate exception or two.

If I wrote two books a year — but I don't. It is more like one every eighteen months. This is chiefly a matter of deliberate choice. The shoddy writing of most crime stories springs in part from the fact of over-production. It is possible to produce a great deal of work on a high level — Simenon has shown that. And it is possible to write two or more highly ingenious mysteries each year — John Dickson Carr gives testimony to it. But these are exceptions. For most authors what happens is that they write a couple of good, reasonably successful books, and discover with delight that it is possible to make a living from this kind of fiction. Then sales remain static or even go down a little, and as the first zest fades, there comes the production of increasingly tired-looking and mechanical work.

One way of avoiding this (obviously there are others) is to do other work, so that you write crime stories only when you feel like it. This is a matter of personal inclination and ability. Over the years I have made part of my living from book reviewing (for ten years it was re-viewing crime stories), from TV plays, from non-fiction books dealing with subjects as various as the sage Carlyle and the swindler Horatio Bottomley, the attempt to save General Gordon at Khartoum, and the British General Strike of 1926. I enjoy the variation these subjects pro-vide and I believe, although this may be an illusion, that taking a rest between crime stories is a good thing. It gives one the chance to con-sider a theme, and what approach one should make to it.

Many crime writers are very touchy, as I have reason to know from the reactions some of them have shown to my criticism of their books. They are in my experience much more easily upset by sharp criticism than what are called "straight" novelists. Many crime writers assert that their purpose is only to amuse, but express indignation if a re-viewer says that they have failed in this modest objective. Most news-paper criticism, in both Britain and America, is not only too kind, but also makes too little distinction between the trivial and the serious.

In all kinds of fiction the best writing is personal, work that springs from beliefs and attitudes genuinely held. To say this is not to suggest that crime novelists ought to take what they do with total seriousness, only that it will be better work if it truly expresses something in a per-sonality. I have only a limited admiration for the James Bond stories, but it is evident that the first half-dozen are much better than the later ones, and this is because in the early books Ian Fleming was exercising his imagination in filling out this wish-fulfillment figure. Something boyish, ingenuous, fresh and personal is mixed with the conscious ex-pertise. In the last stories this has been lost, and the books are produced to a formula. They are production-line and not custom-made jobs.

I don't want to repeat ideas I've already advanced in *Mortal Conse-quences (Bloody Murder* to the British), but since this is largely a personal piece, perhaps it is in place to say what I think I have been doing in my own books. In them there has been a conscious and an unconscious element, a fact I have been helped to recognize by the comments of a television producer, who pointed out some things about the attitudes of my chief characters of which I wasn't aware.

What I have consciously been trying to do in most of my crime stories is to use an act of violence to point up my feelings about the pressures of urban living. An advertising man becomes wholly psychotic, principally because of the meaningless and inhuman work he does; the pressures of life in a "progressive" housing complex involve a roughneck who lives there in acts of violence, possibly leading to murder; when teenagers kill a man, retributory wheels are put in motion, but the people who turn them are not concerned with justice, only with finding a scapegoat. These are among the ideas I have consciously used, retaining almost always the puzzle element of a classical detective story partly because I enjoy it, and partly on Eliot's principle that a book or a play can operate on two levels of meaning. You can read *The Thirty-first of February*, *The End of Solomon Grundy* and *The Progress of a Crime* on the level of a puzzle simply, or you can enjoy the puzzle and also take note of the social ironies suggested. Such ironies tend to be Left-wing, at least in the sense that they criticize the attitudes and behaviour of those in authority. Edmund Crispin once said to me that those who took most pleasure in the classical detective story tend to be conservative, while those who wanted in one way or another to break down the restraints of the detective story as a form were more likely to be radical. If one puts it with that suitable degree of caution, I think he is right. Certainly the conclusions implicit in the books of mine I have mentioned are radical, although generally pessimistic.

What the television producer pointed out to me was that the central characters in my books, particularly the more recent ones, are always looking for a way of escape from their difficulties which will permit them to become totally different people. He took as one instance *The Man Who Killed Himself*, a blackish comedy about a little henpecked man who one day puts on a red wig and beard, and finds his personality transformed. A fairly standard situation in itself, which I tried to enliven with various comic and sinister complications. What I hadn't at all realized, and what the producer rightly said, was that the climactic point of the book came when the little man, having got rid of the various encumbrances that surrounded both of his personalities, set out to make a new life and found that he couldn't do it, that the new life was an illusion.

Warming to his work, he elucidated the same theme in *The Man Who Lost His Wife*, where a respectable publisher suffers an upheaval in his emotional life, visits a foreign country and becomes a different person there, perhaps commits murder — and returns to find the surface of life at home unruffled, so that he inevitably slips back into the skin of his previous personality. By the time he had analyzed a couple more books I was convinced. These characters were all looking for an escape from the pattern of their lives, an escape that proved to be unattainable. That, he suggested, rather than my conscious social ironies, was the meaning of my stories, even though I might not know it myself. The interpretative silent documentary he proposed, consisting partly of an ambiguous figure seen at office conferences, parties, in crowded streets, and partly with this figure emerging from them to walk down endless corridors and through many different rooms, to be confronted at the end with a mirror image showing — what? Nothingness perhaps, or something terrible and unknown — in the end never got made. Perhaps this was as well for my own peace of mind.

These fairly random personal notes drift towards an impersonal conclusion. A novel built on the basis of crime may be worth as much as another kind of novel. The form is limited, but perhaps not so limited as we used to think a few years ago. From a memorable work of fiction we carry away resonances and images, disturbing sounds and archetypal shapes, that perhaps transcend the creator's intention. Such resonances, such images, are not beyond the reach of the crime story.

Paul Bowles, on his terrace at The Shangri-La, Santa Monica,
California, 27 January 1969. Photo by L. D. Stewart.

PAUL BOWLES:
UP ABOVE THE WORLD SO HIGH

By Lawrence D. Stewart

PAUL BOWLES has had so many careers — as poet, composer, critic, journalist, translator, musicologist, short-story writer and novelist — that we should not be surprised at his trying out the detective story. He came to the form well along in his career, but the world of mystery and detection has been familiar to him since childhood when his mother used to read aloud the stories of Poe, with their "combination of repugnance and fascination," and he, sometime later, began "writing a collection of crime stories called 'The Snake Woman Series.'"[1] His first and most familiar novel, *The Sheltering Sky*, as well as his most memorable short stories ("A Distant Episode," "The Delicate Prey," "Pages from Cold Point," "He of the Assembly," and "The Time of Friendship") had detected, even if they did not solve, for his characters what we have come to call "the crisis of identity." It seems, therefore, inevitable that his notion of the detective genre should emphasize the psychological mystery of human personality and of life itself.

Among the first to deduce the direction of his fiction was Alice Toklas. In 1951 Bowles responded to her query about *The Delicate Prey and Other Stories* by defining them as "detective stories." She complimented him upon the label and viewed his work as continuing the tradition of Elizabethan mystery; he had, for her, restored to the genre its essential eeriness — a power that had been fatally lost from 1920 to 1950 in so-called mystery and detective fiction. When Miss Toklas thought that her letter to Bowles had miscarried, she wrote again. This time she analyzed his stories as fulfilling Gertrude Stein's requirement (he had, we should not forget, once been Miss Stein's protégé): the work reveals the "bottom nature" of a character as he responds to that fundamental force he carries within him. No wonder that the end of a story is, for the protagonist, the revelation not of the murderer but of himself — of who and what he, the "hero," really is. Only that interest, said Miss Toklas, could make a mystery story "really modern."[2]

When Bowles disposed of the majority of his manuscripts and papers in the mid-sixties he kept back these letters because he prized Miss

Toklas's observations. Then in 1968, when he was coming to America to teach, he decided to place them in his archive at the University of Texas. "Leaving them around in Tangier would be fatal. Now at least I know they're in Austin and they can be Xeroxed."³ Significantly, the letters had recalled to him the possibilities inherent in a genre he had been raised on. Perhaps they had even contributed to the creation of his fourth novel, *Up Above the World*, when he "tried to recapture the state of mind which had produced the thrillers I had read to the seventh grade in primary school, [and tried] to discover what result that point of departure might give now. The ploy worked: I got caught up in the elaboration of the tale fairly quickly and knew I was going to finish the book" (WS 356-57).

Though he would later remember *Up Above the World* as having been written without difficulty, it actually evolved slowly. He began it in the fall of 1961, telling his parents that "it's nearly seven years since I completed the last novel, which is a long time" (HRC: TLS, PB to his parents, 3 October 1961). The seven years since *The Spider's House* had not seen him a captive of idleness, however. During that period he had developed expertise in two areas that would particularly affect this novel. The first of these was tape recorders. In the mid-fifties he began taping and translating from the Moghrebi the stories and reminiscences of young Berber friends, and in the late-fifties he traveled widely throughout Morocco on a grant from the Rockefeller Foundation, taping native music for the Library of Congress. The other area in which he had become expert was hemp, in all its forms; it afforded him a personal exploration of the potions — as well as close observation of the charms, incantations, and spells — of North Africa. The seven years had also traumatically altered his domestic life: in 1957 his wife Jane had had a cerebral hemorrhage and would, for the rest of her life, be an invalid, crippled increasingly by depression as her vision faded into blindness.

Particularly because of Jane's condition, with its moment to moment uncertainties, Bowles was seldom permitted escape into the untimed world of his fiction. Not until three years after he had announced the projected new novel to his parents did he reach page 125 of the manuscript. By May 1964 there had been a temporary stabilization of Jane's illness, and Bowles was experiencing new calmness. "It's Janie," he explained to me that spring in Morocco, "I don't have to worry about her anymore." He was able, therefore, to take a house on the Old Mountain outside Tangier, on "a cliff overlooking the sea, 400 feet above the waves" (WS 357). "I *was* up above the world, right at the top of this terrible cliff." There, in view of the Atlantic, he lived in solitude, writing out the novel in the notebooks he carried on his walks through the forests on the property, and then typing up the holograph entries daily as they took final shape. "I worked on it very hard, I remember that. I worked on it hard in the sense that I worked on it day and night and wandering around, writing outdoors, not just confining my writing to certain hours of the day, certain circumstances or conditions [as had been the case with *The Spider's House*], but wrote it all the time — was thinking about it all the time. I just shut myself off, to write it" (Tape, LDS).

On August nineteenth he reported that "life is going smoothly and I'm doing what I can to finish my book while I'm here in the house on the mountain" (TLS, PB to author). By mid-October the book was "just about done, save for retyping the entire manuscript, which ought not to take more than three weeks, if I work enough hours each day at it. (Of course, it's not merely a question of retyping, but rewriting as I go.) But the main thing is that I can do that under more or less any conditions, whereas the actual writing seems to require solitude. Which is where this house on the mountain comes in, and why it has been so useful to me all summer. I'm giving it up at the end of the month, and shall be back in the [Tangier] apartment then" (HRC: TLS, PB to his mother, 18 October 1964). But retyping had not got the book exactly as wanted; and in December he was "doing a few rewrites on my new book, in order to have it in perfect condition" (TLS, PB to author, 22 December 1964). By then he had also offered it as a serial to the *Saturday Evening Post*, but they were interested only in new short fiction which he had no time to provide.

On 17 February 1965 he announced that "the new book is completely finished save for a title, and that will have to turn up sooner or later" (TLS, PB to author). (A working title had been "Where the Slades Went.") Despite her own illness and declining vision that was to make reading the book an heroic feat, Jane Bowles had been able to write on February eighth that "we are both eager to have your opinion on Paul's new book. . . . I really want you to see the new book, because I have a feeling it can be a great success, and I'd love to have your opinion and suggestions on how to handle it. Paul does not like to discuss it" (TLS, Jane Bowles to author). Clearly he still felt himself and his work to be an entity; the propitious moment for breaking that fusion, for allowing the novel to assume its separate identity, had not come. Bowles Thermofaxed the typescript at the American Consulate in Tangier and, in the spring of 1965, brought it to his New York agent with the expectation that Random House would be the publisher.

But Random House did not rise to *Up Above the World*, and that American spring Bowles went to Santa Fe in new uncertainty. Though Tangier had been home for himself and Jane since 1947, he now began considering a change. The political situation in Morocco had become increasingly uncertain, and he could no longer foresee safety as an expatriate. (Jane always had reassured herself that as long as they remained in Tangier, a warship could be sent to rescue them if war broke out — whereas if they were down toward the Sahara, which Paul preferred, how ever could they escape?) Just as in 1931 on his first trip to North Africa Bowles had responded to Morocco's temperature and climate, so now in Santa Fe — "the least objectionable city in the United States" (WS 358) — he was invigorated by the purity of air and the novelty of silence. In that restorative atmosphere he looked around at houses; he also re-examined his "completely finished" novel. "I did quite a bit of rewriting (after reflection) on the new book while I was in Santa Fe, and now have got to collate the new sections into what I'd thought was the definitive draft of the manuscript. I still hope to have some sort of decision on it before I leave [New York]" (HRC: TLS, PB to his mother, 17 May 1965).

He returned to Tangier, doubtful of the book's acceptability. Not until July twenty-ninth was he able to write his mother that "Simon & Schuster . . . will be publishing the work, instead of Random House, who didn't understand it and consequently wanted changes made. Grove Press was eager to publish it as it stood, but my agent didn't seem to want to deal with them; agents always prefer to deal with what they call 'big houses' " (HRC). He corrected the proofs in October; and in the spring of 1966 the book was published.

In view of Bowles's life work and the evolution of his aesthetic, it is important to remember this long period of gestation, for during it he modified his earlier theories about the novel and produced, curiously enough, not his longest but his shortest novel. By the time he had finished with it, he was so uncertain of *Up Above the World*'s reception that he proposed issuing it pseudonymously. "I wrote it just as seriously as I would have any other, naturally, or I couldn't have written it. But I thought, because of the subject matter, in the beginning that it was going to be a light novel. I didn't want to write a light novel. I felt that it wouldn't be successful after the others, and that perhaps I should sign it John Smith — simply, you know, so as not to disappoint anybody." But his agent would not hear of such a ploy. "She wouldn't know the difference, you see. To her it was just another novel. I don't think she saw any great difference between it and the previous ones" (Tape, LDS). Bowles wrote his mother on 23 November 1965: "You ask the title of my new book, to appear, supposedly, in February. UP ABOVE THE WORLD. It's a murder mystery about beatniks, decidedly light, and probably will get awful notices. However, I was tired of writing about North Africa" (HRC). Similarly he cautioned Andreas Brown: "It lays itself open to being misunderstood, and I hope the reviewers are bright — at least, some of them!" (HRC: TLS, 7 March 1966). Luckily some were, and the *New York Times* and *Life* notices opened for him the door to a new audience. Bowles has called his novel "very American" (Tape, LDS) and says that of all his works it is "the one that satisfies me most because it's the best-written" (TLS, PB to author, 6 November 1973).

But if we examine the intention that Bowles has privately revealed he had for the book, as well as look into some of the sources of his novel's plot and development, we may see that *Up Above the World* is something far more than a murder mystery about beatniks. It began in the recollection of personal encounters the Bowleses had had on their honeymoon when they themselves were young and healthy wanderers through the world. It ended as a re-examination of Gide's confrontation with determinism and free will — a re-examination prompted by Bowles's own perplexity with the vagaries of life, by the traps he now saw set for the body as well as for the mind.

I

In his childhood Bowles had been uncommonly passive: "I had thought of myself as a registering consciousness and no more. My nonexistence was a *sine qua non* for the validity of the invented cosmos. . . . [My fantasy] enabled me to view, rather than participate in, my own existence. (Much later I read Gide, and understood his feeling perfectly . . . '*Il me semble toujours m'appauvrir en me dessinant. J'accepte volontiers de n'avoir pas d'existence bien définie si les êtres que je crée et extrais de moi en ont une.*')" (WS 52-53).

Gertrude Stein, in her categorization of personality, would have labeled Bowles's a "dependent independent" nature, capable of expression more through resisting than through attacking — those two modes of behavior inevitably linked, for her, to "bottom nature." He had shown great self-reliance, as such dependent independents frequently do — it was, after all, what Miss Stein thought her own nature to be. As a writer, therefore, Bowles began as one who fancied himself the recorder of impressions, one unusually sensitive to his own unconscious and to the material momently erupting from it. His has always been a "habit of never starting to write until I had entirely emptied my mind," getting rid of all conscious thoughts (WS 102). He would never rely totally upon involuntary response or "automatic writing"— he works too slowly and carefully to master the speed implied by such a method. Yet he would attempt not to censor, modify, or suppress the expressions of his unconscious. The act of rewriting, under circumstances improperly controlled, could be for him a betrayal of aesthetic.[4]

Logical form — the rhetorical framework of plot, action, and character — "would require planning. It would require knowing what you

250 Mystery & Detection Annual

are going to write before you write it — which I don't. I sort of open
the door and plunge into this unknown world — and then suddenly
the door of the ending appears, and I go out again. But what's happened
while I was inside, I don't really know" (Tape, LDS). Therefore he
cannot explain his work. The works themselves — particularly the
second and third novels — suggest, however, an increasing attempt on
his part to regularize the visions from the unconscious, to impose on
them a rationality that makes comprehensible the behavior of his
characters. In order to write his second novel, *Let It Come Down*, he
even made charts and diagrams, laying out the action required to get
his characters into the situations that he reasoned necessary. That
novel had released an American from the daily routine of commercial
life in New York, only to entrap him in the commercial world of
Tangier; it then dramatically liberated his unconscious, via kif, and
ultimately brought him to destruction. Bowles's style, which makes
even melodrama pleasantly acceptable in the reader's suspended dis-
belief, helps conceal the basic implausibility of *Let It Come Down*,
where the interest is in the events themselves instead of the characters.

In the years between his third novel, *The Spider's House* (1955),
and *Up Above the World*, Bowles's aesthetic shifted — perhaps due to
his practical work with translation. To write fiction he invariably
worked straight through from detonating scene to its culmination. (If,
as in *Let It Come Down*, that detonating scene did not open the novel,
then he had to plot only the series of incidents that would plausibly
account for it.) Translation had never been more than mechanical
work for him, an almost automatic enterprise. But translation from the
tapes made by Berber storytellers high on kif was a new experience,
since the final manuscript would be a mortising together, an editing
of transcribed ingredients. If a Berber storyteller did not adequately
clarify an incident that might mystify a non-Moslem, Bowles asked
him to expatiate — he invariably did his translating in the presence of
the storyteller himself — and this supplement would then be translated and placed in the manuscript. Perhaps it was such practice with
rational assemblage that made possible the rewriting and alteration in
the manuscript of *Up Above the World*. His practical experience had
trained Bowles to analyze closely the effect of each scene and to assess
its contribution to the tension mounting in his novel. For the first time
his psychological detachment produced critical judgment, a conscious
self-evaluation. It is essential that in *Up Above the World* we not lose
sight of Bowles's process as well as this governance of rationality. The
abrupt changes, switching, and tergiversation of mood within the
novel are not the result of incapacity but of deliberation.

We should now examine the nature of Bowles's proficiency with
tape machines and drugs and the manner in which they have affected

his novel. Both *Their Heads Are Green and Their Hands Are Blue* (1963) and *Without Stopping* discuss his use of tape recorders in North Africa. In Tangier Brion Gysin and William Burroughs showed him new possibilities with taping — in particular how spliced tapes could create unusual effects. For them this technique spun out a singular literature. On one occasion Burroughs even sliced up a portion of *The Sheltering Sky* to instruct Bowles in the benefits of their methodology. Bowles himself has had little interest in such deliberate surrender to caprice, but he knows very well the dramatic possibilities of tape machinery and the distorted sense of reality it can provide.

His profound interest in drugs and medicaments began in a child-hood fascination with potions. One of his juvenilia is "a long story called 'Hadeized,' in which the characters disappeared the moment they swallowed alcohol. (The touch of liquor 'hadeized' them, and they were instantly transported to hell.)" (WS 53). *Without Stopping* records his early experience with marijuana and ether, as well as his later interest in hemp (particularly kif and majoun) and reveals how *A Hundred Camels in the Courtyard* (1962) developed its theme and structure from that interest. He has also followed with some slight curiosity the pharmacological experimentation of Timothy Leary. The drugs in Bowles's fiction, however, are generally concoctions of his own devising and could not easily be duplicated. In "Tapiama," he blended a native drink, the *cumbiamba*, which had peculiar properties: "it's an invention of mine, and there are drinks like that down there [in Latin America] that are very strong and I suppose they put bits of other herbs in them too as well as the alcohol. But it's an invention, it's fiction!" In *Up Above the World* he destroyed his American tourists by giving them an unidentified mixture, only some of whose elements we recognize as LSD, scopolamine, and morphine "combined at differ-ent intervals so that you are taking the psyche and going YANK-YANK back and forth with it" (Tape, LDS). But it is the effects — not the medical causes — that interest Bowles dramatically. Inevitably for him plot is "not as interesting as the real material in life. I think one of the most difficult things is to see the drama that is really in front of one every minute — the drama that follows living. And one often doesn't. Actually see it. And if you can, then you're involved in the most momentous things every minute. They're around you all the time. In other people's lives, I mean. But one doesn't see them. I sup-pose one's protected from them."[5]

Yet the reader of a novel must commence with plot before he can consider "the drama that follows living," and it is partly the manner in which evidence is presented that makes this novel difficult. Unan-nounced flashbacks and the order of narrated events dramatize the fluctuations of the drug experience: the uncertain mixture of the present with the past, merged with presentiments of the future. *Up Above the World* is the story of a retired doctor, Taylor Slade, and his second wife, Day—thirty years his junior—who embark in San Francisco for a trip to "a composite country: Latin-American, definitely . . . [but it's] not supposed to be precisely situated" (Tape, LDS). They land at a small port, Puerto Farol, stay overnight in a run-down hotel, and the next morning entrain for the capital, high in the mountains, where they intend a leisurely visit; in the doctor's "experience the world was a rational place."[6] On shipboard they had become casually acquainted with a Montreal clubwoman, Mrs. Rainmantle, "a Canadian who lived in London and who was in the habit of coming here to visit her son . . . Grover" (UATW 24-25). This rather sloppy and friendly woman disembarks with them, but only after continuing difficulties: her letter of credit seems unacceptable, and her bar bill must be settled before her luggage can be taken off the ship. Despite these impasses she ingratiates herself with Day and ultimately shares Day's hotel room for the night as the doctor unhappily settles for the less secure accommodation that had been assigned Mrs. Rainmantle. (" 'It's the door that makes the room impossible,' Mrs. Rainmantle said in a dead voice" [UATW 31].) When very early the next morning the Slades slip away to their train, they think they have seen the last of their eccentric companion. And indeed they have. But what little they have seen of her is to be their undoing.

In the capital Day encounters a seemingly pleasant young man, Vero Soto, who is half-English, half-Latin. He volunteers to show her his city, and later the Slades go to his penthouse for cocktails. Dr. Slade's drink is spiked, and he is then lured to Vero's seventeenth-century hacienda at Los Hermanos, where he is given intensive treatment to alter his memory. Day, thinking her husband will be returning before long, refuses to go to Los Hermanos; she is put under drugs by Vero in his city apartment and is then taken, with Dr. Slade, to Vero's ranch near San Felipe for further observation. Vero wires their room, pipes in disturbing sounds, and observes them. He may insist that he is "not one for trying to change people" (UATW 103), yet he succeeds in wiping nearly two weeks from the Slades's memory. The remaining question is, What do they still remember? Have they fatally connected him with the woman they had befriended? For Mrs. Rainmantle is Vero's mother — and though the Slades left Puerto Farol unaware, Mrs. Rainmantle had been murdered in her sleep with a syringe of curare that first night on land, and the hotel itself was burned shortly after the Slades went to their train. Vero feels certain that Day, "rather than see herself getting involved, had merely shut the door and gone away, free to tell everything later" (UATW 204). Is it not inevitable, therefore, that the Slades must be destroyed?[7] They never know what they have done or what they have consumed, but are troubled in their moments of waking consciousness that there is malevolence around them, "the slow journey down into the cloaca of horror that had been the disease" (UATW 136). They are powerless to escape; their death is itself the immediate consequence of an accident.

"Things don't happen," Grove has insisted. "It depends on who comes along" (UATW 206). The one who accidentally comes along is, of course, Day, walking through the kitchen garden where she sees some partially burned papers—Grove's "typewritten notes of the sort he was always making" (UATW 207). She glances idly at them but their significance does not register, even though the one complete sentence on the top fragment is "Dawn will be breaking soon." That is the phrase which, in her drugged dreams, had been "whispered across the moving water" of her fantasy. Hearing that phrase had lifted "a great weight . . . slowly from her; little by little her happiness became more complete, and she awoke" (UATW 156-57). As ill luck would have it, her casual inspection of the burned fragments had been observed and reported to Grove, who assumes that she must be on to his plan: "Believe me when I say it's bad," he tells his friend Thorny. "It's as though I'd known all along it was going to be this way. Unbelievable how things can dovetail" (UATW 208). His incorrect deduction calls for the destruction of the Slades. Both are killed — their bodies thrown into the jungle, where they will decay in inaccessibility.

Is *Up Above the World* escape from poetic justice? Perhaps so — at least for the two agents who assist Vero. One is the girl, Luchita, who thinks Vero plots only to seduce Day (Luchita is willing to cooperate so long as that assistance will guarantee her own return to Paris). The agent instrumental to Vero's plot is a fellow Canadian, Thorny, a classmate from McGill, with whom Vero has a sinister alliance. Thorny is the beatnik, the hanger-on whose presence seems unaccountable to Luchita (for surely she can give Vero whatever it is he wants). She does not see that Thorny's special talents as an engineer will be put to needful use; nor does she recognize the strength of evil in his character. For it is Thorny who follows Vero's strategy and murders Mrs. Rainmantle for $100,000 promised him from Grove's inheritance. The act has also given Thorny leverage in his relationship with Vero who, for him, had always been "the one constant in a totality of flux and chaos" (UATW 200). "Grove had always had the power to pull the world out from under his feet, but until now he had not done it" (UATW 197). In these reversed circumstances, Thorny moves into Luchita's empty room and, as Luchita had never been able to, quietly threatens his classmate with domination.

The corollary to this homosexual theme which runs through the novel[8] is that of matricide: the ultimate expression of the hostility that Bowles has, in his work, invariably found between generations as the young assume mastery over their elders and bring about their destruction. The theme had been graphically developed in "Pages from Cold Point," where a son seduces his father in order to guarantee his personal escape into a well-subsidized homosexuality. In *The Sheltering Sky* it emerged as a mother and her twenty-one-year-old son slept together by night and by day affected a British superiority to the "decadence" of North Africans.

But Bowles, remembering an early injunction of Gertrude Stein's that he attend to "description," describes rather than surmises. The determination of "bottom nature" is not an analysis of causes in any customary manner; it is not speculation upon the mother/son difficulty of Mrs. Rainmantle and Grover, it is not an exploration of the causes for the unhealthy attraction between Thorny and Grover. It is not even a clarification of the chemical mixtures and statement of their equations that produce the observed metabolic responses. As Gertrude Stein admonished, and as she herself did, he observes and describes effects, the repetitions of behavior that can reveal "bottom nature." *Up Above the World* does not inquire how matters could be other than they are. Knowledge is inductive; and even a reversal of Newton's third law will not solve this mystery.

II

In the years following *The Sheltering Sky* Bowles began and abandoned two novels, both of which contributed to the creation of *Up Above the World*. We need to look at them in some detail, as well as at the raw material he drew upon for them. "I have . . . written, oh, one or two chapters, thinking that they would gain their own impetus and that I'd be able to go on. And then things have happened and I've just stopped them and decided they weren't such a good idea after all" (Tape, LDS).[9] The first of these was titled "Almost All the Apples Are Gone" and was set in New York. "It was going to go from there to Yucatan or somewhere, I don't remember" (Tape, LDS). He had made several notes for it and had indeed begun writing it in a small notebook when, in December 1949, en route to Ceylon, his ship passed Tangier at night. Bowles on deck was so struck by the sight of his beloved Morocco that he abandoned his novel and, in the notebook that contained it, immediately started another — one set in Morocco in the very scene that the ship was then passing. This became, of course, *Let It Come Down*. Even in its brief development, however, "Almost All the Apples Are Gone" had played with themes which ever were to interest him; and certainly *Up Above the World* is grounded in material first recollected, or collected, for that aborted work.

"Almost All the Apples Are Gone" was to have been the first-person narrative "told all in sort of typical Massachusetts talk" (Tape, LDS).[10] The "principal protagonist was a grammar-school teacher in New York City. . . . She went to normal or training school in Massachusetts, abandoning the idea of a teacher's career shortly after being graduated. Then, after she had been living in New York a while, she decided to follow her original intention, and got a job teaching there in a public school" (HRC: TLS, PB to Daniel Burns, 11 December 1949)..

But the job displeases her, primarily "because she is bored, bored, bored. . . . Paradoxically, the more slowly time seems to pass, the more quickly it seems to have disappeared, even to the point of not having existed at all, when one (looks back on it) considers it in retrospect. That is, empty time is transparent." She "keeps journal to lessen monotony of life. Details of everyday life," but she doesn't make an escape until she enters into correspondence with a planter: "With letter she sends old snapshot in riding breeches, telling herself she hasn't changed at all, or not basically. . . . excitement felt at leaving every thing behind, going into a new life, accomplishing something always desired. . . . When answer finally comes, she finds 'tonic of happiness' it provides makes her feel utterly different." She takes a sabbatical and goes to Central America: "Disparity between imagined tropics and first taste of them. (But at end she says: 'But it is real, and that is saying a lot.') In nearest large town to village where M. x lives she goes to hotel. Has decided not to go to village, to give up the venture. He has sent servant to get her. She goes, without knowing why." They marry, and then "series of short scenes wherein incompatibility of husband and wife is shown increasing. Show native servant becoming a character, gardener slowly emerging from his anonymity." She becomes pregnant by the gardener, but the husband — ignorant of the affair and thinking himself to be the father — dies before the birth of the child, "dark suspiciously to her, light to other inhabitants." When the gardener tries to take over the plantation from the widow, she "arranges subtly for his being accused of murder. . . . He is imprisoned."

The years move on, the estate decays. Bowles's notes outline the planned development of his story:

Growing-up of child (s'inspirer du chapitre 36 de *Tchad*) stress his waywardness with girls. Mother pleased secretly. Always tells son he is white, (the only white,) not to play with other children. . . . One day tells fortune of native woman as pastime. Prophecy comes true, woman tells everyone. She is lancée as fortune-teller. (Cards) Little by little house falls into ruins, she uses only one room, finally moves to gardener's hut. . . . As boy grows, shown to be stupid. Unbelievable vanity. Scenes of childhood. . . . By time boy is adolescent, mother (living as fortune-teller) conceives idea of selling son's services to women of town, both for themselves & their daughters. He remains ignorant of maneuver. Women & girls happen to be there, let themselves be seduced. Reason, all want light children, and luxury, novelty of being with white husband.

Mother pretends to herself she knows nothing about what goes on between son & women. His services go with séance of fortune-telling. They ask about children. "Will I have a child?" She says yes, which always pleases them. Then they ask where son is. . . . Son finally goes off to town. (Scenes of his empty life in the ruined house & garden, slow passage of time, boredom.) Because he is father's son, given clerical job in government — mother, needing money, comes looking for him, tries to get him to go back. Refusal. (Finds white halfwit to take back with her in his place.) Son gives mother some money. She buys brass bed. (Final scene in room with broken ceiling, canvas stretched across like tent, bed beneath.) She spins fantasy. Gardener returns, innocent of her maneuver. Halfwit in garden hut with native woman. Gardener thinks he is her son. Puts woman out. Halfwit furious. Gardener announces intention of remaining. She suggests to halfwit to kill him. He does.

One notation seems particularly significant: "Last part her monstrous world of the senses — Chaos of senses, anarchy of perceptions, not drink or madness — merely decomposition. Not conscious of deformations. On the contrary, Johnny's world must be presented as one of light & clarity. No disorganization here — merely the simple world of the animal" (HRC: MS of "Almost All the Apples Are Gone").

Even the most rudimentary comparison of plot details shows how much the two novels share: the destructive relationship between mother and son, the tropical setting with its lush decadence, and ultimately the charting of a journey from boredom to "Chaos of senses." "Almost All the Apples Are Gone" emphasized that the decomposition was merely that — not a result of drink or madness or, presumably, drugs. *Up Above the World* accelerates that disintegration and draws upon Bowles's enriched awareness of pharmacology and potions, an awareness gained in the years that intervened between the abandoning of the one novel and the commencing of the published mystery.[11]

Bowles himself believes that it was the *second* of his two abortive novels — this one, begun between *Let It Come Down* and *The Spider's House* — which most affected *Up Above the World*. It "was going to be about Ceylon. It was taking place in Ceylon. Actually the situation and the character in it finally found its niche in *Up Above the World.* The woman, Mrs. Rainmantle, was originally the protagonist in one of these, because she was a woman I had met in a very strange situation back in 1938 — fantastic woman named Lady Yvonne Glendower. Really, her story would make a very good book." [12] Bowles and his wife Jane were on their honeymoon when they first

> saw her on ship between Puerto Limon in Costa Rica and Puerto Barrios in Guatemala, and she got off the ship with us and she shared our room in this hotel — the Gran Hotel de la Independencia, which was a real shambles. And that's where I got the idea, she was such a mysterious woman. She was traveling *de luxe* in an enormous first-class cabin on the *Caribia* — it's a German ship that I think was destroyed during the war — and she had trunks all over her cabin. Everything she owned was with her. She had been a chorine in the Folies Bergère or something in her youth, and this wealthy Englishman named Lord (somebody) Glendower had fallen in love with her; and she'd married him and gone to live in his manor in England and had lived there for many years until he died. She had clippings about herself (a diamond necklace had been stolen), clippings from those terrible Sunday graphics like *News of the World*, you know, with ridiculous photographs. She was fascinating. We were only with her for three days. We saw her all the time. Jane thought she was marvelous. She was *filthy*. Her clothes were all spotted, she was drinking heavily. One of these newspapers had finally reached a coffee planter somewhere way in the interior of British Honduras, named Campbell — a Scotsman — and he had written her and said "I'm in love with you" — and she'd got the letter a year later, or something. He'd written to *News of the World* or one of those papers in London, and they'd forwarded it. (She wasn't in England any more: Lord Glendower had died and she was back in France. She was French.)
>
> And he said, "Would you share your life with me?" And she wrote back and said, "Well, you know, what have you got to offer? What's there? Why would I go to live on a coffee plantation? I'm used to Paris and London." And he kept this up and he sent her the fare to come, which she then squandered in Paris and didn't go, of course. This was over a period of several years. Then he kept writing her, and he said "Don't feel guilty if you've spent the money. I'll send you more." So he sent it again — I saw some of his letters, for she showed them to Jane and me, because we were both fascinated — with absurd things like, "I've had a special

bureau built in your room; I think you will like it. It is made of native butterwood (or something) which is a very lovely wood. It's very heavy. I've got curtains at last in your room, the room that you will have. It is the best room in the house." He was going into all of this. [She, of course, thought he was either mad or sick.]

He sent the money a second time, and again she squandered it. (It's really like a fairy tale.) And finally the third time she said, "No! No! I don't want to hear from you any more. I've misbehaved, I just can't look at myself in the looking glass, I feel so guilty. But I had debts, and now I still haven't got the money to pay the passage." So he sent it a third time, and she said, "Well, this time I've got to go." (She had a certain kind of— She was just a dancer in the Folies Bergère — whatever — the Moulin Rouge.)

She looked very strange, too. She wasn't old, but she had let herself go, and she had dyed hair and it was all frizzy, and it wasn't right. She looked exactly like a concierge in an apartment house in Paris and talked like one. (I'll bet she *was* one.) So she was on her way to see him, and she still hadn't met him. And she had taken all her clothing and all the objects that she still had left from Lord Glendower, and her cabin was full of them. She had unpacked all these trunks — they were steamer trunks with drawers. Everything was out all over the place — it was a shambles. [By then she had been on the water for twenty days.] Then when she came to get off the ship they wouldn't let her off in Puerto Barrios because she had a bar bill and she had to go and get the British consul to go out and pay it, but *he* had to get in touch with Mr. Campbell in the interior before he could do it, because she looked so peculiar. He wouldn't trust her. (All this is in *Up Above the World* — just the situation.)

She came to the hotel and she spent an afternoon, taking a siesta in our room. There were two beds, with a space in between, and they had these mosquito nets over them. And she and Jane had the siesta in one, and I had the siesta in the other. And we had our parrot with us, which we'd bought down in Costa Rica, and it was sort of a wild parrot. It had eaten through its cage and it was loose, it was all over the room. And it climbed up under the mosquito netting and began walking on her, and there was an awful shriek and he was sort of pecking at her thighs — she was very fat, incidentally. "*Ahhh! Mon Dieu!*" She thought it was all the horrors of the tropics, which she was very afraid of, and it was quite a traumatic little scene there. And we didn't get much siesta. I think it was later the same day (she didn't spend the night with us — she had no money, of course, not a penny, which was why we let her in, invited her — at least she could take a siesta. It was very hot, horrible weather there. She could lie down and rest) she was waiting for a little launch to come over from a place called Livingstone across the harbor, a long way up, to take her off to a place called Punta Gorda, where Mr. Campbell would pick her up and drive her into the jungle. The last we saw of her she was in this little put-put boat, getting smaller and smaller, going off across the bay.

But, later that year we went to Paris and we went to a hotel there where I had stayed years ago — this is back in '32 — and we'd discussed the hotel with Lady Yvonne, you know, reminiscing about Paris. "You must go there and absolutely without fail tell Madame Dubois that I've arrived safely, because she's very worried about me and I always live in that hotel and even in the summer when Madame Dubois goes out to the country I go with her and live in her little house in the country." They were very good friends. When we got to the hotel in Paris . . . the woman went into ecstasies hearing that we'd seen Lady Yvonne Glendower. "*Ah, comment va-t-elle, la pauvre?*" she said. "She's been having nightmares now for three years about this trip, and I'm so glad to hear that she got there alive. I was sure that she was going to commit suicide on the way. She didn't want to go to live with this awful Scotsman, but she felt compelled to." And then she said, "When we used to go to the country, poor Yvonne — she couldn't even go out to the lavatory, which was in a little shack, you know, in the back, at night. She always had to wake me up and I had to go with her. She was so afraid of the outdoors, to go through the garden alone."

When I thought of this *horrible* country she was going into, what it must have been to her! That's the end of her. I mean, that's the last we ever heard of her, discussing her with the *patronne* of the hotel.

"The episode kept bobbing up like a cork in my memory: Lady Yvonne, and what could have happened to her?" (Tape, LDS). He now believes that he first attempted to put her in a novel after he had completed *Let It Come Down* — even though the protagonist of "Almost All the Apples Are Gone" shared many of Lady Yvonne's experiences — particularly the marriage arranged by correspondence. But it must ever be remembered that Bowles never fancies his fiction as a record of actual events. A recollected experience "sets off a sequence of flashes of memory which somehow combine into making one entity. The memories are the raw material, the stimuli. Sometimes the whole thing is purely invented, they're not really memories at all. It's an attempt to evoke for myself the way I felt during a given experience long ago, so the material could be quite different, the subject matter doesn't necessarily have to be the original subject matter. It's a kind of synthesis to re-create an emotion subsequently, after the fact" (Tape, LDS).

The second of his abortive novels would have tested that theory. That novel was to have been about Thorny and Anne Sims, their trip to Ceylon, and their life there. The novel opened on shipboard and showed Anne's boredom with her conformist husband, a painter. Bowles concluded his notes for the novel with the suggestion: "Set up should be fairly actual. Wife about as Mrs. Copperfield [in Jane Bowles's *Two Serious Ladies*],[13] as far as character and compulsive behavior go, but motive can be left blank, with fear acting as backdrop and general emotional and atmospheric element. (Eventually it must become apparent that her fear is of him, if still irrational.) He must face her with it, demand: But why? Why? She thinks: 'If he doesn't know that, he doesn't know anything in this world.' She says: 'If I knew why, I wouldn't be afraid' " (HRC: MS of untitled novel). Bowles's later recollection was: "I put Campbell in Ceylon as a tea planter, instead of a coffee planter in British Honduras. I was going to tell her [Lady Yvonne's] story and have all the unpleasant adventures which might have happened to her in British Honduras transposed to Ceylon where I was living then half of every year. That would have been fun. I had it all worked out, and then? I don't know. It got heavy for me — perhaps because I had let her go with her son, which wasn't a good idea, a little boy about eight or nine" (Tape, LDS).

Apparently in both of these aborted novels, the mother/son relationship was, for Bowles, inescapable. It had begun to assume such mythic power that when a protagonist witnessed its perversion, he was to face more than degradation. The breaking of the taboo against incest and matricide breaks apart the civilized world. And those who casually witness — or are assumed to — become victims of forces which they cannot understand. Small wonder that they think themselves the targets of the *acte gratuit* in a totally irrational universe.[14]

III

A clue for solving the mystery of *Up Above the World* — in particular the appropriate critical attitude to take toward that novel itself — was provided by Bowles in conversation. "I was thinking of publishing it under another name, when I started it, because it was not a typical novel. I considered it a light novel, an entertainment, as opposed to a novel — what Gide would have called a *sotie* as opposed to a *roman*. I

thought, 'Now I'm going to write a suspense story, not a serious novel
— something else, something that I haven't tried.' I wanted to try
something different. And I thought, 'That's another category — that's
not really a literary category' " (Tape, LDS).

It is not surprising that he turned to Gide for a model. His fascination with the French author can be traced to a spring evening in 1926
when he bought his "first Gide: Knopf's edition of *The Vatican Swindle*. (A later edition was called *Lafcadio's Adventures*; God knows
why.) Like my fifteen-year-old counterparts all over the world, I was
seduced by Lafcadio's *acte gratuit*." And nearly fifty years later,
Bowles was insisting that "I still prefer *Les Caves du Vatican* to Gide's
other novels" (WS 67).[15] In January 1969, when he was thinking of
writers he rereads, he remembered Gide: "Three years ago [about
the time he was completing *Up Above the World*] I reread *Les Caves
du Vatican*, and since then I've reread parts of *Amyntas*. I *have* reread
him" (Tape, LDS). Certainly he had also turned earlier to Gide for
literary inspiration when he drew the structural notion for "The
Hours after Noon" from Gide's *Amyntas*. To speak of *Up Above the
World* as a *sotie* is, therefore, to turn upon it a tiny but powerful
searchlight that suddenly illuminates the novel and brings out not
only its form but that of the larger shadow which looms behind it and
gives it dimension.

When Gide divided his prose works into *soties*, *recits*, and the
roman (only *The Counterfeiters* goes into the third category) he said
there were three *soties: Paludes, Le Prométhée Mal Enchaîné* and *Les
Caves du Vatican*. The label came from fourteenth-century satiric
farces, and there is, undeniably, a degree of ludicrousness in each of
these works; it is produced partly by the editorial asides of the author
and his wryly ironic tone that detach the reader from any vicarious involvement in the actions and agonies of the characters.[16] Perhaps to
Bowles, however, these *soties* were unified not so much by their satiric
attitude as by the theme of *l'acte gratuit* which Gide developed, discussed, and dramatized in them.

Paludes is prefaced with Gide's refusal to explain either his intention
or assumed accomplishment: "what interests me most in my book, is
what I have put in without being aware of it — the part that belongs
to the unconscious, which I should like to call, the part that belongs to
God." [17] From the beginning, Gide implied that a gratuitous act depends upon free will; but the organized unconscious surely militates
against such possible independence. In the first of these *soties* the
narrator would willingly forsake all choice: "I remained alone for a
moment. Now, of that moment what should I say? — Why not speak
of it, just as much as of the instant that followed: do we know which
are the really important things? What arrogance there is in *choice!* —

Let us look upon everything with equal insistence" (Marshlands 76). It is an attitude developed in *Les Caves du Vatican* where the narrator justifies his description of so minor a detail as a wen: "For until I have learnt to distinguish more surely between the accidental and the necessary, what can I demand from my pen but the most rigorous fidelity?"[18] In *Paludes* the narrator wants "not to generate action, but to disengage freedom" (Marshlands 53). He accommodates determinism to free will or choice by writing a journal that projects activities a week in advance; "in this way I go to sleep every evening with a to-morrow before me that is unknown, and yet already pre-ordained by myself" (Marshlands 22). *Le Prométhée Mal Enchaîné* takes a less whimsical attitude toward the emerging problem of *l'acte gratuit* and defines it as "a disinterested act; self-born; an act without an end in view; and therefore without a master; a free act; an autochthonous Act."[19] That *sotie* shows that no matter how obscure the motivation behind an act, each act is itself productive of inescapable consequences. Only Zeus "whose fortune is infinite, can act with absolute disinterestedness; man cannot" (Prometheus 151).

But it is *Les Caves du Vatican* which builds action from this concern. Early in his conversation with his half-brother Lafcadio, Julius insists that "there is no such thing as inconsequence — in psychology any more than in physics" (Lafcadio 98). Specifically, "the author of a crime is always found out by the need he had to commit it." The next step in the logical argument is clear: "There is no reason that a man who commits a crime without reason should be considered a criminal" (Lafcadio 229). The fancied *acte gratuit* thus seems freed from moral considerations. Surely this parallels Bowles's own definition of an existentialist character as "one who plays it by ear — and every moment afresh from the given situation. He's infinitely adaptable, I would say. He thinks of everything in terms of the immediate situation, not according to credos and traditions" (Tape, LDS).

In an essential conversational exchange in *Les Caves du Vatican*, Lafcadio hazards the idea that "When one's traveling . . . there's no fear of consequences." Protos admits "Oh! . . . all the things one would do in this life if there were no fear of consequences. . . . If one could only be sure that it wouldn't lead to anything! . . . But what astonishes *me* is that a person as intelligent as you, Cadio, should have thought it possible to quit a society as simply as all that, without stepping at the same moment into another; or that you should have thought it possible for any society to exist without laws" (Lafcadio 249, 256).

Lafcadio's delusion is what Grove's will be when he associates guilt only with a physical act. "Life's . . . about who's going to clean up the shit," says Grove. "The work's got to be done. If *you* don't want to do it, you've got to be able to make somebody else do it. That's what life's about" (UATW 180). He therefore disassociates responsibility for action from the action itself, cause from effect; by giving Thorny pills that strengthen his resolve, he assures that Thorny will fulfill their agreement and murder Mrs. Rainmantle. And since Grove himself does not plunge the hypodermic into his mother's flesh, he fancies that act as separable from its conception. In his fractionalized perception he exclaims "What? . . . Tie myself to that kind of guilt for the rest of my life? God!" (UATW 199). He does not realize that the severance from his mother is a fatal joining with his companion — just as Lafcadio's act, designed to demonstrate free will, now ties him irrevocably to his old conspirator, Protos, whom he thought he had eluded.

The parallels between Grove and Lafcadio seem more than accidental. Lafcadio's cryptic journal finds its counterpart in Grove's tapes, where he talks to himself and shapes the future: "he improvised these one-sided conversations, recorded them, and then wrote out notes on the more convincing passages. Using these, he plotted the course of a verbal procedure from which he allowed himself almost no deviation when the moment came for actual speaking" (UATW 94). There is a parallel as well in their multiple identities. As a schoolboy, Lafcadio had learned respect for *the slim*, "a genus who, for one reason or another, did not present to all persons and in all places the same appearance" (Lafcadio 252). Grover/Grove/Vero: we have the same multiplicity as the basis of deception; for the Slades never do identify Mrs. Rainmantle's Grover with the Vero that they know. In the ending of each book there is a parallel mystery: Will the protagonist surrender, will the forces within his unconscious bring about that final dramatic gesture which will end his personal freedom?

Gide himself, of course, did not accept belief in *l'acte gratuit*. In his notebooks for *The Counterfeiters* he stressed "the need to go farther and farther back to explain any given incident. The slightest act requires an infinite motivation." [20] Ultimately explanation is impossible: "The secret motive of our acts — I mean of the most decisive ones — escapes us; and not only in memory but at the very moment of their occurrence." [21] And to the same degree that explanation of motivation is impossible, so is freedom from motivation itself delusional.

"Chance encounters, an adventure in life that was particularly significant to the surrealists, form in reality a new structure of the world. . . . Like an elaborate detective story, like a parody on a fantastic adventure story . . . [this novel] unfolds in an atmosphere where chance seems to dominate, and yet where chance seems to be devised by the mastermind of the novelist." [22] Wallace Fowlie's description is not of *Up Above the World* but of *Les Caves du Vatican*; yet its aptness reinforces their parallels.

Gide himself insisted that what is called *l'acte gratuit* is only an act which lacks external motivation. To one with omniscient vision there is always an apparent cause. In *Up Above the World* the Slades see this as a rational world with only moderate restrictions. "We just move around where we please, when we please," says Day. "It's the only way to do it. Group travel's a degradation. The whole point is to be free" (UATW 101). Similarly Dr. Slade believes "that what he called negative emotions immediately ceased to exist once they had been exposed to the blazing light of reason" (UATW 42). When they finally conclude that everything happening to them is gratuitous, theirs are "the incomplete powers of perception" that invariably plague intellectuals in Bowles's world.[23] To the reader who has, by the author, been given more comprehensive powers of perception, there is less of a mystery. We know eventually what happens to the Slades because we can see what Grove and Thorny have done to them. But even those more comprehensive powers do not reveal the interior causes that produce these awful responses. To classify the protagonist as insane is not to explain causation. But it does explain a work's classification as a *sotie*. As Mr. Fowlie reminds us, "the *sots* of a *sotie* [are those] in whom the real self has been dispossessed by manias."[24]

It is not Bowles's intention to show us something outside of ourselves that frightens us. Rather, he shows the beast within — what he has called "the unleashed id." *There* is, of course, the source of terror in a Bowles story and particularly in this novel. Not only are we the potential victims of indiscriminate forces whom we have unintentionally alienated and aroused; we can ourselves become those victimizers as the unconscious within us gains mastery over us by the casual taking of a drug, the smoking of kif, the ingestion of an herb. "Whatever kif or any drug gives you is not determined by the kif itself," says Bowles. "The kif is simply the key which opens a door to some particular chamber of the brain that lets whatever was in there out. It doesn't put anything in. It doesn't supply the matter. It liberates whatever's in, that's all" (Tape, LDS).

In *Up Above the World* there is, of course, a master criminal and his accomplice. But although Taylor and Day Slade are the targets of Grove and Thorny, they are even more significantly the victims of themselves — Day, distrusting the intuitions which should have protected her; Taylor, falsely relying upon his reason and his degree of professional knowledge. The novel develops the contrast between the Slades and builds on their marital discord. Day dislikes truth encased in language: words "were not what she wanted: they might only make it all the more real" (UATW 42), even though "words were deceptive, the very short ones most of all" (UATW 155). When she first sees Grove she thinks that "no man could look ['wholly and dramatically handsome'] as this one did and not have ended by taking unfair advantage of it" (UATW 48). But she does not place faith in such protecting intuition. For his part, Taylor Slade invariably plays the rationalist — but unconvincingly: despite his medical background he can neither recognize the odor of marijuana nor, even in his waking clearer moments, appreciate that his delusions have been chemically induced. When he fantasizes that an acquaintance may be psychopathic he misreads the symptoms and selects Mrs. Rainmantle rather than her son. Individually such personal flaws may be trivial; but collectively they make the Slades fatally vulnerable to the stress of events.

The potions the Slades take, the tapes they hear, merely liberate the self-destructive images that they have always carried within them. "From fantasy to actuality is often a much shorter distance than one imagines" (WS 207). Once drugged, Dr. Slade "was aware of the outside world rushing away, retreating before the onslaught of a vast sickness that welled up inside him, and he knew that soon there would be only the obscene reality of himself, trapped in the solitary chambers of existence" (UATW 107). Similarly, as Day sinks into her drugged state, she sees her own disintegration: "Inside, in the dark vault of her consciousness, there was an endless entry into Hell, where cities toppled and crashed upon her, and she died each time slowly, imprisoned at the bottom of the wreckage" (UATW 120). As "bottom nature" is thus freed, it wreaks havoc upon the body that has, all its life, enslaved it. And therefore this is truly, as Alice Toklas observed, a modern mystery story: the victim has been murdered by himself.

In such writing there is no place for the author — other than as satiric viewpoint which Gide adopted for himself in his *soties*. Bowles requires an almost scientific detachment from his stories. "I don't ever want to be in them at all. I am *not* in them. That's why I object when people say 'That's you!' or also, 'What was your idea in writing this, what was your method?' Well, I didn't have any idea or method — not that I'm aware of — so I can't answer these questions." He draws a parallel to the painter, Francis Bacon. "I think he's extraordinary — he lived a lot in Tangier, so I used to see a lot of him. And he used to explain how he worked, and I understood it so well. He works, I think, in rather a different way from most painters because he works without conscious intervention. He just paints — paints, paints, without knowing what he's painting. And when a given moment comes he knows it's ready, he mustn't touch it again, or else he takes a knife and slashes the whole canvas and begins again on something else" (Tape, LDS).[25] Like Bacon, Bowles too is "very secretive." The external world may see his work only when that work is finished and ready for display. By such time the work is no longer a part of that mysterious fusion of artist and composition, that valued entity for which privacy is an essential. The work has achieved its own identity and, live or die, it cannot be again touched by the artist who was its agency for existence.

When Bowles titled his novel *Up Above the World* he did not place the epigraph of "Twinkle Twinkle Little Star" on his title page. "I thought it was unnecessary. I thought it was most obvious. But nobody got it! I don't think anybody ever realized — except you — that it [the title] came from the nursery rhyme." He particularly liked the two words suggested by, and immediately following, the title — "so high" — with their connotation of geographical elevation as well as drugged exaltation: "one's supposed to think of that, too. But nobody ever did. I guess people don't know the words" (Tape, LDS).[26]

But the lines that begin the nursery rhyme are equally evocative:

> Twinkle twinkle little star,
> How I wonder what you are. . . .

The novel investigates human wonderment: the questioning of ourselves, of others, of the universe. Neither the nursery rhyme nor Bowles predicates a changing galaxy. Only in apocalyptic vision, such as William Blake's, do the stars throw down their spears and liberate human nature from the shackles of self-imposed delusion. In *Up Above the World* stars twinkle with the resonant assurance of immutability. They shine upon a humanity which, if unalterable, may nonetheless be ultimately revealed and comprehended. The force behind the stars is the mystery that Bowles does not explore. But that nature which the stars shine upon is a constant mystery to which there may indeed be a solution.

NOTES

Parenthetical abbreviations: HRC: Paul Bowles Collection, Humanities Research Center, University of Texas at Austin; Lafcadio: *Lafcadio's Adventures (Les Caves du Vatican)*; LDS: Lawrence D. Stewart; Marshlands: *Marshlands (Paludes)*; MS: manuscript notebook; PB: Paul Bowles; Prometheus: *Prometheus Misbound (Le Prométhée Mal Enchaîné)*; Tape, LDS: my taped conversations with Paul Bowles; TLS: typed letter, signed; UATW: *Up Above the World*; WS: *Without Stopping*.

[1] Paul Bowles, *Without Stopping:An Autobiography* (New York: Putnam's, 1972), pp. 33, 66. "In each tale there was a death which, although unexpected, could be reasonably laid to natural causes. However, in each case the reader had to explain away the brief but inexplicable appearance on the scene of a woman named Volga Merna. Since the other characters were not able to remember what she looked like or what she was doing, she was never suspected. Nor was it explicitly stated that she had any part in the crimes; the reader could decide" (WS 66).

[2] The two letters from Miss Toklas are dated 9 January 1951 and 28 March 1951 and are in the Paul Bowles Collection, Humanities Research Center, University of Texas

at Austin. The letters themselves are quoted in my *Paul Bowles: The Illumination of North Africa* (Carbondale, Illinois: Southern Illinois University Press, forthcoming). For a discussion of Gertrude Stein's theory of detective fiction and "bottom nature," see my "Gertrude Stein and the Vital Dead," in *The Mystery & Detection Annual* (1972), pp. 102-23.

3 Paul Bowles in taped conversation with the author, in Santa Monica, California, 17-21 January 1969.

4 In this regard, see his later comment: "it's much less likely that a good work will come out of a free association than out of planning. You're taking a much greater risk, that's all. . . . However. I think calculation should only come in at a certain point. It's not a substitute for imagination, and it can be very dangerous — in certain work, not all. . . . I don't think one could follow the Surrealist method absolutely, with no conscious control in the choice of material, and be likely to arrive at organic form" (Oliver Evans, "An Interview with Paul Bowles," *Mediterranean Review* 1 [Winter 1971], 14).

5 Ibid., p. 6. The notion was one shared by Gertrude Stein and William James.

6 Paul Bowles, *Up Above the World* (New York: Simon & Schuster, 1966), p. 14.

7 Bowles himself emphatically disagrees with this aspect of my interpretation: "I don't see the destruction of the Slades as inevitable. If the memory manipulation had proven successful, at least to Grove's satisfaction, he would have let them go. What finally decided him on their liquidation was only an accident, and had nothing to do with the Slades or their reaction to his treatment" (TLS, PB to author, 6 November 1973). Bowles sees Grove as rationally responsive to logical evidence; I, to the contrary, think that the protagonist is insane. I can find no evidence in the novel suggesting, to me at least, that his paranoia could have been assuaged by any sort of reassurances. (Did Mrs. Rainmantle once have Grove committed? Or are we to regard his assertion that she did as merely an aspect of his nightmare? The puzzling reference is on p. 89.)

8 Originally Bowles had thought of developing the relationship between Day Slade and Mrs. Rainmantle as a lesbian one, at least as seen by Dr. Slade. The plot outline had read: "Mr. S. levels his charge of lesbianism at her. She is startled, furious. All you need is a good psychiatrist. When they get back to hotel she leaves bedroom, goes to Mrs. R's room for a minute, returns and says that she has invited Mrs. R. to share her room, and that he must sleep in other room." A cancelled note for Dr. Slade stated: "He wondered if by any chance Mrs. R. were a lesbian, perhaps an unconscious one. Still, he knew that certain aggressive matronly women had an unexplained but generally admitted power of attracting very feminine women like his present wife. He supposed a basic irregularity like that could explain her more salient characteristics, such as disregard for her appearance and general air of irresponsibility. The theory explained several things, yet he was not convinced." The published novel suppresses most of such evidence. Confessedly, when Dr. Slade mentions to his wife their anniversary, Day's thoughts turn instantly to Mrs. Rainmantle — and if Dr. Slade will not join them for drinks, she could not care less. There lingers suspicion in Dr. Slade when "he saw his wife lay her hand on the older woman's arm as they went through the door, and he had an immediate premonition of the way in which the situation was going to be resolved" (UATW 32). But the theme of their relationship, as published, is not sexual but philosophic: the joining up with Mrs. Rainmantle is partly that inevitable association of foreigners who share a language; more important, it is itself a gratuitous act — certainly there is no external motivation given, and we are not encouraged to look inward and speculate about sexual needs. The act merely happens. As for the relationship between Thorny and Grove,

Bowles states: "I don't see it as a homosexual attraction, since I don't think sex is implicit in it. Perhaps frustrated unconscious sexual feelings on Thorny's part, but no more. Hero-worship, exploited by Grove to feed his power fantasies" (TLS, PB to author, 6 November 1973).

9 "He has started a couple of novels but discarded both — after they were quite a way along. He seems to feel that there is nothing that can be done to straighten out a book once it has gone askew" (My diary for 30 October 1958).

10 A notebook entry suggests, however, that it was partly to have a journal form, such as had been used in "Pages from Cold Point": "go perhaps continually from journal to straight 3rd person, back & forth, indicating changes in situation, through journal, thus having two moving points which eventually meet at some strategic spot" (HRC).

11 When I suggested to Bowles that he described the making of drugs in Morocco as though it were the formulating of an Anacin tablet, he responded: "That's the way it exists over there, and it's part of the culture. Certainly it's no more absurd than any religion is, really. It's a part of their life, that's all. . . . A curse can even be cast without the knowledge of the victim, especially the ones which involve the imbibing of foreign elements, which attack the nervous system and make one suggestible and malleable" (Tape, LDS).

12 Lady Yvonne Glendower and Mr. Campbell are fictitious names.

13 He once said that he could see that Jane had used some of his characteristics for Mr. Copperfield in her novel.

14 In discussing "The Frozen Fields," a story based on some of his childhood experiences and particularly his initial observation of a homosexual relationship, Bowles remarked that "I thought I might do a series of stories based on memories of childhood. . . . I did toy with the idea, around '63, before I started *Up Above the World*" (Tape, LDS). Perhaps that suppressed impulse also had an effect on the novel. (The confusion in a correct starting date for the composition of *Up Above the World* also occurred in the interview Bowles gave to Oliver Evans: "I started it [*Up Above the World*] about seven years ago, then laid it aside. Then a year or so later I looked at it again, got some more ideas and wrote some more, then laid it aside a second time. Finally, the third time I started working on it in earnest, and finished it" [*Mediterranean Review* 1 (Winter 1971), 11].)

15 He read Gide's *Counterfeiters* in 1927, and in 1929 carried with him on his first trip to Europe Gide's "working notes for the novel, *Journal des Faux-Monnayeurs*" (WS 81). In 1931 he met Gide in Paris, but "I was so elated by the idea of being face to face with the master that I had no precise idea of what we were talking about" (WS 108).

16 Jean Hytier, *André Gide*, trans. Richard Howard (New York: Frederick Ungar, 1967), pp. 68-69, emphasizes the enigmatic quality in the *soties*: "Their very mysteriousness has a specific purpose. A work must make us work — make an effort; it must not leave us as we were when we began it, it must instruct us, 'broach' us, as Gide says, and in order to do this, is not the best way to disturb us? 'A splendid function to assume; that of disturber,' he writes in the *Nouvelle Pages de Journal*." Readers disturbed by the enigmatic quality in *Up Above the World* have perhaps not understood Bowles's belief that enigma is needful.

17 André Gide, *Marshlands and Prometheus Misbound: Two Satires*, trans. George D. Painter (New York: New Directions, 1953), [p. 13].

18 André Gide, *Lafcadio's Adventures (Les Caves du Vatican)*, trans. Dorothy Bussy (New York: Knopf, 1943), p. 17.

19 "Prometheus Misbound," in Gide, *Marshlands*, p. 107.

20 "Journal of *The Counterfeiters*," trans. Justin O'Brien, in André Gide, *The Counterfeiters*, trans. Dorothy Bussy (New York: Modern Library, 1955), p. 391.

21 André Gide, *If It Die . . . An Autobiography*, trans. Dorothy Bussy (New York: Vintage, 1935), p. 251.

22 Wallace Fowlie, *André Gide: His Life and Art* (New York: Macmillan, 1965), pp. 74-75.

23 "All absolutes are only results of the workings of the human mind with its incomplete powers of perception. . . . [I] continue my round of eating, sleeping, defecating and receiving consciousness. . . . I say 'receiving' because that is what I mean, yet I am aware that it is not clear. I do not make or give or be that consciousness; I am on the receiving end of the impulses. They arrive, are refracted or recorded, — in any case, experienced —, and that is all. It would be saying too much if I stated that I *am conscious*." Paul Bowles, "Pages from Cold Point," in *New Directions in Prose and Poetry*, no. 11 (New York: New Directions, 1949), p. 202. This version of the short story, the one closest to the original draft of the story, has not been reprinted elsewhere; the version of the story first collected in *The Delicate Prey and Other Stories* (New York: Random, 1950) and subsequently anthologized does not contain the passage I have quoted.

24 Fowlie, *Gide*, p. 73.

25 The process has, however, a respectable tradition and had earlier been recognized by Gertrude Stein. In 1938 she discussed the Heroic Age of Cubism (Max Jacob's terminology) with particular regard to Picasso: "All ages are heroic, that is to say there are heroes in all ages who do things because they cannot do otherwise and neither they nor the others understand how and why these things happen. One does not ever understand, before they are completely created, what is happening and one does not at all understand what one has done until the moment when it is all done" (*Gertrude Stein on Picasso* [New York: Liveright, 1970], p. 14).

26 Bowles observed of this section in my manuscript: "it occurred to me [last night] that there was a third meaning of the title that I had meant to imply: it is an expression of Grove's assessment of his own metaphysical status. He is accountable to no one, because he is he" (TLS, PB to author, 7 Nov. 1973).

AFTERNOTE

WHILE THIS article was in press I discovered in Dashiell Hammett's *Red Harvest* evidence which illustrates Gertrude Stein's theory of bottom nature as well as anticipates Bowles's attitude toward the revelations made during a drug experience. My 1972 *M&D* essay, "Gertrude Stein and the Vital Dead," pointed out that Miss Stein admired Hammett's novels for their early presentation of the corpse, which allowed the reader's endless meditation upon that corpse's bottom nature. Miss Stein had little interest in the detective himself, for the corpse was the "hero"; and presumably once the detective's bottom nature had been determined, there could be no continuing mystery about him — the detective being around to answer questions and clarify uncertainties. But a distinction needs now to be drawn between the theory of Miss Stein and that of her companion, Alice B. Toklas. Miss Toklas, herself a great admirer of Hammett, seems to have had more conventional expectations from detective fiction. Certainly she was not so comfortable with unanswered questions as was Gertrude Stein, and she was also willing to accept the detective as "hero" if there could be a temporary mystery about his bottom nature. But because she required integrity, she wanted the end of a detective novel to reconcile the novel's events with the central figure's bottom nature. (Integrity was ever an aspect of identity for Miss Toklas, even on the simplest domestic level; her father had reminded her, and she never forgot, that "a hostess should never apologize for any failure in her household arrangements, if there is a hostess there is insofar as there is a hostess no failure." Bottom nature will never admit of behavior that contradicts one's identity, no matter whether it is a hostess carving a roast or a murderer carving his victim.)

In *Red Harvest* the Continental Op is sent on one assignment and then arbitrarily enlarges it as the original duty takes on moral obligations. When his client is murdered, the Continental Op decides to clean up Poisonville by turning criminal against criminal in a purgation of blood. But the successful series of murders begins to worry the operator behind them: "This damned burg's getting me. If I don't get away soon I'll be going blood-simple like the natives. There's been what? A dozen and a half murders since I've been here," he tells Dinah Brand. "I've arranged a killing or two in my time, when they were necessary. But this is the first time I've ever got the fever. . . . Play with murder enough and it gets you one of two ways. It makes you sick, or you get to like it. . . . Poisonville is right. It's poisoned me." Has he really changed because of these experiences? Has the Continental Op's bottom nature finally been revealed as one which uses an independent dependent (i.e. attacking) nature only to bring about, and rejoice in, the destruction of others, no matter how justified?

To answer these questions we must focus on the events immediately following the quoted conversation. The Continental Op voluntarily drinks gin laced with laudanum, passes out, and wakes up to find that, seemingly, he has become a participant in the ritual of blood-letting: for his hand grasps the handle of an ice pick whose blade is buried in Dinah Brand's left breast. Has he killed her in his drugged insensibility? Hammett depicts the Continental Op's opium dream; but that phantasmagoria of images perplexes as much as does Bowles's creation of Grove's marijuana fantasy. At the end of *Red Harvest* Dinah Brand's murderer describes the actions of that mysterious night: the Continental Op had galloped into the room, "coked to the edges, charging at the whole world with both eyes shut"; tumbling into Dinah Brand he had clutched at the handle of the ice pick which had already killed her. Before he learns these facts, and even when confronted with the "evidence" of his complicity in the crime, the Continental Op had had sufficient faith in his bottom nature to distrust the ocular proof of incrimination: "I was all hopped up that night, and had a lot of dreams, with bells ringing and voices calling, and a lot of stuff like that. I got an idea maybe it wasn't straight dreaming so much as hop-head nightmares stirred up by things that were happening around me." Significantly the strange actions were not internalized, were not produced by his liberated bottom nature; they were "happening *around me*." In their drugged state the Slades cannot make this distinction, any more than they can recognize that theirs are hop-head nightmares.

Hammett and Bowles would agree that drugs do not distort our bottom nature, they do not change us into what we were not. Drugs merely liberate bottom nature (if it has been suppressed) and dramatize it. Both *Red Harvest* and *Up Above the World* demonstrate Alice Toklas's notion, as expressed in her letters to Bowles, that in the most effective — the modern — detective stories the hero is ultimately brought to a confrontation with, or confirmation of, his own bottom nature. *Up Above the World* has revealed in the Slades a bottom nature they had not suspected. *Red Harvest* validates the Continental Op's bottom nature which, even in his drugged state, he would not disavow. Hammett's novel thus contrasts helpfully with Bowles's, showing as it does that the drugged state need hold no surprises in the revelation of bottom nature.

WEST

By Henry Binder

The girls walked west
Passing Wabash Avenue
And crossed the stone bridge over the rail tracks
where an iron dust blew up from the yards below.

The wind turned shoreward from the lake
and bits of paper whirled at the curbsides
And they kept on, foolish and chatting,
As the dark buildings enclosed them.

Along Canal Street
An old car passed jarring over the pavement
As the street lamps cast hinges to the walks.

Telephones had begun to ring
And the lines pulsed like nerves through the city
As the car swung west, out of town.

The city stiffened like dying leathers

As no hunts led to the door of the room
where a man with his arms folded
lay out on an iron bed
beneath a bulb
that dropped from the ceiling.

He paused,
resting outside the edges of the search
that probed in the streets.

By the corner of a woods
The girls were lifted out from a black drain,
Shapeless.

Topanga Canyon, 1973

THE MYSTERIES OF *GAUDY NIGHT:*
FEMINISM, FAITH, AND
THE DEPTHS OF CHARACTER

By Laura Krugman Ray

FEW TWENTIETH-CENTURY WRITERS have brought to their work more varied interests and talents than Dorothy Sayers. Best known for her detective novels and stories, she also produced lyric poetry, religious dramas, lay theology, a translation of Dante, and essays on a wide range of literary topics. Certainly no mystery writer has endowed the whodunit with so much manner and meaning without reducing it to either farce or allegory. The significance of *Gaudy Night*, her finest piece of detective fiction, is in fact three-fold. In terms of technique it handles the characters of a mystery novel with the psychological depth of modern serious fiction; in terms of theme it treats the issue of feminism in the chaotic world of the 1930's; and in terms of Sayers's own development it anticipates the concerns of her later theological writings and thus constitutes in some sense a farewell to her detective art.

Clearly *Gaudy Night* is a book that declines to fit easily into the detective-story mold, and its author was perfectly aware of its irregularities. In an article written only two years after the novel's publication, Sayers described her conviction that "if the detective story was to live and develop it *must* get back to where it began in the hands of Collins and Le Fanu, and become once more a novel of manners instead of a pure crossword puzzle."[1] For a writer who considered *The Moonstone* "probably the very finest detective story ever written,"[2] a novel of manners meant a carefully constructed plot that relied on setting and conversation as well as ingenuity to hold its audience. In the two novels that preceded *Gaudy Night, Murder Must Advertise* and *The Nine Tailors*, Sayers attempted to "get back to where it began" by combining the detective interest with two slightly exotic settings from her own experience. She chose a London advertising agency (she had worked briefly as a copywriter after college) and a small cathedral town in East Anglia (she grew up in the fen country). One book is filled with the lore of advertising agencies, the other with campanology, and in both the solution to the mystery depends on Wimsey's— and Sayers's—expertise in these diverse fields.

Gaudy Night too has an unusual setting, a woman's college at Oxford, but here the setting determines more than the solution to the crime. Through it Sayers approaches what she calls, in Arnold's phrase, "a criticism of life."[3] And just as the modern novel aims at such judgments on the quality of experience through analytic and mimetic rendering of its characters' mental processes, Sayers too adds a new depth of characterization to the detective novel. In *Gaudy Night* the setting is closely involved in the psychological dilemma of the heroine, Harriet Vane, a successful mystery writer who had already been acquitted of the charge of murdering her lover through the efforts of Peter Wimsey in *Strong Poison*, an earlier Sayers book. The remarkable thing about *Gaudy Night* is the way the two seemingly separate elements, Harriet's bewilderment over her feelings for Wimsey and the poison pen who is attacking Shrewsbury College, collide in the novel's denouement. The solution to the crime becomes as well the solution to the heroine's life, and the reader's satisfaction comes as much from the resolution of Peter's protracted courtship as it does from the unmasking of the culprit. And because this is a psychological novel, the culprit's psychology is an explanation of her motives *and* an illumination of Harriet's reluctance to accept her own feelings for Wimsey.

That Sayers intended the structure of *Gaudy Night* to function in this double way is clear from her own admission. "The new and exciting thing," she writes, "was to bring the love-problem into line with the detective-problem, so that the same key should unlock both at once."[4] And the key is found in the novel's setting, the integrity and detachment of the scholar's world at Oxford. It is possible to examine *Gaudy Night* as first of all an academic novel, because it is saturated with the details and routines of college life. Shrewsbury is clearly based in part on Somerville College, where Sayers took a first in medieval literature in 1915 as one of the earliest women to receive an Oxford degree. Harriet, who took her first in English and then made her way as a mystery writer, returns to Shrewsbury feeling that she has betrayed her Oxford years by her affair with another writer and her trial for his murder. To explain her residence while she investigates the college poison pen, Harriet researches a biography of Le Fanu; Sayers herself promised, though she never delivered, a biography of Collins, her second idol. It seems fair to assume, then, that both heroine and author are interested in reconciling the modern detective story with its more illustrious antecedents. Harriet's return to Shrewsbury raises the problem of the mystery novel's literary value, and *Gaudy Night* ironically offers an internal commentary on its own experimentation. When Peter suggests a psychological motivation for a character's behavior in Harriet's current book, she responds with reluctance:

> "Yes — he'd be interesting. But if I give Wilfrid all those violent and lifelike feelings, he'll throw the whole book out of balance."
> "You would have to abandon the jig-saw kind of story and write a book about human beings for a change."
> "I'm afraid to try that, Peter. It might go too near the bone."[5]

The difference, then, between mystery novel and literary novel is the addition of convincing characters who deflect some of the interest from the design of the plot to themselves.

And Harriet's fear echoes the reservations of Sayers's critics — such emphasis on character can destroy the perfect balance of the "pure crossword puzzle." A. E. Murch charges that "in *Gaudy Night*, with its well-sustained portrayal of college life and its acutely-reasoned discussions of intellectual integrity and psychological problems, there is scarcely sufficient real detection to sustain even a short story."[6] And H. P. Rickman concedes that "in *Gaudy Night* itself, the form of the novel meant purely for entertainment is already strained by serious characterization and a sense of the complexity of human problems."[7]

The technical problem facing Harriet as a writer is a variant of her personal problem. Peter has saved her life and has, for the five years since her trial, loyally proposed marriage to her at regular intervals. Embittered by the affair that ended in murder, Harriet determines to avoid any further emotional involvements, not to risk the balance she has painfully established in her life. And her stay at Oxford serves to reinforce her retreat from emotion. The calm and devotion of the dons at Shrewsbury to their academic projects, the seeming absence of any disruptive emotion, the perfect integrity of their conduct, all seduce Harriet away from the claims of her own passions. The contest seems to be between London and Oxford, Peter and Le Fanu, commitment and detachment.

The technical problem facing Sayers in *Gaudy Night* is just the reverse of Harriet's worry over Wilfrid. If Sayers *didn't* find a way to give her hero "violent and lifelike feelings," he would throw out of balance a novel of psychological depth and interest. As he emerges in *Gaudy Night*, Peter is far more complicated than in the earlier novels and stories, where fewer demands were made on his frail nature. The specter of the original Wimsey, who first appeared in *Whose Body?* in 1923 as a somewhat foppish and insolent, though keen-witted, detective, haunts the pages of Sayers's critics. He has been called "a caricature of an English aristocrat conceived with an immensely snobbish loving seriousness" whose "speech strongly resembles that of Bertie Wooster,"[8] a description only slightly less damning than Edmund Wilson's: "a dreadful conventional English nobleman of the casual and debonair kind, with the embarrassing name of Lord Peter Wimsey."[9]

Since her detective was in *Whose Body?* a near relation of Wodehouse's Bertie Wooster, Sayers was forced to recall Peter's earlier inanities as she remade him into a serious character capable of feeling as well as detecting. The challenge was to transform Peter from a flat to a round character, to add emotional depth without discarding the distinguishing marks that had long made him Lord Peter Wimsey:

> If the story was to go on, Peter had got to become a complete human being, with a past and a future, with a consistent family and social history, with a complicated psychology and even the rudiments of a religious outlook. And all this would have to be squared somehow or other with such random attributes as I had bestowed upon him over a series of years in accordance with the requirements of various detective plots.[10]

Her strategy was to deflect the absurd babble and patrician assurance onto Saint-George Wimsey, Peter's nephew and a student at Oxford, thus preserving family consistency and at the same time freeing Peter from his worst excesses. When Harriet runs into the young man accidentally, she identifies him as a Wimsey by his conversation: "I recognized the voice before I looked at him at all" (p. 237). And Saint-George's rambling speeches make use of the same coy circumlocutions, the same foolish swagger that tied Peter in the early novels to Bertie Wooster. Here Saint-George tells Harriet about his hold over his uncle:

> "Besides, you see, I've got the bulge on Uncle Peter. If the worst comes to the worst, I can always threaten to cut my throat and land him with the strawberry leaves."
>
> "With the what?" said Harriet, fancying that this must be the latest Oxford version of giving the raspberry.
>
> "The strawberry leaves," said the young man. "The balm, the sceptre, and the ball. Four rows of moth-eaten ermine. To say nothing of that dashed great barracks down at Denver, eating its mouldy head off." Seeing that Harriet still looked blankly at him,

he explained further: "I'm sorry; I forgot. My name's Saint-
George and the Governor forgot to provide me with any brothers.
So the minute they write d.s.p. after me, Uncle Peter's for it."
(p. 144)

In contrast, Peter now uses the Wodehouse manner of his nephew only
for a purpose. When someone reports to Harriet that Peter was seen at
a dog show "giving a perfect imitation of the silly-ass-about-town,"
she replies that "he was either frightfully bored or detecting something" (p. 32). That Peter now employs his former shallow personality as a deliberate disguise is an index to his new complexity.

Sayers now describes Peter as a lonely survivor of the old order, ill-
equipped in some ways for the new democracy of scholarship students
at Oxford and post-war levelling of class barriers. Harriet is a liberated
woman of the thirties, a child of the middle class earning her living,
defying sexual conventions, demanding independence. And though
Peter accepts the new world and shows himself free of class and sex
prejudices, he still demonstrates a nostalgia for the England of his
ancestors. Sayers herself combined an ardent feminism with a generally conservative attitude toward the traditional humanist values,
and we hear a plaintive note in Peter's speech on his family seat:

> "Harriet, will you come with me one day to Denver and see the
> place before the new civilization grows in on it like the jungle?
> I don't want to go all Galsworthy about it. They'll tell you I don't
> care a damn for the whole outfit, and I don't know that I do. But I
> was born there, and I shall be sorry if I live to see the land sold for
> ribbon-building and the Hall turned over to a Hollywood Colour-
> Talkie King." (p. 238)

The jungle image is an exact echo of Waugh's *A Handful of Dust* of
just a year earlier, where Tony Last is literally expelled from his
family home to a South American jungle, while Hetton becomes a
flourishing silver fox farm. Sayers shares with Waugh a regard for
the dignity and order of aristocratic England, but in the marriage of
her blue-blooded detective with a self-made woman she allows a class
balance that accommodates the old order to the new, a synthesis that
Waugh never envisions.

*   *   *   *   *

If a novel is to contain a significant "criticism of life," it must concern itself with the conditions under which life is actually lived. Sayers

therefore broadens the scope of Harriet's dilemma to include the plight of the educated woman in reconciling her public and private roles. *Gaudy Night* appeared in 1935, when the liberating effects of World War I on women in England were waning. Economic depression and unemployment brought resentment of women who held men's jobs, and abroad the Nazi doctrine of *Kinder, Kirche, Kuche* questioned the security of gains at home. Sayers is not a social historian, but she allows hints of these external forces into her novel to complicate Harriet's situation. This conversation between Padgett, the college lodge-keeper, and a workman suggests that the women of Shrewsbury are not yet fully secure:

> "Young ladies," Padgett was heard to say, "will 'ave their larks, same as young gentlemen."
>
> "When I was a lad," replied the foreman, "young ladies was young ladies. And young gentlemen was young gentlemen. If you get my meaning."
>
> "Wot this country wants," said Padgett, "is a 'Itler."
>
> "That's right," said the foreman. "Keep the girls at 'ome. Funny kind o' job you got 'ere, mate. Wot was you, afore you took to keepin' a 'en 'ouse?"
>
> "Assistant camel 'and at the Zoo. Very interesting job it was, too."
>
> "Wot made you chuck it?"
>
> "Blood-poison. I was bit in the arm," said Padgett, "by a female."
>
> "Ah!" said the foreman decorator. (p. 101)

One woman scholar is an ardent proponent of eugenics and encourages educated women to propagate; another is the author of an anti-Nazi study, *The Position of Women in the Modern State.* Even inside the quiet enclave of Shrewsbury the debate over feminism continues, and Peter's exchange with Dr. Baring, the college warden, underscores the precarious hold of women's education, even at Oxford. The warden begins:

> "But probably you are not specially interested in all this question of women's education."
>
> "Is it still a question? It ought not to be. I hope you are not going to ask me whether I approve of women's doing this and that."
>
> "Why not?"

"You should not imply that I have any right either to approve or disapprove."

"I assure you," said the Warden, "that even in Oxford we still encounter a certain number of people who maintain their right to disapprove."

"And I had hoped I was returning to civilization." (pp. 275-76)

Harriet's imagined choice between independence and marriage or between intellect and emotion reflects the tenuous hold on her professional freedom the educated woman feels she has; Harriet's situation is offered as a dramatic instance of a fairly common difficulty.

All the psychological and sociological material that Sayers includes is necessary background to what must be the center of any detective novel, the crime. In this case there is no murder, no single act of violence demanding a single and clear-cut response from the reader. Instead, a member of the college community sends obscene and threatening messages to various dons and students, engages in acts of vandalism calculated to bring embarrassment to the college, and tries to drive a withdrawn but brilliant student to suicide before attacking her real enemy. The college authorities, fearing the effect of any publicity on their position, ask Harriet to conduct a private investigation. Like Harriet, they come to assume that the perpetrator is one of themselves, a spinster warped by sexual repression and isolation who is determined to humiliate her fellow academics, in short, the popular stereotype of an educated and celibate woman. Only Peter Wimsey, offered Harriet's evidence, can see through such distorting prejudices to identify the culprit as a vindictive widow whose husband was driven to suicide after his falsified thesis was exposed by a Shrewsbury don. That the culprit is a married woman, and the mother of two daughters, reveals the anti-feminist impulses of the educated woman, her unconscious complicity in the prejudices against her. In keeping with the psychological slant of the novel, the guilty woman is treated medically, not legally; her crime stems not from malice but from a failure of perspective. As a feminist novel, however, *Gaudy Night* is stern in its exposure of the enemy within and ironic in its use of the aristocratic male as the only unswerving proponent of sexual equality.

If the women of Shrewsbury prove to be flawed feminists, they also prove to be unshakable in their professional integrity. All the members of the Senior Common Room agree that, whatever the consequences, a single fact may never be falsified and a falsification may never be condoned. Miss de Vine, the historian who ruined Annie Wilson's husband, is portrayed as a scholar whose vocation is the result "of a powerful spiritual call, over-riding other possible tendencies and desires" (p. 109). She has, in years past, ended an engagement when she realized that her research, not her fiancé, was her "job." Annie stands at the opposite end of the female spectrum, discarding integrity in favor of an unjudging devotion to her man: "If he'd been a thief or a murderer, I'd have loved him and stuck to him" (p. 372). Like two characters in a psychodrama, these two women act out the conflicting impulses of Harriet's personality. She is drawn toward the life Miss de Vine represents as toward a crusade, what in her imagination she sees as "a Holy War, and that whole wildly heterogeneous, that even slightly absurd collection of chattering women fused into a corporate unity with one another and with every man and woman to whom integrity of mind meant more than material gain" (p. 28). And if her physical nature is drawn toward the emotional indulgence and the protection Peter offers, she finds that between two such incompatible forces she must choose the integrity of Oxford.

What Sayers offers as the solution to Harriet's life is the idea of balance, the reconciliation of two seemingly irreconcilable positions. The scholar's integrity demands that not a single fact be concealed, and in a precisely parallel way the personality's integrity resides in its ability to take account of all its inclinations. It is one thing for a devoted scholar like Miss de Vine to renounce any personal ties, but for Harriet this would amount to a betrayal of self. And Peter too must demonstrate his integrity by allowing Harriet to see, in Annie Wilson, what she fears most and what Sayers terms "emotion uncontrolled by intellect."[11] Harriet must understand the risks of unrestrained passion as clearly as the dangers of its opposite state, "intellect starved of emotion,"[12] before accepting Peter's proposal. One of the many balances posited by the novel, then, is that of intellect and emotion, head and heart, scholarship and passion, and the structure of *Gaudy Night* reflects this balance by planting a love story amid Oxford's cool Gothic towers — even Peter's final proposal and Harriet's acceptance are spoken in Latin. And it is this conjunction of setting, plot, and theme that Sayers herself values in her book:

> To make an artistic unity it is, I feel, essential that the plot should derive from the setting, and that both should form part of the theme. From this point of view, *Gaudy Night* does, I think, stand reasonably well up to the test; the setting is a women's college; the plot derives from, and develops through, episodes that could not have occurred in any other place; and the theme is the relation of scholarship to life.[13]

The delicate balance achieved by Harriet and Peter is expressed by

Gaudy Night in a variety of ways, and it is here that Sayers brings to the detective novel the techniques of the modern novel. The balance she has in mind is related in theory to the star equilibrium of Ursula and Birkin in *Women in Love*, the union of two discrete and independent individuals in a relationship of tension and support. But where Lawrence has his characters explain their relation through conscious metaphor, Sayers uses symbolic incident and careful ambiguity. As her lovers are drawn closer together, their activities suggest the cooperation of a complementary relationship. They go punting together on the Isis, where Harriet takes the pole and Peter steers in an auspicious reversal of traditional roles. Shopping at an antique store, they sing Elizabethan duets and Peter remarks that "anybody can have the harmony, if they will leave us the counterpoint" (p. 323). And in the most striking instance of such frictional collaborations, Harriet and Peter share the authorship of a sonnet. In a musing moment, Harriet writes the octave in the notebook she compiles of her investigation:

> Here, then, at home, by no more storms distrest,
> Folding laborious hands we sit, wings furled;
> Here in close perfume lies the rose-leaf curled,
> Here the sun stands and knows not east nor west,
> Here no tide runs; we have come, last and best,
> From the wide zone through dizzying circles hurled,
> To that still centre where the spinning world
> Sleeps on its axis, to the heart of rest. (p. 189)

But finding "no turn for the sestet to take, no epigram, no change of mood" (pp. 189-90), she abandons the poem. Later, when Peter borrows the notebook, he completes the sonnet:

> Lay on thy whips, O Love, that we upright,
>   Poised on the perilous point, in no lax bed
>   May sleep, as tension at the verberant core
> Of music sleeps; for, if thou spare to smite,
>   Staggering, we stoop, stooping, fall dumb and dead,
>   And, dying so, sleep our sweet sleep no more.
>   (pp. 303-04)

It is perhaps unfortunate for the feminism of the book that Peter's sestet is so much better than Harriet's octave, but the image of tense balance is successfully supplied by both the form and the theme of the sonnet. It accomplishes in miniature the same artistic unity that Sayers claimed for the novel. Even the image of the poem on the notebook page, like one of Herbert's shaped verses, suggests the same motif to Harriet, who finds it "a little unbalanced, with her own sprawling hand above and Peter's deceptively neat script below, like a large top on a small spindle" (p. 303). And the sonnet itself is a poetic expression of precisely the equilibrium the lovers can hope for, a balance not stagnant but dynamic, a repose that exists only in motion and pain.

Peter contains within himself further harmonious discords. He is an aristocrat with "six centuries of possessiveness, fastened under the yoke of urbanity" (p. 344), yet he clearly demands equality rather than submission from his wife. Sayers elsewhere called her detective "an eighteenth-century Whig gentleman, born a little out of his time,"[14] a label he rejects when offered by Harriet: "The perfect Augustan? No; I'm afraid it's at most a balance of opposing forces" (p. 254). These opposing forces are due in part to Peter's change from a charming stereotype to a complicated personality, but they reveal as well an instability that is finally anchored by Harriet's staunch and sensible nature. It is interesting to note that in the union of Harriet and Peter, Sayers saw one more balance, the enduring complementary natures of man and woman. In her introduction to Dante's *Purgatory,* she points to the eternal distinction art and life have made between the sexes:

> And art and literature, as well as experience, bear witness that on the whole woman's preoccupation is not with the subtleties of love but with the practical problems of marriage and household. Women are interested not in sex, but in love-affairs; not in passion but in people; not in man but in men. . . . The sentiment, "Man's love is of man's life a thing apart; 'tis woman's whole existence" is, in fact, a piece of male wishful thinking, which can only be made to come true by depriving the life of the leisured woman of every other practical and intellectual interest. Lovers, husbands, children, households — these are major feminine preoccupations: but not love. It is the male who looks upon amorous adventure as an end in itself, and dignifies it with a metaphysic.[15]

Her lovers in *Gaudy Night* are intended not as sexual stereotypes but as embodiments of what she considers the male and female principles:

> The essential Peter is seen to be the familiar figure of the interpretive artist, the romantic soul at war with the realistic brain. Harriet, with her lively and inquisitive mind and her soul grounded upon reality, is his complement — the creative artist; her make-

up is more stable than his, and far more capable of self-depen-
dence. On the surface he is a comedian; his dislocation is at the
centre: she is tragic externally, for all her dissatisfactions are
patent, but she has the central unity which he has not.[16]

If Peter is the superior poet, Harriet is the literary craftsman; if Peter
is confident of his role in society, Harriet is confident of her inner
poise. That Peter's romanticism is steadied by Harriet's realism seems
a weakening of Sayers's call for sexual equality in marriage, but she
continues to insist that these distinct roles are equal in responsibility
and value.

To illustrate this theme, the final rapprochement of the lovers
occurs at a Bach concert, and it is in terms of a great fugue that their
union is accomplished:

> "Peter — what did you mean when you said that anybody
> could have the harmony if they would leave us the counterpoint?"
>
> "Why," said he, shaking his head, "that I like my music poly-
> phonic. If you think I meant anything else, you know what I
> meant."
>
> "Polyphonic music takes a lot of playing. You've got to be more
> than a fiddler. It needs a musician."
>
> "In this case, two fiddlers — both musicians."
>
> "I'm not much of a musician, Peter."
>
> "As they used to say in my youth: 'All girls should learn a little
> music — enough to play a simple accompaniment.' I admit that
> Bach isn't a matter of an autocratic virtuoso and a meek accom-
> panist. But do you want to be either?" (p. 382)

At this point symbolic incident becomes conscious metaphor, as it so
often does in Lawrence. Sayers fills a traditional form with her progressive meaning — the precarious balance of two separate individuals conceding only their need to blend emotion with intellect, union
with detachment, impulse with convention. And like the buildings of
Shrewsbury, "built by a modern architect in a style neither new nor
old, but stretching out reconciling hands to past and present" (p. 7),
this union embraces the dignity of Peter's family heritage and the
dignity of Harriet's personal achievement.

*   *   *   *   *

After *Gaudy Night* Sayers wrote only one more novel, *Busman's
Honeymoon*, which she subtitled "A love story with detective inter-

ruptions" and based on her stage play of the same title. She then turned her attention to presenting, in her numerous theological essays, a possible fusion of Christianity with the experience of modern life. It is clear that even in *Gaudy Night* the idea of balance includes as well a harmony of the secular and religious. Oxford itself, with its values of truth and discipline, finds a partner in what Sayers terms "the great Anglican compromise." Attending the university sermon, Harriet ponders the peculiar sympathy of Christian philosophy and atomic physics:

> Here were the Universities and the Church of England kissing one another in righteousness and peace, like the angels in a Botticelli Nativity: very exquisitely robed, very cheerful in a serious kind of way, a little mannered, a little conscious of their fine mutual courtesy. Here, without heat, they could discuss their common problem, agreeing pleasantly or pleasantly agreeing to differ. (p. 231)

In *The Mind of the Maker*, published six years after *Gaudy Night*, Sayers alters her image of harmony from partnership to hierarchy. The scholar's dedication to truth is still an incomplete means of apprehending experience, but instead of a union of intellect and emotion, Sayers now advocates the subordination of intellect to creativity: [17]

> We have begun to suspect that the purely analytical approach to phenomena is leading us only further and further into the abyss of disintegration and randomness, and that it is becoming urgently necessary to construct a synthesis of life.[18]

She attributes to "the desire of being persuaded that all human experience may be presented in terms of a problem having a predictable, final, complete and sole possible solution"[19] the popularity of detective fiction, but she argues that in her own *Gaudy Night* not all the problems posed by the book are solved in the traditionally resolute way. The identity of the poison pen at Shrewsbury is disclosed, and a method of uniting Harriet and Peter is supplied, but even this union is not closed and permanent — it remains fluid and speculative, available to change and adjustment. And the central issue of the book, "Is professional integrity so important that its preservation must override every consideration of the emotional and material consequences?",[20] is answered not in a universal edict but only for the Shrewsbury situation.

In *The Mind of the Maker*, Sayers maintains that in the act of creation the human mind is analogous to the Divine mind of the Creator. The disciplined and sober work of analysis is only the second phase of the creative act; it is the initial Idea that illuminates a problem and permits the less inspired but necessary labor of exposition. In *Gaudy Night* this initial idea is the one problem that remains unsolved:

> The enriching (and also catastrophic) quality of Integrity is thus the Father-Idea of the book, providing the mechanics of the detective problem, the catalyst that precipitates the instability of the emotional situation, and also a theme which unites the microcosm of the book to the macrocosm of the universe.[21]

To Sayers, then, in retrospect, the detective element of *Gaudy Night* is almost incidental to the life of the book, to its connection with a universe of moral and human problems that dwarf its own limited plot of crime and sleuthing.

Such an attitude is clearly subversive of the very premises of detective fiction. In 1934, Sayers asserted that "the detective story seeks to leave nothing unexplained; . . . [it] belongs essentially to the literature of knowledge."[22] But when an author of detective fiction decides that not everything *can* be explained, that as the genre moves closer to the realm of serious literature it must accept more and more ambiguities, then her satisfaction with her own plots may well weaken. Once she tapped the deeper mysteries of human psychology and Christianity, Sayers perhaps became reluctant to produce any more of the tidy mysteries that had secured her reputation. At any rate, from 1937 to her death twenty years later, she occupied herself with the writing of neo-medieval plays, theological essays, and her translation of Dante, reportedly declining even to provide an introduction for a new edition of her detective stories. In *Gaudy Night* Dorothy Sayers attempted to make the literature of knowledge a little less omniscient than it had been before, and she produced a rich and complicated novel that brought detective fiction to the brink of literary legitimacy before she abandoned Lord Peter in favor of a higher Lord.

NOTES

[1] Dorothy L. Sayers, *"Gaudy Night,"* in *The Art of the Mystery Story*, ed. Howard Haycraft (New York: Simon and Schuster, 1946), p. 209.

[2] Sayers, ed., *Great Short Stories of Detection, Mystery and Horror* (London: Victor Gollancz, 1928), p. 25.

[3] *"Gaudy Night,"* p. 209.

[4] *"Gaudy Night,"* p. 215.

[5] Sayers, *Gaudy Night* (New York: Avon, 1970), pp. 255-56. All references will be to this edition and will be given parenthetically in the text.

[6] A. E. Murch, *The Development of the Detective Novel* (London: Peter Owen, 1958), p. 223.

[7] H. P. Rickman, "From Detection to Theology," *Hibbert Journal*, 60 (1962), 291.

[8] Julian Symons, *Mortal Consequences: A History, from the Detective Story to the Crime Novel* (New York: Harper & Row, 1972), p. 109.

[9] Edmund Wilson, "Who Cares Who Killed Roger Ackroyd?" in Haycraft, p. 392.

[10] *"Gaudy Night,"* p. 211.

[11] *"Gaudy Night,"* p. 214.

[12] *"Gaudy Night,"* p. 214.

[13] *"Gaudy Night,"* p. 217.

[14] Sayers, *The Mind of the Maker* (New York: Harcourt, Brace, 1941), p. 131.

[15] Sayers, Introduction to the *Purgatory* of Dante (Harmondsworth: Penguin, 1955), p. 33.

[16] *"Gaudy Night,"* p. 219.

[17] Rickman argues that Lord Peter himself is a symbol of the intellect (Rickman's term is the Enlightenment) and that Sayers's dismissal of Wimsey after *Busman's Honeymoon* is symptomatic of her rejection of pure intellect in favor of a reason blended with faith. See Rickman, p. 293.

[18] *Mind of the Maker*, p. 181.

[19] *Mind of the Maker*, p. 188.

[20] *Mind of the Maker*, p. 190.

[21] *Mind of the Maker*, p. 191.

[22] Sayers, ed., *Great Short Stories of Detection, Mystery and Horror, Third Series* (London: Victor Gollancz, 1934), p. 15.

THE PASSAGE

By J. E. Harrison

Hold my hand—
Let's try this corridor.
We can hardly see.
A chill dankness settles close
As mould to the cheek.
Far off a clock face glimmers
In arched shadows beyond the hall
Where our steps echo into a distance
Waiting, beyond time, for us to arrive.

Suddenly, as we pass, a click,
A faint whirr of metal wheels—
The clock strikes.
We look up; the light-spun disk hangs
simple as cheese, pale as curds
no numbers counting the circle
Giving us sense and momentum,
No hands spacing our life;
We do not catch time.

From its long, boxed belly
A scratching, like rats in a coffin,
Something fumbling the catch,
A wincing of the door outwards
As it struggles past;
Stiff hands beat the air
Black shapes point the way
In a rush of smoke, a smell
Of dead roses . . . unrelenting it goes.

We cringe against the cold wall,
Feel plaster crumble under our nails. . . .

REVIEWS

Graham Greene. *Graham Greene on Film: Collected Film Criticism 1935-40*, ed. John Russell Taylor. New York: Simon and Schuster, 1972. $12.50.

In the introduction to his collected film criticism, Graham Greene suggests that reviewing films was an escape, not from the depressing social problems of the thirties, but from the pressures of writing fiction.

> These films were an escape—escape from that hellish problem of construction in Chapter Six, from the secondary character who obstinately refused to come alive, escape for an hour and a half from the melancholy which falls inexorably round the novelist when he has lived for too many months on end in his private world. (p. 1)

Yet it is precisely his novelistic qualities that make his film criticism valuable. Contributing little to film theory, Greene's reviews usually summarize the plot and comment on the acting in a witty, impressionistic style. But what really distinguishes them is their power to evoke the experiential quality of the cinema—an achievement that is rare in any age.

Unlike the literary critic, the film critic uses a different medium from that of the art about which he is writing. To capture the special qualities of a particular film, he cannot merely quote a passage from the text, but must try to express the film's visual and auditory texture through his own imaginative use of language. He must, like the novelist, employ rich verbal imagery to recreate the multi-sensory experience that is his subject. In his film criticism, Greene does not escape from this novelistic task; in fact, it is the primary source of his achievement. With the vivid descriptive powers so characteristic of his fiction, he can successfully evoke the face of Peter Lorre,

> Those marbly pupils in the pasty spherical face are like the eye-pieces of a microscope through which you can see laid flat on the slide the entangled mind of a man: love and lust, nobility and perversity, hatred of itself and despair jumping out at you from the jelly. (p. 11)

or the laugh of Fernandel,

He can carry half a minute of film with a laugh alone, the camera fixed on the huge mouth and the great mulish teeth. Watch him in the cafe with the crook as he suddenly realizes that he doesn't love his wife; the sudden disconcerting bellow, then the splutter, the attempt to explain, the feeble flap-flap of one hand, the hopeless movements of the equine head, and laughter welling out, bursting between the big rocky teeth, unstemmable, like an oil-gusher running to waste over a whole countryside. (p. 238)

or the unique comic style of Alexandrov,

This at any rate is completely original: Alexandrov's use of a moving camera to convey the grotesque in his long panorama of a crowded bathing beach. The wealthy woman in pyjamas swaying her munificent hips along the shore in pursuit of the famous conductor is followed by the camera behind a close-up frieze of enlarged feet stuck out towards the lens, of fat thighs, enormous backs, a caricature of ugly humanity exposing pieces of itself like butcher's joints in the sun. (p. 24)

Although he sees film as an escape, Greene is not really condescending toward the medium. True, his reviews are teeming with literary comparisons, sometimes illuminating (e.g., he puts *It Happened One Night* and *Arms and the Girl* in the tradition of Restoration comedy, and compares Charlie Chaplin with Joseph Conrad as two artists who have a few simple ideas that could be expressed in the same words: "courage, loyalty, labour: against the same nihilistic background of purposeless suffering," p. 53) and sometimes humorous (e.g., seeing a Garbo movie is like reading a book by Carlyle: "Good, oh very good, but work rather than play," p. 271). Yet he grants film its autonomy from literature, insisting that its comprehensive scope, agile speed, and concrete realism give it advantage over the stage play and novel. This conception of the unique qualities of cinema—particularly its capacity for realism—is fairly conventional.

Where Greene departs from other critics is in suggesting that one of the medium's unique features is its capacity for "lyrical absurdity" or "ecstatic happiness," precisely those qualities that make film a form of escape.

Only the cinema is able in its most fantastic moments to give a sense of absurd unreasoning happiness, of a kind of poignant release: you can't catch it in prose: it belongs to Walt Disney, to Clair's voices from the air, and there is one moment in this film

[*Paris Love Song*] when you have it, as the Count scrambles singing across the roofs to his mistress's room; happiness and freedom,
nothing really serious, nothing really lasting, a touching of
hands, a tuneful miniature love. (p. 7)

Although Greene finds this quality in humorous detective films (like
The Trunk Mystery, The Thin Man, Star of Midnight, and we see it
as well in Greene's own *Our Man in Havana*), he implies that this
potentiality is most fully realized in farce—especially in the films of
Rene Clair, Grigori Alexandrov, Walt Disney, and Fred Astaire. The
recognition of this lyrical absurdity is what leads him to the witty insight that Fred Astaire is the "nearest approach we are ever likely to
have to a human Mickey Mouse."

> He might have been drawn by Mr. Walt Disney, with his quick
> physical wit, his incredible agility. He belongs to a fantasy world
> almost as free as Mickey's from the law of gravity, but unfor-
> tunately he has to act with human beings and not even Miss
> Ginger Rogers can match his freedom, lightness and happiness.
> (p. 30)

But it is in discussing René Clair and his special genre (combining
fantasy, satire, and realism) that Greene develops his conception of
this special cinematic quality most fully. In reviewing *The Ghost Goes
West*, he insists that the silliness of the basic story, so inferior to Clair's
usual material, gave him the chance to see a more deeply imaginative
Clair.

> It is only in memory that the silly tale begins to outweigh Clair's
> direction, for it is so much easier to carry a subject in the mind
> than a treatment. But even in the cinema there were moments
> when one realized the conflict between the scenario and Clair's
> poetic talent. . . . One remembers the long drift of white cumulus
> while the voice of the dead father condemned the cowardly ghost;
> the moment on the ramparts at midnight when the great lace
> sleeve fell in close-up across the corner of the screen and with all
> the sudden shock of a stroking clock one knew the ghost was there,
> just beyond the dark edge of one's vision; the seconds when the
> camera slowly climbed the long worm-eaten cobwebbed stairs and
> paced beside the cracked panelling. (p. 41)

The ultimate escape seems to lie in a triumph of style over matter,
which results in a transformation of experience. The filmmaker who

is in control of his medium creates a unique visual style that reshapes the dramatic or literary material and alters its meaning. It is the primary function of the critic to discover this unique non-discursive quality. These films by Clair with their elusive images and tone give us the chance to see a more deeply imaginative Greene: one of the few critics who can use his creative powers of language to help us remember the treatment and make it outweigh in our memories the prosaic subject, theme, or plot.

Given this preference for escapist farce, it is not surprising that Greene is hard on what he sees as pretentious films—those offering us Shakespeare or other great literary classics with limited visuals, the life of a great "artiste," a scholarly view of an historical period, or opera singing with open mouths and bogus pomposity. In fact, in reviewing *The Gay Desperado* he remarks that many of the shots remind him of images from Eisenstein's serious documentary *Que Viva Mexico!*, but surprisingly he argues that these images are more effective in comedy.

> In a serious film the effect of the careful compositions might have seemed precious and unconvincing, but in artificial comedy these lovely shots of cacti like cathedral pillars, of galloping horses before old Spanish churches, of sombreros against skyscapes, are like a framework of fine and mannered prose. (p. 117)

Although it leads to a perceptive insight about *The Gay Desperado*, here his recognition of cinema's capacity for lyrical absurdity begins to become a prescriptive norm, limiting his appreciation of other modes and intentions. Greene insists that cinema is a popular medium that must appeal to a mass audience; hence, his preference for westerns, comedies, farces, and detective thrillers.

> It is wrong to despise popularity in the cinema—popularity there is a *value*, as it isn't in a book; films have got to appeal to a large undiscriminating public: a film with a severely limited appeal must be—to that extent—a bad film. (p. 228)

Of course, this distinction is arbitrary since the novel and theater have been submitted to similar pressures historically, and cinema seems to be a large enough medium to include many kinds of film—the avant-garde and underground film, which he completely ignores, as well as the popular movie. But this rather dubious assumption leads him to capture another unique quality of some of his favorite farces.

There are very few examples of what I mean by the proper popular use of the film, and most of those are farces: *Duck Soup*, the early Chaplins, a few "shorts" by Laurel and Hardy. These do convey the sense that the picture has been made by its spectators and not merely shown to them, that it has sprung, as much as their sports, from *their* level. (p. 94.)

Interestingly, many underground filmmakers are striving precisely for this sense of audience participation.

I do not mean to imply that Greene is open solely to farce and comedy. He is very perceptive in discussing documentary (particularly *Song of Ceylon* and *Dark Rapture*) where he presents some of his most evocative and detailed descriptions of the visuals, with strong literary overtones. The few films he deems truly "great" are not entertaining farces, but heavier melodramas: Fritz Lang's *Fury*, Frank Capra's *Mr. Deeds*, and Julien Duvivier's *Pepe Le Moko*. He suggests that all three films exploit the medium's capacity for realism, all deal with significant themes of freedom and justice, all have a sense of spiritual integrity, all have expressive visual imagery, all have a mass appeal. Yet they lack that "sense of absurd unreasoning happiness" that cinema is capable of expressing and which lies at the center of Greene's escapist vision. This polarity between the two kinds of film that he admires is, of course, analogous to the two kinds of fiction that dominate his career as a novelist. Yet in the context of film, Greene implies that by pursuing this line of entertainment, cinema eludes the demands of great art and retains a "sense of fun." From the vantage point of the seventies, we can see that the accomplishments of the medium have clearly shown the limitations of such an attitude. Yet it does not undermine what Greene does have to offer as a film critic. He is one of the few writers on the cinema who is able to locate the non-discursive qualities of a group of films (limited though they may be) and to evoke their experiential qualities through his own prose style. In his hands, a film retains its sense of life. One cannot say that about many film critics.

MARSHA KINDER

SWEDEN AND DETECTIVE FICTION

Jan Broberg. *Mordisk familjebok*. Uddevalla: Zindermans, 1972.

Jury. Tidskrift för deckarvänner. Bromma.

DAST-Magazine. Strängnäs.

SWEDISH POLITICAL and economic experiments have gained international attention, but Swedish literature remains little-known outside its homeland. Strindberg, of course, and perhaps Pär Lagerkvist appear in college survey courses in modern European literature, but how many readers ever encounter the works of Verner von Heidenstam, Erik Axel Karlfeldt, or Selma Lagerlöf — all of whom were Nobel Prizewinners?

The recent popularity of Maj Sjöwall and Per Wahlöö (a husband and wife team) in this country marks a happy breakthrough on two fronts — the addition of a genuine new talent in the genre of crime and detective fiction, and the emergence of Swedish literary efforts in the international market-place.

But the Wahlöös's "novels about crimes" (as they prefer to call them), besides being cultural expressions of a country still somewhat unfamiliar to Americans, remind us as well that Sweden is one of the largest per capita consumers — and producers — of detective fiction in Europe. To understand the success of the several Sjöwall/Wahlöö novels already available, we need to survey briefly the attitude of Swedes toward detective fiction.

One of the best beginnings for such a study is Jan Broberg's recent critical volume *Mordisk familjebok* (1972 — the title puns on the word *mord*, murder, and the name of the Swedish family encyclopedia, *Nordisk familjebok*). Mr. Broberg is eminently qualified to lead Swedes through the complicated world of crime and detective fiction. Although just forty years old and a professional writer for less than a decade, he has already published scores of articles in half a dozen literary journals in Sweden, discussed his favorite genre many times on the Swedish national radio, and is the crime and detective reviewer for *Kvällsposten*, Malmö's largest evening paper. In addition he is a member of Mystery Writers of America, Crime Writers Association of London, Poeklubben of Copenhagen, and the President and founder of the brand-new *Svenska Deckarakademin* — the mystery writer's version of the rather more famous model, the Swedish Academy. Among his literary productions are six anthologies of short American and British detective fiction, for which he furnished translations of his own when no previous Swedish version was available.

Mr. Broberg's literary career began with the first solid book of criticism and commentary on detective fiction ever to appear in Swedish. It was entitled *Mord för ro skull* (Murder for the fun of it—1964) and *Mordisk familjebok* is, essentially, a continuation of that work and a reassessment of his earlier literary evaluations.

Both works are basic surveys and cover a staggeringly large number of authors and works, although the most recent volume tends not to recapitulate the earlier volume so much as to enhance it. The bibliography of *Mord för ro skull*, for example, lists some one hundred and thirty reference works, while the index contains more than three thousand authors and titles. In his most recent work, the critical bibliography is almost twice as long, with three indices (Detectives, Authors, and Titles) similarly expanded.

Broberg, of course, is writing for a Swedish audience, which means that most of his material is drawn from sources in English already familiar to readers of *The Mystery & Detection Annual*. Nevertheless, his methodology is fresh and unusual, and his expertise impressive enough to warrant a brief survey of his newest volume as the appropriate introduction of him to his American counterparts.

Mordisk familjebok opens with a stimulating reappraisal of J. Austin Freeman, the creator of Romney Pringle and Dr. John Thorndyke, based largely on the recent study by Norman Donaldson in *The Armchair Detective*, Vol. 1, No. 2 (1968). (Dissatisfied with Freeman's undeserved oblivion, Broberg had included a translation of "The Art of the Detective Story" in his anthology *Meningar om mord* five years ago. A translation of "The Aluminium Dagger" had appeared in an earlier Broberg anthology of locked-room mysteries [*Mord i slutna rum*, 1967], but before that only the short story "The Singing Bone" was still in print.) Broberg rates Freeman as one of the all-time masters of the genre, because of his ability to experiment with the *form* of the genre, as well as to master its essential intrigue. Broberg, in fact, finds the believability of the intrigue to be about the most important element of good crime and detective fiction. However, he also praises those authors who, because of a fine sense of place, period or characterization, have contributed essentially literary aspects which have made the genre "respectable."

Broberg's chapters on Ellery Queen, Agatha Christie, John Dickson Carr, Eric Ambler and Georges Simenon briefly discuss each author and his or her *oeuvre*, without adding much that has not been more thoroughly treated in earlier English or American sources. Other chapters, however, would certainly interest English-speaking *aficionados*.

Broberg interviewed Michael Gilbert and Mary Gilbert in 1970, H.R.F. Keating (creator of Inspector Ghote) in 1968, and the Swedish authors Sven Sörmark and Vic Suneson (Sune Lundkvist) in 1971. The last-named is probably the best detective writer in Sweden today, alongside Maj Sjöwall and Per Wahlöö, a personal conclusion with which Broberg happily concurs. While no major revelations were un-covered in Broberg's interviews with English writers, Suneson related several interesting points of view on his own unique brand of detective fiction.

Beginning in 1948 as a follower of the "classical" English and Amer-ican authors of the '30's (Christie, Carr, van Dine), Suneson has gradually moved away from the intrigue-for-its-own-sake toward the "procedural school" of Ed McBain and Hillary Waugh. Says Suneson:

> There is no conscious reason why I've come more and more to concern myself with police methodology, but I get so damned mad at these amateur detectives who make the police look stupid just so that they in turn will appear more genial. The police, of course, aren't stupid—and Swedish homicide investigators are of inter-national quality. (Broberg, *Mordisk familjebok*, p. 104)

In 1956, Suneson wrote an article, "Hur jag mördar . . ." ("How I murder . . ."), in which he indicates his belief in the Sayers "Golden Rule"—fairness to the reader. He is also convinced of the rightness of B.J.L. Stolpers's recipe for a good detective novel — ½ Sherlock Holmes, ¼ P. G. Wodehouse, ⅛ pure adventure, and ⅛ something that is the author's specialty.

Broberg discussed Vic Suneson in a *Mord för ro skull* article which dealt exclusively with Swedish products in the crime and detection field. Entitled "Svenska svagheter" ("Swedish weaknesses"), it is a serious critique of the derivative and imitative work done by most of the practitioners of the art in pre-Sjöwall/Wahlöö days. Only Suneson then received highest marks from Broberg, who considers him to be of international quality, like the above-mentioned homicide investiga-tors of Sweden.

Another sharp criticism of Scandinavian detective fiction appeared in *Poeklubbens arsbok 1967-1968* (Annual of the Poe Club, 1967-1968), written by Klas Lithner. Even more severe a critic than Broberg (the latter greatly admires the works of Sjöwall and Wahlöö which do not much impress Lithner), Lithner gave Vic Suneson—the only Swede on his list—the highest praise ("med utmärkt beröm god-känd").

Broberg has not limited himself merely to short surveys of various authors' best and worst books. In *Mord för ro skull*, he treated the hybrid of science-fiction and detective themes (for example, Isaac Asimov's "Caves of Steel" and Paul Anderson's "The Martian Crown Jewels"), but found the new genre usually violates the Golden Rule:

> The reader ought, at least theoretically, to have a chance to be able to solve the mystery in question himself. If, however, one writes a detective story in which one presents murder methods which depend on technological developments from the *future*, one pulls the rug out from under the reader's logical thought processes, which are based on deductions from the *present*. (p. 126)

Although he does not abandon his position in *Mordisk familjebok*, Broberg *does* admit that science fiction and detective literature can occasionally be blended effectively and mentions Randall Garrett's *Too Many Magicians* (1968) and Hans Stefan Santerson's *Crime Prevention in the Thirtieth Century* (1969) as excellent examples.

Other special areas that Broberg treats range from historical detective fiction (Josephine Tey's *The Daughter of Time*, for example, or John Dickson Carr's *Most Secret*) to the roles played by archeologist-, priest-, writer- and minority-detectives in the genre.

For our purposes—which is to detect the Swedish point of view—his concluding chapter to *Mordisk familjebok* provides some of his most entertaining observations, Broberg invited eleven well-known Swedish and Danish critics of crime and detective literature to choose the best Swedish detective novel. Among the judges were Barbro Alving, the detective fiction critic for one of Sweden's largest newspapers, *Dagens Nyheter*; Bo Lundin, prolific enthusiast of the genre and critic in Göteborg; Kjell Stensson, book reviewer for the Swedish National Radio; and Sven Sörmark, detective story writer and critic for the Stockholm daily *Aftonbladet*. Eight out of eleven votes went to Maj Sjöwall and Per Wahlöö's *The Laughing Policeman*.

Recently, there appeared a new journal named *Jury. Tidskrift för deckarvänner* (Jury. Journal for detective fiction enthusiasts), edited by the highly-gifted, prolific, and erudite Ted Bergman (author of, among other works, *Sherlock Holmes, 1891–1916: A Bibliography Enumerating and Describing Eighty-three Original and Variant Editions of the Swedish Translations of Dr. John H. Watson's Sherlock Holmes Stories*). The attractiveness of the journal owes as much to the highly professional layout as it does to the sophisticated level of the contents. Ted Bergman provides an interesting overview of the development of Sherlockian societies in the North. The first was The Creeping Man of Lidköping, founded by Jörgen Elgström in 1955,

which later developed into a much larger lodge, De ensamma cyklisterna (The Solitary Cyclists). Its members have discoursed learnedly
on a number of the thornier canonical problems: in 1953 Gösta Ry-
brant identified the "tra - la - la - lira - lira -lay" tune; and another
member, Curt Berg, made a good case for identifying 221B Baker
Street with number 111, destroyed by Nazi bombs (in retaliation for
the destruction of the master spy von Bork?). It might be added that
the late Vilhelm Moberg (author of *The Emigrants*) was the most
celebrated member of De ensamma cyklisterna; his debut lecture
concerned Dr. Mortimer's article in *Journal of Psychology* (1883),
from *The Hound of the Baskervilles*.

Bo Lundin's review of C. Day Lewis's Nigel Strangeways mysteries
critically surveys one of the more interesting academic-detective writers of the 1930's, while Hans Stertman's thorough investigation of
"kiosk" detective stories (approximately our pulp fiction) explores
the social dimension of a literature which has too often been seen as
divorced from the cultural context which produced it. In fact, it is this
societal aspect of detective fiction which seems most evident in Swedish
criticism as well as certain Swedish products of the genre. Another
article, which should appeal to English-speaking audiences, is K. Arne
Blom's elaborate pedigree of the "procedural school" detective novel.
He sees this type as descending directly from the "criminal" novel,
which has a policeman as a main character; its main tools are still
those of the "mystery" novel's amateur sleuth: logic and the ability to
analyze rationally. The procedural school goes somewhat farther,
utilizing the scientific methods of the whole police department to solve
the crime with realistic accuracy. Further, the procedural school sees
the crime in its social spectrum, and not merely as an intellectual
puzzle for an excited amateur detective. Blom has six points which
mark the product of the procedural school at its best:

A. It describes a phenomenon actually being debated in our
    time: the police.
B. It describes people in our society in different situations or
    settings which function as adjuncts to the crime.
C. It portrays the society, the setting, and the social circum-
    stances which make the crime a reality.
D. It describes, and it *analyzes* through its description, the po-
    lice, the person, and the crime, and its origins in today's
    social system.
E. It is exciting and stirring.
F. It causes us to reflect.
    (*Jury*. Nr. 1, p. 46)

In a short article in the same number of *Jury*, Maj Sjöwall and Per Wahlöö write on "Kriminal-romanens förnyelse" ("The Renewal of the Criminal Novel") in a manner which touches K. Arne Blom's argument at almost every point. While this is by no means their first theoretical explanation of their ten-volume "history," it is as admirably abridged a statement of their basic ideas as is likely to appear. For that reason, and because they seem to be riding the crest of an international wave of popularity which none of their fellow countrymen has ever seen, a fuller investigation of their career is in order.

Their obvious mentors have been "crime novelists" like Julian Symons (whom Jan Broberg interviewed in 1961—see *Mord för ro skull*, pp. 81-83)—all three find Dostoyevsky's *Crime and Punishment* among the finest crime novels ever written—and the "procedural school" writers such as Hillary Waugh and Ed McBain/Evan Hunter. The Wahlöös write:

> Our purpose in the Martin Beck series has been to arrive at an analysis of a bourgeois welfare society—an analysis in which we try to see its criminality in relation to its political and ideological doctrines. It is the basic idea in a long novel of some 3,000 pages, divided into ten independent parts or, if you prefer, chapters, to analyze criminal behavior as a social function and that function's relationship to the present society and to the moral life patterns of different kinds which surround society. (*Jury*, p. 10)

They point out the essentially bourgeois nature of the classical detective novel—"the absence of realism which is really a conscious distancing from reality"—with its upper-class settings in castles, country estates, and elegant town houses; with its wealthy amateurs and their cool contempt for the bumbling policemen. The Wahlöös see the new crime novel as one which demands "psychological balance, realism, sociological analysis and also social consciousness." Modern readers desire

> something radically different from mysteries and puzzles; they are conscious and want a conscious literature. In many cases, they also get what they merely dream of: literature for the present, but also for the future. If anyone a hundred years from now wanted to read a book about how New York City really looks today, we don't think he could find a better description than, for example, Hillary Waugh's *The Young Prey*—whose author once, in a moment of very penetrating observation, described as "too true to be good."

We believe that the key to this whole discussion lies in these words. The goal of the modern crime novel seeks to be true on a wholly objective plane. It is more important and more meaningful that it serve as a social alarm clock, that it have a meaningful and psychologically accurate content, than that it should dazzle with its formal problem complex and its juggling with abstract logic.

And perhaps this literary form is now at hand (*Jury*, pp. 9-11).

While many would disagree with the ideological didacticism (despite "objectively" and "truth") with which Sjöwall-Wahlöö criticize the Swedish welfare state, very few would call the Martin Beck books "escapist." The care with which the authors fashion the situation, the crime, and the solution have a monumental inevitability in which tired men pursue trivial clues for long and bone-wearying hours until the final quiet denouement. The books—with the publication of *The Abominable Man from Säffle*, all seven in the series are now in English—have sold well in America and in England. (Sales are highest in the Warsaw Pact nations, shattering theories about political partisanship limiting readers' taste.) Bantam paperbacks has issued them in large impressions, and *The Laughing Policeman* was recently made into a film.

Yet neither the Martin Beck series nor the earlier Inspector Jensen books (*The Thirty-first Floor*) have attained a commensurate popularity in Sweden itself. Jan Broberg's criticism of other Swedish detective and thriller writers for their stodginess and mediocre, derivative plots seems to substantiate the fact that Swedes, contrary to what the Wahlöös stated, are not ready for such socially conscious crime novels. Instead they prefer more traditional—what the Wahlöös would undoubtedly call "escapist"—detective fare. Why should this be so?

A facile answer, fashionable with critics of the Swedish welfare state, is that Swedes are, quite simply, bored. They have seen the reality of their economic and political creation, they acknowledge its imperfections, but when they turn to literature for entertainment they expect to be entertained, not forced to renew the debate.

But this argument does not account for the general literary trend in Sweden, which, in fact, does tend toward socially aware literature. Most of the better-selling authors on the scene right now are disciples of Jan Myrdal and reflect his deep concern for the role of affluent nations in the underdeveloped nations of the world. Some, like P. O. Enquist, treat the problems of creating a truly egalitarian classless society amid the tumults of conflicting political ideologies and rapid socio-economic flux. Others, like Sara Lidman and Eva Moberg, deal more specifically with the shifting tide of the feminist movement, charting its changes into the future. All of them share the same vigorous social awareness as Maj Sjöwall and Per Wahlöö, but they sell many books and the crime novelists do not. Nor, as I have tried to indicate, is this a reflection of a lack of interest on the part of the Swedish reading public who love detective fiction, either classically good or hard-boiled, violence-filled pulp literature. Broberg's works testify abundantly to the size of his audience and the level of their sophistication.

A different interpretation of the facts might lead us to somewhat speculative conclusions. A look at book lists of translations into Swedish of foreign works over the years reveals that even before the modern welfare state had evolved into its present form, Swedes were avid readers of detective fiction. Their taste has not changed. Fifty years ago, they read Dorothy Sayers, Agatha Christie, Ellery Queen and John Dickson Carr, and those are the authors always in heavy demand. Over the years, this basically conservative taste has accommodated newer voices, but the dates of translation are usually many years after publication in the original language.

Bo Lundin, detective fiction reviewer for *Göteborgs-Tidning*, discussed the problem of popularity in a recent article for that paper, reprinted in *DAST* (an acronym for the unfortunate term "Detective - Agent - Science fiction - Thriller." The magazine is edited by Iwan Hedman of Strängnäs, owner of one of the largest collections of crime and detective material in Scandinavia). Lundin finds the classical conservatism of "Golden Age" detective fiction symptomatic of the genre's function as "entertainment for the middle class." It has been and will continue to be, says Lundin, a genre characterized by snobbishness, distinctly anti-Labor sentiments, upper-class respectability, and an uncomfortable sense of embarrassment for anyone who has to earn a living by the sweat of his brow.

Lundin recounts mercilessly the reactionary and imperialistic political orientation of almost all post-Sherlockian detectives—Bulldog Drummond, with his task to keep England free of Communists, Jews, and Labor politicians; Dennis Wheatley, who equates Marxism with Satanism itself; *et al*. And, although the climate is quickly becoming more liberal, the "classical school" authors of Sweden—Vic Suneson, Maria Lang, Stieg and Trenter—continue to set their stories in a comfortable suburban upper-class milieu, peopled with, in Lundin's phrase, "congenial industrial snobs." A newcomer, Bo Baldersson, has written two thrillers which attack the present Social Democratic government and which are, despite their somewhat puerile hysterics on behalf of the right, well-constructed political thrillers.

Lundin believes, apparently, with "Nicholas Blake" (C. Day Lewis) that:

> The working class does not read detective novels of the classic type; but prefers the products of the "hard-boiled school." The reason for this is that the police are always regarded as the working-man's enemy, which naturally disinclines the working-man from reading stories of how the police emerge triumphant from every controversy. The detective novel is therefore the literature of the other classes—the middle class above all.
>
> (*DAST*, No. 12, p. 16.)

If we judge by the silent testimony of sales, his case seems correct, despite the international successes of Maj Sjöwall and Per Wahlöö.

LARRY EMIL SCOTT

Chandler Before Marlowe: Raymond Chandler's Early Prose and Poetry, 1908-1912. Edited by Matthew J. Bruccoli. Foreword by Jacques Barzun. Columbia, South Carolina: University of South Carolina Press, 1973. Limited first printing of 499 copies, boxed. "Numbers 1 through 400 are for sale, and numbers 401 through 499 have been distributed as complimentary copies to various persons involved in the creation and the marketing of the book." $25.00. (Prepublication price: $14.95.) Second edition. $4.95.

SHOULD ANYONE doubt the scholarly popularity of Raymond Chandler, he need only consider the auspices and success of the latest Chandler publication. In the 3 August 1973 *Times Literary Supplement* (London) appeared the discreetly triumphant notice: "The University of South Carolina Press regrets to announce that eight weeks before the announced publication date of July 2 [1973], all copies had been sold of the limited first edition of *Chandler Before Marlowe*." Such "unexpected demand" has more than justified the press's quick decision to bring out an inexpensive second edition.

Mr. Bruccoli's preface makes modest claims for the apprentice pieces; he finds these " 'lost writings' . . . good—but not remarkably so —for the first published work of a writer in his early twenties. It is important and worth publishing only because it is Raymond Chandler's." The scholarly stance is unassailable: "If Raymond Chandler's novels are as good as some of us think they are, then all of his published work ought to be conveniently available for the sake of the light it sheds on his career."

Half of the volume is taken up by Chandler's verses, about which, says Jacques Barzun, "there is little to say except that they are without merit of any kind." Chandler's own appraisal of his poetry is not much of an endorsement either: "I had, to be frank, the qualifications to become a pretty good second-rate poet, but that means nothing because I have the type of mind that can become a pretty good second-rate anything, and without much effort." Why bother, then, to give almost half a volume to twenty-seven poems written from 1908-1912 and two poems (including a sonnet in two drafts) written between 1955-58? Because, despite their confessed inadequacy, these poems stimulate speculation about the development of a singular intelligence. Consider these quatrains, for example:

> There is no thought born in man's brain
>   Which I too have not known;
> There is no single joy or pain
>   I have not made my own.
>
>   .   .   .   .   .
>
> O tyrant with the sneering face,
>   O victim 'neath the knife,
> O saint sublime and sinner base,
>   I too have lived your life.

Chandler called that poem "The Poet's Knowledge." It's easy now to call it Marlowe's.

The half of the volume that reprints Chandler's early prose (eight essays and sketches and four reviews, all 1911-12) is more immediately inviting. In 1949, however, Chandler even recollected this work with undue harshness; he said his reviews and essays were "of an intolerable preciousness of style, but already quite nasty in tone. . . . Like all young nincompoops I found it very easy to be clever and snotty, very hard to praise without being ingenuous." (He once said that his sketches were "the sort of thing Saki did so infinitely better.") Perhaps Mr. Barzun's reaction is over-compensatory, when he finds great merit in these pieces: "The obsessive character of his thought, which gives the novels much of their power, is right here, full force, in these youthful pages, so happily gathered and restored to our inquisitive but sympathetic glance." It is the "full force" in Mr. Barzun's statement that seems excessive. Mr. Bruccoli's evaluation is more judicious: "Chandler apprenticed himself to the wrong muse and the wrong master. The Raymond Chandler who wrote his first detective story, 'Blackmailers Don't Shoot,' in 1933 was the same man but a different writer." It is the style in the essays, unlike the style of the poems, that promises achievement.

This handsome volume encourages each reader to be his own detective, seeking clues for Chandler's then-latent genius. I myself like his assertion in "The Genteel Artist" that the personally immaculate artist may have only a modest conception of what it is to be a genuine one. "A gentleman standing elegantly before the easel . . . might be a charming companion, he was more than well-groomed, and he was very possibly more than usually clever. But the beholder felt quite sure that he was not a great artist. He had never felt the sweet bitterness of the garret." If, as a matter of record, he had, "at a simpler age," indeed been so bitterly garreted, than "the experience had left no mark, and had not made him any more cunning in his work." The shabbiness of Marlowe is not merely the realistic shabbiness of the private eye; it underscores Chandler's idealistic belief that the evidence of involvement with life must be made visible. "The garreteer, whether he eventually dies famous or completely unknown, has been worthy of his craft." The young Chandler said that the artist's life could, justifiably, "cause its devotees to miss a meal or to bundle a friend out of the room with a vigorous rudeness." It produces exhaustion and "the sweat of a terrible toil." Maybe it is as that special kind of a sincere artist that Marlowe has his own vocation and his meaning.

In his *Down These Mean Streets a Man Must Go*, Philip Durham refers to a 1961 *Times Literary Supplement* series of articles which praised Chandler. Durham believes that while the articles would have pleased the man, they "would have ... saddened [him], too, for in none of the articles was there a discussion of style, of the magic of words. And after all, he would have thought, if you do not have magic in writing, what do you have?" The notion had been expressed by Chandler as early as his 1912 essay, "Realism and Fairyland," in which he had stated: "To be an idealist one must have a vision and an ideal; to be a realist, only a plodding, mechanical eye. . . . To those who say that there are artists, called realists, who produce work which is neither ugly nor dull nor painful, any man who has walked down a commonplace city street at twilight, just as the lamps are lit, can reply that such artists are not realists, but the most courageous of idealists, for they exalt the sordid to a vision of magic, and create pure beauty out of plaster and vile dust." *Chandler Before Marlowe* evidences that this writer had had, from the beginning, a concern for the magic of words and the power of transformation. But his genius would become apparent to all, only when he had found his milieu and created pure beauty out of the plaster and vile dust of Los Angeles.

Lawrence D. Stewart

Edith Wharton. *The Ghost Stories of Edith Wharton*. New York: Charles Scribner's Sons, 1973. $8.95.

THE FINAL thing one should read in any book is the Preface. Frequently written last, with any luck it will do a reviewer's job for him. Mrs. Wharton's Preface is most accommodating in this respect, and it is a pleasure to reaffirm that she is not capable of a failure of perception. The Preface offers some justification for her kind of ghost story and a good-natured expression of pity for those without the background or insight to sympathize. Although (to use Mrs. Wharton's dichotomy) I am not a Latin and therefore automatically incapable of understanding ghosts, neither am I a Celt with an intuitive ability to respond, to "shiver." That, I suppose, puts me in the middle ground along with almost all of Mrs. Wharton's other readers—willing to go along, needing to be convinced.

It is just this need to be convinced, however, that provokes Mrs. Wharton's most stubborn disclaimers. Indeed, in arguing that a reader who needs convincing can't be convinced, she rather forlornly appeals for a "common medium between myself and my readers, of their meeting me halfway among the primeval shadows, and filling in the gaps in my narrative with sensations and divinations akin to my own." Mrs. Wharton has hit the mark exactly: her narrative suffers from gaps of sensation and divination. But does she have any right to ask her readers to meet her halfway?

Just as the Preface defines the nature of her failure, a Postscript to this handsome volume of eleven stories suggests a possible cause. As Postscript the publishers print a few unpublished paragraphs from the manuscript of her autobiography, *A Backward Glance*. These concern the childhood origin of her interest in ghosts and conclude with the astonishing statement that "till I was twenty-seven or eight, I could not sleep in the room with a book containing a ghost-story and . . . I have frequently had to burn books of this kind, because it frightened me to know that they were downstairs in the library!" What is astonishing is not the obsessive power of Mrs. Wharton's feelings, but her failure, once they were mastered, to bring them to life in her art. And the cause of her failure must surely lie in the very power of these feelings, in an imagination where the slightest stimulus yielded the greatest response. But readers, including this one, are notorious for lacking imagination. Unfortunately, no one is going to burn this book.

The main weakness is her easy reception of these ghosts. They appear on the scene with as little trouble as one of her butlers delivering a calling card. Gathered together, and imposters all, they certainly lower the tone of her drawing room. There is Mr. Jones, servant to an early nineteenth-century master, who doesn't like it one bit when the long-unoccupied house gets a new owner one hundred years later. Or a young, greyish man, driven to suicide by a swindler, who comes back long enough to make his enemy vanish. Or a lady's maid who leaves no tracks in the snow when running about outside and otherwise walks the corridors of the servants' quarters—restless—knowing more than she ought about her ailing former mistress. Or a pack of dogs who rip out, I am delighted to report, the throat of the French nobleman who had strangled them one by one, and who are now very good company indeed, because silent. Since most of the stories are slight things with weak characterizations, anecdotal plots, and conventional country-house settings, the whole burden of interest falls upon these ghosts. Feeling strongly herself, Mrs. Wharton seems to think that to compel horror she only needs to present or identify the ghost. But easy identification and fright do not encourage anything more than a conventional notion of what a ghost is.

Even more damaging is her failure to define the ghostly state. Existence implies a state of existence. If ghosts exist they exist somewhere, in accordance with some agency or power, in time or beyond it, at the behest of someone or something, as a reflection of some consciousness, their own or, more mysteriously, someone else's; and they must act as the supreme embodiment of will—mindless, perhaps, or directed, but capable of relentless energy. This catalogue is not meant to be exhaustive, and in any case it has little to do with Mrs. Wharton. Her ghosts merely appear: a fatal error—for a ghost may be disembodied in every respect except in respect of its existence. Even when they act her ghosts commit their horrors of retribution timidly, almost reluctantly, as if themselves expecting to be scared away from the awful deed. When Mrs. Boyne told her ghostly visitor that her husband wasn't receiving anyone that morning, the ghost turned away disappointed and only returned to his murderous task after Mrs. Boyne, having taken pity, called him back. Mr. Jones strangles an inoffensive housekeeper out of mere petulance, but offstage, out of hearing. In this book one looks in vain for the complex world of moral, indeed physical, imperatives which give, in an example which cannot be avoided, the ghost in *Hamlet* its frightening power. Not surprisingly, therefore, the best of these stories, "The Triumph of Night," lacks a proper ghost, although it does have a personified vision of evil. Flawed by an epilogue which explains the obvious, it is the only story in this collection to engage Mrs. Wharton's interest. Only in the presence of a congenial theme—the failure of a timid innocence to recognize and thus to cope with malevolence and evil—does her prose rise to an eloquence not possible in the company of the pallid ghosts of her other stories.

Some of Mrs. Wharton's ghosts are driven to revenge. In raising them again one wonders what the publishers had in mind, what sense of deprivation or hurt they felt these apparitions could put right for them. Anticipated again by Mrs. Wharton, who knew that her ghosts had little chance to compete with "the conflicting attractions of the gangster, the introvert and the habitual drunkard" of 1937, a reviewer can only assume that the new audience for the occult, jaded after two generations of scary movies, all recently seen on television, is not likely to be satisfied with the little tingle that her well-mannered visitors arouse. Finally, these stories do nothing for Mrs. Wharton's reputation. Once laid to rest they should not, in all decency, have been asked to walk again.

W. B. VASELS

Charles Dickens. *The Mystery of Edwin Drood*. Margaret Cardwell,
    editor. Oxford: The Clarendon Press, 1972. $15.25. (£4.50 net
    in U.K.).

AT LAST, the Clarendon edition of *The Mystery of Edwin Drood*.
Which is another way of saying: at last, the definitive edition. Here—
again: at last—we have an authoritative text, one that has been compared with the manuscript, with the texts of the first English and
American editions, and with such proofs as were available; and one,
moreover, in which we are granted all those accessories that an ideal
edition of this book should have: the original illustrations by Luke
Fildes, the cover of the monthly parts, Dickens's title notes and number
plans, and the enigmatic 'Sapsea Fragment' which was unexpectedly
discovered (if John Forster is to be believed) among Dickens's papers
after his death. There is an introduction by the editor, satisfying in its
completeness, and we are provided as well with various appendices: a
discussion of the illustrations, an examination of the first American
editions, a glimpse of the artist's proofs now in the Beinecke Library at
Yale, and an informative essay on the novel's "After History 1870-
1878." In short, this physically handsome book is, and is likely to remain for some while, *the* edition of Dickens's last, fated novel, the
Compleat *Edwin Drood*.

Miss Cardwell's introduction traces the vicissitudes that the book
has undergone in its various guises: latently, as an idea of Dickens's (as
far as that can be reconstructed from outward evidences), as manuscript, as proofs and as published texts. There has been so much mis-
information published these last sixty or seventy years about Dickens's
problems in writing the book, that it is a pleasure to have here in a convenient form a knowledgeable summary of what he actually did. The
various shifts he was put to by his serial mode of publication will now
be plain to everyone and should have a sobering effect upon speculation. For one thing, it will be obvious that his numerous cuts from the
fifth number, many of which concerned the much-discussed Datchery,
were prompted primarily by limitations of space; and, for another,
those who have thought that the author didn't know what he was doing
when he transposed Chapters 18 and 19 will find they have reason to
change their minds.

Miss Cardwell is cautious, in the Introduction and elsewhere, in
speculating about the story itself. Quite rightly so. To speculate on *The
Mystery of Edwin Drood* is a venture fraught with peril, one which
perhaps should be left to those who have no scholarly or critical reputa-

tions to lose. But her commendable desire to preserve at all times a detached and judicious tone, to merely suggest here and there a possibility, may be what causes her an occasional obscurity: one mutters "What was that?" and goes back over a paragraph or two to make out her meaning. In one case, this softness of focus results in an unintended, but rather serious and undeserved, injury to Dickens's reputation. I suspect that it will now be widely believed, on the supposed basis of what will surely be regarded for years as the most authoritative single piece of writing on *Drood*, that Dickens stole a significant part of his story from another man. To explain this matter at all, I must give it what may seem a disproportionate amount of space; but I trust I am justified in doing so, both by the potential seriousness and by the intrinsic interest of the subject.

About the first of September, 1869, when Dickens was mulling over the story that was to become *The Mystery of Edwin Drood*, he received from Robert Lytton, the son of Bulwer Lytton, a long narrative that he then published in his magazine *All the Year Round* as *The Disappearance of John Ackland* (18 Sept.-16 Oct. 1869). But on the first of October, he wrote to Lytton, saying:

> I am assured by a correspondent that John Acland has been done before. Said correspondent has evidently read the story—and is almost confident in Chamber's Journal . . . I should not have mentioned it at all, but as an explanation to you of my reason for winding the story up (which I have done today) as expeditiously as possible. . . .

"The whole tone of the letter," comments Miss Cardwell, "is reassuring and kindly," adding in a footnote (same page, *xix*) that "this intention [to spare any embarrassment on the part of the young writer] is reiterated in an unpublished letter of 21 Oct. (MS Lytton Papers) in which Dickens expressed his conviction that it was better not to institute a search for the original," *i.e.*, for the previously published piece. "There is no reason," she says, "to suspect Dickens's motives in bringing the story to so rapid a conclusion."

The reader may wonder what is the suspicion being rejected. She enlightens him in another footnote (p. *xx*): "There is no resemblance between the two stories [*John Ackland* and *Edwin Drood*] in respect of character, character-relationships, setting, or emphasis of interest. What possible links there are, are purely 'detective plot features'" which she proceeds to list. No "link" is striking in itself ("the mystification of the reader over the question of murder, the production of jewelry in evidence, a broken love affair") but chained together they are impressive enough; and it will inevitably cross the mind of the reader that perhaps Dickens has detected in *John Ackland* certain elements that he would like to use in his own projected work and so has contrived this very thin pretext that Lytton's story is not original in order to suppress it, that his own may flourish in its stead. In other words, it appears that Dickens in effect accused the young man of plagiarism, to disguise the fact that he himself intended to plagiarize Lytton's story!

As it happens, Angus Wilson has already voiced a suspicion along these general lines—though not so brutally expressed—in his review of the Clarendon *Drood* in *The Dickensian* (LXIX [1973], 49). Miss Cardwell, says Mr. Wilson, is skating "over thin ice a little too gracefully" in this matter. He speaks of Dickens's "ambiguous tact" in refusing to institute a search for the original of Lytton's "plagiarism," and remarks that the older man's consideration for the younger's feelings "can hardly have made happier Lytton's knowledge that his story had been violently truncated in publication."

What Miss Cardwell has not sufficiently emphasized—although she does give the story's full title, which includes the tag, '*A True Story in 13 chapters*'—is that *John Ackland* (or "*John Acland*," as she consistently misspells it, following Dickens in his 1st October letter to Lytton) is not a work of fiction but, however embellished and padded, an account of an actual murder that had been committed some years before in the United States. "In the case of a good story—as this is," Dickens wrote to Lytton in the letter twice mentioned, "liable for years to be told at table—as this was—there is nothing wonderful in such a mischance" of someone else having written it up before. And Dickens did not, as Mr. Wilson would have it, "violently truncate" the story. He did just what he had said he was going to do: he wound it up as expeditiously as possible, printing the remaining nine chapters in the next three issues of this magazine, rather than in the next four or five as had been originally intended. He quite evidently condensed the last few chapters (the last installment reads, here and there, like a synopsis) but the story as such is obviously complete.

In short, there are no grounds for suspecting Dickens of plagiarism. Of course, Miss Cardwell has not intended to accuse him. Her reason for introducing the matter was to make a sensible observation on Dickens's retitling of the earlier story—Lytton had submitted it as *The Murder of John Ackland*—and what that implies about the title of his own story, and her exposition contains nothing that is in error. But her obstinate, her almost perverse, innocence in phrasing points in such a way that *they* seem to incriminate Dickens ("While *John Acland* was reaching its abrupt end, *Edwin Drood* was beginning to take shape") inescapably reminds one of Winkle testifying at the trial of Pickwick.

Possibly the most interesting of the various appendices is Dickens's notes for the novel. It is difficult to reproduce these in typescript (a glance at the photograph facing p. 219 of Dickens's manuscript plan for the fourth Number will show why) but we are given the best readings to date. They are far freer from error than the same notes as represented in Felix Aylmer's *The Drood Case* (1964), but they are nevertheless flawed, it seems to me, by two misreadings. Miss Cardwell construes a note about the Landless twins on the left-hand side of the plan for the second Number as "Mixture of Oriental blood—or imperceptibly acquired nature—in them"; but I, and several others before me, have read the entry as "Mixture of Oriental blood—or imperceptibly acquired mixture—in them." The other misreading (as I think) occurs in a discarded title for Chapter xvii. The eventual title was "Philanthropy professional and unprofessional," but Dickens first wrote and then cancelled some other words in place of the last three. She reads the obliterated words as "in several phases" (also Aylmer's reading), but I read them as "in divers places," *i.e.*, in the offices of the philanthropic organization of which the bullying Honeythunder is the head, and at Staple Inn.

But the text — surely, the text is the important thing! And this one is very close to being perfect. It is the only text since that of the first to be "compared" with the manuscript—far more carefully than the first was, actually. As with the previous volume in the Clarendon Dickens series, *Oliver Twist*, we are given interesting variants in running foot-lines on nearly every page: the author's erasures and discrepancies between the manuscript and proofs and published texts. (It would seem that the editor has made no attempt to recover every obliterated passage in the manuscript—wisely, perhaps, as some are irrecoverable or, anyway, would not repay any reasonable amount of effort. But I would have liked to have seen her reading of two blotted sentences in Chapter xix, in which Jasper, speaking to Rosa, accuses Neville Landless of having murdered Edwin Drood.)

This consultation with the manuscript may not make a critical difference for most of the book, as an author's published text may be presumed to have an authority superior to that of his manuscript; but it makes a very decided difference where the last two chapters are concerned. Dickens never saw the proofs of these, as they were only in manuscript form when he died, and the printers passed a great many misreadings into the published text, where they have remained for more than a century. The speech of the candid Mrs. Billickin, for example, was consistently bettered for the worse. The Clarendon *Drood* restores it to its pristine impurity, although even here there are two unnecessary, as it seems to me, lapses into correct English. Mrs.

Billickin declines, on page 194, to "put a deception upon" Mr. Grew-gious, but the word in manuscript looks to me like "deceptin"; and I believe that the 1870 printing in the American magazine, *Every Saturday*, was unaccountably right when it had Mrs. Billickin advise Miss Twinkleton not to "put suppositions betwixt my lips, where none such have been imported by myself"—although the first English edition, and the Clarendon, have it as "imparted by myself."

My reading of these last two chapters differs from Miss Cardwell's in a few other small instances also. Miss Twinkleton is, I think, an admired reader, not an admirable reader (p. 201, bottom); Jasper's reply to the opium woman's question, "Who was they as died, deary?" was "A relation," not "A relative" (205); and when the opium woman apostrophises Jasper's unconscious form, she says — But, never mind. It would not only be ungenerous of me, but perhaps misleading, to pursue this line of criticism further: She has doubtlessly sent me back to the manuscript (or to my microfilms of it, rather) far oftener than I could send her.

I find myself in disagreement with her in only one substantial matter, the dating of the so-called Sapsea Fragment — that broken bit of manuscript, written on sheets of paper of the size that Dickens ordinarily used for his notes. Lightly, even thinly, humorous, it describes how a too deferential young man, Poker, a stranger in Cloisterham, ingratiates himself with the pompous Sapsea. Miss Cardwell writes (p. xlviii):

> The fragment is written partly in blue, partly in the brown-coloured ink, and, as the latter is found elsewhere only in chapters x and xvii, it seems possible that Dickens was writing, on the latter of these two occasions, a preliminary try-out for chapter xviii, "A Settler in Cloisterham."

This seems plausible enough at a glance, because Poker is obviously a discarded first version of that self-styled settler in Cloisterham, Datchery. But there are considerations that suggest, rather forcefully, that the Fragment was written earlier. Most of its humor derives from Mr. Sapsea's fatuous assumption that he appears to be someone connected with the Church, a part of the early comedy of Sapsea that Dickens dropped after the auctioneer became mayor of Cloisterham. And, in fact, Mr. Sapsea is quite evidently *not* the mayor in the Fragment, so it must have been written before Dickens appointed him to that position: that is, some time before he wrote chapter xii in the third Number — in other words, about the time he wrote chapter x, which is in the same number and is the other place where the rust-colored, or brown, ink is used. My own guess (I have argued this matter more fully in *Dickens Studies*, II [1966], 39-44) is that Dickens wrote these half-pages just after he was informed by his printer that his first two Numbers were, altogether, twelve printed pages too short. This meant that he had to use in his second Number material that he had intended to use in the third and, generally, to advance his story beyond his original plans. He must have felt that the introduction of new material would be necessary and it was while he was conjecturally (as I suppose) working up Poker, who shows such a sly interest in the future magistrate Sapsea, that he was struck (as I suppose) with the idea that the stranger should be someone in disguise, or seemingly in disguise: in short, with the idea of Datchery. This would tie in too with another change that must have been made about the same time: The three uniformed policemen bounding up the steps of the spiral staircase after the top-most pointing figure in Collins's sketch for the cover of the monthly parts became, in Luke Fildes's finished drawing of that cover, two men in plain clothes: "possibly," as Miss Cardwell shrewdly remarks (p. 241), "with a view to the greater concentration and interest to be achieved by keeping the whole mystery and detection essentially private"—a thought that has an obvious bearing upon Datchery.

But, to criticize is to distort. I have passed by many things that might be of most interest to other readers—such as Miss Cardwell's discussion of the genesis of the novel and its early posthumous history — and my editorial preoccupations have naturally led me to bring into prominence features that are negligible in the over-all effect of the book. Her handling of the *John Ackland* matter is to be regretted, as it inadvertently insinuates a notion that is likely to have great staying power, and her dating of the Sapsea Fragment is suspect; but such textual errors as the book might have can hardly be said to mar it, they are (compared to any previous printing of the novel) so very few. The Clarendon is, after all, much the best edition of *The Mystery of Edwin Drood* that is likely to be published in several life-times . . . and so any complaints that one might make are like the waves beating upon Gibraltar.

Arthur J. Cox

CONTEMPORARY NOVELISTS, Second Volume, *Contemporary Writers of the English Language series.* Edited by James Vinson. New York: St. Martin's Press, 1972, $30.00.

The thin-skinned enthusiast of crime and detective fiction approaches a reference volume like *Contemporary Novelists* prepared — even eager — to be offended. Certainly a 1422-page tome, covering about 600 present-day novelists-in-English, should contain at least a fair representation from the mystery field. But, just as certainly, academic snobbery will prevail and the great crime writers will be by-passed in favor of minor and little-read "serious" novelists.

However, in the present volume this anticipated snubbing does not come to pass. The crime fiction field is being taken more seriously these days, both as literature and as social history, and a dozen writers are included here whose reputations as novelists are based on their works under the crime-mystery-detection-suspense-espionage umbrella: Eric Ambler, Agatha Christie, Len Deighton, Nicolas Freeling, William Haggard, Patricia Highsmith, John Le Carré, Ira Levin, Ross Macdonald, Helen MacInnes, Ngaio Marsh, and Julian Symons. There are also many writers here who have contributed significantly to the field, though their main fame may be based on other works: Kingsley Amis, Isaac Asimov, C. Day Lewis (Nicholas Blake), August Derleth, Daphne Du Maurier, Howard Fast (E. V. Cunningham), Graham Greene, Chester Himes, Evan Hunter, C. P. Snow, Francis Steegmuller (David Keith), J. I. M. Stewart (Michael Innes), Gore Vidal (Edgar Box), Colin Wilson, P. G. Wodehouse, Philip Wylie, James Yaffe, and numerous others.

Selection of the novelists included was based on the recommendations of 26 advisors, a distinguished group (for example, Anthony Burgess, Leslie Fiedler, Anthony Powell, Kenneth Rexroth, Mark Schorer) of novelists, critics, academics, and publishers. Each entry includes a *Who's Who*-type biography, a bibliography of the author's works, a list of published critical studies and bibliographies, a comment by the author in cases where he or she chose to comment, and a signed critical essay on the author's fiction. There are about 200 critical contributors, identified in a section in the back.

There are some shocking omissions, of course. If Marsh and Christie are included, how can Ellery Queen, John Dickson Carr, and Rex Stout possibly be left out? If Ross Macdonald makes it, why is John D. MacDonald passed over? Regular appearance on best-seller lists has obviously been a contributing factor in some selections, but best-seller-

dom has been no assurance of inclusion in or out of the crime field —
though Arthur Hailey and Leon Uris find a place here, Irving Wallace
and Harold Robbins do not. Quibbles over inclusions and exclusions
could easily fill the rest of the space available, but it will probably be
more profitable to discuss what is actually in the book.

The bibliographic material is accurate for the most part, though
some lapses have been noted in the entry on August Derleth. His Solar
Pons books (short story collections) and his *Wisconsin Murders* (a
collection of true crime essays) are listed with his novels. Also, his
Chronicles of Solar Pons is listed as a 1971 publication. Though announced for 1971, this volume was not actually published until 1973,
publication having been delayed by the author-publisher's death on
4 July 1971.

The main question to be addressed for our purposes is this: how well
and how seriously is the crime writer treated in this volume? Is he
treated like any other novelist, going forth to examine the human condition, or is he looked at condescendingly? For the most part, the
former is happily the case. In fact, there is only one blatant example of
the snobbish approach: Elizabeth Evans's essay on Helen MacInnes,
highlighted by the following stuffy admission: "Although the scholar
will not subject such writings to serious critical consideration, the fact
remains that many literate people have read and enjoyed Miss Mac-
Innes's books" (p. 804). The perfect finishing touch would have been
to make it "otherwise literate people." Later, Dr. Evans writes, "One
is tempted to label such books as sub-literary and if they are compared
with the work of a serious artist like Henry James, the label is justified" (p. 805). Undoubtedly, Dr. Evans sees herself as a staunch defender of Helen MacInnes, but her patronizing and apologetic tone
does not befit an advocate.

The most bleak appraisal of the state of the crime fiction art comes
not from one of the critics but from the creator of Inspector Van der
Valk, Nicolas Freeling, who writes,

> The crime novelist who attempts art, his rational function and
> legitimate ambition, is asking for trouble.
>
> Few commercial crime novelists make the attempt. Most are
> content to work in purely mechanical fashion, with no artistic or
> literary pretension whatever. The result is that they receive no
> critical attention — indeed they need none, for their public rarely
> bothers with book reviews and has small interest in literary effort
> — and have small ambition being content with a commercial op-
> eration and financial success. (p. 429)

Having thus disposed of most of his colleagues and having denigrated most of their (and his) readers, he then aligns himself with Raymond ✓ Chandler as one who is trying to make literature of the mystery form.

Many of the critics, however, see detective fiction not as a collection of cumbersome conventions that must somehow be transcended for a writer's work to have genuine value, but as a form within whose bounds great things can be achieved. Ross Macdonald, perhaps taken most seriously by the literary establishment of any present-day crime writer, has never deserted the traditional whodunit structure, any more than his predecessors Dashiell Hammett and Raymond Chandler did. John M. Muste writes, "Among the chief virtues of Macdonald's work are his observations of the manners and mores of affluent Americans, his sharp delineation of unusual characters among those who have not made it or whom society has rejected, his objective portrayal of the grimness of urban American life" (p. 800). These are the kinds of achievements all novelists strive for, and the private eye novel happens to be an ideal vehicle for them.

J. C. Reid, writing on Agatha Christie, salutes her pre-eminence in the field of the formal puzzle, remarks on her undistinguished but efficient style and her frequently stereotyped characterizations, then makes a statement about the continuing theme of her fiction and its value as social history: "She has tried to mirror the transformation of English society in her lifetime, but at the same time, she is naturally conservative and clings to older values of life and conduct, as shown especially in her somewhat outdated village setting. . . . Ambivalently, she clings to belief in the possibility of a stable, ordered world, yet she recognizes inevitable changes and the defects in the older class system" (p. 257).

Such comments effectively counteract the idea that if mystery writers and other popular writers mirror their times or make any kind of a social statement, they are doing it by a happy accident, not by design, and that their works should be viewed as documents or exhibits, not as works of art.

Another critical tendency in the past has been to deny that crime and mystery stories by eminent authors (e.g., William Faulkner's *Intruder in the Dust*) actually belong to the genre, a practice that has also annoyed enthusiasts of science fiction and western stories. ("If you do it really well, you aren't really doing it.") This tendency is less common in this book and in other recent criticism — if anything, the tendency is being reversed. Detective fiction is sometimes used metaphorically in discussing writers not generally associated with the field. For example, James Gindin writes of John Fowles, "Part of the pleasure in reading Fowles's work inheres in appreciating a highly sophisticated detective process, a piecing together of clues and references that carry a thematic meaning" (p. 423). And Mark Van Doren's *Wind-*

less Cabins, neither published nor reviewed as a mystery in 1940, is described as one here.

When writers have worked both in the crime field and in the "mainstream," the attention given their criminous output varies. Slightly more than half the discussion of J. I. M. Stewart is given over to the Michael Innes books, and approximately the same proportion of the C. Day Lewis article is devoted to his work as Nicholas Blake. Howard Fast's books as E. V. Cunningham get an approving sentence or two. Gore Vidal's novels as Edgar Box are ignored in the critical discussion, probably to Mr. Vidal's satisfaction. C. P. Snow's one pure detective novel, the excellent *Death Under Sail*, is not discussed and, surprisingly, the strong influence of detective fiction in all his work is not remarked upon. Isaac Asimov's successful fusion of science fiction and the formal detective story is duly pointed out. P. G. Wodehouse's strong interest in, and influence on, detective fiction is not mentioned. August Derleth's detective fiction is mentioned only in passing, and his Solar Pons works are mentioned only in the bibliography, as discussed earlier.

As the artificial distinction between popular writers and "literary" writers fades, and with it the distinction between the aims and objectives of mainstream writers and those of crime writers, the whole stale question of legitimacy may soon become a dead issue. In general, this valuable reference book treats novelists as novelists, gauging what they have attempted and how well they have achieved it, not ghettoizing or pigeonholing them. Once mystery readers get over the outrageous exclusion of several worthy authors, above all Ellery Queen, they should be quite pleased with *Contemporary Novelists*.

JON L. BREEN

BOOKS RECEIVED

The First Hundred Years of Detective Fiction. 1841-1941. Compiled and edited by David A. Randall. Bloomington: The Lilly Library, Indiana University, 1973. (no price).

First Editions, Detective Fiction, Mysteries and Crime. Chicago: J & S Graphics, 1972. J & S Catalogue 15. $10.00.

For many years, detective novels, like children's books, have tended to be bought impulsively, read for immediate pleasure, and then casually thrown aside. Now that the detective genre is well into its second century we turn to bibliographies and look back in astonishment at the thousands of titles by hundreds of mystery authors, titles that (for all most of us can tell) have disappeared from the face of the earth. Were all copies read to pieces by their enthusiastic but bibliographically careless owners? Were they pulped during two world wars? Did they ever, in fact, exist?

The solution to the Mysterious Disappearance of the Detective Thrillers lies, no doubt, in the fact that for many readers such books were not "real literature" and had no claim to be treated with any more respect than last week's newspapers. Until recent years, comparatively few serious book collectors thought of specializing in the detective novel. It was a rare bookseller, prior to fifteen or twenty years ago, who troubled himself with such books. And even fewer libraries (again, until recent times) made any attempt at assembling comprehensive collections of mystery and detective fiction.

Yet it is to these percipient collectors, dealers and libraries that we owe much of our detailed knowledge of the history of the genre. Eager collectors like John Carter, E. T. Guymon, Jr., and Fred Dannay, starting as early as the Twenties and Thirties, built distinguished collections of mystery, crime and detective fiction. Happily for us who are late on the scene, these notable collections have been acquired — through gift or purchase — by university libraries and are now available for study by fans and scholars. The collection of Fred Dannay, specializing in the detective short story, is at the University of Texas. The extensive collection of mystery and detective authors in first editions assembled by E. T. Guymon is now part of the Department of Special Collections at the Occidental College Library. And John Carter's own collection, built in the Twenties and early Thirties, found its way (via Charles Scribner's in New York) to the Lilly Library at

Indiana University, where in the succeeding years it has been substantially augmented.

David A. Randall, Librarian of the Lilly Library and well known for his *Dukedom Large Enough*, has compiled a valuable annotated checklist of certain Lilly holdings to accompany an exhibition held at the Library from July to September, 1973. The scope of the exhibit is indicated by the pamphlet's subtitle: *The First Hundred Years of Detective Fiction. 1841-1941. By One Hundred Authors On the Hundred Thirtieth Anniversary of The First Publication in Book Form of Edgar Allan Poe's "The Murders in the Rue Morgue" Philadelphia, 1843.*

What makes this "Lilly Publication Number XVIII" of lasting interest to every collector of detective fiction is the choice of items on display, the accompanying illustrations, and the annotations to each entry. The publication (which claims that it "is the first comprehensive exhibition of the genre to be attempted") is divided into seven sections: "In the Beginning: Poe" (which includes, inevitably and necessarily, the first appearance of "The Murders in the Rue Morgue"); "Sherlock Holmes" (among other items is the original autograph manuscript of "The Adventure of the Red Circle"); "Gaboriau to Simenon—France" (where Gaboriau's *L'Affair Lerouge* is described as "the first full-length detective novel"); "England to 1914" (besides the expected works by Dickens and Collins such rarer titles as Charles Martel's *The Detective's Notebook* and B. L. Farjeon's *Devlin the Barber* appear); "England since 1914" (the first appearances of H. C. Bailey, Agatha Christie, Dorothy Sayers, Francis Iles and others); "America to 1920" (among the titles listed is a collection of tales by Julian Hawthorne who as a crime writer is unfortunately little known to modern readers); and finally "America since 1920" (where one will find the original manuscript of S.S. Van Dine's *The Scarab Murder Case* and the original edition of *The Maltese Falcon* in immaculate dust-jacket).

The extensive priced catalogue of *First Editions, Detective Fiction, Mysteries and Crime* appeared in Chicago last year. The list, which runs to 4,561 items in 340 pages, forms a useful checklist for the collector. To be sure, it is not as comprehensive as such more formal bibliographies as Barzun's and Taylor's *Catalogue of Crime* or Hagen's *Who Done It?*. But it has the virtue of generous illustrations, frequent annotations, and prices. Except for well-known "rarities," prices for detective titles are not well established among book dealers and tend to vacillate widely, depending on the bookshop one deals with. The J & S catalogue establishes prices which, at the time of issuance, may have seemed high. But with inflation they appear more just. The chief objection to be raised about the catalogue is that it is in no sense a bibliography or checklist of rare titles (for the simple reason that such rare titles have been scarce, often unprocurable, for many years). Many of the books in the catalogue are comparatively run-of-the-mill, and a sizable number of them appears to be in indifferent or poor condition. All the same, the list is extensive and the prices provocative. This is a catalogue that many collectors of detective fiction will welcome for reference purposes and for browsing; as Charles Lamb said of another book, it is "a book we would rather have than *not have* . . . for it is replete with instruction and interest."

Cosmopolitan Crimes, Foreign Rivals of Sherlock Holmes. Edited by Hugh Greene. Harmondsworth and Baltimore: Penguin Books, 1972. 95 cents.

The Further Rivals of Sherlock Holmes. Edited by Hugh Greene. Baltimore: Penguin Books, 1974. $1.50.

Gothic Tales of Terror. Volume One, Classic Horror Stories from Great Britain. Edited by Peter Haining. Baltimore: Penguin Books, 1973. $2.50.

Gothic Tales of Terror. Volume Two, Classic Horror Stories from Europe and the United States. Edited by Peter Haining. Baltimore: Penguin Books, 1973. $2.75.

Detective Fiction, Crime and Compromise. Edited by Dick Allen and David Chacko. New York, Chicago, San Francisco and Atlanta: Harcourt Brace Jovanovich, 1974. Price not set.

A major problem for any person who wants to sample the work of nineteenth-century and pre-World War I mystery and detective writers is where to find their stories. In the last few years publishers have been coming to our rescue with valuable anthologies of early detective fiction. Hugh Greene's successful and much-talked-about *The Rivals of Sherlock Holmes* (Harmondsworth and Baltimore: Penguin Books, 1971) has been followed by two additional books of selections: *Cosmopolitan Crimes* and *The Further Rivals of Sherlock Holmes*. These appeared in Britain in 1971 and 1973 respectively, and are reprinted in the Penguin format one year later in each case. *Cosmopolitan Crimes* introduces the modern reader to such writers as Jacques Futrelle, Arnold Bennett, Maurice Leblanc and E. Phillips Oppenheim (whose reputations are still reasonably intact) and to Grant Allen, George Griffith, Robert Barr and H. Hesketh Prichard (who have been virtually forgotten). *The Further Rivals*, which Hugh Greene expects to be the last of his collections of early detective fiction (because of limited quality supply), returns to some of the authors used in the original collection — Arthur Morrison and Ernest Bramah, for example — and to these adds representative tales by J. S. Fletcher, Victor Whitechurch, Catherine Louisa Pirkis, and the Theosophical and prolific Fergus Hume.

Having perused all three collections of "Rivals of Sherlock Holmes" one comes away with mixed feelings: gratitude for having had these authors called to one's attention, yet dismay at the galloping assumptions, the use of improbable clues, and the convoluted plots in the stories. The reader certainly gains a new respect for Conan Doyle as craftsman. If he was guilty of dubious assumptions and shaky plotting once in a while, he covered his weaknesses superlatively well. Narrative skill and clever characterizations were vital requirements for the detective writer seventy years ago as they are today. And in these two respects the writers in the three collections edited by Hugh Greene cannot be seen as very serious rivals to the great Holmes.

One other impression is left by the Hugh Greene assemblages (it is an impression sometimes left from a reading of the Sherlock Holmes stories themselves): it is astonishing how often the detectives or policemen are blandly willing to break the law — sometimes to be grossly dishonest — in order to trap the criminals. So many stories in which the end justifies the means! These tales throw the modern reader into thoughtful musing about the years from 1890 to 1914, years in which a popular fiction was produced that resolutely refused to examine the moral assumptions behind the social facade.

To Penguin Books we are also indebted for an important pair of anthologies of *Gothic Tales of Terror*. The first of the two collections deals with "Classic Horror Stories" from Great Britain, and the second similar stories from Germany, France and America. The two collections are edited by Peter Haining, who has been (as the half-titles tell us) "an avid student of the macabre and the occult for many years" and is the author of four books in the Gothic vein. Haining chooses his tales (or, in a few cases, excerpts) widely, providing an informative prefatory essay for each selection. The result is that the 543 pages of Volume I offer a comprehensive survey of the genre in Britain throughout the eighteenth and nineteenth centuries, from Horace Walpole to Sheridan LeFanu. Samples are provided of the work of Ann Radcliffe, "Monk" Lewis, William Beckford, Charles Maturin, Dr. John Polidori, Percy Shelley, Mary Shelley, Byron, Harrison Ainsworth, De Quincey, James Hogg and Thackeray. In most cases the stories are little known and rarely to be found except in large public or institutional libraries (and even there they are difficult to search out). The reader who works his way through the collection of British tales of terror will have acquired an excellent survey knowledge of the Gothic form, and will instantly be able to spot each clichéd element in twentieth-century "Gothics."

Haining's second volume — stories from Germany, France and the United States — has less historical authority, for the obvious reason that neither Germany nor France possessed such a lengthy and profuse Gothic literary tradition as did England. America does have such a long tradition, from Poe to the twentieth century, yet the selections here are only ten in number and are chiefly by Poe, Brockden Brown, Hawthorne and Irving. The American selections, then, are rather thin; but they are balanced by the twelve German tales and the eight stories from France, most of these probably unfamiliar to British or American readers. The number and nature of the selections do tend to teach the reader that the Gothic frame of mind is most congenial to the Germans and the English (and Scots and Irish) and least appealing to the French. (Perhaps the alleged pragmatism and skepticism of the French makes them suspicious of Gothic flimflam and stagy supernaturalism.)

Those of us who teach in colleges and universities are quick to recognize the academic anthology: the title accompanied by a subtitle promising philosophic inquiry; the introduction addressed to the intelligent but naive student; the selections grouped under broad generalizations; the "Questions for Discussion" after each selection; the "Suggestions for Further Reading" following the selections; and — finally — the six or eight pages of "Topics for Writing and Research." *Detective Fiction, Crime and Compromise* soon declares itself such an anthology. The teacher's heart may sink at the sight of yet another such thematic anthology (even though it is, as far as I am aware, the first to deal with detective fiction). But such a response does a disservice to a superior anthology.

The book is divided into four parts, the first of which (called "Manifestations") deals with "the main philosophical and social problems with which the book is concerned." These problems are illustrated by selections as diverse as Browning's "My Last Duchess," Hemingway's "The Killers" and Graham Greene's "The Destructors" — none of them, properly speaking, detective tales but all significantly related to the concept or assumptions behind detective fiction. The second section, called "The Detective," reprints eleven stories (Poe, Doyle, Chandler, Hammett, Simenon, etc.) which assure us "there will be answers — that, in fact, the answers are here before us, if only we knew where, or more importantly how, to look properly. . . . The grand solution, appearing almost miraculous, is the end result of the use of our powers of observation and of reason."

"The Genre Extended," the third section of the book, attempts to show what writers of wider scope can do with the notion of "search and discovery": Henry James and Jorges Luis Borges, for example, and William Burroughs and Donald Barthelme. The anthology concludes with seven documents about detective fiction: Dorothy Sayers's important introduction to her *Omnibus of Crime*, Chandler's familiar and oft-quoted (too oft, one sometimes thinks) "Simple Art of Murder," Auden's perceptive "The Guilty Vicarage," and several other and more recent essays.

Wilkie Collins. *Tales of Terror and the Supernatural*. Selected and introduced by Herbert van Thal. New York: Dover Publications, 1972. $3.00.

J. S. LeFanu. *Best Ghost Stories of J. S. LeFanu*. Edited by E. F. Bleiler. New York: Dover Publications, 1964. $2.00.

Algernon Blackwood. *Best Ghost Stories of Algernon Blackwood*. Selected by E. F. Bleiler. New York: Dover Publications, 1973. $3.00.

R. Austin Freeman. *The Stoneware Monkey and The Penrose Mystery*. New York: Dover Publications, 1973. $3.50.

Howard Phillips Lovecraft. *Supernatural Horror in Literature*. New York: Dover Publications, 1973. $1.50.

Eight Dime Novels. Edited by E. F. Bleiler. New York: Dover Publications, 1974. $3.50.

Dover Publications continues its inexpensive and well-printed paperback series, one of which is dedicated to resuscitating supernatural stories and novels that have fallen out of print and out of readers' memories. Previous to this Dover had issued LeFanu's *Uncle Silas*, *Ghost and Horror Stories of Ambrose Bierce*, Beckford's *Vathek* and Polidori's *Vampyre*. Now Dover continues the list with six important reprints. Wilkie Collins ranks second only to Dickens as the most fertile and inventive of Victorian novelists; why his tales should have fallen from sight is hard to say, for certainly they deserve a modern hearing. Sheridan LeFanu and Algernon Blackwood are well known to enthusiasts of supernatural fiction, and the two selections of their ghost stories contain stories that are already famous (Blackwood's "The Willows," for example, which H. P. Lovecraft thought the finest of all supernatural tales) or that deserve such wide acclaim (LeFanu's "Green Tea," "Mr. Justice Harbottle" and "Carmilla" are all here along with thirteen other supernatural stories). R. Austin Freeman has presented a special puzzle to detective readers. He has surely come closest to Conan Doyle in the creation of novels and short stories that possess the ambience, mood, characterizations and plotting of Holmesian tales. Yet his novels have been out of print for many years. What a pleasure, then, to welcome two novels within the covers of one book: *The Stoneware Monkey* and *The Penrose Mystery*.

Howard P. Lovecraft, who died in 1937, wrote in 1927 a historical essay on weird fiction which was intended for magazine publication. It came out in *The Recluse*, "a folio-sized magazine with a dark gray cover," and then apparently disappeared both in physical form and in memory. Dover has now reprinted this brief survey of the sub-genre of supernatural fiction. It is only 106 pages in length and attempts to survey the supernatural from the Gothic novel of the late eighteenth century to "Modern Masters," to discuss Poe's contributions, to investigate the weird tale on the Continent, and to outline the development of the form in Britain and in America throughout the nineteenth century. These aims are much too ambitious to allow for much depth, and indeed the modern student can find better and more detailed information in other histories of the Gothic form. Still, Lovecraft's special knowledge and his personal expertise as a creator of supernatural horror will commend the book to collectors of Lovecraft's writings and to students of mystery fiction.

Eight Dime Novels is a celebration of that Great American Invention, the cheaply-printed, mass-produced, widely read dime novel. This sampler includes examples of the major kinds of dime fiction: the Western, the detective, the self-improvement, and the early science fiction. The several detective tales printed in this collection are "The Bradys and the Girl Smuggler, or Working for the Custom House," by Francis W. Doughty, "a New York Detective"; "Frank James on the Trail" (an anonymous 1882 story that is as much a "sensational" tale as detective story); and "Scylla, the Sea Robber," which introduces "Nick Carter and the Queen of Sirens."

Barry Perowne. *Raffles Revisited, New Adventures of a Gentleman Crook*. New York, Evanston, San Francisco, London: Harper and Row, 1974. $8.95.

Norman Donaldson. *Goodbye, Dr. Thorndyke*. Culver City, Calif.: Luther Norris, 1972. $4.00.

Hardened detective enthusiasts are never satisfied. Like Oliver Twist they constantly want more. Holmesians pine for more exploits related by Dr. Watson, Poe fans would give arms and legs for just one more ratiocinative tale, Chandler buffs weep that there are no more of the great Hollywood novels. But despair is premature. Once in a while such wistful hopes can be gratified. Here are fourteen stories in which the renowned Raffles (a little modified in behavior, perhaps) makes a return bow, and one last tale about the great John Thorndyke.

E. W. Hornung's amateur cracksman, Raffles, has always been an acquired and somewhat specialized taste. Even in his heyday at the turn of the century, A. J. Raffles — old school boy, splendid cricketer, perfect English gentleman, and consummate burglar — came close to being a parody of himself. But his adventures with the faithful Bunny (who had fagged for him in school and continued a devoted worship into adult life) displayed a good deal of exciting adventure and a modest but adequate amount of detecting, all set against the glittering facade of English society in Victoria's last days and the early years of Edward's reign. With the coming of the war and the transformation of the world then and in the Twenties, Hornung's Edwardian settings took on the charm of faded postcards.

Hornung himself died in 1921, and though his tales continued to be reprinted again and again after his death, the public thirsted for new adventures by Raffles and Bunny. In 1932 a twenty-four-year-old crime writer, Barry Perowne (whose real name was Philip Atkey), was commissioned to write a new series of Raffles stories, to be published in a British periodical, *The Thriller*. The editor of *The Thriller* wanted tales with hard and fast action, and Perowne obliged. Further Raffles adventures were subsequently published in books like *The Return of Raffles* (1933) and *She Married Raffles* (1936), this last a novel in which Perowne attempted to put Raffles to rest by marrying him off.

In 1950 Frederic Dannay persuaded Perowne to write a new series of Raffles tales, this time for an audience hungering for adventures closer to the style and settings of the original Hornung tales. Perowne obliged, and the stories were published in *Ellery Queen's Mystery Magazine*, the *Saint Magazine* and *John Bull Magazine*. Harper and Row have now collected them in book form for the reader of the Seventies who, if he is historically minded, can look back to see how a crime writer of forty years ago set about duplicating the atmosphere and plotting of another man's fiction written thirty years earlier.

Norman Donaldson, author of the authoritative biography of R. Austin Freeman, *In Search of Dr. Thorndyke*, has written in *Goodbye, Dr. Thorndyke* a Final Problem that explains how and why the famous Dr. Thorndyke retired from active practice. As Donaldson explains in his "Introduction," Thorndyke's last official appearance (in "The Unconscious Witness") suggests that Thorndyke, though plainly in his seventies, continued his career even through the troubled events of the second World War. Surely Thorndyke deserved an honorable and peaceful retirement? Was he to be left, for eternity, confronting Armageddon?

And so Norman Donaldson has written this urbane last adventure. Its detecting is quite up to the level of Freeman's originals, and the setting — though damaged in a night bombing raid — rings true. Without revealing too much of the plot, it must be explained that in this last bow Thorndyke loses the invaluable services of Polton, who gives his life, like a faithful dog, to protect his master. Thorndyke, desolated at the loss of his devoted co-worker and disoriented by the damage inflicted on the Inner Temple by the German bombers, decides to retire to the country, where Donaldson leaves him in a permanent and serene happiness.

DONALD K. ADAMS

"DEVIANT SEX" AND THE DETECTIVE STORY

By Vern L. Bullough

Popular literature, if only because of its appeal to a mass audience, tends to reflect the concepts, the ideals, the physical setting of the period in which it was written somewhat better than the work of more "serious minded" authors who seemingly care nothing for popular taste. This means that popular literature itself serves as a valuable index to the historian on what individuals of any particular time were thinking and feeling (since only rarely does the author insert material which would grate on the sensibilities of his readers). To remain popular the author, if he is active in a period of changing sensibilities, must also indicate his awareness of these. One of the most obvious of recent changes is the rewriting of many of the early juvenile Nancy Drew stories to remove references to "darkies" and other similar stereotypes. No such rewriting as yet has been done in the sex field, and for this reason the detective story seems peculiarly well fitted to serve as a kind of litmus test for changing public attitudes. The purpose in writing this brief article is to indicate what I have found about what is regarded as "deviant" sex in mystery fiction and to ask interested readers to contribute any information which they might have.

On a superficial level, several things seem evident about the detective story, and one of the most obvious is the differences between English and American attitudes towards sex. If mystery fiction is any criterion, the American has been much more openly sexual than his British cousin. Americans included sex earlier in their mystery fiction, and with an accent on greater variety than did their British cousins. It was not until Ian Fleming appeared upon the scene that sex became a major subject in British mystery fiction, although sex in Fleming was not any more realistic than in his American competitors. In his *Snobbery with Violence* Colin Watson summed it up:

> The sexual encounters in the Bond books are as regular and pre-
> dictable as bouts of fisticuffs in the "Saint" adventures or end-of-
> chapter red herrings in the detective novels of Gladys Mitchell,
> and not much more erotic. Yet it often has been claimed that these,
> in conjunction with carefully described scenes of cruelty, form
> the pornographic core of the Fleming lodestone . . . . In 1953, when
> the first of the Bond stories, *Casino Royale*, was published, many

people in Britain and America—probably the majority—had inherited and unthinkingly absorbed the notion that merely to read about certain sins was very nearly the same as committing them. The range of such sins was limited, admittedly: felonies such as fraud, robbery, arson and murder were not deemed to contain an element of communicable pleasure, whereas all venereal offences, from bottom-pinching to rape, were. . . .[1]

Fleming's sexual overtones were anticipated by Mickey Spillane and any number of other American writers although sex in their novels was not any more realistic than that in Bond.

Perhaps the typical masculine hero of British detective fiction in an earlier period was Tiger Standish as created by Sydney Horler, the British writer of the Thirties. Horler conceived Standish as a thoroughly likable fellow, always ready to smile in the eye of danger, the soul of courtesy, and hostile to any kind of deviation. Horler himself, like his hero, had almost a horror of sex and he wrote that D. H. Lawrence was a "pathological case," for his emphasis on sex, while he dismissed Michael Arlen as the "only Armenian who never tried to sell me a carpet," and called Marcel Proust a neurotic and decadent Frenchman whose "habits and views on life are naturally abhorrent to most healthy human beings." Horler periodically tried to get Scotland Yard to make up a special detail to deal with homosexuality which he felt was a disgrace to mankind.[2] In effect Horler and his hero both reflected attitudes that were held by the average Britisher and American. With such attitudes how are unusual sexual practices portrayed?

One of the earliest portrayals of "deviant" sex is the incidents of transvestism recounted in Mark Twain's *Pudd'nhead Wilson* (1894). In this story the villain, the false Tom Chambers, liked to dress up in women's clothes, and it was while he was so attired that he murdered Judge Driscoll. He was eventually uncovered by David Wilson, an eccentric lawyer who was interested in palmistry and fingerprinting. But how did Twain's transvestite villain reflect popular prejudices since this novel was essentially one of Twain's potboilers? The false Chambers turns out to be really a light-skinned Negro who in infancy had been substituted for the true Chambers. The implication is quite clear that only a Negro could engage in such "degenerate" behavior. Whether Twain was making fun of prejudices against the Negro or whether he subscribed to them himself is debatable, but the thinking of that day makes the former, rather than the latter, more likely. Just how much Twain was adopting current beliefs is evident from a description of a transvestite ball that appeared in *The Alienist and Neurologist* in 1893, the year before *Pudd'nhead Wilson* was published. The author, a physician named C. H. Hughes, was shocked to find that there were numbers of men who dressed as women but his shock was lessened when he found that the phenomenon was confined to Negroes. After all what else could one expect of a Black man.

> I am credibly informed that there is, in the city of Washington, D.C., an annual convocation of negro men called the drag dance, which is an orgie of lascivious debauchery beyond pen power of description. I am likewise informed that a similar organization was lately suppressed by the police in New York City.
>
> In this sable performance of sexual perversion all of these men are lasciviously dressed in womanly attire, short sleeves, low-necked dresses and the usual ballroom decoration and ornaments of women, feathered and ribboned head-dresses, garters, frills, flowers, ruffles, etc., and deport themselves as women. . . . Among those who annually assemble in this strange libidinous display are cooks, barbers, waiters, and other employees of Washington families, some even higher in the social scale—some being employed as subordinates in the Government departments.[3]

Twain, in effect, was reflecting widely accepted opinions about transvestism. In fact it was not until over a decade later that Hughes began to realize that transvestism was not confined to the black ghettoes, although he still regarded such activity as more likely to occur among "degenerate" groups such as Negroes.[4]

If Twain's view of transvestism represented the prevailing opinion, the question then arises whether Mickey Spillane in his 1950 *Vengeance is Mine* reflected a changing attitude? In this typical Mike Hammer story the master criminal turns out to be Juno Reeves, by whom Mike was both attracted and repelled:

> I dragged myself over to the lifeless lump, past all the foam rubber gadgets that had come off with the gown, the inevitable falsies she kept covered so well along with nice solid muscles by dresses that went to her neck and down to her wrists. It was funny. Very funny. Funnier than I ever thought it could be. Maybe you'd laugh, too. I spit on the clay that was Juno, queen of the gods and goddesses, and I knew why I'd always had a resentment that was actually a revulsion when I looked at her.
>
> Juno was a queen, all right, a real, live queen. You know the kind.
>
> *Juno was a man!*

Obviously such a discovery was regarded by Spillane as shocking, but he did not consider it as beyond the ken of his readers. Transvestism existed, and though transvestites might be rather odd creatures, people had heard or at least could imagine such individuals, and they came from all classes of people. Spillane's success with Juno led to a number of other stories and novels which featured transvestism and crime in one way or another.

The taboos dealing with transvestism, perhaps because of the fame of such female impersonators as Julian Eltinge, and in more recent times, Flip Wilson, were as nothing compared to the difficulties in dealing with homosexuality. If my rather haphazard researches are correct, homosexuality entered detective fiction through the backdoor, as sort of an inside joke which only gradually became apparent to the wider reading audience. Hostility to any kind of mention of homosexuality in mystery fiction meant that writers such as Dashiell Hammett and Raymond Chandler used euphemisms to get the implication across. The first such euphemism was "minion," an old English term which described a lover who owed everything to the favor of a patron, and by implication it very early implied a kept male lover. When Hammett and Chandler used such terms did they refer to the homosexuality of some of the characters in their stories? There is considerable evidence that they did. There is a widely circulated but undocumented story that when their editors objected to the continued use of the term "minion" because of its homosexual connotations, they satisfied them by using the word "gunsel" which had the same implications but did not affront the sensibilities of the editors.

The origin of the word "gunsel" is unclear, but it entered detective fiction from the argot of tramps and hoboes. In hobo talk a "guntzel" was the boy traveling companion of an older hobo, the boy who rustled food for him and served his other needs, including his sexual ones.[5] The term was first described in some detail by a "Josiah Flynt" in an appendix to Havelock Ellis, *Studies in the Psychology of Sex*.[6] There is still some scholarly debate over the origin of the word, with most scholarly opinion tending to the belief that it came from the Yiddish *genzel* (gosling), a term applied to a naïve young male kept for purposes of "dubious" morality. Other terms implying the same thing, all of which entered the hard-boiled school of detective fiction, were "punk," "gazooney," "lamb," or "prushun." When Wilmer in *The Maltese Falcon* is referred to as a "gunsel" Hammett's implication is quite clear, as is Chandler's in his various novels. It was only gradually that homosexuality could appear more openly. Roderick Thorp's *The Detective* might well be a turning point in this respect but to my knowledge it was not until 1970 that the first believable homosexual hero appeared in detective fiction, namely David Brandstetter in Joseph Hansen's *Fadeout* (Harper & Row, 1970). Brandstetter is a homosexual insurance investigator who in this case inquires into the death of a folk singer whose white convertible is found smashed in an arroyo. His homosexuality is incidental to his job since in this respect he is simply a man doing a difficult and a hazardous task who happens to be homosexual. His sexual problems also furnish the major themes in Hansen's second homosexual novel, *Death Claims* (1973), when Brandstetter lives with another homosexual who has had experiences similar to his own. Does this indicate that in popular opinion it is now all right to be publicly a homosexual? If my thesis is correct it does and it ties in with the current confessional trend for well-known figures such as W. H. Auden, Christopher Isherwood, Merle Miller and Tennessee Williams publicly to declare their homosexuality. Perhaps readers of *The Mystery & Detection Annual* can give me other references to the acceptance or rejection of various kinds of sexual behavior in the detective story. When such an incident first appears is important in dating a willingness of both author and publisher to reflect a change in public sentiment. I know that in the last few years we have had a rather sympathetic view of social nudism (by John Ball, who also introduced the Negro detective as a major figure in his *The Heat of the Night*). How many other sexual "deviations" have come to be accepted?

NOTES

1 (London: Eyre & Spottiswoode, 1971), p. 237.

2 Watson, pp. 86-90.

3 C. H. Hughes, "Postscript to Paper on 'Erotopathia,' " *The Alienist and Neurologist*, 14 (October 1893), 731-32.

4 C. H. Hughes, "Homo Sexual Complexion Perverts in St. Louis," *The Alienist and Neurologist*, 28 (1907), 487-88.

5 See H. L. Mencken, *The American Language* (4th ed., corrected and revised, New York: Knopf, 1960), p. 582.

6 (2 vol. edition, New York: Random House, 1936), I, iv, 359-67.

THE DUST JACKETS OF
THE GREAT GATSBY AND
THE LONG GOODBYE

By Lawrence D. Stewart

LEON HOWARD's article about *The Long Goodbye*'s relationship to *The Great Gatsby* is so persuasive we must believe that Chandler had Fitzgerald's novel in mind while writing his mystery. There is less likelihood, on the other hand, that Walter H. Lorraine, the dust jacket illustrator for *The Long Goodbye*, was modeling his wrapper upon that which originally encased Fitzgerald's novel. While the curious parallels between these dust jackets may be no more than coincidental, their effects are quite different. Fitzgerald's wrapper seems to have been designed to help him, fortuitously, in the creation of his book; Chandler's, to help the reader in his reading.

Dust wrappers have long passed the stage where they were created merely to protect a volume's binding. With respect to the jacket for *The Great Gatsby*, for instance, there is a tradition that it had a conceptual effect upon the novel's content. Fitzgerald was going abroad in May of 1924 to complete the manuscript of his book; but before he left New York he was shown a roughed-out sketch by F. Cugat which was proposed as the novel's jacket. Late that August, Fitzgerald wrote from France to Maxwell Perkins, his editor at Scribner's: "For Christs sake dont give anyone that jacket you're saving for me. I've written it into the book." Critics ever since have seen that the billboard of Dr. T. J. Eckleburg came into the novel because of Cugat's design. But there is a problem with so deft an explanation, and Matthew Bruccoli states it succinctly:

> It is possible that Fitzgerald got the idea for the billboard from the Cugat illustration; but in point of fact it is not known what the trial jacket looked like, for no surviving correspondence describes it. . . . On 10 April 1925, publication day, Fitzgerald told Perkins, "The cover (jacket) came too and is a delight" — which sounds as though he might have just seen the final dust jacket for the first time.[1]

Since that published dust jacket depicts no billboard but shows a woman's eyes (with nude figures reclining in the pupils) brooding over the bright lights of an amusement park or carnival, the jacket may combine one theme of the published novel (the haunting aspect of Daisy Buchanan) with the images of an earlier version (the forbidden amusement park in "Absolution," a story which was part of *Gatsby* in a draft that no longer exists but which may have been shown Cugat[2]). Even if we see Daisy's eyes as reflecting her aversion to Gatsby's Trimalchioan world (a world that "offended her — and inarguably, because it wasn't a gesture but an emotion"), the dust jacket is an enigma in which even the images cannot be identified with certainty. The illustrator has created a mystery which is probably not susceptible of solution.

The Long Goodbye's dust jacket is also dominated by a face and eye; but this jacket is a mystery which baffled the novelist and may baffle his audience, since it reflects the illustrator's personal reaction to the events of the novel and the most compelling of its clues. Chandler himself had not always been happy with his dust wrappers. A new edition of *Farewell, My Lovely*, for instance, had prompted his complaint, "Is it permissible to wonder why the people who do illustrations and covers can't pay some attention to the text?"[3] When he saw the wrapper for *The Long Goodbye* he exploded:

> Some day someone ought to explain to me the theory behind dust jacket designs. I assume they are meant to catch the eye without offering any complicated problems to the mind, but they do present problems of symbolism that are too deep for me. Why is there blood on the little idol? Why is the idol there at all? What is the significance of the hair? Why is the iris of the eye green? Don't answer. You probably don't know either.[4]

Six months later he was still fuming about the "incorruptible genius [who] designed the cover for *The Long Goodbye*. I still don't like it. Houghton Mifflin's covers tend to an extravagance of design which is supposed to suggest something rather than hit you on the nose with it. Even . . . their senior editor didn't know what the last cover was supposed to mean, but it looked rich."[5] And in discussing the dust wrapper for *The Little Sister* he concluded with his credo: "Someday, just for the hell of it, a dust jacket artist ought to submit to the excruciating agony of reading the damn book."[6]

Is it possible that Chandler was wrong and that the dust wrapper for *The Long Goodbye* is something more than a collection of images, casually drawn from the story and assembled according to Walter H. Lorraine's visual aesthetic? Let us consider the details chosen: half a face stares out at us, its eyeball reflecting a small medallion. Long grey hair gives a contour to the face and swirls down to encircle other images — a totemic idol stained with blood; an open bottle of spilled capsules; a silhouette of a man with a suitcase. The spilled capsules and the man-with-suitcase present no difficulty: they relate to key incidents in the plot. But beyond these images, we may only speculate. The most confusing seems to be the idol. Terry's wife, we are early led to believe, is killed by a bronze statuette of a monkey. It is that which has been transformed into this bloodied idol? Chandler saw no connection, but the small amount of blood on the idol strengthens the identification: "when the statuette was used to beat her face to a pulp, it was beating a dead woman. And the dead, Mrs. Wade, bleed very little." We presume that the half face is the original Terry (i.e. Paul Marston) — only half of whose face had not been plastic reconstruction during World War II. The grey hair may be a distorted darkening of the bone white hair which all assert that Terry has. But why its length? Is it a confusion of the Terry that we know with the Cisco Maioranos he will become? ("You've got nice clothes and perfume and you're as elegant as a fifty-dollar whore," Marlowe tells Terry at their final encounter, though Terry insists he's not "just a piece of fluff.") And what of the medallion in Terry's eye? Is it the one that allegedly he had given during the war to his sweetheart? The medallion worn by Eileen Wade "consists of a broad dagger in white enamel with a gold edge. The dagger points downwards and the flat of the blade crosses in front of a pair of upward-curling pale blue enamel wings." Yes, that seems to be depicted with no uncertainty.

Is it possible that the illustrator's selected images are his own cluing toward the solution? Customarily dust jackets are not designed to give away plots but to arrest attention. Yet of all the images Lorraine has depicted, the most compelling is the insignia in the eye. Not only does it closely approximate Chandler's description, it is placed in the pupil which, the dictionary reminds us, is "the tiny image of oneself seen reflected in another's eyes." It is this insignia which ties Terry to Eileen, but far more tightly than in a mere historical relationship. Near the end of *The Long Goodbye* we learn that if the medallion had ever become known to Terry, it had become so only years later: the medallion had not even existed during World War II when supposedly it had been bestowed. But it is the physical evidence that Eileen Wade has required to validate her fantasy — it is the faked evidence that brings all apparent "facts" into question. Like Gatsby's shirts, Eileen's medallion is the essential device that bridges fantasy and reality.

Terry doesn't deceive himself about this aspect of the past, nor about his feelings for Eileen: "It's pretty tough to turn a woman in for murder — even if she never meant much to you." But he recognizes in her mad faith an intensity of belief akin to his own. Leon Howard's article makes possible an answer to Chandler's final question. Like the green light at the end of Daisy Buchanan's dock, the green iris of Terry's eye implies that one can create his own reality and, even as a boat against the current, go forward through the past. Paul Marston has become Terry Lennox; and Terry Lennox has become Cisco Maioranos. A pretty good plastic reconstruction of half a face has made possible a pretty good life; now a totally invented face assures a totally invented life. It may be as fake as the medallion reflected in his eye, but it will also be as successfully self-sustaining.

No, whatever charges may be made against Walter Lorraine's selection of images, we cannot charge him with having missed the book's essential thesis. The clue which indicated that Terry had not died but would survive again — that clue had been strategically positioned on the dust jacket for all who would have an eye to see.

NOTES

1 Introduction to *F. Scott Fitzgerald "The Great Gatsby": A Facsimile of the Manuscript*, ed. Matthew J. Bruccoli (Washington, D.C.; Microcard Editions, 1973), pp. xvi, xviii.

2 For a discussion of the putative relationship between the story and the novel, see my " 'Absolution' and *The Great Gatsby*," in *Fitzgerald/Hemingway Annual, 1973* (Washington, D.C.: Microcard Editions, 1974), pp. 181-87.

3 To Freeman Lewis, 15 May 1951, in *Raymond Chandler Speaking*, ed. Dorothy Gardiner and Kathrine Sorley Walker (Boston: Houghton Mifflin, 1962), p. 155.

4 To Paul Brooks, 1 March 1954, ibid., pp. 168-69.

5 To Roger Machell, 1 Sept. 1956, ibid., pp. 171-72.

6 To Hamish Hamilton, 26 Oct. 1956, ibid., p. 172.

CONTRIBUTORS

Donald K. Adams, general editor of *The Mystery & Detection Annual*, is Professor and Chairman of the Department of English and Comparative Literature at Occidental College, Los Angeles.

Henry Binder, a graduate of the California State University, Northridge, is presently a doctoral candidate in English at the University of Southern California.

Jon Breen, head reference librarian at the California State College, Dominguez Hills, is the author of numerous short stories and articles in the field of detective fiction and has contributed to such journals as the *Ellery Queen Review, Ellery Queen's Mystery Magazine*, the *Wilson Library Bulletin* and the *Library Journal*.

Vern L. Bullough has written a round dozen books, the latest of which is *The Subordinate Sex, a History of Attitudes Towards Women* (1973). He is a specialist in the history of medicine and science and is Professor of History at the California State University, Northridge.

Steven R. Carter, who resides in Cuyahoga Falls, Ohio, wrote his master's thesis on Ross Macdonald's novels. He presently is a graduate student in the English Department at The Ohio State University.

Robert L. Chianese is Associate Professor of English at the California State University, Northridge. He is the editor of *Peaceable Kingdoms: An Anthology of Utopian Writings* (1971).

Arthur J. Cox is a Dickensian scholar who has published articles in *The Dickensian* and *Dickens Studies*. He is the textual editor of the recent Penguin edition of *The Mystery of Edwin Drood* (a volume in the Penguin English Library series).

Benjamin Franklin Fisher IV, the author of numerous articles on Poe and other nineteenth-century authors, British and American, has taught at the University of Pennsylvania and is on the staff of The Hahnemann Medical College and Hospital of Philadelphia.

J. E. Harrison was educated at schools in England and in the United States at Ohio University. Having returned to Britain she now teaches at the Northhampton College of Education and continues actively to write poetry. In 1971 she published a collection of her poetry as *The Magic of Reality*.

Leon Howard is well known as the author of many books on American literature, among them studies of Herman Melville, James Russell Lowell and Jonathan Edwards. He is professor of English at the University of New Mexico.

Albert D. Hutter is Assistant Professor of English and Comparative Literature, University of California, Los Angeles, and Research Clinical Associate of the Southern California Psychoanalytic Institute. He has published articles on Dickens and on psychoanalysis.

Marsha Kinder is Associate Professor in the Department of English and Comparative Literature at Occidental College. A specialist in eighteenth-century English literature, she is also a scholar of the cinema and in the field has published articles and a book (*Close-up* [1972], written in collaboration with Beverle Houston).

Mark McCloskey is a widely published poet, currently living in San Francisco. He formerly taught at the University of Southern California.

Horace McCoy, novelist and screenwriter, best known for his novel, *They Shoot Horses, Don't They?* (1935), also wrote *No Pockets in a Shroud* (1937), *I Should Have Stayed Home* (1938), *Kiss Tomorrow Goodbye* (1948) and *Scalpel* (1952).

Ngaio Marsh, one of the most distinguished of mystery novelists, lives in New Zealand. Several of her recent novels were reviewed in *The Mystery & Detection Annual*, 1972.

Mary W. Miller is a teaching assistant and doctoral candidate in comparative literature at the University of California, Los Angeles.

Thomas D. O'Donnell is a specialist in the study of the twentieth-century French novel and teaches in the Department of French and Italian at the University of Minnesota.

Laura Krugman Ray, who holds degrees from Bryn Mawr and Yale, is Assistant Professor of English at the University of Bridgeport. She specializes in the Victorian novel and in British writers of the Twenties and Thirties.

John Robertson is a graduate in English of the California State University, Northridge. "Consider, Sir, the Hyacinth Hair" is his first published poem.

Martin Roth is Associate Professor of English, University of Minnesota, and—as his article indicates—is a long-time student of Poe. His scholarship includes *Washington Irving's Contributions to "The Corrector"* (1968).

Larry Emil Scott took his Ph.D. from the University of Washington, taught in the Scandinavian Section of the Department of Germanic Languages, University of California, Los Angeles, and is now teaching at the University of Texas.

Ralph Bruno Sipper is the proprietor of Joseph the Provider, a bookstore in Inverness, California, specializing in twentieth century first editions.

Wilbur Jordan Smith was, until his recent retirement, for many years Head of the Department of Special Collections, University Research Library, University of California, Los Angeles.

Editha Spencer lives with her husband on a farm in Connecticut and divides her time between being a housewife and painting. Her work has been exhibited extensively on the East Coast.

Eric Spencer, like his mother Editha, is a resident of Connecticut and is currently studying at the Rhode Island School of Design in Providence, Rhode Island.

Ann Stanford is a California poet whose most recent books include *The Weathercock* (1966) and a verse translation of *The Bhagavad Gita* (1970); her study of Anne Bradstreet will appear soon. Her poems have appeared in *The New Yorker, Poetry, Sewanee Review,* and many other journals. She is Professor of English at the California State University, Northridge.

Lawrence D. Stewart is Associate Professor of English at the California State University, Northridge. His and Edward Jablonski's revised and enlarged edition of *The Gershwin Years* was published in 1973. *Paul Bowles, The Illumination of North Africa* appeared in 1974.

Thomas Sturak took his doctorate at the University of California, Los Angeles, and is now an editor for a Santa Monica research corporation. He published "Horace McCoy's Objective Lyricism" in *Tough Guy Writers of the Thirties* (1968); his "Horace McCoy, Captain Shaw, and the *Black Mask*" appeared in *The Mystery & Detection Annual,* 1972.

Julian Symons is widely known as novelist, critic, biographer and poet. He lives in London, reviews detective fiction for British journals, and writes crime novels, the most recent of which is *The Plot Against Roger Rider,* which appeared in late 1973.

W. B. Vasels lives in Corona, California, where he continues to take an interest in ancient history, book collecting, indoor gardening, cats, and international finance (not necessarily in that order).

J. Stuart Whiteley is a British psychiatrist, and is Medical Director of the Henderson Hospital, Sutton, Surrey.

1500 copies of the

MYSTERY & DETECTION ANNUAL

1973

were printed by Grant Dahlstrom

at The Castle Press,

Pasadena, California

in November 1974.

The type used is Intertype Waverly,

a version of a baroque letter

otherwise known as Walbaum.

The paper is

Northwest Mountie Offset